RELIGION AND CULTURAL STUDIES

RELIGION AND CULTURAL STUDIES

Edited by
Susan L. Mizruchi

PRINCETON UNIVERSITY PRESS
PRINCETON AND OXFORD

Copyright © 2001 by Princeton University Press
Published by Princeton University Press, 41 William Street,
Princeton, New Jersey 08540
In the United Kingdom: Princeton University Press,
3 Market Place, Woodstock, Oxfordshire OX20 1SY
All Rights Reserved

"The Place of Ritual in Our Time" was first published in
American Literary History 12, Fall 2000.

Library of Congress Cataloging-in-Publication Data

Religion and cultural studies / edited by Susan L. Mizruchi.
p. cm.
Includes bibliographical references and index.
ISBN 0-691-00502-8 (CL : alk. paper) —
ISBN 0-691-00503-6 (pbk. : alk. paper)
1. Religion and culture—United States.   2. United States—
Religion.   I. Mizruchi, Susan L. (Susan Laura)

BL2525 .R454 2001
200′.973—dc21   00-045328

This book has been composed in Galliard

The paper used in this publication
meets the minimum requirements of
ANSI/NISO Z39.48-1992 (R1997)
(*Permanence of Paper*)

www.pup.princeton.edu

Printed in the United States of America

10 9 8 7 6 5 4 3 2 1

10 9 8 7 6 5 4 3 2 1
(Pbk.)

Contents

Contributors

Eytan Bercovitch, is an Independent Scholar living in Berkeley, California. A cultural anthropologist, he has taught at Stanford, the University of Chicago, and the Johns Hopkins University.

Karen McCarthy Brown, author of *Mama Lola: A Vodou Priestess in Brooklyn* (California, 1991), teaches anthropology and sociology of religion at Drew University.

Gillian Feeley-Harnik, Professor of Anthropology at the University of Michigan, Ann Arbor, is author of *Green Estate: Restoring Independence in Madagascar* (Smithsonian Institution, 1991) and *The Lord's Table: The Meaning of Food in Early Judaism and Christianity* (2nd ed., Smithsonian Institution, 1994).

Richard Wightman Fox, Professor of History at the University of Southern California, is author of *Reinhold Niebuhr: A Biography* (Cornell, 1985) and *Trials of Intimacy: Love and Loss in the Beecher-Tilton Scandal* (Chicago, 1999), and coeditor, with James Kloppenberg, of *A Companion to American Thought* (Cambridge, 1995).

Jenny Franchot, Associate Professor of English, University of California, Berkeley, was author of *Roads to Rome: The Protestant Antebellum Encounter with Catholicism* (California, 1994).

Giles Gunn, Professor of English and of Global and International Studies at the University of California, Santa Barbara, is author of *The Culture of Criticism and the Criticism of Culture* (Oxford, 1987) and *Thinking across the American Grain* (Chicago, 1992).

Geoffrey Galt Harpham, Professor of English at Tulane University, is author of *Getting It Right: Language, Literature, and Ethics* (Chicago, 1992) and *Shadows of Ethics* (Duke, 1999).

Bruce B. Lawrence, Nancy and Jeffrey Marcus Professor of Religion at Duke University, is author of *Shattering the Myth: Islam beyond Violence* (Princeton, 1998) and *The Complete Idiot's Guide to Religions Online* (Macmillan, 1999). His monograph on Asian American spirituality, *New Faiths/Old Fears*, is forthcoming from Columbia.

Jack Miles, Senior Advisor, J. Paul Getty Trust, and Contributing Editor at *The Atlantic Monthly*, is author of *God: A Biography* (Vintage, 1995), which was awarded a Pulitzer Prize.

Susan L. Mizruchi, Professor of English and American Studies at Boston University, is author of *The Power of Historical Knowledge* (Princeton, 1988) and *The Science of Sacrifice* (Princeton, 1998).

Jonathan Z. Smith, Robert O. Anderson Distinguished Service Professor of the Humanities at the University of Chicago, edited *The HarperCollins Dictionary of Religion* (San Francisco, 1995); his books include *Imagining Religion: From Babylon to Jonestown* (Chicago, 1982).

Introduction

AMERICANS have never been more religious than they are now, at the dawn of the twenty-first century. By all reports, attendance rates at traditional places of worship (churches, mosques, synagogues, and temples) are high and rising; the influx of new immigrant religions (since the 1960s) has revitalized standard faiths and drawn in those who had strayed from them. There are popular television shows like "The Simpsons," which features characters who go to church every Sunday, speak to God, and live next door to Evangelical Christians; and special events like the 1998 outdoor mass in Worcester, Massachusetts for a comatose girl believed to have miraculous powers (e.g., eliciting human blood from Communion hosts), which attracted 10,000 people from all over the world; and "God Talk" was a predominant rhetoric of the millennial presidential campaign. *The New York Times* reported in 1997 that 96% of Americans say they believe in God; 93% own a Bible; 90% think there is a heaven; and 87% consider themselves Christians.[1]

At the same time, the category, "Christian" has undergone a sea change in recent years, with Jehovah's Witnesses, Assemblies of God, and Church of God in Christ reporting increases in worshipers on the order of 119%, 211%, and 863% respectively.[2] Moreover, the growth of Islam and Buddhism in America has been dramatic, with the number of Muslims, 3.5 million, equaling the number of Presbyterians, and Buddhists estimated at 750,000. To be sure, American observance overall has been consistent throughout this past century (comparative figures for 1947 show that 96% of Americans professed faith in God). What *has* intensified over the past fifty years is the multicultural dimension of this worship. I refer to the increasingly complex hybridity of religious forms in this country, described, for example, by Bruce B. Lawrence in his account of how the arrival of new immigrant religions has coincided with the rise of the Internet.

The contributions to this volume are united by three distinct but related premises. First, religion is understood as nonuniversal in practice and in theory. Religion is an historically particular phenomenon only apprehended through language, which is itself historically particular. Thus, the analytical terms we apply to the religious instances we study are themselves subject to historical scrutiny.[3] Second, no religion is pure and unique unto itself. Religions are, by definition, "polythetic" as opposed to "monothetic": they are amoebas rather than clams, which is to say that their survival depends on their capacity for transformation and incorporation, to borrow, influence, and be influenced, to maintain coherence in the face of diversity and crisis.[4] Third, the methods that are most suitable to the conceptualization of this particularity and diversity are multidisciplinary as well as interdisciplinary. The attention paid to religion in the past decade by analysts who have been especially attuned to the value of cross-disciplinary methods and exchanges has done much to revitalize its study. Religion is now a "cutting edge" field of research, and some of the most exciting academic work in disciplines such as literary criticism and history is now being done in specializations devoted to the subject of religion. While each of these disciplines has significant traditions of such work, each had also seen a waning of those traditions in the late 1960s, 1970s, and well into the 1980s.

It is fair to say that during those decades, historians and literary critics interested in "culture" in the modern sense—as an intellectual category with a history—tended to shy away from religion as a field of inquiry.[5] For instance, the "besieged" state of historians working on religion in the 1970s was attributed to the advent of social history, and to the eclipse of the mainline Protestant denominations, which had defined much of the canon for investigation up to that time.[6] In literary studies, the powerful impact of poststructuralism, with its skepticism toward universals and transcendence, created a general resistance toward religion as a subject of analysis. This was underscored by the rising visibility in the 1980s of America's religious right, which reinforced an earlier tendency to identify religion with the forces of reaction. Like its companion term, the "aesthetic," religion has until recently been considered the special province of cultural conservatives. All this has changed. The boundary line of religion and culture at the turn of the twenty-first century is a major site of intellectual action and interaction.

This collection aims to be part of this intellectual ferment. It brings together major scholars from the fields of anthropology, history, literary criticism, and religion in order to foreground the ties between religion and cultural studies. Prominent analysts of religion and culture have helped to articulate the prospects of this engagement. The philosopher of religion Cornel West has insisted on the centrality and variety of American religious life, all the "religious sects and groups and cults and denominations . . . through which folk come together." The historian David Hollinger posits as a key point of reference for contemporary intellectual historians the question, "Why is there so much Christianity here?"[7] And the literary critic Fredric Jameson calls religion "a very large and basic component of American mass culture," which has been "decidedly underanalyzed and underrepresented in the field of Cultural Studies."[8] Such sentiments and questions unite the contributions to this volume. To apprehend religion for these authors is to grasp in the deepest way the constituents of culture. Each essay can be seen as a sustained meditation on the implications of bringing the subjects of religion and culture together. Despite the variety of disciplines represented by this group of scholars and the variety of cultures explored in their essays—from fifteenth-century Flemish Asceticism and nineteenth-century African-American Spiritualism to Russian blood-libel trials and Alien Abduction Reports in the twentieth century—their common ground is the question of religion's place in current American academic analysis, and more broadly in American life today. Understanding religion, according to these essays, means recognizing its inextricability from culture. We aim to highlight, for those engaged in the study of culture and for those engaged in the study of religion, how profoundly each of these two fields is enriched by the conjunction between them.[9]

A primary condition of this project is the recognition of religion as multicultural. This is an insight confirmed by American novels from James Fenimore Cooper's tale of national beginnings, *The Last of the Mohicans* (1826), to Robert Stone's tale of global endings, *Damascus Gate* (1998). When Natty Bumpo declares himself "a man without a cross," for instance, he inadvertently conflates religious and racial identifications. Cross bearing can be a voluntary symbol of Christian affiliation or an involuntary sign of cultural identity (borne on the skin). Alienness in early America may be equally a matter of blood and of ritual. It is a testimony to the staying power of this colonial bind of body and soul to find it reimagined in *Damascus Gate*, where every act of worship stages the ongoing hybridity of faith itself, customs clinging to one another over time, a hybridity denied by perpetual conflict among rival religious traditions.[10] Indeed, the fervor with which worshipers battle to protect the boundaries of their faiths is fueled in great part by the tenuousness of those boundaries. Religion is yet another American story in which the "not me" is discovered already living within.

Kenneth Burke's pathbreaking *The Rhetoric of Religion* (1961) is notably sensitive to the irony of this situation. "Religion has often been looked upon as a center from which all other forms of human motivation gradually diverged." Yet the history of religions, he immediately reminds us, is one of continuous "discord. . . . The rich man's prayer is not the poor man's prayer. Youth's God is not the God of the aged. The God of the wretch to be hanged is not the God of the lucky chap who just won at bingo under ecclesiastical auspices." From the recognition of religion's multiplicity, Burke proceeds to argue for the fundamental role of language in understanding the construction and experience of transcendence. Human thoughts on the nature of the divine are ex post facto thoughts about the nature of language itself—while language, in turn, as it moves into the literary, is profoundly shaped by religious imperatives, practices, traditions, and texts.

These two insights—regarding religion's multiplicity and its relation to language—have helped guide this volume's collective inquiry into the nature and status of religion in an era of cultural studies. To argue for religion as a significant and under-studied instance of the "multicultural" is also to recognize that articulating histories of religions depends upon unearthing the particular languages that have voiced faith in any given era. The social or literary historian of religion, so understood, is inevitably an anthropologist who benefits from the investigation of materials and cultures that may at first appear anomalous. At the same time, religious faith and practice distinguish themselves from other cultural practices by their insistence upon being *beyond* culture. The essays in this collection are all efforts to probe this contradiction and to track religion's various articulations of the transcendent in, through, and against culture. The study of religion is here understood, then, as an exercise in disruptive classification, interrogating earlier modes of classification regarding religion and culture while at the same time developing categories for capturing what has been mystified (as opposed to specified in contemporary theory) and unified (as opposed to fractured or fragmented in historical practice).

To identify the time frame of this volume as the era of cultural studies, is to designate an historical context. While notoriously—and purposefully from the perspective of many practitioners—difficult to define, "cultural studies" can be broadly characterized. Cultural studies, by whatever program or practice, involves a commitment to elaborate the mutual constitution of cultural forms and historical forces, to articulate relationships between cultural practices and relations of power, to challenge divisions between elite and popular culture, and to maintain a skeptical if not critical view of academic disciplines as such.[11] The contributors to this volume are all, to varying degrees, in sympathy with this "desire,"[12] or set of desires, as they seek to make sense of religion in our post-modern moment. They recognize, from the perspectives of their different disciplines, how recent critical developments inform the contemporary analysis of culture. Among these are the political and economic changes associated with multiculturalism and globalism, the academic attempt to redress formerly ignored claims and interests (of the colonized; of gays and lesbians; of racial "others"; of women; of working classes), the preoccupation with texts of all sorts (from written to visual to virtual), and the theoretical fascination with fragmentation and dispersal, with the indeterminate, illusory, and constructed. At the same time, this volume is designed to focus a widespread conviction on the part of intellectuals that they need to deal seriously with spiritual and ethical issues.[13]

In highlighting the interdisciplinary character of this collection, I am, in one sense, merely emphasizing basic differences among the contributors in academic training and professional identification. These differences are valuable and hard won. They are the product of long years of education, apprenticeship, and participation in a wide range of group-defining activities (from departmental work and service to scholarship and conferences).[14] But in another sense, I mean to call attention to a cultural situation they all share. Perhaps this commonality is best defined by a historic contrast. Where self-aware postmodern academics strive to speak across their bounded specialties, and in so doing, to become "inter-disciplinary," self-aware moderns of a previous century sought to become "disciplinary." The plague or promise of Enlightenment knowledges was their hybridity, the perilous proximity of literary criticism and social commentary, the lack of distinction between, for example, aesthetic and political endeavors. The late-nineteenth-century push toward institutionalization and professionalization in numerous academic fields led to a privileging of boundaries. Disciplinary distinctness held out the prospect of distinction. Differentiating one's discipline from neighboring disciplines (anthropology, as against psychology or sociology) was the guarantor of institutional sovereignty, academic authority, and public support. The current tendency of scholars to pursue interdisciplinary connections has been seen as a betrayal of that century-long struggle for coherence. In fact, it confirms the vitality of the humanities and social sciences in our time.

Those connections *extend* rather than subvert the separateness of disciplines, for true exchange *among* disciplines depends on the integrity *of* disciplines. Indeed, hybridity is a characteristic of disciplinary practices. This is why all of the essays collected here are, at least in part, self-conscious allegories about the states of their respective disciplines, whether Richard Wightman Fox reflecting upon the difficulty historians have had in coming to terms with a "grand and slippery notion" like "Love," Karen McCarthy Brown analyzing the difficulties of making alternative spiritual knowledges audible to academics, or Gillian Feeley-Harnik contemplating the proliferation of anthropological definitions of "culture."

Religion and Cultural Studies is an effort to deepen our understanding of individual disciplines as well as to foreground the intellectual value of collective interdisciplinary works of this kind. This requires an historical-mindedness about disciplines and subjects: the recognition that methods are as historically embedded as religion and culture. Alert to the ways in which the unique genealogies of their respective fields have shaped their approach to religion, each author makes that genealogy integral to the analysis.

Jonathan Z. Smith's essay, "Close Encounters of Diverse Kinds" (chapter 1), is a remarkable case in point. His subject is the gradual displacement in the seventeenth century of biblical understandings of singularity and diversity. At what moment did the biblical explanation that asserted the fundamental unity of humankind become impossible, and the "invention" of race thereby necessary? He wants to isolate the circumstances that led to these twin acts of repudiation and discovery, a purpose which is realized through close investigations of two examples, remote from one another in time and place, yet epitomizing, each in its way, the intellectual struggle aroused by contact with altogether alien beings. His first example is "Alien" Abduction Reports, testimonials by humans recounting their experiences as captives of extraterrestrials, and he begins with a careful review of their typical narrative structure. Later, the scene shifts to ancient narratives: the biblical version of human origins (revised but basically preserved by the Greeks and Romans), an eminently adaptable tale of human singularity that goes unchallenged until the post-Columbian response to the nature of the Americas. Smith dwells on the dominant note of wonderment, the essential and respectful quiet of these discourses. The fundamental recognition of alterity that emerges from these accounts has the effect of undermining permanently the Noachic model. The grasp of the essential status of difference arises in great part, Smith makes clear, from the experience of the unexpected. Smith writes, "It was neither Orientals nor Blacks, who had long been mapped on the old Greco-Roman and biblical taxonomy, that gave rise to the intellectual problematics of race. Rather it was the unanticipated presence of native Americans." He concludes that in culture as in language, it is difference which generates meaning, a meaning that is best pursued through cultural and comparative theories equally informed by the inadequacy and the necessity of translation.

Karen McCarthy Brown, in "Telling a Life through Haitian Vodou: An Essay Concerning Race, Gender, Memory, and Historical Consciousness" (chapter 2), is also attentive to the contradictions of the translation enterprise. A reflection upon the relationship of Brown and Mama Lola as they deal in their respective ways with the reception of Brown's book, *Mama Lola: A Vodou Priestess in Brooklyn* (1991), the essay has as much to say about the translation of "author" into "friend" as it does about the translation of "Vodou Priestess" into "Visiting Artist." The tension and affection between Brown and Mama Lola becomes an intimate recreation of academic struggles with the issues of identity, alternative cultures, and their politics. But this unlikely pair never lets us forget that it is on the human level that such abstractions are realized. In Brown's essay, translation takes many forms, ranging from the compression of a living "subject" into a "character" whose "life" is limited by the scope of narration, to the brutal transformation of free Africans into captive slaves on the beaches of Ouidah. While translation, in Brown's account, is often a process of reduction—the academic construction of other cultures as "voices," or the interpretation of spirit possession as pathology—it is not always negative. At best, it is identified with *wanga*, the Vodou charms created through ritual binding and bundling with ropes, chains, or padlocks. Of principal concern to Brown are the variations of memory, whether embodied unconsciously in gestures or speech, or captured deliberately by notebook or tape recorder. Brown describes the different suppressions inspired by the heritage of slavery—her own denial of the Bermudian slave-owning merchants on her mother's side, and Mama Lola's configuration of the family tree so as to eliminate her Dahomean slave ancestors. "Transatlantic slavery is to history as black holes are to the reaches of space," Brown writes; "we know their presence by the warping effect they have on what surrounds them."

The view of religion's susceptibility to fragmentation and memorialization that is shared by Smith and Brown is reconceived in the language of icon, miniature, and trope, by Jenny Franchot and myself. In essays that are formal as well as historical, Franchot and I confirm the capacity of religion and literature to inspire both curiosity and reverence. Jenny Franchot's subject in "Unseemly Commemoration: Religion, Fragments, and the Icon" (chapter 3) is the status of religious experience as an object of interpretation, a status which stems from the Enlightenment, and condemns religion irrevocably to "visual scrutiny" and "memorial appropriation." Religion becomes a province of loss and memorabilia, a collector's cabinet of images and texts that testify to someone else's encounter with the divine. Belief is that which is not ours, a condition identified with others who believe, with otherness itself. From the perspective of postcolonial theories of othering, religion appears as a stereotype of lost belief. "Belief's transformation into pastness," Franchot observes, "is, in fundamental respects, the narrative of Western culture's birth into the modern." Like childhood, religion represents primitive origins that seem powerfully authentic as well as safely diminutive. The identification of the sacred with the fragmentary and the visual is especially acute, Franchot suggests, in nineteenth-century America, where anxiety about secularization is expressed in a Protestant preoccupation with material vestiges of Roman and African spirituality. Settling on exemplary scenes in major American novels—the recovery of a Madonna engraving entangled in seaweed by the Protestant heroine of Harriet Beecher Stowe's *The Minister's Wooing* (1859) or the Vodou item shaken loose from the clothing of the priestess Clemence, symbolizing the lost arm of a tortured slave, in George Washington Cable's *The Grandissimes, A Story of Creole Life* (1880)—Franchot reveals a national becoming marked by "theological ruin and racial violence."

The identification of religion with loss and ruin is also the starting point of my own essay, "The Place of Ritual in Our Time" (chapter 4).

This is for me an echo of ancient tradition, where ritual acts regularly expressed nostalgia for greater spiritual promise and communal coherence, and uncertainty about the authenticity of ritual procedure. Focusing on representations and actual instances of ritual sacrifice in the twentieth century, I show how they fulfill a typical pattern of restoration (of a lost relationship between humans and gods) and atonement (for offenses against powerful spirits). Sacrifice in our time symbolizes antiquity become intensely real. A basic assumption of my argument is the ordinariness of sacrifice. One sign of this is the fact that sacrifice is grounded in eating, and I begin accordingly, with the most common of objects, a box of breakfast cereal. I then turn to a biblically inspired domestic murder that looks aberrant, but is actually rather conventional in its basic aspects. My final and fullest example comes from high culture: Bernard Malamud's *The Fixer* (1966), a novel based on the 1913 ritual murder trial of Mendel Beilis in Kiev, Russia. My essay is designed to demonstrate the reach of sacrifice in postmodern America: from an item of popular culture, to a way of expressing rage, worship, or fear, to a mode of historical reflection and explanation.

Where Franchot and I explore the intersections of the literary and the religious at particular historical moments, Giles Gunn and Geoffrey Galt Harpham attempt to identify specific spiritual lineages for contemporary literary criticism. In "Human Solidarity and the Problem of Otherness" (chapter 5), Giles Gunn addresses a subject of central concern to Smith, Brown, and Franchot. His essay might be seen as an exploration in political terms of the philosophical axiom articulated by Jonathan Z. Smith: "In culture as in language, it is difference which generates meaning." But Gunn observes in the West at present an "abundance of difference," a world scene where cultural as well as personal identity seems to require, beyond mere differentiation from others, their demonization. Emphasizing the reparative prospects of genealogical modes of analysis, he notes that since the Enlightenment the sense of solidarity has enjoyed the moral valence of a god-term. In works by "secular theologians" such as Tocqueville, Marx, and Durkheim, the concept of a unitary humanity symbolized the nature of the human bond not only within cultures but between them. A century of ethnic cleansing across the globe, however, has provided dramatic evidence for the disrepute of the solidarity concept. Working through a variety of theories (including those of Kenneth Burke, Michael Ignatieff, Emmanuel Levinas, and Jacques Derrida) and testing possibilities in different literary examples (Conrad's *Heart of Darkness*, Coetzee's *Foe*, and Celan's "Death Fugue") Gunn arrives at a "pragmatist" solution to the adversarial relations that have plagued twentieth-century cross-cultural exchange, in academia as well as in practical politics. A "sense of fundamental kinship with the enemy," he suggests, might yet provide a model for global solidarity. This sense involves the recognition that even in their "total antagonism, 'self and other' remain constructs that are at once implicated in one another's fabrication and necessary to each other's moral constitution."

Geoffrey Galt Harpham shares Gunn's interest in the moral histories of scholarly concepts. His subject in "Ascetics, Aesthetics, and the Management of Desire" is the spirit of asceticism in modern art, and he begins by highlighting the deep affinities between aestheticism and asceticism, two systems of value with a common understanding of desire as a process involving translation or conversion. Art is traditionally conceived, Harpham suggests, as compensation for the flaws or inadequacies of human existence, while terrible suffering is transformed, through the logic of asceticism, into assurance of eternal reward. Creativity often requires aescetic behaviors: successful performance depends on discipline; the hardships of poets and painters are legendary. Ideals of artistic seclusion and Christian models of monasticism and hermeticism subscribe equally to a law of compensation, where sexuality is the repudiated desire. The modern notion that beauty (both its creation and its reception) represents a sublimation of sexuality, Harpham points out, is rooted in fifteenth-century asceticism. And he proceeds to a detailed analysis of a fifteenth-century Flemish painting depicting the holy embrace of St. Anthony and Paul the Hermit. The painting, by Sassetta, affirms, in Harpham's words, not only "a momentary relief from the intense solitude suffered by each . . . but an astonishing interval of sensation." For while the two holy men carefully avoid genital contact, leaving a space between their bodies, that avoidance results in the placement of their hands on each other's buttocks. As Harpham observes, "no conversion converts without a remainder, without creating fresh opportunities and needs for further conversion." The homoerotic embrace may stand as *the* model for piety in an ascetic context, he concludes, precisely because it is forbidden.

In the ascetic tradition Geoffrey Harpham writes about, sexuality is sublimated to higher ends. In the contemporary historiographic context which is Richard Fox's concern, sexuality is on everyone's mind, while love goes unexplored. How can historians redress the balance, giving historical substance to an idea and an experience that have often been considered trans-historical? This is the main question of Fox's essay, "New Baptized: The Culture of Love in America, 1830s to 1950s." From the purview of the historian, universals, such as "Love," only become meaningful when examined in specific cultural circumstances. Hence Fox attempts to capture some of the human experiences that the category has helped to express, and some of the social uses to which it has been put. He emphasizes that love in nineteenth-century America was as much a religious phenomenon (love of Jesus) as it was secular and romantic (love of Juliet). It is characteristic of Fox's purposes in the essay, that his title is drawn from another time and place. A Shakespearean sanctification of private passion ("Call me but love and I'll be new baptized") is used to make a local point. "Religiosity and secularity have not been zero-sum combatants in the United States," Fox writes, "they have deepened one another's hold." The historian of love must be alert to causal and formal complexity: love is sacred and mundane; experience as well as idea; a story of individual feelings and of broad social forces; an affirmation of convention or a route to transgression.

No field has been more intimately involved than anthropology in the task of defining "Culture." Yet the historical basis of this theoretical project is not widely known. In her essay "'The Mystery of Life in All Its Forms': Religious Dimensions of Culture in Early American Anthropology" (chapter 8), Gillian Feeley-Harnik proposes to recuperate some of the historical-material circumstances which surrounded the emergence of the culture concept in mid-nineteenth-century American anthropology. Drawing upon her archival and ethnographic research into the life and work of Lewis Henry Morgan (1818–81), whom his contemporaries named "the father of American anthropology," Feeley-Harnik argues that the idea of culture derives from debates in Morgan's time on the respective explanatory powers of science and religion. These debates, which issued in the formation of separate "natural" and "social" sciences, were focused in particular on the problem of design, or, in Morgan's words, the "mystery" of "life in all its forms." Feeley-Harnik suggests that Morgan intends "mystery" in a theological sense, and, more importantly, that current uses of "culture" still retain this religious connotation. In books such as *Systems of Consanguinity and Affinity of the Human Family* (1871), *The American Beaver and His Works* (1868), and *The League of the Ho-de'-no-sau-nee* (1851), Morgan sought answers to questions as diverse as the origins of life, the relationship between verbal and non-verbal language, and the last judgment. To trace the former social and political organization of the Iroquois, to pore over the Iroquois relics turned up by the plows of upstate New York farmers (sometimes a kettle or pipe, sometimes actual human bones), was for Morgan to confront the very question of atonement—why the innocent were sacrificed for the guilty. What united Morgan's vast researches methodologically was the imperative of interpretation: linguistic, cross-cultural, biblical, religious, and scientific. What united them morally and spiritually was the irony of progress: that "civilizing" intentions wrought such destruction and slaughter.

Feeley-Harnik brings together threads of history that have been analytically separate due to disciplinary divisions. A hybrid intellectual like Lewis Henry Morgan recognized the web of associations that united the elaborate dam-building of beavers, Euro-American constructions of kinship, and Indian efforts to revitalize their devastated civilization in the Handsome Lake Movement of the 1840s. Writing the histories of disciplines allows us to reclaim foundational points of affinity that are obscured by modern disciplinary practices.

Among the most significant relationships uncovered by Feeley-Harnik's research on Morgan, is the interconnectedness of nineteenth-century ecology and theology, an interconnectedness which is confirmed for the late twentieth century but with quite different implications, by Jack Miles's essay. In "Global Requiem: The Apocalyptic Moment in Religion, Science, and Art" (chapter 9), Miles addresses the widespread conviction that the environmental assurances of wisdom literature are no longer tenable. The biblical testimony that posits individual death against the eternal return of earth and species, Miles contends, is losing ground among scholars, artists, and journalists. As illustration, he describes a variety of works, from William Ashworth's somber history of *The Late Great Lakes* (1987), to Malcolm Browne's memoir *Muddy Boots and Red Socks* (1993), which concludes that the human species "exhibits all the pathological features of cancerous tissue." Our demise, Miles predicts, "will not come as it does in the disaster movies that are now so strangely popular . . . it will come rather as an accumulation of ignored warnings from scientists." But it will come with time to spare, remote enough for full-fledged despair. If we are doomed, scientifically speaking, Miles believes we'll be confronting this fate with our eyes open. His question then becomes the potential consequences for art and religion: what type of aesthetic, of spirituality, is suitable to this apocalyptic moment—the final days of humanity? A central paradox of Miles's analysis is the way a Judaeo-Christian legacy has helped to authorize the end of life as we know it by fostering such unwavering faith in its continuation: the persisting belief that the earth and species will endure has justified disregard of genuine threats to their endurance. Given the limits of this tradition, it's not surprising that in conclusion Miles looks beyond it, promoting a multicultural blend of religious resources as the best prospect for human renewal or comfort.

In contemplating the state of a domestic and global ecosystem, Jack Miles identifies the postmodern limits of Judaeo-Christian wisdom. Exploring the spiritual contours of an altogether different culture, Eytan Bercovitch discovers the vitality of Christian practice. In "The Altar of Sin: Social Multiplicity and Christian Conversion among a New Guinea People" (chapter 10), Bercovitch describes the powerful role of Christianity in parts of the world most deeply associated in the popular Western imagination with indigenous religions. He notes that the majority of New Guineans consider themselves Christians, as do many of the peoples of Africa, South America, and Australia. "By necessity and choice," Bercovitch observes, "anthropologists who study such areas are increasingly making Christianity a focus of their research." Based on his three years of fieldwork among the Atbalmin, a group of three thousand who live in the Star Mountains of Papua New Guinea, Bercovitch's analysis seeks to assess what it means for a group to convert to Christianity. Conversion, he points out, is never complete: Atbalmin faith represents a complex blend of Christian and indigenous traditions. In order to sort out the various forces impinging on the religious experiences of the Atbalmin, Bercovitch introduces the concept of "social multiplicity," which he defines as "a situation where people possess several, often contradictory sets of beliefs and practices." What distinguishes "social multiplicity" from previous concepts devised to account for coexisting social practices, is Bercovitch's emphasis on conflict. Where concepts such as "pluralism," "syncretism," or "compartmentalization" posit a harmonious coexistence or synthesis of values, "social multiplicity" highlights the ambivalence aroused by adherence to diverse beliefs. And Christianity may provide, according to Bercovitch, the ideal script for ministering to such ambivalence. The Atbalmin's loyalty to indigenous religions actually intensifies the force of Christianity in their lives. Their example reveals how Christianity is constituted fundamentally in relation to that which is non-Christian, and how its focus on sin and temptation makes it peculiarly adaptable to the religious dilemmas spawned by cross-cultural confrontations.

Christianity, at the verge of the twenty-first century, remains one of America's most prominent exports. Yet the country has, since its beginnings, been renewed continuously by spiritual imports of different kinds. How is the inherent pluralism of American religious life, its receptivity to alternative customs and beliefs, affected by the information technology revolution? This is the question posed by Bruce B. Lawrence in his essay, "God On Line: Locating the Pagan/Asian Soul of America in Cyberspace" (chapter 11). Drawing on the work of Manuel Castells, Lawrence cites the technological advances that will make a globally interactive communication system available and indispensable to all levels of society by the early twenty-first century. While noting the potential for a bifurcation of the multimedia world into "interacting" and "interacted," Lawrence also professes optimism about the savvy of the "netizenry" in exercising control over its virtual options, especially in the area of religion. The culture of the information age, Lawrence suggests, is one of "real virtuality": a culture in which the message *is* the message, is ideally suited to the representation of a "higher" reality, especially a multiple one. "God on line becomes the representation of the unrepresentable," Lawrence writes, "the surplus of meaning that becomes the property of multiple 'traditional' religions, and also others that are not traditional."

Asian and pagan religions, he points out, have proven especially adaptable to the do-it-yourself spirituality of popular media, especially those of cyberspace. The Immigration Act of 1965 prepared the way for new Asians, which included spiritual teachers whose influence has been widespread, while the unique spiritual pragmatism of pagans allows them to "imagine technology as both a metaphor and a tool for ritual." These two traditions, one established yet alien, the other rarely accorded anything like religious respectability, have been consistently linked as offerings in the smorgasbord of New Age spirituality. The promise of cyberspace, Lawrence concludes, is the opportunities it affords for the exploration and appreciation of "the religiously 'other,' who is not less American for being non-Abrahamic."

The shared subject of religion and culture reveals striking continuities of theory, theme, and method. In conclusion, I want to focus on three of the most significant of them. The first is a theoretical continuity: an interest in the origin of analytical categories, the forces that combine to make certain concepts seem necessary at some historical junctures, or outmoded at others. As confirmed by Jonathan Z. Smith on the invention of "race" in seventeenth-century Europe, and Gillian Feeley-Harnik on the emergence of "culture" from nineteenth-century debates on the explanatory merits of science versus religion, major concepts, however long their intellectual genealogies, are finally spurred by shocks to the social system. For Smith, it is the surprise of Indians in North America that pushes Europeans over the edge into theories of polygeny. For Feeley-Harnik, it is the confluence of Darwinism and colonialism that gives rise to the social science of culture. In keeping with the attention to how terms evolve, other contributors seek to repair terms that have gone out of favor (Giles Gunn on "solidarity"), or to coin terms required by the phenomena they seek to describe (Eytan Bercovitch on "social multiplicity").

The second is a continuity in method: the emphasis on popular as well as on elite cultural forms, and the acknowledgment of religion's deep structures as aural and visual as well as cognitive. Cereal boxes, covers from *Life* magazine, paintings from fifteenth-century Flanders, photographic portraits from antebellum family albums, the music of John Cage, all appear in these essays as central expressions of the religious imagination. Richard Fox's nineteenth-century culture of love includes the mass of Jesus worshipers "entranced by the impassioned rhetoric of preachers on the stump," in addition to self-conscious utopian radicals like John Humphrey Noyes and Emma Goldman. Jonathan Z. Smith's analysis of "close encounters" between "diverse kinds" sets best-sellers like Whitley Strieber's *Communion: A True Story* (1987) beside high intellectual tomes like Gregorio Garcia's *The Origin of the Indians of the New World and the West Indies* (1607). And Bruce B. Lawrence considers academic textbooks such as W. G. Oxtoby's *World Religions* and witch-craft websites such as www.witchvox.com equally reflective of that ever-changing "ideological fault-line," world religions.

Finally, there is continuity in theme itself: as in the assumption of religion's root association with violence. In Franchot's essay, America's nineteenth-century foundations are laid by the vestiges of alternative cultures and spiritualities annihilated in the process of national development. In my account, what makes the image of sacrifice arresting and potent, from the perspective of advertisers, is the hint of brutality that is subliminally recognized as basic to the ritual. For Geoffrey Harpham, to grasp ascetic practices as fundamental to a modernist aesthetic is to expose "the sheer violence of the modern work of art." Jack Miles sees the possibly irreversible ravage of nature by the West in general, and America in particular, as an outcome both authorized and assuaged by biblical wisdom. And Karen McCarthy Brown understands the affective power of Vodou *wanga* or tying charms, as issuing in part from the African experience of enslavement.

The volume's range of vocabulary and subject matter is aimed at enriching what is still an underdeveloped critical discourse about religion and culture. Only in the past few years have cultural studies scholars come to recognize the field's near complete inattention to the subject of religion. Ours is among the first volumes explicitly aimed at exploring religion's position in or against cultural studies through essays that are both thematic and theoretical in stance. It is our hope that our collective effort will initiate scholarly interest in the field of religion and cultural studies, correct a substantial bias against the study of religion in cultural studies, and finally, help vitalize and deepen intellectual inquiry in the academy today.

Let me end on a personal note. The genesis of this collection was my discovery of work in a different field, which seemed to address questions I'd been pursuing for years, in ways that were not only strangely familiar, but powerfully new. In his brilliant book, *Imagining Religion*, Jonathan Z. Smith explored problems of classification in the study of early Judaism, and analyzed such varied phenomena as the rituals surrounding bear hunting in the northern hemisphere, and the implications for religious studies of the mass suicide in Jonestown, Guyana. Among the most significant aspects of Smith's work for me, was the way in which it crossed disciplines (bringing together methods drawn from literary theory and anthropology, as well as religion), and also mediated divisions between academic and popular investigations of religion (both through the striking range of its subjects and the clarity of its reflections).

Smith's work provided the inspiration for a panel I organized at the Modern Language Association Meetings in Toronto in 1997, "Imagining

Religion in an Era of Cultural Studies," which brought together scholars of religion and English, in order to stage a dialogue about the complex ties between "religion," "culture," and the area of recent critical analysis dedicated to probing the thorny political history of the culture concept, cultural studies. The panel, which included Jenny Franchot, Giles Gunn, Andrew Delbanco, Jonathan Z. Smith, and myself, was designed to fill a vacuum in postmodern conceptualizations of religious experience and moral inquiry overall. It addressed what seemed to me a split, or even chasm, between the richness and intensity of religious life in American society in general, and the relative impoverishment of academic discussions of religion, especially among those most disposed to reflect deeply upon the various and highly contested meanings of "culture." This was the first MLA panel ever to conjoin the subjects of religion and cultural studies, and it attracted enough interest from scholars and editors in the Toronto audience, and beyond it, to legitimate the idea of a larger collection centered on expanded versions of the panel papers.

Because I had long admired the extraordinary scholarship of Jenny Franchot, a literary critic and historian of nineteenth-century American religious life at the University of California, Berkeley, I asked her to co-edit the prospective book with me. Our collaboration had only just begun at the time of her tragic death in the fall of 1998. This book is dedicated to her.

Notes

1. Mark I. Pinsky, "Faith Finds Unlikely Home on 'Simpsons,'" *Orlando Sentinel*, August 26, 1999; Patrick Flaherty, "Believing in the Blessedness of Audrey," *Boston Globe*, August 10, 1998; "Belief by the Numbers," compiled by Russell Shorto, *New York Times Magazine*, special issue: "God Decentralized," December 7, 1997.

2. At the same time, the Episcopal, Methodist, and Roman Catholic denominations reported decreases of 44%, 38%, and 3%, respectively, "Belief by the Numbers," *New York Times Magazine*, December 7, 1997.

3. Jonathan Z. Smith has called this, borrowing from Arnold Van Gennep, "the pivoting of the sacred." "There is nothing," Smith writes, "that is inherently sacred or profane. These are not substantive categories, but rather situational or relational categories, mobile boundaries which shift according to the map being employed" (*Imagining Religion: From Babylon to Jonestown*, Chicago: University of Chicago Press, 1982, p. 55 and passim). I have drawn here also on Talal Asad, *Genealogies of Religion: Disciplines and Reasons of Power in Christianity and Islam*, chapter 1, "The Construction of Religion as an Anthropological Category," pp. 27–54.

4. These terms, along with the inspiration for thinking of religious classifications as analogous to biological or botanical classifications, are from Jonathan Z.

Smith's essay, "Fences and Neighbors: Some Contours of Early Judaism," in *Imagining Religion*, pp. 1–18.

5. Among the many contributions to recent academic debates over definitions of the category of culture, the most precise and illuminating include Raymond Williams, *Keywords: A Vocabulary of Culture and Society* (New York: Oxford, 1976), pp. 87–93; Gillian Feeley-Harnik, in her essay below; and Talal Asad, *Genealogies of Religion*, especially pp. 248–53. See also the essay on "Culture" by Tomoko Masuzawa, as well as the essay on "Religion, Religions, Religious" by Jonathan Z. Smith, in *Critical Terms for Religious Studies*, ed. Mark C. Taylor (Chicago: University of Chicago Press, 1998), pp. 70–93 and 269–84.

6. This is not to deny that even during this period of eclipse, some of the most respected historians worked on religious subjects, including Puritanism and slave religion. Harry S. Stout and D. G. Hart describe religion's changing fortunes as a subject of research in their Introduction to *New Directions in American Religious History* (New York: Oxford University Press, 1997), p. 3, a collection which exemplifies the extent of the current revival of interest in religion among historians in general. See also on this subject, Robert Orsi's "Snakes Alive: Resituating the Moral in the Study of Religion," in Richard Wightman Fox and Robert B. Westbrook, eds., *In Face of the Facts: Moral Inquiry in American Scholarship* (New York: Cambridge University Press, 1997), pp. 201–26. Exemplary historical studies on religion published in the 1960s and 1970s include Edmund Morgan, *Visible Saints* (1963); David Hall, *The Faithful Shepherd* (1972); Eugene Genovese, *Roll, Jordan, Roll* (1972); and Albert Raboteau, *Slave Religion* (1978).

7. Cornel West, "The Postmodern Crisis of Black Intellectuals," *Cultural Studies*, eds. Lawrence Grossberg, Cary Nelson, and Paula Treichler (New York: Routledge, 1992), p. 695; David Hollinger, *Science, Jews and Secular Culture: Studies in Mid-Twentieth Century Intellectual History* (Princeton: Princeton University Press, 1996), p. 21.

8. "On Cultural Studies," eds. Jessica Munns and Gita Rajan, *A Cultural Studies Reader* (London: Longman, 1995), pp. 614–45.

9. All this will come as no surprise to those familiar with the classics of religious studies, such as Emile Durkheim's *Elementary Forms of the Religious Life* (1916) and Perry Miller's two-volume exploration of *The New England Mind* (1939, 1953). For these authors there is no separating religion from culture, which is to say that there is no separating religion as a conceptual field from its practical enactments and effects.

10. Consider the scene where the visionary, Adam De Kuff, inspects the "sacramentals" of the former Jewish Sufi Master: "kippa, *tallit, tefillin* . . . a band of saffron-colored cotton cloth from a temple in Sri Lanka, and incense sticks and, wrapped in a silk cloth, a crucifixion icon in imitation of the one by Dionysius the Monk at the Ferapont Monastery in Russia." Each icon carries the residue of a culture, registering a way of life of a particular people, in a particular time and place. As he proceeds to bind the *tefillin* in the manner of "the accursed Gnostics and Nazarenes," represented to him in a dream, De Kuff pays homage to yet another entanglement of religious affiliation and human affinity. *The Last of the*

Mohicans (New York: Signet, 1980), pp. 35, 40, 73, 83, 92, 148, 216, 314, 316, 318, 325; *Damascus Gate* (New York: Scribner, 1998), pp. 146–47.

11. The introductions to *Cultural Studies*, eds. Lawrence Grossberg, Cary Nelson, Paula Treichler, and *A Cultural Studies Reader*, as well as Tomoko Masuzawa's essay, "Culture," in *Critical Terms for Religious Studies*, all provide useful efforts to think through the implications and ends of cultural studies while avoiding its definition.

12. Fredric Jameson in "On Cultural Studies," pp. 614–15. Jameson also observes here that persisting efforts to establish unified purposes and methods have tended more to divert from than to serve the ends of scholarship.

13. See Lawrence Buell's introduction, "In Pursuit of Ethics," to *PMLA*'s special issue on "Ethics and Literary Study," vol. 114, no. 1 (January 1999), pp. 7–19; and Richard Sennett's *The Corrosion of Character* (New York: Norton, 1998), an analysis of the contemporary workplace, consistent with Sennett's previous critical sociology, full of statistical references, global comparisons, and anecdotal descriptions of the American managerial classes, which concludes with an appeal to the ethical-spiritual theories of Levinas as one means to alleviating some of the ills highlighted by the study.

14. These differences are, if anything, intensified by the fact that the roles and obligations of academics in all disciplines seem increasingly in flux, susceptible to the climate of rapid change that is a chief component of this early-twenty-first century moment. It's not always clear whether a literature professor's ideal forum is a scholarly journal or a mass circulation magazine; or whether the most appropriate site for fieldwork is some "alien" pocket in the anthropologist's home town or some select locale across the globe; or whether a historian's best audience is the somnambulant viewers of early morning "C-SPAN" or a conversant group of colleagues from his or her own field.

RELIGION AND CULTURAL STUDIES

1

Close Encounters of Diverse Kinds

> Noah sail'd round the Mediterranean in Ten
> Years, and divided the World into Asia, Afric and
> Europe, Portions for his three Sons. America
> then, it seems, was left to be his that could catch
> it.
>
> John Locke, *Two Treatises of Government*
> (1698), Treatise One, ch. XI, par. 142.

I

To signal at the outset, as Steven Spielberg has done, the indebtedness of my title, I remind you of the labors of the late Chicago-area professor, J. Allen Hynek, to put the study of unidentified flying objects (UFOs) on a scientific basis.[1] In Hynek's typology, "close encounters of the first kind" are where alien ships are sighted; in the "second kind," the UFOs leave some physical mark of their presence; "close encounters of the third kind" are where contacts with the occupants of a UFO are made.[2] It will be with a variant of the latter "kind" with which we shall initially be concerned, considered, recently, by some to be a distinctive new type, "close encounters of the fourth kind."[3]

Since the fall of 1957, when a Brazilian farmer, Antonio Villas Boas, reported that a spaceship had landed on his farm, the occupants taking him aboard and performing a variety of physical acts on him,[4] a specific mode of American UFO tale has emerged, and found a secure, iconic place in popular culture: the Abduction Report.[5]

The first North American version was that of Betty and Barney Hill in the White Mountains of New Hampshire on the evening of September 19, 1961; it was widely disseminated through the television movie, *The UFO Incident,* and more recently reconfigured in a characteristically ingenious fashion in the late, lamented TV series, *Dark Skies*.[6] The Travis Walton narrative (Arizona, November 1975), recounting his five-day capture, the subject of the Paramount film, *Fire in the Sky,* is, perhaps, best

known, having received nationwide media attention.[7] The most developed, all but canonical report, is the Betty Andreasson narrative.[8] The
most popular account remains Whitley Strieber's best seller, *Communion*
(1987), presented as an autobiographical recounting of a series of experiences undergone by this well-known writer of horror stories.[9]

In all, by 1987, some 1200 North American abductions were filed
under the name of the abductee; 600 to 700 narratives had been collected; 300 of these were carefully studied by the folklorist, Thomas E.
Bullard, with 103 considered by Bullard to be "high information cases."[10]
Bullard's comparative studies suggest that there is a persistent structure
to Abduction Reports, with the same episodes recurring in invariant order in 80% of the "high information" narratives.[11] "A single deviation
accounts for failure of sequence in almost all of the remainder."[12] Bullard
distinguishes eight episodes.[13] By his own statistics, I would reduce the
number to seven.

1. *Capture*. The aliens take the individual aboard a UFO.[14]
2. *Examination*. The aliens subject the individual to both physical and
   mental tests.[15] The first two episodes, capture and examination, are
   the most developed segments of the Abduction Reports. With the
   obvious addition of the penultimate episode, the return, they recur
   most frequently and contain the highest degree of repetitive
   elements.

To elaborate on the examination episode: once aboard, the human is
taken to the examination room, a central, circular location, with a dome,
dominated by an examination table, and usually lacking all other furni-
ture. The placement of the room suggests that the ship was constructed
with examination as its primary purpose. The abductee is stripped,
cleaned, and placed on the table where she or he is subjected to a searching physical examination. The first stage is manual; the second, scanning
with a mechanical device. Next, various needle-like instruments probe
beneath the skin, with specimens of various sorts, especially bodily fluids,
being taken. Either the ovaries or the testicles are probed in what seems
to be the preoccupation of the examination with the reproductive system.
(In one report, a male's examination was terminated and he was abruptly
released because he had had a vasectomy). Finally, neurological tests are
administered, at times climaxed by the insertion of some sort of miniaturized electronic device in the brain.

Significantly, it is most often in the context of the examination episode
that we are given the fullest physical description of the aliens. While more
than one hundred types of alien beings have been described in UFO
reports and classified in taxonomic studies by Jadar U. Pereira, Eric
Zurcher, David Chance, Patrick Huyghe, Kevin Randle, and Russ Estes,[16]

most commonly, in North American abduction narratives, they are represented as humanoids, three to five feet tall, with soft gray skin. Popularly referred to as "the Grays," they have large hairless heads with tapering chins. Their eyes are large, extending around the sides of their heads like wraparound sunglasses. Their ears are tiny or absent, the nose and mouth are small holes. Their limbs are thin, with arms that reach to their knees. Their fingers are elongated, with less than five visible digits. Their legs are often short and oddly jointed, producing an awkward gait. They are most often represented as clothed in a neutrally colored, close-fitting garment which appears to be a uniform, at times belted or with a hood. There are usually no visual sexual characteristics. One alien, in some reports taller than the others, in other reports indistinguishable from the rest, serves as leader and liaison, both directing the examination and communicating with the human, frequently in a reassuring manner.[17]

3. *Conference.* The effects of the examination on the abductee are often described in terms ranging from discomfort and embarrassment to pain and terror consistent with its nature as a rape-like violation of a helpless subject. However, following the examination, the next reported episode is a conference between the aliens and the human, usually by means of telepathic communication, which, without supplying the reasons, claims a shift in attitude by the abductee towards the aliens from fear and hostility to friendly, positive feelings.[18]

Beginning in the mid-1980s, a different sort of narrative has emerged which describes the examination as sexual abuse, often related to an alien project of producing human-alien hybrids. This focus brings about a concomitant decline in the number of reports of a positive conference, the conference often being replaced by a horrified viewing of the hybrid embryos or children.[19]

4. *Tour.* The conference is usually followed by an escorted tour of the ship.[20]
5. *Journey.* The ship then leaves its landing site and conveys the human to a "strange place," usually not identified as the aliens' home base. In a very few cases, a "divine" figure is encountered.[21]
6. *Return.* A necessary part of the narrative structure of the Abduction Report, the return tale is usually quite brief, often reversing the capture sequence. The human is escorted out of the ship, frequently to the place of initial contact, and watches the UFO's departure.[22]
7. *Aftermath.* A distinctive feature of Abduction Reports is that they do not conclude with the reintegration of the abductee into society or the resumption of ordinary life. She or he remains strongly marked by the experience, exhibiting a variety of often puzzling

symptoms.[23] Acute thirst and the need to bathe are the most immediate. Later, there will be nightmares, flashbacks, anxiety attacks,
and noticeable personality changes, often relieved by remembering
the experience under hypnosis. Others report further paranormal
experiences, incidents of extrasensory perception, or visions of
"men in black," a subtype, studied by Peter M. Rojcewicz, which
seems to be one of a number of subordinate elements which interpret the abduction experience as demonic. (Note that the recent
Columbia-Amblin film, *Men in Black*, has quite inverted the significance of these figures).[24] In a few cases, further abductions, or rec-
ollections of previous abductions, are reported.

It will serve little purpose, here, to pause over the question of the truth
of these reports, or to rehearse the various theories, from the psycho-
analytic to the folkloristic, that have been brought to their interpretation.[25]
For our reflections, their nature as narratives allow them to be linked
with Mark Rose's "paradigm" for science fiction: texts that "are composed within the semantic space created by the opposition of human . . .
and non-human,"[26] and our attention is directed to their most elaborated
episode and theme, the examination.

It may seem a simple conclusion to assert, with Bullard, that in these
narratives, "the examination appears to be the real purpose of the encounter,"[27] and yet, this is quite remarkable. When one reads in the wider
UFO literature, and, most particularly, in the alien contact or encounter
literature produced by the stunning variety of UFO religions,[28] a variety
of other motivations prevail: they are from a superior culture and bring
us wisdom; they are from a threatened culture and bring us warning; they
are from a dying planet or species which needs something from us; they
come to lead; they come to share; they come to give; they come to
exploit; they come to punish; they come to replace; they come to destroy.
Whatever the scenario, there are interests at stake, be they ours, theirs, or
mutual. By contrast, in the Abduction Reports, there are rarely explicit
motivations.[29] Rather than interests, there seems only to be interest, or,
better, disinterested observation, a curiosity often felt to be prurient by
the abductee.

At one level, the Abduction Reports seem to be a modernist version of
the literary subgenre, reverse anthropology, well known through texts
such as *Gulliver's Travels*. Americans are captured as specimens. They are
helpless. They are manipulated (literally) without regard to their feelings
as if they were not of the same order as their examiners. The humans are
stripped, cleaned, and probed for incomprehensible reasons. Their only
acknowledged function is that of providing data. And yet, faithful to the
all but pornographic male fantasy of the ethnographic enterprise, the ab-

ductees' own emotions at being violated begin with fear and hostility and end with good will. It is only the concluding episode, the aftermath, which challenges this dominant scientific romance as the narratives go on to record the aftershocks, the posttraumatic effects of the encounter. Once examined, nothing is (or will be) ever the same again.

While it is tempting to develop these themes into a contemporary fable, one which would invoke a host of images from discipline and panopticons to the ambivalences of post-colonial discourses, something does not fit. Above all, it is the silence—not a lack of communication, but a lack of interrogation.[30] The aliens betray no interest in human culture, and impart nothing of their own. There is no trace of the interspecific, interlocutory agendum of cultural encounter which informs ethnographically sophisticated science fiction novels such as Chad Oliver's *Unearthly Neighbors* (New York, 1960); which underlies the recent essay by Jonathan vos Post, "How to Talk to an Extraterrestrial"[31]; or which was raised at the 1970 Annual Meeting of the American Anthropological Association in their symposium, "The Role of Anthropology in Outer Space."[32] Indeed, as has been noted, while not the explicit subject of the reports, there is a silent, mutual examination of bodies, ours and theirs. It is from a comparison of these bodies that I shall derive my fable for our reflection.

What the aliens seem to be interested in, above all, what they appear to most want to understand, is difference. As their bodies are represented to us in the Abduction Reports, it does not matter whether they are clothed or unclothed; either way they are uniform, neutrally gray, with no distinguishing features, whether of physiognomy or status. This uniformity was strikingly replicated in the 1997 collective suicide of the Heaven's Gate group with their erasure of difference by means of identical dress, haircuts, and traveling cases as well as the neutered males, as they awaited transportation to an alien ship hidden behind the Hale-Bopp comet.[33] In the Abduction Reports, the aliens are neither naturally nor culturally marked in any way visible to their human subjects. Their observed activities—search, seize, probe, release—could just as readily and interchangeably be performed by NASA-style robots. In archaic language, they are "protoplasts," "homunculi," existing permanently in this preformative state without any apparent imprinting mechanism to give them characteristics. They lack even the mysterious contagious processes of mimicry, of simulation, by which the protoplasts in the pods in the now thrice-made film, *Invasion of the Body Snatchers*, assume the personal appearance, habits, character, and memory of those human individuals to which they are placed in close proximity. In the Abduction Reports, there is no transfer, only collection; and while there is concentrated interest in the human reproductive system, there are no processes of reproduction.

The aliens' attention to the body, to that which is, at one and the same time, most typical and most individual in any complex species, is an examination of that site at which difference, whether evaluated as natural or cultural, is most immediately apparent. The aliens' preoccupation with probing beneath the surface of the skin both the human reproductive system and the brain, while ignoring other, equally significant physiological systems,[34] is to focus on precisely those systems in which the problematics of difference are most complex and rich in information.

The comparison of bodies, theirs and ours, which underlies the central episode of the Abduction Reports might be expressed in the technical terminology of classical taxonomy as follows: the aliens' bodies, in their pre-formative uniformity, appear as essential; the humans' bodies, in their variegation, appear as accidental. The fable I want to construct out of the Abduction Reports for our further reflection is one of singularity and diversity. While the genre of fable requires relative brevity, this very characteristic often compels its exegesis and application to take the "long way round." In this case, the detour is necessarily historical, an element in the histories of the western imaginations of difference which will lead us to isolate the intellectual moment that made the invention of "race" necessary—the first, new, influential anthropological theory since the classical period, and one that made urgent the emergence of the human sciences.

II

It is a commonplace to speak of western intellectual history as an interrelationship between Athens and Jerusalem. Within the sphere of anthropological thought, at least through the sixteenth century, it is undoubtedly true. The biblical account of human origins and subsequent relations, especially the genealogical and territorial map of Genesis 10, was overlaid upon the rich Greek and Roman ethnographic tradition, especially as categorized and transmitted by classical and Christian encyclopaedists. The resultant system exhibited remarkable flexibility, ever accommodating to new elements. For example, as late as the fifteenth and sixteenth centuries, aided by the pseudo-Berossian forgeries of Annius of Viterbo,[35] new segments were added to both the Noachic genealogies and migrations to account for the origins of the population of all of known Europe, as well as Africa and Asia, as may be seen, for example, in the well-known ninth chapter of Jean Bodin's *Method for the Easy Comprehension of History* (1565).[36]

It was a system that, by its very elasticity, prevented surprise whenever similarities or differences were encountered in the peoples mapped upon it. For the genealogies that underlay the system, as well as the biblical narration of anthropogony, guaranteed the essential unity of humankind. All were children of Adam and Eve, even though their lineages must be traced through Noah's three sons: Shem, Japhet, and Ham. Differences were, therefore, accidental. Drawing upon Greek and Roman theories, these were explained by the effects of climate, especially for somatic characteristics, and as the results of migration or diffusion for cultural divergencies. Similarities and differences were perceived as having documentary characteristics, allowing the mapping of spatial and temporal associations. Adopting the archaic Christian apologetic language for the relations of Christianity to classical culture, a notion of anthropologically significant survivals was developed in which the Christian scholar sought "seeds," "sparks," "traces," "footprints," "remains," or "shadows" of the original, essential unity of humankind amidst its palpable, contemporary diversity, and through which one could discern placement and reconstruct historical relations.[37]

Take, for example, the encounter with the Mongols (or, Tartars) in the thirteenth and fourteenth centuries, the occasion for the first new ethnography in the West since Roman times. Older Christian pseudo-Sibylline oracles were updated to place the Mongols within the framework of an apocalyptic scenario that associated them with the Scythians, one of the borderlines of humanity on the old Herodotean ethnographic map, and, through them, with the release of the feared, biblical tribes of Gog and Magog, walled in by Alexander the Great in Jewish and Christian versions of the *Alexander Romance*.[38] In support of this, a new version of the pseudepigraphical *Letter of Alexander to Aristotle Concerning the Wonders of India* was produced, proclaiming the presence of apocalyptic trials and associating them with the advent of the Mongols.[39] Other initial reports of the Mongol incursions displayed more positive biblical placements: the first notice (1221) identified Genghis Khan with King David,[40] while the Hungarian Dominican, Brother Julian (1238), as well as the *Alexander to Aristotle* letter, declared them to be "sons of Ishmael."[41] An interpolation into a set of fourteenth-century French manuscripts of *Mandeville's Travels*, confusing Khan and (C)ham, connected the Mongols with the Noachic Hamitic lineage.[42] The Mongols were hitherto unknown to the West, but their presence constituted no surprise; they could be classified as another "remnant" of biblical ethnography. The literature on the Mongols, taken as a whole, demonstrates the power of the amalgamation of the Greco-Roman ethnographic tradition and the biblical. Even in times of extreme distress and military conflict, the flexibility of the system proved able to assimilate new elements while holding the map intact. Differences remained in the realm of accident; similarities in that of essence.

I know of no serious challenge to this interpretative system until the post-Columbian debates over the nature of the Americas. It is here, for the first time, that a strong language of alterity emerges. America is an "other world," a "new world."[43] I shall not take time, here, to review the slow and difficult history of this perception,[44] but pause only to note that, as such, the American continent was a world wholly unknown to either the Greco-Roman or the biblical authors. In that regard, both sets of writings were irrevocably impeached. True, the Noachic model was reexamined, including the suggestion that there were two Arks, one that repopulated the familiar three-lobed world island of Africa, Europe, and Asia, a second that sailed, with its cargo of quite different species, to the new world[45]—an hypothesis most likely based on an observation of the effects of interweaving the so-called "J" and "P" Flood narratives, which, among other doublets, results in Noah, his family and the animals entering the Ark twice (Genesis 7.7–9[J]/Genesis 7.13–15[P]).

Other authorities expanded the migratory model in the face of the dilemma created by Noah having three rather than four sons. For example, in Gregorio García's enormous encyclopaedic work on *The Origin of the Indians of the New World and the West Indies* (1st edition, 1607), theories that the Americas were populated by Jews, Carthaginians, Greeks, Romans, Phoenicians, Egyptians, Africans, Ethiopians, French, Cambrians, Finns, Frisians, or Scythians are reviewed.[46] As an appendix to this naval, Noachic, transatlantic catalogue, another possibility is raised, returning to the original Columbian misidentification of the native Americans as "Indians," but, in fact, now a correct understanding, that the Americas were populated by an overland migration of Chinese or, more likely, Mongols.[47] Once this theory was isolated and disseminated, most famously by Edward Brerewood's *Enquiries Touching the Diversity of Languages, and Religions through the Chiefe Parts of the World* (1614)[48] and by John Ogilby's *America, Being the Latest, and most Accurate Description of the New World* (1671),[49] the old genealogical enterprise was resumed as to the Noachic genealogy of the Mongols, with descent from Japhet now being the most frequently argued connection.[50] But the haunting and shattering conclusion could not be long avoided; the elasticity of the old system finally proved insufficiently flexible. The Americas were a novelty that resisted absorption. There were no "traces." The native Americans were untraceable. The "new world" was not merely newly discovered, it was not merely different, it was "other" in its very essence—a radical conclusion first and more readily made with respect to its flora and fauna. Thus Acosta (1590), in a passage much discussed in seventeenth-century works on the implications of America for biblicist anthropology:

> What I say of the *guanacos* and *pacos* I will say of a thousand varieties of birds
> and fowls [in the Americas] that have never been known [previously] by either

name or appearance, nor is there any memory of them in the Latins or Greeks, nor in any nations of our [European] world over here. . . . It is well to ask whether these animals differ in kind and essence from all others, or if this difference be accidental . . . . But, to speak bluntly, anyone who in this way would focus only on the accidental differences, seeking thereby to explain [away] the propagation of the animals of the Indies and to reduce them [to variants] of the European, will be undertaking a task he will not be able to fulfill. For, if we are to judge the species of animals [in the Americas] by their [essential] properties, they are so different that to seek to reduce them to species known to Europe will mean having to call an egg a chestnut.[51]

This radical zoological conclusion could even be deployed analogically in seventeenth-century arguments for extraterrestrial life, as in Otto von Guericke (1672): "Anyone who would deny the presence of living creatures on the planets because he is not capable of imagining any creatures other than those he sees here on earth should know that in America there is no wild animal of exactly the same kind as in Europe, Asia or Africa."[52]

The zoological and botanical discoveries of essential difference with respect to the Americas foreshadowed the same sort of revision within anthropology. The novelty and the alterity of the Americas introduced surprise.

III

It is in the context of this disarray with respect to the centuries-old amalgam that a previously refused resource within theories associated with Greco-Roman ethnography was recovered and re-situated at the center of the European anthropological enterprise. The biblical narrative, and, therefore, western ethnologic theory was, up to this point, relentlessly monogenetic. There was a single ancestral pair from whom all humankind descended; there was a single locus, traditionally understood as somewhere in the Armenian mountains, from which all the intrafamilial diversities of humankind ultimately diffused. However, such an account could not be sustained if, as the novelty and the alterity of the Americas suggested, difference was an affair of essence rather than of accident.

Deep within the Greco-Roman theories of migration and diffusion, mixture and borrowing, climate and ecology as the explanations for cultural similarities and differences was a second, oppositional structure which emphasized immobility and originality: that of autochthony.[53] While best known as an Athenian political topos (autochthony equals autonomy), the notion, more widely applied as in emergence myths, suggested not only that some people were sprung from the very soil they inhabit, but implied, as well, a plurality of places of origination. Rejected by the monogenetic presuppositions of the biblically oriented Christian anthropology, autochthony was a theory of polygenesis.

Even at the present time, when we have returned to a Darwinian rather than a biblical notion of monogenesis, the concept of polygenesis persists in some of our most common ethnic designations: "aborigine" (classically understood as the Latin equivalent of autochthony), a people who has been in this or that place from their beginning; "indigenous," "creole," and "native," a people first born (or, created) in the place they inhabit. Ironically, these terms in colonialist discourse shifted from expressing their firstness to ours, becoming a designation of the inhabitants found in a place when we first "discovered" it.

Some scholars find anticipations of polygenetic theory in the Renaissance hermeticists, especially Paracelsus and Bruno.[54] The scattered references are far from clear and seem to reflect speculations about spontaneous generation. By the seventeenth century, these hints would be fully developed. One of the earlier, unambiguous polygenetic accounts of the Americas is by an anonymous author, L. P., Master of Arts, in a work entitled *Two Essays, Sent in a Letter from Oxford, to a Nobleman in London* (1695):

> The West Indies and the vast regions lately discovered towards the South abound with such a variety of inhabitants and new animals not known or even seen in Asia, Africa or Europe that the origin of them doth not appear so clear . . . especially seeing that there are no records or monuments of their migrations out of Asia or any other known parts of the world, either before or after the Flood; and their differences from all the rest of the Globe, in manners, languages, habits, religions, diets, arts and customs as well as in their quadrupeds, birds, serpents and insects, render their derivation very obscure and their origin uncertain, especially in the common [biblicist] way and according to the vulgar opinion of planting all the earth from one little spot. [In their] great zeal to maintain a Jewish tradition . . . every corner of the earth is searched to find out a word, a rite, or a custom in order to derive from thence many millions of different peoples. . . . [But] all nations agree in some words and in some customs, therefore a resemblance in a few of them is no proof. . . . I can see no way at present to solve this new face of nature by old arguments fetched from Eastern rubbish or rabbinical weeds. . . . Let them all [i.e., the new world humans, flora, and fauna] be *aborigines*.[55]

Although L. P.'s essay was not widely circulated, it contains, *in nuce*, the paradigmatic logic of the polygenetic argument: (1) given the utter novelty of the Americas, (2) the biblical account must be rejected (here the rejection contains an anti-Semitic element), (3) as must be the quest for "traces"; (4) the solution is that the life forms of the Americas are autochthonous: "let them all be *aborigines*."

The polythetic logic had already been fully elaborated in its theological rather than its anthropological implications in one of the most controversial and widely known works of the seventeenth century, Isaac de la Peyrère's books collectively entitled *Prae-Adamitae* ("The Preadamites," 1655; English translation, *Men Before Adam*, 1656).[56]

Peyrère represents that longstanding fear of Catholicism, the lay Bible reader. He tells us that he has spent twenty years pondering Romans 5.12–14, the classic Augustinian and Reformation proof text for original sin, itself a monogenetic notion.[57] On the basis of the phrases "sin was not imputed when the Law was not" and "even over those whose sin was not like the transgression of Adam," he concluded that "sin was in the world before Adam" although "it was not imputed until Adam." Therefore, there were many sorts of humans before Adam; Adam was not the ancestor of humankind.

With this established, he turns to an exegesis of the opening chapters of Genesis. Genesis 1.26–27 shows that God created, by the power of the Word, vast numbers of humans (i.e., Gentiles) just as the deity created all of the different sorts of animals and plants. Genesis 2 records the special creation of Adam, the first Jew, out of clay. Turning his attention to a set of well-known conundrums, Peyrère notes that the Cain and Abel story indicates the presence of numerous other peoples: If the brothers were farmers and shepherds, who made the knife that killed Abel? Where did Cain's wife come from? Who are the others who would kill Cain? Who inhabited the cities that "covered" the world at that time?

More generally, he asserts, the Jewish biblical chronology is strictly limited. It comprises no more than some 5000 years. But Peyrère knows of older histories: the Chaldaeans record 470,000 years of history, the Mexicans and Peruvians write of thousands of suns, and Chinese history extends back 880,000 years.

Drawing upon the biblical criticism of his friend Richard Simon, Peyrère then argues that Moses wrote an epitome of earlier records at a comparatively late date. In Genesis chapters 1–11, Moses compressed a series of long works into several brief chapters, being more interested in his own time than in prehistory. Thus, Moses was being no more than hyperbolic when he declared Adam to be the first human rather than the first Jew; the Flood was a limited phenomenon, confined to parts of Palestine which were easily repopulated by Noah's three sons. Hence all parallels between the biblical account and other cultures are merely superficial.

The polygenetic accounts of L. P. and La Peyrère in principle freed anthropology from its biblical framework. The Bible was reduced to a parochial document, the history of the Jews of a relatively early period. It was no longer to be understood as the universal history of humankind.

Human diversity now became an urgent intellectual problem. While these radical conclusions would be debated throughout the seventeenth and eighteenth centuries, they contributed to the formation of the first, new western theory for explaining human similarities and differences, the theory of race, the possibility that the genus *homo* might be divided by essential rather than accidental characteristics into separate species of differing lineages—a possibility first put forth by François Bernier in an article in the *Journal des Savants*, April 24, 1684.[58]

It was neither Orientals nor Blacks, who had long been mapped on the old Greco-Roman and biblical taxonomy, that gave rise to the intellectual problematics of race. Rather it was the unanticipated presence of native Americans, a surprise of profound implication, rendered even more certain once it was clear beyond doubt, post-Magellan, that America was not a part of Asia.

IV

To expand fully on the history of race theories and polygenesis would require a lengthy study, recalling the judgment of George Stocking, Jr.: "It seems fair to say that polygenism—or more broadly the problem of race—was the central concern of pre-Darwinian anthropology."[59] I can, here, give only a few conclusions, shorn of their necessary historical narratives which would, among other matters, have to trace the development of two complex terms and ideas, the new sixteenth-century coinage, "race," and an old term, now reconfigured, "species."

Simply put, monogenesis celebrated similarity, polygenesis, diversity— the latter leading, for the first time, to the development of a complex vocabulary for describing and explaining difference, limited by the unfortunate eighteenth-century decision to correlate biological and cultural characteristics. From the point of view of difference, with respect to biology, the intellectual choice was whether to understand the human "races" as "varieties" (i.e., accidents) or "species" (i.e., essences). If difference was understood to be accidental, a monogenetic account could be fashioned where difference was accounted for by environmental and historical causes. If difference was understood to be essential, then a polygenetic account which held the races to be irreducible was required. From the point of view of similarity, with respect to culture, a monogenetic account would need to refurbish the old language of diffusion and derivation. A polygenetic theory would have to emphasize parallel, independent development. In the biological language introduced by Richard Owen in the nineteenth century, for monogenetic approaches, cultural resemblances would be "homologies"; for polygenetic approaches, they would be "analogies."[60] From these choices, combined with questions of hierarchy, a necessary component in any classical taxonomic enterprise, one can generate the central debates which dominated eighteenth- and nineteenth-century anthropological discourse, and, still, to a large degree, rule popular perceptions, processes, and notions of cross-cultural comparison.

Having undertaken an historical detour, we can return to the Alien Abduction Reports. The central episode, the examination, appears to be a displacement onto "them" of our popular notion for understanding human difference as chiefly an affair of bodies, as being only "skin deep." The uniformity of their bodies, in contradistinction to the differentiation of ours, is a striking exaggeration of our commonsense belief, derived from the Greco-Roman and biblical amalgam, that there is an essential core of human sameness and, therefore, that difference is accidental, transferred, in the narratives, to the imagination of an unambiguously polygenetic situation: alien and human. But, in the examination episode, it is the silence that remains, be it expressed in the lack of either the interrogative or the indicative with respect either to the aliens' culture or to ours, or in the lack of recognition of the problematics of communication, within and between cultures, let alone across phyla, expressed in the Reports as the aliens too ready use of English or extralinguistic mental telepathy.

To this one must respond, whether with respect to popular belief or professional procedure, that the issue of human differentiation will not be settled by more observation at the somatic level, but rather by theories of an intellectual sort. It will not be settled by taxonomies of differential exclusion, but by comparative structures of reciprocal difference. It will be settled, at the level of culture, only by thoughtful projects of mediated discourse, by enterprises of translation, recalling that, whether intracultural or intercultural, translation is never fully adequate, there is always discrepancy. *Traduttori traditori.* And that, therefore, central to any proposal of translation are questions as to appropriateness or "fit," expressed through the double methodological requirement of comparison and criticism. As Isaiah Berlin framed it, in the course of one of his meditations on Vico: "In a sense, the mere existence of an extraordinary variety of very dissimilar languages . . . is itself an index or, one might say, a model of the irreducible variety of human self-expression, such that even in the case of cognate languages, complete translation of one into any other is in principle impossible; and the gap—indicative of difference in ways of perceiving and acting—is at times very large indeed."[61] To which I need only add that in culture as in language, it is difference which generates meaning.

The novelty of the Americas gave the West its first compelling language of difference, shattering, thereby, the older synthetic theory of essence and accident. We have yet to set forth a set of equally compelling cultural and comparative theories adequate to this new language. This remains, today, the unfulfilled challenge to the human sciences.

Notes

1. J. A. Hynek, "Epilogue," in S. Spielberg, *Close Encounters of the Third Kind* (New York: Dell Publishing Co., Inc., 1977): 253–56.

2. J. A. Hynek, *The UFO Experience: A Scientific Inquiry* (New York: Ballantine Books, 1974): 31–34, et passim; Hynek, "Epilogue": 253–54.

3. The terminology gained some currency by its inclusion in the Glossary of A. Pritchard, D. E. Pritchard, J. E. Mack, P. Kasey, C. Yapp, eds., *Alien Discussions: Proceedings of the Abduction Study Conference held at MIT, Cambridge, MA* (Cambridge, MA: North Cambridge Press, 1994): 680: "CE-IV is not part of Hynek's original classification but is used to mean abduction by entities." C. D. B. Bryan entitled his account of the conference *Close Encounters of the Fourth Kind: Alien Abduction, UFO's, and The Conference at M.I.T.* (New York: Alfred A. Knopf, 1995). In fact, the new terminology was little used in the published proceedings. My understanding of the abduction narrative is echoed by David Webb, at the conference, "We have a huge catalogue of CE-III cases of which the abduction cases are a subset" (Pritchard, et al., *Alien Discussions*: 99).

4. G. Creighton, "The Amazing Case of Antonio Villas Boas," in Ch. Bowen, ed., *The Humanoids* (Chicago: Henry Regnery, 1969): 200–38; C. and J. Lorenzen, *Encounters with UFO Occupants* (New York: Berkley Books, 1976): 61–87; K. Randle and R. Estes, *Faces of the Visitors: An Illustrated Reference to Alien Contact* (New York: Simon & Schuster, 1997): 133–41. As Boas's reported experience included compelled sexual intercourse, it more closely resembles a later stage in the development of abduction narratives. (See below, n. 19.)

5. See T. E. Bullard's classic work, *UFO Abductions: The Measure of a Mystery* (2 vols.: vol. 1, *Comparative Study of Abduction Reports*; vol. 2, *Catalogue of Cases*; Mount Rainier, MD: Fund for UFO Research, 1987). He gives a general definition of the Abduction Report as a narrative where a "witness is captured and held in unwilling temporary detention by extraordinary and apparently alien beings usually aboard a flying craft of unconventional design and usually for purposes something like a medical examination" (1: vii). See below, for Bullard's description of typical plot elements.

6. J. G. Fuller, *The Interrupted Journey* (New York: Dial, 1968) is the richest account, widely known through its abridged serialization, "Aboard a Flying Saucer," *Look*, October 4, 1966, 44–48, 53–56; October 18, 1966, 111–21. The television film, *The UFO Incident*, first aired on NBC, October 20, 1975. See further the important synoptic treatment of the Hill narratives in Bullard, *UFO Abductions*, 2: 79–93.

7. T. Walton, *The Walton Experience* (New York: Berkley, 1979).

8. R. E. Fowler, *The Andreasson Affair* (Englewood Cliffs, NJ: Prentice-Hall,

1979); Fowler, *The Andreasson Affair, Phase Two* (Englewood Cliffs, NJ: Prentice-Hall, 1982).

9. W. Strieber, *Communion: A True Story* (New York: Avon Books, 1987). Strieber's narratives have continued in a series, from *Transformation: The Breakthrough* (New York: Avon, 1988) to *Confirmation: The Hard Evidence of Aliens among Us* (New York: Avon, 1998). Strieber's relations with the wider UFO community have become increasingly tense. See the account by S. Casteel, "Q&A: Strieber Sounds Off," *UFO* 8:5 (1993): 20–23.

10. Bullard's works, since his dissertation, "Mysteries in the Eye of the Beholder: UFO's and their Correlates as a Folkloric Theme Past and Present" (Indiana University, Bloomington, 1982), have been central. In addition to his foundational study, *UFO Abductions*, also summarized in Bullard, *On Stolen Time: A Summary of a Comparative Study of the UFO Mystery* (Mount Rainier, MD: Fund for UFO Research, 1987), see, among others, "UFO Abduction Reports: The Supernatural Kidnap Narrative Returns in Technological Disguise," *Journal of American Folklore*, 102 (1989): 147–70; "Hypnosis and UFO Abductions: A Troubled Relationship," *Journal of UFO Studies*, n.s. 1 (1989): 3–40; "Folkloric Dimensions of the UFO Phenomenon," *Journal of UFO Studies*, n.s. 3 (1991): 1–57; as well as his several contributions in Pritchard, et al., *Alien Discussions*: "A Comparative Study of Abduction Reports: Update," (45–48), "The Rarer Abduction Episodes," (72–74), "The Well-Ordered Abduction: Pattern or Mirage" (81–82), "The Variety of Abduction Beings" (90–91), "The Relation of Abduction Reports to Folklore Narratives" (389–92), and "Addendum: The Influence of Investigators on UFO Abduction Reports: Results of a Survey" (571–619; on the latter, cf. Bullard, *The Sympathetic Ear: Investigators as Variables in UFO Abduction Reports* [Mount Rainier, MD: Fund for UFO Research, 1995]).

11. Bullard, "Folkloric Dimensions": 23; Bullard, *UFO Abductions*, 1: 52–57.

12. Bullard, *UFO Abductions*, 1: 47–57, et passim; Bullard, "UFO Abduction Reports": 153–54.

13. Bullard, *UFO Abductions*, 1: 58–63.

14. Bullard, *UFO Abductions*, 1: 58–63. Bullard distinguishes four subelements in this segment of the narrative. (a) Alien intrusion by the UFO. (b) Entry into a "zone of strangeness" where ordinary physical laws seem suspended. (c) A time lapse in which the individual becomes, in some way, mentally impaired. Most frequently expressed as amnesia, it remains a curious (and troubling) feature of the abduction experience that the majority of them have been recovered under hypnosis. (See Bullard, "Hypnosis and UFO Abductions"). (d) The actual procurement of the individual is often described as a series of events: a beam of light strikes the individual, pulling him or her towards the ship; aliens approach and a brief conversation, by speech or telepathy, follows which pacifies the subject who is then escorted (frequently "floated") to the ship. If there has not been a previous impairment of the faculties, the abductee often experiences "doorway amnesia" upon entering the craft, which is usually described as the familiar "flying saucer." Inside, there is uniform antiseptic lighting with no visible source. Temperatures are cold; the atmosphere is misty and it is difficult to breathe. Doors open and close without apparent seams. See, now, B. Hopkins "The Abduction Experience: Acquisition," in Pritchard, et al., *Alien Discussions*: 49–52, which re-

flects the shift, in the later phase of Abduction Reports, from outdoors to the subject's bedroom. See the perceptive remarks on this shift in J. Dean, *Aliens in America: Conspiracy Cultures from Outerspace to Cyberspace* (Ithaca, NY: Cornell University Press, 1998): 100–101.

15. Bullard, *UFO Abductions*, 1: 81–103. Compare the section, "Medical Examination and Subsequent Procedures," in Pritchard, et al. *Alien Discussions*: 53–64.

16. J. U. Pereira, "Les Extra-Terrestres," *Phénomènes spatiaux*, special issue 2 (1974); E. Zurcher, *Les Apparitions d'humanoides* (Nice: Alain Lefeuvre, 1979); P. Huyghe, *The Field Guide to Extraterrestrials* (New York: Avon, 1996); D. Chance, *A Visual Guide to Alien Beings* (n.p., 1996); K. Randle and R. Estes, *Faces of the Visitors*. Cf. Bullard, *UFO Abductions*, 1: 239; D. M. Jacobs, et al., "Descriptions of Aliens," in Pritchard, et al., *Alien Discussions*: 86–99.

17. Bullard, *UFO Abductions*, 1: 238–99.

18. Bullard, *UFO Abductions*, 1: 104–111.

19. The sexual-abuse narrative provides the focus of works such as B. Hopkins, *Intruders: The Incredible Visitations at Copley Woods* (New York: Ballantine Books, 1987); D. M. Jacobs, *Secret Life: Firsthand Accounts of UFO Abductions* (New York: Simon & Schuster, 1992); Jacobs, *The Threat: The Secret Alien Agenda* (New York: Simon & Schuster, 1997); and J. E. Mack, *Abduction: Human Encounters with Aliens* (New York: Charles Scribner's Sons, 1994); and it was a major component in the reports and discussions at the 1992 M.I.T. Abduction Conference, see Pritchard et al., *Alien Discussions*, esp. D. M. Jacobs, "Subsequent Procedures," (pp. 64–68); C. D. B. Bryan, *Close Encounters of the Fourth Kind*: 17–20 et passim. As articulated in the pithy comment of J. Dean, *Aliens in America*: 101: "Rather than an outside event, happening mostly to men on the road . . . in the early sixties and . . . in the seventies, abduction in the late eighties happens inside, in bedrooms." See the few instances of this element in earlier reports in Bullard, *UFO Abductions*, 1: 91–92, 350–60; 2: 66–75.

20. Bullard, *UFO Abductions*, 1: 111–12.

21. Bullard, *UFO Abductions*, 1: 112–17. Bullard classifies the encounter with a divine being as a sixth separate episode (pp. 117–18). On the basis of his statistics, it is uncommon enough to be subsumed as a component in the journey-episode.

22. Bullard, *UFO Abductions*, 1: 63–66.

23. Bullard, *UFO Abductions*, 1: 143–73.

24. P. M. Rojcewicz, "The 'Men in Black' Experience and Tradition: Analogues with the Traditional Devil Hypothesis," *Journal of American Folklore*, 100 (1987): 148–60. Compare the novel by S. Perry, based on the screenplay by E. Solomon, *Men in Black* (New York: Bantam, 1997) which represents the Men in Black as a government agency dedicated to tracking down, regulating, and/or destroying alien life-forms disguised as humans.

25. See the review of the literature in Bullard, "Folkloric Dimensions."

26. M. Rose, *Alien Encounters: Anatomy of Science Fiction* (Cambridge, MA: Harvard University Press, 1981): 31–32.

27. Bullard, "UFO Abduction Reports": 157. This has been a persistent theme in Bullard's work; see *UFO Abductions*, 1: 90, "the examination is the major goal

of the abduction, perhaps its only goal"; 1: 358, "examinations are the heart of abductions"; see further, 1: 122–23, 354 et passim.

28. For a valuable overview, see the collection, J. R. Lewis, ed., *The Gods Have Landed: New Religions from Other Worlds* (Albany: State University of NY Press, 1995).

29. A few narratives do give reasons comparable to those listed above (Bullard, *UFO Abductions*, 1: 108–109, 123, 125– 26, 136–38), but they are a distinct minority. The narratives of sexual abuse (see above, note 19) often provide hybridization as a rationale.

30. Bullard, *UFO Abductions*, 1: 110–111, 119–20.

31. J. vos Post, "How To Talk to an Extraterrestrial," in B. Fawcett, ed., *Making Contact: A Serious Handbook for Locating and Communicating with Extraterrestrials* (New York: Avon Books, 1998): 54–98.

32. M. Maruyama and A. Harkin, eds., *Cultures Beyond the Earth: The Role of Anthropology in Outer Space* (New York: Vintage Books, 1975).

33. I rely on contemporary news reports. It should be noted that the Heaven's Gate group, under a variety of names, had been active with respect to UFO mythology since 1973, and had been well studied by sociologists since 1975. See R. W. Balch, "Waiting for the Ships: Disillusionment and the Revitalization of Faith in Bo and Peep's UFO Cult," in Lewis, *The Gods Have Landed*: 137–86, and the bibliography by J. G. Melton and G. M. Eberhart in Lewis: 275–76.

34. Bullard, *UFO Abductions*, 1: 90–91.

35. Johannes Annius of Viterbo, *Commentaria super opera diversorum auctorum de antiquitatibus* (Rome, 1498). See the discussion of this work in D. C. Allen, *The Legend of Noah* (Urbana: University of Illinois Press, 1963): 114–16.

36. Jean Bodin, *Methodus ad facilem historiarum cognitionem* (1565), in the English translation by B. Reynolds, *Method for the Easy Comprehension of History by Jean Bodin* (New York: Columbia University Press, 1969): 334–64.

37. See further, M. T. Hodgen, *The Doctrine of Survivals: A Chapter in the History of Scientific Method in the Study of Man* (London: Allenson & Co., 1936).

38. R. E. Lerner, *The Powers of Prophecy: The Cedar of Lebanon Vision from the Mongol Onslaught to the Dawn of the Enlightenment* (Berkeley: University of California Press, 1983): 9–24 et passim. For the Gog-Magog traditions, see A. R. Anderson, *Alexander's Gate, Gog and Magog, and the Enclosed Nations* (Cambridge, MA: Medieval Academy of America, 1932; vol. 12 in the series, Publications Medieval Academy of America), esp. 58–86.

39. Lerner, *Powers of Prophecy*: 12, n. 5, referring to an unpublished text, MS UB Innsbruck 187 (fol. 8r–v).

40. F. Zarnacke, *Der Priester Johannes* (Leipzig, 1879–83): 4–59. Note that King David, while understood as a "recirculation" of the biblical figure, is here identified as the son of Prestor John.

41. G. A. Bezzola, *Die Mongolien in abendländischer Sicht, 1220–1270* (Bern, 1974): 41–43.

42. For example, Fitzwilliam Additional MS 23, fols. 144–45, in J. B. Friedman, *The Monstrous Races in European Art and Thought* (Cambridge, MA: Harvard University Press, 1981): 102–103 and 237, n. 68. See also, M. Letts, ed.,

Mandeville's Travels: Texts and Translations (London: Hakluyt Society, 1953), 1: 154–55.

43. See the useful collection of the terminology of novelty in K. Kretschmer, *Die Entdeckung Amerikas und ihre Bedeutung für die Geschichte des Weltbildes* (Leipzig, 1892); 360–69.

44. See my discussion of this, with the essential bibliography, in J. Z. Smith, "What a Difference a Difference Makes," in J. Neusner and E. S. Frerichs, eds., *'To See Ourselves as Others See us': Christians, Jews, 'Others,' in Late Antiquity* (Chico, CA: Scholars Press, 1985): 21–44.

45. See the critique of this view of an "*otra Arca de Noé,*" in José de Acosta, *Historia natural y moral de las Indias* (Seville, 1590), Book I, chapter 16, in the edition of E. O'Gorman (Mexico City, 1962): 45.

46. G. García, *El origen de los Indios de el Nuevo Mundo e Indias occidentales,* 1st ed. (Valencia, 1607); 2nd ed., A. Gonzalez de Barcia, ed. (Madrid, 1729). I cite the reprint of the 2nd ed., edited by F. Pease (Mexico City, 1981): 41–308.

47. García, *El origen*: 239–48, 315.

48. E. Brerewood, *Enquiries Touching the Diversity of Languages, and Religions through the Chiefe Parts of the World* (London, 1614): 96–102.

49. J. Ogilby, *America, Being the Latest, and most Accurate Description of the New World* (London, 1671): 35–42.

50. See, among others, A. Tornielli, *Annales sacri, ab orbe condito ad ipsum Christi Passione repartum, praecipus ethicorum temporibus apte ordinateque dispositi* (Milan, 1610), 2: 239; A. de la Calancha, *Cronica moralizada de la Orden de San Augustin en el Perù* (Barcelona, 1639), 1: 41–46.

51. Acosta, *Historia natural y moral*, IV.36 in O'Gorman: 202–3. For its use in debates, see, among others, Matthew Hale, *The Primitive Organization of Mankind, considered and examined according to the Light of Nature* (London, 1677): 198–201.

52. Otto von Guericke, *Experimenta nova (ut vocantur) Magdeburgica de Vacuo spatio* (1672; rep., Aalen, 1962): 216, as cited in K. S. Guthke, *The Last Frontier: Imagining Other Worlds from the Copernican Revolution to Modern Science Fiction* (Ithaca, NY: Cornell University Press, 1990): 178.

53. The classic study remains that of N. Loraux, "L'Autochthonie: Une topique athénienne," *Annales, Economies, Sociétés, Civilisations,* 34 (1979): 3–26, English translation, N. Loraux, *The Children of Athena* (Princeton, NJ: Princeton University Press, 1993): 37–71. See further, E. Montanari, *Il mito dell'autoctonia* (Rome, 1981); V. J. Rosivach, "Autochthony and the Athenians," *Classical Quarterly,* 81 (1987): 294–306.

54. For example, Paracelsus, *Astronomia magna* (1537–38), in K. Sudoff and W. Mattiessen, eds., *Paracelsus: Sämtliche Werke* (Munich, 1922–33), 12: 35, 114, 469. Giordano Bruno, *De immenso, innumerabilibus et infigurabilibus* (1590), in F. Fiorentino, et al., eds. *Jordani Bruno Nolani, Opera latine conscripta* (Naples, 1879–86), 1.2: 282.

db55. L. P., Master of Arts, *Two Essays, Sent in a Letter from Oxford, to a Nobleman in London. The First, concerning some Errors about the Creation, General Flood, and the Peopling of the World. In Two Parts. The Second, concerning the Rise, Progress, and Destruction of Fables and Romances. With the State of Learning*

(London, 1695), reprinted in J. Somers, *A Third Collection of scarce . . Tracts* (London, 1751), 3: 291–308 (rep., London, 1814). I follow the convenient reprint of extracts from the latter in J. S. Slotkin, *Readings in Early Anthropology* (New York: Werner-Gren Foundation for Anthropological Research Inc. [no. 40 in the series, Viking Fund Publications], 1965): 82–83. Another reprint of the relevant passages may be found in T. Bendyshe, *The History of Anthropology* (London: Trübner and Co., 1865): 365–71 (same as Memoirs of the Anthropological Society of London 1 [1863–64]: 335–458). See the polemic rejoinder by J. Harris, *Remarks on some late Papers (by L.P.) relating to the Universal Deluge* (London, 1697). The only extended treatment of this important essay is G. Gliozzi, *Adamo e il nuovo mondo* (Florence, 1976): 585–93.

56. Isaac de la Peyrère, *Prae-Adamitae, sive Exercitatio super Verbibus duo-decimo, decimotertio et decimoquartyo, capitia quinti Epistolae D. Pauli ad Romanos. Quibus inducuntur Primi Homines ante Adamum conditi* (n.p. [Amsterdam], 1655); anonymous English translation, *Men Before Adam. Or a Discourse upon the twelfth, thirteenth, and fourteenth Verses of the Epistle of the Apostle Paul to the Romans. By which are Prov'd that the first Men were created before Adam* (London, 1656). See further, D. Pastine, "La origini del poligenismo e Isaac La Peyrère," *Miscellanea Seicento*, Instituto di Filosofia della Facolta di Lettere e Filosofia dell' Universita di Genova, 1 (1971): 7–234; R. H. Popkin, *Isaac la Peyrère: 1596-1676* (Leiden: E. J. Brill, 1987), with rich bibliography.

57. Hence Pius XII's attack on polygenesis, along with other modern scientific theories, in the encyclical, *Humani Generis*, August 12, 1950.

58. F. Bernier, "Une nouvelle division de la Terre d'après les différentes espèces des races d'hommes qui l'habitent," *Journal des Savants*, April 24, 1684.

59. G. W. Stocking, Jr., *Race, Culture and Evolution: Essays in the History of Anthropology* (New York: Free Press, 1968): 40.

60. R. Owen, *Lectures on the Comparative Anatomy and Physiology of the Invertebrate Animals* (London, 1843). See further, E. R. Lankester, "On the Use of the Term Homology in Modern Zoology, and the Distinction Between Homogenetic and Homoplastic Agreements," *The Annals and Magazine of Natural History*, 6 (1870): 34–43.

61. I. Berlin, *The Crooked Timber of Humanity: Chapters in the History of Ideas*, ed. H. Hardy (London: John Murray, 1990; rep., Princeton: Princeton University Press, 1997): 61.

2

Telling a Life through Haitian Vodou: An Essay Concerning Race, Gender, Memory, and Historical Consciousness

KAREN MCCARTHY BROWN

NEARLY two years after the publication of *Mama Lola: A Vodou Priestess in Brooklyn*, with no warning and much to my regret, Lola announced: "I hate that book. I hate it!" Several tension-filled months passed before she told me, in a way I could hear, why she hated a book she once loved and displayed prominently in her altar room. "Why do you hate the book?" I asked repeatedly. "Please tell me. I *need* to know." One day she got exasperated with my questions, and an answer we both understood popped out. "I hate that book," she said, "because it does not change . . . and I do."

The text is now back on her altar, our friendship is no longer marked with tension, but the point Lola made that day has stayed with me. Mama Lola wanted something a printed book cannot give—although a "virtual" one might one day be able to. Lola wanted a book with a central character whose story continued after the publication date. She wanted an open-ended text. "Mama Lola is a natural postmodern thinker," I thought to myself. "She perceives her identity as open-ended and fluid and, what is more, she has a good nose for the power issues embedded in discourse."

This paper will suggest some of the more important ways in which Mama Lola's life, and my interaction with her, changed in the years immediately following the publication of our book. In terms of theoretical concerns, this is a paper that moves on several levels simultaneously. On the most obvious level, I am focused on the way experiences becomes memories, and memories are collected into narratives, some of which take on the authority of history. In relation to this process, I am particularly interested in cultural differences in the arts of memory. I will also

A shorter version of this paper, titled "Telling a Life: Race, Memory, and Historical Consciousness," appeared in the spring 1999 issue of *Anthropology and Humanism* (24 (2) 1–7) devoted to essays by winners of the Victor Turner Prize in Ethnographic Writing, an annual award given by the Anthropology and Humanism section of the American Anthropological Association.

give attention to the reverse process by which subsequent experiences deconstruct narratives and literally rewrite history. On another level, as characters in the narrative, individual and collective, struggle for power and for the right to tell the definitive stories that count as history, I will take note of the roles played by issues of race and gender in these struggles. Toward the end, I focus on the tying of *wanga*—that is, on the manufacture of Vodou ritual charms using string, rope, chains, and padlocks—and, by doing so, I will extend the discussion of memory and history into embodied forms of remembering. Entering the realm of magic and other ritual technologies also will allow me to deal more directly with power issues involved in the formation of historical narratives.

Telling Lives

I tell here a complex story about events in the lives of Mama Lola and myself that occurred during the two-year period following the publication of the book I wrote about her. The book appeared in April 1991 and the two major events described here took place in early October '92, when Mama Lola and I made our first joint appearance on the academic speakers circuit, and in the first three weeks of February '93, when Mama Lola, her daughter Maggie, and I went to Africa.

The product of more than twelve years of overlapping research and writing, *Mama Lola* was a difficult book to produce. In the writing itself, the problem of voice troubled me more than any other. Who got to speak in this book and from what perspective? Rather than resolving itself with a single answer, the tension behind my question eased only when a wide range of voices emerged simultaneously from the hundreds of pages of field notes collected in two fat black binders on my desk. My own voice had several registers. There was my analytical scholar's voice, my personal voice, and my ethnographic storytelling voice. Mama Lola's voice was several as well. She was quoted often and at length when she spoke as herself, and then again, in passing, when her body and voice had been taken over by the Vodou warrior spirit Ogou, or the fierce domestic woman-warrior Ezili Dantò, or another more irenic Vodou spirit, such as the persona of the Haitian market woman, Kouzinn Zaka.

The Problem with Voice as Synecdoche

In late October 1992, a scholar with an interest in post-colonial studies invited Mama Lola and me to visit the small liberal arts college where she teaches in New York State. Lola's daughter Maggie went along as well.

For three days we collectively filled a cross-cultural visiting professor slot. We participated in a faculty discussion group, a class and, on our last evening, a community-wide event billed as "A Demonstration of the Haitian Vodou Approach to Life." Cecily, a woman born in Barbados and raised in the United States, was a thoughtful host. The schedule she created for us was humane, and enough Caribbean food had been prepared that Mama Lola never had to eat anything suspect. So it was not for want of careful planning that things rather quickly became strained.

On the first sunny, fall afternoon we found ourselves in a comfortable oak-paneled library with the members of the women's faculty seminar seated in chairs around the edges of the small room. Homemade oatmeal cookies and red fruit punch were being served. I spoke first, as I had agreed to do. I talked about what Mama Lola and I hoped to accomplish with the book, our relationship, and our collaborative work. When I finished, questions were immediately addressed to Lola. She responded to the first one (I no longer remember what it was) with one or two halting, fragment sentences. I realized that she was more nervous than I had anticipated.

Suddenly, with a loud whoop, her body went rigid, the glass of punch in her right hand flew toward the ceiling, and she fell to the floor. Maggie moved quickly to help her mother as she routinely does in Vodou ceremonies when the spirits arrive. Lola's dress was pulled down to a more decorous level, her shoes removed, and, after the spirit was "seated" in her head, that spirit was helped to his feet and a red scarf tied tightly around his upper arm. A seemingly angry Ogou had arrived. His eyes protruded from his head and darted from side to side in a mood of hyper-vigilance. His chest was puffed out and his arms crossed over it. From time to time he beat on his chest with a balled fist and grunted. The women faculty members were nervous, confused, and a little frightened, but what they "voiced" was concern for Mama Lola's health and safety. Uncharacteristically Ogou, who usually has quite a lot to say, that day said nothing. In the midst of much huffing and puffing, however, he did greet several people with a brusk handshake. Then the spirit quickly departed. Maggie glossed the event by explaining that Papa Ogou had simply arrived to say hello. He had no special message, so he did not stay long.

In an odd way, the arrival of Ogou created intimacy in the group, and the talk after that was more personal and slower in pace. Yet, not a single person subsequently referred to Ogou's visit or asked any questions about it—not that day and not during the next two days we spent on campus. It was as if the event had not happened. This is an example of an experience so out of the ordinary, so far from the safe and predictable, that misrecognition is the only way to deal with it. The faculty women continued to interpret what happened in terms of illness. At the end of the session, several asked if she were feeling better, thus unwittingly pathologizing her religion and handily putting her back in "her place," a place whose boundaries she had transgressed when ridden by the powerful, white, male warrior figure, Ogou, a fierce presence who chose to remain mute in a world of words. A similar reading of her possession practice happened several years later when Ezili Dantò sought to "ride" Mama Lola on the stage in the auditorium of the Fowler Museum at UCLA. Even after Ezili Dantò arrived in a fairly gentle way (Lola did not fall to the ground) and sang a very sweet song to the audience, guards still brought a wheelchair to the edge of the stage.

Possession is usually not remembered by the "horse" of the spirit. So, after Ogou left, Mama Lola sat in her previous place on the sofa in the college library, looking unperturbed and only a little fatigued. At one point, her eye fell on her empty punch glass. With mild curiosity, she asked, "What happened to my punch?" Mama Lola did not know about Ogou coming to the seminar until two days later. Maggie told her in the car on our way back to New York City.

There is sound thinking behind the desire of the academy to hear voices like Mama Lola's, but those persons whose religions and cultures are of interest to the academic world are still required to come onto academic turf as *voices*, a role Mama Lola found to be both too much and too little, and she steadfastly resisted it during her three days as a visiting dignitary. As a result, the last event, our demonstation of the "Vodou Approach to Life," came close to being a fiasco. The plan was that for the first part of the evening Lola, once a professional singer, and her daughter Maggie would sing a cycle of songs routinely used to open Vodou ceremonies. After that, Lola and Maggie would move one by one through a list of the most important Vodou spirits, offering a song or two for each, demonstrating dances, showing the spirits' costumes, and discussing the foods and other offerings presented to them. In the latter part, I was going to assist. Much to our surprise, the turnout that evening represented a substantial portion of the student body; even the floor space in front of the low stage where we were seated was filled with people.

When it came time to start, Mama Lola froze. Nothing came out of her mouth. Not a refusal to participate, not an attempt to sing. Nothing. After a few awkward moments, Maggie switched on a tape of Haitian drumming and sacred songs that had been prepared for use later in the evening. Maggie and I both clapped enthusiastically, trying to bring in the audience and get everyone (especially Mama Lola) into the mood. It did not work. So the ever-resourceful Maggie eventually jumped up and began to demonstrate dances; she even coaxed a student here and there to come up on the stage and dance along with her. The rest of the evening was choreographed in quick whispers between Maggie and me. At one point, I even showed and discussed slides that had been intended only to provide images behind the singers. Mama Lola remained silent until the private dinner following our painful public performance. One of the student evaluations of the event—several were sent to me a week or two after our visit—strongly suggested I "ought to allow Mama Lola to do more of the talking."

Mama Lola understands herself as a teacher and she knows how to teach well, but not in the form that teaching is done in the academy, not immobilized behind a podium and limited to words, words addressed to other immobilized bodies. The complaint she has routinely made about me is that I ask too many questions and do not spend enough time helping her do the actual work of healing: lighting candles, pouring libations, "refreshing" the spirits whose icons are on her altars by spraying them with a mist of water, rum, or perfume; tying yards and yards of string around bottles to produce *wanga*, healing charms; pushing one hundred and one straight pins into thick black wax candles while repeating a vow with each thrust, or collecting and preparing the herbs, fruits, and liquors used for healing baths. When I visit Mama Lola, most of the time I want to talk, but most of the time, she wants to teach me by example about spiritual practices.

It is also likely that, on this our maiden visit to an academic institution, Mama Lola had difficulty comprehending what it could mean to teach people she does not know, anonymous people whose life crises are invisible to her and therefore cannot mobilize particular responses from her, people who have no urgent need for her wisdom. The idea of learning for its own sake should be deeply puzzling to a woman who believes that to live is to suffer and that *konesas,* spiritual knowledge, is the most important tool we human beings have for dealing with that suffering. Some in the academy have a bad habit of thinking colleges and universities are neutral spaces and that any kind of knowledge, that is *real* knowledge, can be imported into our domain. If such knowledge is not directly recognizable, it may be assumed that careful translation can render it so. At times, we become convinced that, given good intentions and cultural sensitivity, any knower who really does know something important can be invited into our world and can communicate with us, more or less on our terms. We are only beginning to understand the politics of our construction of knowledge and the pitfalls of "epistemological imperialism," to borrow a phrase from Judith Butler.[1]

In light of this experience and of Lola's belated critique of the book I wrote about her, I have begun to consider the epistemological imperialism in my decision to configure the book about Mama Lola as a cluster of voices. My career-long tendency to focus on women's issues was no doubt one of the reasons I made this choice. When I began the project feminists frequently spoke about "voices" and the need to "recover" or "locate" the "voices" of women that had been "lost" or "ignored." We spoke uncritically of the voice as synecdoche for the whole person. Now I question whether that tendency to privilege voice is not a version of the same epistemological bias that, in post-structuralist discussions, gives discourse a nearly exclusive role in the social construction of what we call reality. This is all a bit embarrassing, since words are, after all, the scholar's métier.

Modes of Remembering—I

Mama Lola, Maggie, and I had accepted the invitation to play visiting professors in upstate New York because we were trying to make money in order to finance a trip to Africa. We had been invited to attend a "Reunion of Vodun Cultures," to be held in February 1993, in the Republic of Benin, formerly known as Dahomey.

Nicephore Soglo's election to the presidency in Benin marked the end of a government that had strongly opposed traditional religious practices. Large numbers of priests had been killed, shrines had been destroyed, and sacred groves had been cut down. According to traditional priests in Benin (where the spirits are called by the generic term Vodun), Soglo almost did not survive winning the election. I was told by more than one person that he became very ill shortly before his inauguration and no medical doctor could find out what was wrong with him. Finally, it was a traditional healer who saved his life. Healers in Benin perform a kind of psychic surgery and one such healer was reported to have removed a piece of chain and a padlock from Soglo's stomach.[2] It supposedly had been placed there by an act of sorcery. President Soglo had been "locked up" by a political opponent, and it took a traditional healer to get him loose. It is said that gratitude to the Vodun community prompted Nicephore Soglo to promise the people of Benin that he would host a reunion of all the Vodun populations scattered across the globe. Mama Lola, Maggie, and I received an invitation to be part of "the American delegation." The Beninoise government agreed to pay for our accommodations and to provide us with a car and a driver, but we had to raise the money for general expenses and for our airfare.

All official correspondence for the Benin festival was addressed simply to "Mama Lola" (a name she never used before the book came out) with no last name, and when we entered the packed, bustling airport in Cotonou on the first day of the Vodun reunion, that was the name called out to let us know we could breeze through customs straight to the navy blue, air-conditioned Mercedes that waited for us at the curb. We drove immediately to our hotel in the historic town of Ouidah, once a major embarkation point for slaves and still the religious capital of the coastal region of Benin. Our driver took the car straight down the middle of a thirty-mile highway, horn tooting, flags snapping, and headlights flashing. All other traffic stopped. Motor bikes and cars pulled over. Overburdened mules, peasant farmers, and market women carrying loads on their heads spilled off the road on either side of us.

The much anticipated "Reunion of Vodun Cultures" turned out to be at least two separate events. Artists, scholars, and diplomats attended colloquia, dinners, and receptions in the capital city of Cotonou, while we stayed in Ouidah, in the world of the Vodun. Those who serve the Vodun staged a monumental, lavish, day-and-night, two-week-long celebration, drawing only on their own resources. The *couvents*, "convents," as they call temples in this former French colony, were refurbished; new costumes (some making profligate use of cowrie shells and red parrot feathers) were sewn for members of the *couvents*, sometimes one hundred or more persons; masks were refurbished that had not appeared in public during the lifetime of many participants, and more familiar ones danced through the streets of Ouidah every day; ceremonies were held that had last been performed nearly half a century ago, and sumptuous meals were prepared for the Vodun and for the faithful.

Followed by a retinue of wives, local kings processed through the streets under massive twirling umbrellas fashioned from colorful cotton applique. Important priests of the Vodun did the same, but rather than being followed by their wives, it was the members of the *couvent*, in full ritual regalia, who provided the entourage. On several occasions Mama Lola was asked by both kings and priests to process with them under the twirling umbrellas.

Formal delegations in full ritual regalia from the various *couvents* in town came to greet her at our hotel. It confused a woman such as Mama Lola, who considers herself a child of the Vodou spirits and a good Catholic at one and the same time, to realize that, after several of these visits had occurred, a local Catholic priest felt it necessary to exorcise the lobby of our hotel and put up an altar to the Virgin Mary there.

It was moving to catch glimpses of how much this temporary knitting up of the raveled sleeve of the African diaspora meant to traditional religious leaders on both sides. Previously such transatlantic connections were infrequent for the people of Benin and almost unheard of for all except the tiny group of financially privileged Haitians known as "the elite." Servants of the Vodun in Africa were eager to compare notes with Mama Lola, and occasionally to instruct her on the apparently forgotten *règlement*, "rules," of one or another of the spirits that she confessed to serving in ways different from theirs. In the end, there were only two religious leaders from the other side of the Atlantic who managed to raise money to come to the festival; the other was a Shango priestess from Trinidad. It was Mama Lola who spoke French, the official language of Benin, and, within twenty-four hours of our arrival, she was in great demand.

Strangers stopped Mama Lola on the streets of Ouidah, and at least one member of the Haitian upper class, someone who probably would not have given Mama Lola the time of day in Haiti, went down on his knees in the middle of a restaurant and kissed her hand. Television and documentary film crews followed her around Ouidah. During our two weeks in Benin Mama Lola was like a lightning rod, receiving everyone's projections. To the Beninoise she was clothed in the halo of history. She was the remnant of all those lost to slavery. (In Benin, traditional priests still perform ceremonies for family members enslaved centuries ago, as well as for the progeny of those souls lost to the lineage.) To journalists Lola was the epitome of the exotic. Mama Lola was often off balance. In one television interview, she claimed to have written the book that bears her name as title.

As Maggie, Mama Lola, and I moved more deeply into the world of the Vodun in Benin, the cameras came to feel intrusive and irritating. We laughed at how European cameramen clambered over one another to film the last drop of blood from a pigeon sacrifice. We had originally tried to finance our trip by working with a film crew of our own. The plan did not work out, yet I will never forget the parting words of the Fox Television producer. "Take a video camera. Even if you miss some things because you are working with the camera, you can study it as much as you want when you get back. Without a camera you only get to see things once!" I never regretted leaving the video camera at home, but it *was* hard to get to see things only once. So much was happening in such a short period of time.

Also, Africa in general is hard on travelers, and Benin is one of the poorest countries in the hump of West Africa. Things tended to break down—cars, telephones, and hotel air conditioners. We had trouble finding out what was happening where and when, and how important it was for us to be there. We all became tense. The considerable power of some of our experiences made this worse.

Embodied History

At the beginning of our second week in Benin, at twilight on a Sunday evening, we visited the site next to the ocean where, between 1710 and 1810, more than one million slaves embarked on the Middle Passage.[3]

This site was part of an historical restoration of the "Route de L'Esclave," Slave Route, and it was nearing completion at the time of the Vodun festival. A narrow sandy path led from the town to the sea; contemporary art works rich in Vodun imagery stood at intervals along the path. Half way to the sea, on the left-hand side of the road, there was a tree labeled "The Tree of Forgetting." The story on the attached placard said slaves on their way to the ships bound for the Americas were made to walk three times around this tree, a ritual act intended to wipe all memory of the Dahomean homeland from their minds. Memory-less they would then board the ships for their journey west—questionable history but apt imagery.

At the end of the road, only a few yards from the beach, a monument was erected to all the enslaved people who had passed through Ouidah's port. In front of the monument, placed like strangely hobbled guardians on either side of the gate were two life-size statues of slaves, one male and one female. They were on their knees, ankles shackled and hands bound in front with heavy rope. At the time Maggie and I did not understand what was happening when Lola sank to her knees, put her hands on the face of the woman, and began to sob. As she stroked the face of the slave woman, she appeared to be apologizing: "I'm sorry. I'm really sorry. I didn't know. We did not know." Later Lola explained that almost as soon as we arrived at the memorial, she began having strong flashback memories of someone in her family passing through that very spot in Ouidah, on the way to the slave ships. The Dahomean connection in Lola's family is actually not unlikely. Many people were taken from Dahomey to Haiti, and several names of towns in the old Dahomean Empire appear as words in *languy*, the sacred language of Mama Lola's family Vodou practice.

Later in the evening, Lola talked about being overcome by fear and sadness in the midst of this "memory." She was clearly moved. I have never heard of another Haitian Vodou practitioner having an ancestor's memory, yet it is not inconsistent with the general understanding of human connectedness operative in Vodou. The living routinely have dreams whose messages are intended for one another; and the ancestors, who do not cease to exist with physical death, frequently appear in dreams to give help to the living. However, what happened to Mama Lola near the beach of Ouidah, she was clear, was not a dream but a "memory."

Throughout the first fifteen years of our friendship Mama Lola consistently maintained that there were "no slaves in our family." "We are French," she would say, "from Bordeaux." It is not unusual for people from the Caribbean to locate their identity entirely in the colonial part of their heritage. I now see that she had even configured her family tree is such a way as to give this story greater plausibility. Lola chose as the originating ancestor on her otherwise matrilineal family tree a sailor from Bordeaux; he was either white or light-skinned and had jumped ship in Haiti around the middle of the nineteenth century, decades after slavery had ended there. The Haitian woman who bore his children has been erased from the genealogical record.

It was sometime after our Africa trip and partly as a result of it that I realized I routinely did something very similar with my own family tree. I identified myself as the descendant of Irish immigrants fleeing the second potato famine. This is not inaccurate, in a narrow sense of the term, but it is partial. By ignoring the seventeenth- and eighteenth-century Bermudian merchants, pirates, and privateers on my mother's side of the family, I neatly avoided my family's involvement in chattel slavery. Transatlantic slavery is to history as black holes are to the reaches of space: we know their presence only by the warping effect they have on what surrounds them.

Configuring our family trees, Mama Lola and I had both taken the route of misrecognition—in Pierre Bourdieu's language, *mèconnaisance* (1977)—to avoid the connection with slavery. Of course, we had very different connections to avoid. Yet she had retrieved a "memory" that deconstructed her prior history in an instant, the instant in which she encountered the statue of the bound and shackled female slave. Where could that memory have come from?

Bourdieu's concept of the *habitus*, a key to his theory of practice, may help to unfold this puzzling event. *Habitus* refers to deep habits of the socialized body-mind (my language). It is created by the process of transforming social structures such as language and economy into durable dispositions of the body. For *habitus* to play its role the body must be educated, but not through rote learning, rather through intergenerational body-to-body *mimesis*. "The child imitates not 'models' but other people's actions," Bourdieu observes. "Children are particularly attentive to the gestures and postures which, in their eyes, express everything that goes to make an accomplished adult—a way of walking, a tilt of the head, facial expressions, ways of sitting and of using implements, . . . a tone of voice, a style of speech, and (how could it be otherwise?) a certain subjective experience." In Bourdieu's words, *habitus* is "embodied history, internalized as a second nature, and so forgotten as history." This is what makes his theory of practice relevant to Lola's ancestral "memory."[4]

In Haitian Vodou there is a pervasive contrast between a state of being that is bound, tied, chained, or blocked and that state characterized by the energy of a free-flowing stream. This opposition is fundamental to the practice of Vodou, and it is far more complex than the opposition between a good thing and a bad thing, a feared state and a desired one. Sometimes binding is good, or at least necessary to bring about the good. The manufacture of healing charms or *wanga,* for example, often require that they be bound many times over.

Surprisingly, slavery is a topic virtually never voiced in Vodou ritual. There are no Vodou songs that make use of the Creole words *esklav* or *esklavaj,* slave or slavery. Yet slavery is constantly being referred to and commented on in Vodou ritual technologies. My field notes from 1994 describe the manufacture of a *màye djol,* a tie-the-lips charm, designed to stop the wagging tongue of a gossip, in which the bottle holding the active ingredients for the treatment was so thoroughly tied up that it ended up looking like a small mummy. Bundles of herbs known as Pake Kongo, used for healing ceremonies in Haitian Vodou, are wrapped in brightly colored cloth and then bound round and round with ribbon of contrasting colors. In a cleansing ritual known as an *expedyson,* seven lengths of string measured out on the client's body are laid side by side and then, by executing seven knots seven times, a single thick cord is finally produced. This then becomes the stand-in for the human body in the cleansing ceremony. After nearly forty years working as a Vodou healer, Lola's hands have literally bound and tied miles of string, ribbon, and rope.

Also, Vodou altars often contain chains; some altars even have authentic slave chains. In fact, chains are part of the routine iconography of some members of the "hot" class of Vodou spirits known as Petwo, and they are central to the iconography of those spirits even fiercer than the Petwo. Chains and padlocks appear in the *wanga* Lola makes for wandering husbands. Thus Lola had both a visual and a kinesthetic intimacy with the binding and shackling the Ouidah slave had to endure. I want to suggest that this is what made it possible for her to "remember" that such shackling had occurred in her own family. It was the rich performative practice of tying and binding, control and confinement, mimed across several generations of women healers, from body to body, that harbored Lola's elusive connections with the experiences of her slave ancestors.

Mama Lola's ancestral memory was no intellectual breakthrough; it was an eruption of memory propelled by fear and sadness. "The body believes in what it plays at," says Bourdieu. "It weeps if it mimes grief. It does not represent what it performs, it does not memorize the past, it *enacts* the past, bringing it back to life. What is 'learned by body' is not something that one has, like knowledge that can be brandished, but something that one is."[5]

It should be noted however that this tying and binding aesthetic was not invented to deal with slavery. Speaking of *bocio,* the Dahomean cousin of a *wanga,* Suzanne Blier, who has done extensive work in Benin, says that "works of this sort no doubt were made and used prior to the slave trade."⁶ But there is equally no doubt that the history of slavery added to their affect. The power lies not in the ideal *wanga* as object, but in the training of the body and its sensibilities through the reiterative practices of making and using *wangas*.

Modes of Remembering—II

Differences between the ways Mama Lola and I relate to memory emerged with a force on the Africa trip. On this trip, I went after experiences, or more precisely after memories, the form in which experiences can be held in the hand (so to speak), as if they were collectible objects. I am so wedded to contemplation as a major mode of comprehension that I wanted to take the memories home with me in some tangible form that would allow me to postpone at least part of the process of contemplation until a time when I was less fatigued and less stressed. I was also anxious that I get all the important memories (Mama Lola's, Maggie's, and mine) into my tape recorder. I was constantly vigilant, fighting to stay conscious, lest I lose memories through forgetting. By contrast, on at least one occasion, the one when she approached the statue of the slave at the old embarkation point on Ouidah's beach, it was remembering that Mama Lola feared. And, when she did "remember," she did so with a kind of surrender of vigilance.

For the first half of our trip Mama Lola, Maggie, and I managed to preserve without friction an evening ritual we had agreed upon before setting out. Each night before going to sleep we talked into my tape recorder, an instrument I have an indefensible habit of trusting more than a camcorder. We talked for at least half an hour, reminding each other what had gone on during the day, and what we thought and felt about it. On the evening we visited the slave memorial at Ouidah, I decided to forget the tape recorder. Emotions were too raw.

On the morning after that experience, as Mama Lola and I sat across a table from one another in the bright sunshine outside our hotel, I found her studying my face intently. "Boy," she said, "you are really blonde . . . blonde, blonde, blonde." Then she sucked her teeth. Later in the day she said something that indicated she blamed me for the difficulties of our trip. That evening Mama Lola flatly refused to talk for the tape recorder. "Aw, come on Karen. I'm tired. Okay? Turn it off!" I panicked. These were the captured words that would compensate for memories badly disorganized by fatigue and stress. Those audio tapes were the mnemonic devices that would evoke the sights, smells, sounds, emotions, and ironies that made memory tangible. Those words were the lifeline to my work. I walked out of her room, quietly closed the door to mine, and then picked up an empty suitcase and hurled it against the wall.

Twenty minutes later there was a knock on my door. "Aren't you coming?" Mama Lola asked. "Coming? . . . Where? . . . For what?" "With the tape recorder," she offered in a small noncommital voice. "I thought you said you didn't want to," I responded. "Okay. That's it!" Lola pronounced and went into her room, slamming the door for good measure. I did deep breathing exercises, picked up my tape recorder, and went once more to her door. After all that acting out, the three of us had a good, long talk—and it was on the record.

The next day we went north to Abomey, the capital of the old Kingdom of Dahomey, a city that grew fabulously wealthy during the eighteenth century by trading with the Portuguese, English, and French. At one point the exchange rate was fifteen slaves for one cannon. This trade contributed significantly to one of the largest and most brutal forced migrations in human history.

While going through the museum in Abomey, Maggie and Mama Lola learned for the first time that Africans had sold other Africans into slavery. Each reacted in her own way. Maggie got mad and wanted to get even. She wanted to use her bare hands to tear apart a skull-encrusted throne in the palace museum. Lola could not quite take it in. She got distracted by birds and lizards in the museum courtyard; she moaned loudly and bent over double with the onset of stomach pains later attributed to bad food. All three of us fell silent before the final exhibit: cloudy reproductions of old photographs of slaves on an auction block. It was impossible to tell where these photographs had been made. Next to the photographs a thoughtful curator with no budget had taped to a moveable chalkboard considerably clearer blow-ups of photos of Nazi death camp survivors, their ankles rubbed to raw meat by heavy leg irons. We did not talk for the tape recorder on that night either.

The tension between Mama Lola and me got worse. It had been exacerbated a few days earlier by an incident on the way to Abomey. Even though we had set our schedule with a visit to Allada in mind, Mama Lola told the driver not to stop at the monument to Toussaint L'Ouverture, erected just outside Allada, the small town where the liberator of Haiti is said to have been born. "Why we got to stop here? I don't need to see no Toussaint L'Ouverture," she said adamantly. She relented, as usual, but not without tension and then for only five minutes and one photograph: a sour, glowering Lola standing beside the bust of Toussaint, ironically presented to Benin by the French government during the bicentennial of the French Revolution, an event that changed European history and sparked the slaves in Haiti to stage a revolution of their own.

Fluid Subjectivity

Early on in the trip Mama Lola had made a connection with a leader in the world of the Vodun. He is known as Daagbo Hounon, and some call him the Pope of Vodun in Benin. (Others dispute his, or anyone's, right to such a title.) Family is the pervasive metaphor for social organization in both West Africa and Haiti, so Lola was clear that she was in the position of child in relation to Daagbo, a role complicated for her by his flirtatiousness. Daagbo interpreted her deference to him in ways that were more demeaning than she could take. The two of them struggled for position for the entire week before we went to Abomey. He would demand that she spend the entire following day at his temple. She would counter that she could not come until 6 P.M.. Then she would show up at 9:30, only to be told that he had already retired for the night. And so it went. Everywhere she turned Lola felt controlled, if not by me (I was in charge of scheduling and money) then by Daagbo. Lola could afford to fight with me, but with Daagbo the time was too short and what was at stake was too important. In fact, her tug-of-war with this patriarch reached a kind of resolution not long after we returned from Abomey.

Finally consenting to receive her late in the evening, a sleepy Daagbo sat on his throne and talked with the three of us. In the course of the conversation, Mama Lola suddenly became possessed. This was the first time it had happened in Benin. Again, it was the Haitian spirit Ogou, the master of self-protection and self-assertion, who showed up that night. Lola had not yet seen Daagbo's altars and thus did not know if he venerated the African Ogun, so in this context Lola's Haitian Ogou called himself Hevioso, a Dahomean spirit unknown in Haiti, but one whose character and iconography is similar to Ogou's and one whose *couvent* Lola had visited on one of our first days in Benin.

Once firmly in control of his "horse," Ogou/Hevioso asked for tobacco and liquor. Daagbo deferred to the spirit's wishes and sent someone to buy them. Then the spirit inspected the priest's hands and declared they were "clean." The spirit said Daagbo had nothing destructive "hidden in the corners of his house." Ogou thus set the ground rules for Daagbo's behavior with Mama Lola by establishing an authoritative description of who he, Daagbo, was and how he functioned in the world of the spirits. As for Mama Lola, although she did not want to stop at the monument to honor the memory of Toussaint L'Ouverture, she did make contact with him in another way. In a sense, she became him. She was ridden by Ogou, the brave soldier whose image in Haitian Vodou is a condensation of Haiti's revolutionary history. Touissaint L'Ouverture was one of the most important of Haiti's great military leaders.

Mama Lola had not been happy with her performance in the opening ceremony of the Vodun Reunion. She was nervous and only managed to whisper, "Thank you for inviting me." Also, her hands were shaking visibly when she poured the libation. Lola was determined she would do better in the closing ceremony, and, with Maggie and me as witnesses, she rehearsed her speech and the song she would sing along with it dozens of times during our stay in Benin. She worked especially hard at memorizing the lines she wanted to say in the traditional language of the Fon people. When the time came, there was little to worry about. She looked magnificent in a new African dress. She was introduced as the "leader of Vodou in the United States," a job title that had been spontaneously inflating since the opening ceremony when she had been identified as "an important priestess from New York." Mama Lola spoke well and electrified the crowd with her rendition of a song for Ogou that she used to sing as a member of Haiti's Troupe Folklorique. Her closing words, saluting the President and the people of Benin in their language, were delivered in a shout of joy with both arms thrown up in the air. The closing ceremony was broadcast throughout the country on television and radio. It was a love affair between Mama Lola and the people of Benin.

At the end of the ceremony President Soglo came to greet us. "Nicephore Soglo," he said, smiling broadly and sticking out his hand. "I'm Mama Lola," she said. "I know who you are," the president replied, with a sly smile. "This is my daughter," Mama Lola said putting her arm around Maggie and drawing her close, and then tossing a hand back over her left shoulder, vaguely in my direction, she added, "my writer."

It is presumptuous to craft the narrative of another person's life, especially when that person is still alive. It was hard for Lola to *be* Mama Lola in Benin when she entertained even a suspicion that this character might be as much a construct of my narrative as a persona continuous with her previous life. For the time being, she needed to make me disappear a little. Thus my presence became more problematic to her than it usually was. I had searched for the words to characterize her in my book, and she performed the same sort of objectifying exercise on me when she studied my face in the sunlight and pronounced me "blonde, blonde, blonde."

Lola's acknowledgment of slavery in her family sparked her observation of my blonde otherness. In Benin during the Reunion of Vodun Cultures, race identity was the most enduring and the deepest of issues. It shaped everything, even though very little was said about it at official levels. The Route de l'Esclave project was after all a commemoration of the systems that gave birth to race and racism as we know them today in the United States. This occasion urged Lola to mark the differences between herself and me more than she usually does. Yet at the same time when Lola needed to trump Daagbo in order to gain some leverage in a troublesome relationship, she did so by allowing Ogou to ride her. Ogou Badagris is a white man. He is also Lola's main spirit, and therefore this way of being in the world is thought to be close to her own personality or character. Mama Lola has four or five other spirits who are important to her, and collectively they articulate who she is. These spirits are male and female, black and white, privileged and poor. They are interactive, differently empowered dimensions of her character while being simultaneously aspects of the larger social and natural worlds.[7] Mama Lola acts out of a fluid, open-ended subjectivity. The gender and race pluralism in her character support Euro-American theories about the socially constructed nature of gender and race.

Mama Lola continuously re-creates herself and her spirit world through the reiterative practices of trance possession, and she "refreshes" (a Vodou term) her contact with history through endless repetition of ritual technologies. Through tying and binding ritual practices such as the manufacture of *wanga*, Mama Lola's body has preserved a dense tangle of affect, an embodied sense of the control and confinement of enslavement. Every time Mama Lola makes a *wanga* with yards and yards of string, her body rehearses the technologies of binding and loosing so central to the service of the Vodou spirits. Through her hands she touches on an experience of the sheer power of slavery, one passed on to her through generations of healers in her family.

Notes

1. Judith Butler, *Gender Trouble: Feminism and the Subversion of Identity* (New York: Routledge, 1990), p. 13.

2. This is not the only version of President Soglo's illness. Suzanne Blier, who has done extensive field research in Benin, reports that she heard President Soglo was poisoned by a barber who rubbed something into Soglo's face as he shaved him. She had not heard the chain-and-padlock story. Personal conversation, February 9, 1999.

3. Suzanne Preston Blier, *African Vodun: Art, Psychology, and Power* (Chicago: University of Chicago Press, 1995), p. 23.

4. Pierre Bourdieu, *Outline of a Theory of Practice* (Cambridge: Cambridge University Press, 1977), and *The Logic of Practice* (Palo Alto: Stanford University Press, 1990); the quotations are from p. 74 of *Outline* and p. 56 of *Logic* respectively.

5. Bourdieu, *Logic*, p. 73.

6. Blier, *African Vodun*, p. 80.

7. Karen McCarthy Brown, *Mama Lola: A Vodou Priestess in Brooklyn* (Berkeley: University of California Press, 1991), pp. 112–13, 315.

3

Unseemly Commemoration: Religion, Fragments, and the Icon

JENNY FRANCHOT

> The sacred is invested in the trace that is at the
> same time its negation.
> Pierre Nora, "Between Memory
> and History: *Les Lieux de Memoir*"

1

What is the status of religious experience as an object of interpretation in intellectual culture today? I would like to approach this question by examining two scenes from nineteenth-century American fiction, one in Harriet Beecher Stowe's *The Minister's Wooing* (1859) and the other in George Washington Cable's *The Grandissimes, A Story of Creole Life* (1880). In these and similar nineteenth-century novels, I believe, we can trace a larger cultural experience of the loss of religious belief and its re-creation as visual memory, or more precisely as souvenir and entertainment, one fit for visual scrutiny and memorial appropriation as the "seen."

In the wake of the Enlightenment, the status of religion in intellectual culture is that of a loss, a collection of images and texts that are now irrevocably a recollection, a memorial of past faith, or, depending on one's perspective, of past illusion. This condition of belief, the attachment to invisible realities, is ours through not being ours. We know of others' belief or attachment to the invisible only through the visible traces left behind, through the images and texts that attest to an encounter with the unseen. In a sense, the situation of intellectual culture vis-à-vis religious experience reenacts the classic problem of distance from the divine familiar to theological and mystical traditions: those who approach divinity and then report on it dwell always in the trope of inexpressibility. A double exasperation haunts Western culture's encounter

From *American Literary History* 9, Fall 1997.

with its deity—an exasperation not only with "his" overbearing yet neglectful, raging yet rueful character, but also with our ability to represent that character. We are made in his image, according to Biblical tradition, but cannot discern his image. Records of encounters with the deity are always pointing to an insufficiency, even a failure of witnessing. He is fragment, a backside vanishing from Moses. But in becoming subject of our recollection, in becoming a memento of a lost faith, this exasperation has often been minimized, sometimes even replaced, by the colonizing conviction that our past Western selves—the Other in this case—constitute a whole, an object of our condescension or nostalgia, surveillance, and repressed desire. Contradiction, alienation, and loss belong to the conqueror; neither the native nor the past self is granted depth.

If we consider the Anglo-American past in terms of postcolonial conceptions of othering and strategies of the "gaze," religion emerges as a "stereotype" of the kind that, according to Homi Bhabha, figures the colonized as a mode of representation dependent on contradictory urges toward "fixity" and "ambivalence." Stereotypes of lost belief appear most typically in museums, on public television, or in history movies: in all three places visuality is critical. We gaze on accoutrements and art of past centuries—saintly faces, Biblical scenes, church interiors, crucifixes. Or we encounter their representations in books where print, born in the era of Protestant iconoclasm, set itself in conscious competition with the image: the visibility of text—shorn of color, shape, and the libidinal, idolatrous lure of graphic representation—potentially offers unmediated contact with an invisible deity.[1] Such images and texts filling museums and libraries are, for secular culture, the Other, the loss by which, ironically, we have come to know ourselves: we are *not* belief. We are that which we have lost.

Belief's transformation into pastness is, in fundamental respects, the narrative of Western culture's birth into the modern. The Other to modernism, religion has become a repository of the visual and has itself become a mental image. Just as the past is "religious," religion itself is a sign of the quaint, scaled down into a memory like our conception of childhood, which, Susan Stewart argues, is seen "as if it were at the other end of a tunnel—distanced, diminutive, and clearly framed." As memorabilia or as pathology, religion is imagined as an "other" state of being that is stranger and smaller—the "doll-like Middle Ages" that so fascinated Henry Adams in *Mont-Saint-Michel and Chartres* (1913), a perspective that now characterizes our bemused scrutiny of contemporary cults. Religion has become its own relic, its pastness an insignia of the inaccessible but also, as with our childhoods, of the authentic. Religion's scaled-down dimensions register our possession of it instead of its possession of us. As memento of our Western childhood, religion is thus miniaturized into objects available for visual appropriation as commodity, souvenir, or ornament.

The effort of early Protestant reformers to arrive at a purified form of Christianity is central to this othering and miniaturization—this construction of faith as something to be remembered through being scaled down to the "seen." Augustine's argument that knowing God ultimately entails an act of remembering that which he had always known is important to later Protestant efforts to construct a purified Western memory of Christ that knows itself by the superiority of its internal sight of Christ to the visual artifacts of a repudiated Catholic culture. The elder William Bradford, setting out to learn Hebrew in his last years so that he could acquire the language God spoke, is a classic instance of this Protestant memorial project to circumvent the contaminations of Roman Catholic materiality, to get back to a pure time not through the image but through the greater purity of words. Such procedures of memorial purification, at once iconoclastic and nostalgic, ironically enough contributed to the othering of religion: Catholic culture was denigrated into the seen in order to establish the purified precincts of Protestant spirituality. Critical thought today moves within the wake of this iconoclasm, still positing itself against the claims of adequate representation, melancholically content with the fragments produced by its iconoclastic energies. Current appreciation for the fragmentation and hybridity of diasporic consciousness and voice is one among many instances in contemporary cultural studies where we encounter these pleasures of iconoclastic skepticism.[2]

In becoming subject to critical reflection, religion now dwells in front of us as a visual and textual fragment to be remembered precisely as that which is not us: a subject not only *for* memory but deeply constitutive of Western memory. We possess religion through encounters with text and image, a "seeing" that understands itself as a not believing. Central to this process of secularization, this experience of liberation and loss, is the descent of belief into private and material domains as personalized object. The sacred falls into the mundane region of the seen, the knowable, the fragment.

A disassemblage of a prior unity, the Judeo-Christian tradition has, since the eighteenth century, fallen into iconic fragments—the detritus of a once powerful, overarching, and "invisible" ideology. Was the Protestant "part" a unity by virtue of its claims to having restored Christianity to its apostolic purity? If so, how did it both emerge from Catholic corruption and yet claim purity? Or was the Protestant "part" a fragment, shamefully broken off as Catholic polemicists accused and condemned to a derivative, impure status until returned to its proper place in the encompassing unity of Rome? Voicing such anxieties over the fragmentary status of Protestantism, nineteenth-century Anglo-American writing is pre-occupied with alternative religions, especially Catholicism and to a lesser but significant extent, in the postbellum era, with voudou. Both Rome and Africa emerge as metaphoric sites of fetishized consciousness, a depository of material items forced into illicit, even grotesque assemblage that bespeak libidinal power. Centuries of iconoclastic rhetoric have produced not only literal and metaphoric fragments but a continuing preoccupation with the dangers of the idol, the fetish, the miniature object hidden within.[3] Subject to the iconoclastic energies of reform, the space between deity and believer has been swept clean of the visual, and yet, paradoxically, religion now rests before us as a collection of the visible, wrested from ideology into the humbled dimension of the artifact. In this case the visible does not refute skepticism, but rather, as talisman of undecidability and and inescapable materiality, it signifies the absence of proof.

2

Walking along the Newport beaches in the late eighteenth century, the Protestant heroine of Stowe's *The Minister's Wooing* improbably stumbles across one such religious fragment: an engraving of the Madonna lying tangled in seaweed. Washed ashore (presumably from the Old World), the Catholic image is immediately adopted as a "waif" by our rigorous Calvinist heroine whose purity exceeds that of the Virgin Mary (a comparison hinted at throughout the story). Stowe's account of her Protestant heroine's eventual marriage, not to the Edwardsean Calvinist minister but instead to a more attractive suitor, sets as its fundamental narrative problem the project of female asceticism within the obligations of the marriage plot. How is the Protestant heroine to be at once saint and wife, an ascetic and a procreative homemaker? *The Minister's Wooing*, both sentimental novel and manual of personality development, details the construction of interior spirituality in a Calvinist culture that disdains external aids to or representations of spiritual work. The portrait our Protestant Mary stumbles upon is central to this characterological project of passionless procreation, for it functions as Other and fragment to her invisible and whole interiority. Her encounter anticipates the reproduction of Christianity entire as fragment, as memorial accessory to secular culture.

In an act of delicate ethnic cleansing, the Protestant Mary nails her Catholic Mary on the wall of the secret garret where she retires to meditate and spin yarn, producing bundles of literal whiteness. Hung directly opposite a portrait of a woman who suffered martyrdom during the

Salem witchcraft crisis, Mary's Madonna serves as marginalized image
and raw material for the production of her invisible sentimental piety.
Eighteenth- and nineteenth-century gothic, sentimental, and eventually
realist narratives are replete with similar visual encounters with Catholic
religious fragments that bespeak loss and ruin in a context of possessive
appropriation: the religious past, humbled into the fragmentary, iconic
dimension, functions as visual accessory in the development of novelistic
character and of the novel's "inner language" as it is produced in the
experience of reading.[4] Religious warfare gives way in the eighteenth and
nineteenth centuries to acts of stylistic religious appropriation. Stowe's
heroine can pick up Catholicism entire in an act of ecumenical housewif-
ery, reincorporating Protestant New England's hated Other as accessory
to sentimental female identity.[5]

This pious Protestant rhetoric of iconoclasm is characterized then by
disavowal of its own violence. The assault upon an abandoned competi-
tor faith's political and ethnic cultures involves the fragmentation and
appropriation of the image as commodity or souvenir. The Madonna's
transit from her status as mother of God to ornament in the Protestant
Mary's garret emblematizes this iconoclastic process whereby preservation
of the image masks its loss of significance. One can excoriate the seen as
the "Whore of Babylon," the "Anti-Christ," the scheming "Jesuit"—
demonizations that gain force from the reduction of ideology into figure,
into bodies that can then be disassembled. Such reduction of a rival faith
to the scale of the body is reenacted in Mary's treatment of the Madonna: as a portrait walling Mary's private interior, the mother of God is
reduced to a bodily Other whose boundaries mark the limitless reach of
the disembodied.

Hung on the garret wall, the portrait of the Madonna becomes a memorial site for the reformulation of the sacred from a collective tradition
to an improvisational style of spiritual being. The Madonna can appear
opposite the Salem witchcraft victim because, from the novel's devotional
perspective, they go together nicely as versions of alternative feminine
spirituality. Secularization records coincident processes of iconoclasm:
fragmentation of the image and privatization of religious meaning out of
corporate consensus. The nineteenth-century cult of domesticity, which
has drawn so much critical attention in the past three decades, provides
us with an archive of these aftereffects of iconoclasm. In Victorian novels
like Charlotte Bronte's *Villette* (1853), George Eliot's *Middlemarch*
(1871–72), Nathaniel Hawthorne's *Scarlet Letter* (1850), and Henry
James's *Portrait of a Lady* (1881), visual fragments of an abandoned
"Romanism" function as vestigial traces for what must remain, ideologi-
cally speaking, the invisible processes of an improvisational, Protestant
perfectionism. Such broken sacramental signs are critical to these novels'

postsacramental semiotics, for, as material markers at once numinous and fallen, these Catholic fragments deploy the ambiguity of the fragment to testify to the superior immateriality and wholeness of fictional character.

The uneven descent of sacred objects from holiness to inauthenticity typically elicited nostalgia for a prior, more communally sanctioned sacramentalism and disquiet toward the materiality newly perceived by the iconoclastic eye in viewing religious objects as separated items or fragments, ineluctably divorced from the wholeness of spirit. In particular, the nostalgic perception of Catholic fragments recorded in Protestant novels' encounters with monastic ruins, sacred iconography, or Rome itself was laced with the libidinal anxiety of othering. This linked yearning and distaste ambiguously positioned the religious fragment both within the bourgeois subject (as erotic or subversive enticement) and without (as supernatural force). Gothic fictions like M. G. Lewis's *The Monk* (1796) configure this dual position by dramatizing the monastery as a memorial site of commemoration and incarceration. The implicitly Protestant (or even post-Protestant) reader's progress through such founding gothic fictions is at once a touristic movement "out there" into a newly colonized space of religious otherness—a spatialized terrain of corridors and cells inhabited by the religious Other (the raging, libidinal monk)—and an intrapsychic movement "down into" the Western past.

The trope of incarceration is of course crucial to gothic discourse in the Enlightenment as it seeks to liberate Western thought from the "confinements" of superstition. The washed-up portrait of the Madonna reveals sentimental fiction's eventual inversion of this trope of incarceration: the frightening religious past is now diminished and framed, the monastic corridor has opened onto the beach, the cell onto the decorated garret. The portraits that haunt gothic fictions no longer haunt, but decorate, serving as stylistic models for sentimental piety's perfection of personality. Furnished with the Madonna, Mary's garret is an early figuration of the space of advertising, where the commodified representations of spiritual perfection depend upon acquisitions, ones that will wall the interior space of personality in contemporary culture.

Historical novels like Stowe's *The Minister's Wooing* and Cable's *The Grandissimes* construct history as the material site for locating this purified national character. History in such novels serves not only as place and time but also as "body," a space of the carnal that gives form to what Hawthorne anxiously referred to as the ghostliness of literary character. As image, or that which is seen, history is the place of the fragmented, repudiated body that anchors the iconoclastic energies of the fictional imagination as it seeks to create character and plot out of emptiness. The past holds the body as Hawthorne's narrator observes of the Elizabethan females who crowd in to watch Hester on the scaffold: "Morally, as well as materially, there was coarser fibre in those wives and maidens of old English birth and breeding, than in their fair descendants" (37). The theological ruminations of *The Scarlet Letter*'s narrator suggest America's past as an abandoned eroticism associated with the iconic domain of the Catholic image. To tell the story of America in the historical novel is to recount progressive forgettings of this bodily past, purifications from old- and new-world religious, class, and racial contaminants, emptyings of the image. The narrative of American national identity is a story of refine- ment, disembodiment, and forgetting.

Paradoxically, what enables this process of forgetting is the image, the visible shred of the past—whether it be a portrait of the Madonna or the rag of scarlet cloth Hawthorne picks up in "The Custom-House." Such relics initiate a process of remembering crucial to the organization of these nineteenth-century historical fictions—"mixed, hybrid, mutant, bound intimately with life and death," these memorial sites provide the carnality of history that empowers fiction's iconoclastic critique.[6] Intoxi- cated with the pleasures of religious othering—the displacement of tradi- tional asceticism by improvisational processes of "refinement"—the nine- teenth-century Protestant novel silences the flesh in its new preoccupation with sentimental sentience, the breathless "now" of Amer- ican purity. Central to this memorial national project, iconic fragments such as we shall see in Cable's *The Grandissimes*, the voudou amulet construct the past as visual fragment promising a criminal materiality at the heart of national origin. The image serves at once as speech and dis- cretion, voice and shroud. Not text, the image at once remains subordi- nate to the imperial powers of discourse to emplot and interpret, while, as we know from reading *The Scarlet Letter*, it disdains the global reach of discursive interpretation, eluding its grasp. Generated by the iconic fragment, the project of American historical romance is to "remember" a past otherwise censored by language, to provide a visible form for other- wise repressed truths. The logic of historical romance then is deeply para- doxical: to correctly, deeply, fully remember by fabricating memories, to know their fictionality through bodily memorial sites.

3

In 1803 a New Orleans slave woman is sent by her quadroon mistress to kill a white man. Although the quadroon is universally feared in both the white and black Creole communities for her skills as a voudou priestess, her talents backfire when her accomplice is captured. The slave woman, Clemence, is caught in a steel trap laid by a member of the white Gran- dissime clan, a man who is intent on catching whomever has been "fixing" his uncle with voudou charms. This describes in brief the setting for one of the most troubling scenes in nineteenth-century American fiction: the death by torture of a woman at the hands of a white supremacist, a character as irritated by the slave religion of voudou as by race, a man "beset with the idea that the way to catch a voudou was—to catch him; and as he had caught numbers of them on both sides of the tropical and semitropical Atlantic, he decided to try his skill privately" (Cable 311).

Filling the penultimate pages of Cable's *Grandissimes*, Clemence's lynching at the hands of Captain Jean-Baptiste Grandissime is a double murder: Clemence's protracted death marks not just an intimately physical destruction of an individual but the killing of an entire religion, or more precisely, of that of Clemence and of a religious stereotype—"voodoo"—as constructed by the Euro-American colonial imagination from its centuries-long encounter with African and New World African religious practice.

Students of the black Atlantic and the American South have studied voudou both as remnant of West African cultures after the trauma of enslavement and diaspora and as evidence of African spiritual and political resilience in the new world.[7] Perhaps the best known literary treatment of voudou's creative potential, Zora Neale Hurston's *Of Mules and Men*, presents the rites of "hoodoo" as providing access to an ultimate authenticity, the richest site of hidden folk culture and of incipient female authorial power. Karen Brown's recent anthropological classic, *Mama Lola: A Vodou Priestess in Brooklyn*, presents immigrant Haitian voudou as a regenerative polytheism and feminism that can heal our impoverished, secular sensibility. In its depiction of voudou ceremonies and ritual behaviors in French colonial New Orleans, Cable's novel anticipates these recent appreciations of voudou as a beguiling instance of racial and religious heterogeneity, a multicultural practice that therapeutically mixes not only the races but, theologically speaking, the flesh and the spirit. Mulattoes, Creoles, full Africans—virtually everyone in *The Grandissimes* except for the Anglo- and German-Americans—practices voudou and often together.

Cable's representation of this colonial religious culture provoked deep anger among local readers. An anonymous pamphlet published shortly after the novel accused Cable of being a jackal whose ironical but probing portrait of Creole culture's involvement with voudou disinterred a "cherished corpse"; Cable's exposé was equivalent to miscegenation, charged the author, with no less than the famed New Orleans voudou priestess herself, Marie Laveau. While Cable's various local color sketches of voudou practice constitute a good deal of the novel's touristic charm, the scene of Clemence's death reveals voudou's paranoid position in the Euro-American imagination. In the chapter title sarcastically denoting Clemence's death as "Voudou Cured," we see the interplay between the intimacies of bodily suffering and the abstractions of racial and religious othering as quaintness balloons into horror. Clemence is the "Voudou" and, crucially, Clemence *is* "voodoo": she is stereotype and scapegoat, the point of fixity for an abstraction's materialization and contraction.

Critically, Clemence's capture moves from interrogation into murder with the abrupt disclosure of an iconic fragment: the sculpted arm of a murdered slave, itself enclosed in a tiny coffin that is shaken loose from her clothing. The moment, rich with the violence of illicit seeing, marks the ultimate revelation of the religious Other in a novel that otherwise provides merely enticing glimpses into New Orleans voudou practice. "He removed the lid and saw within, resting on the cushioned bottom, the image, in myrtle-wax, moulded and painted with some rude skill, of a negro's bloody arm cut off near the shoulder—a *bras-coupé*—with a dirk grasped in its hand" (314). This miniaturized object has been designed by Palmyre, the voudou priestess, as a signature for Clemence to leave at the murder site. The cut-off arm memorializes the death by torture some decades earlier of a slave who, on being sold into slavery, had named himself "Bras-Coupé" to signal his now useless status to his tribe and whose ensuing resistance to slavery cost him his life. A relic of slave insurgency, Palmyre's sculptured arm radically condenses the narrative complexities of Bras-Coupé's story that otherwise filter through the novel's master narrative as the fragmentary legend that everyone is seeking to hear and to tell. The coffin finally arrests Bras-Coupé for our readerly curiosity and dominion. The miniature limb is also the visual evidence that spurs Grandissime on in the torture of Clemence. As icon of the religious Other, it is instantly deciphered as evidence of her criminality, while its moment of disclosure subtly repositions that criminality as curio of Anglo-American postbellum regionalism. With the visual emergence of the waxen arm, voudou emerges as the site of an ultimate violence, which is duplicated in a considerably milder register by the narrative's stance of genial Protestant condescension to voudou practice as infantile superstition likely to attract the colonial Catholic imagination but rightly giving way to the novel's master narrative of bourgeois progress.[8]

Clemence's lynching ruptures the genteel conventions of historical romance otherwise deployed with local charm in the story's parallel marriage plot that happily pairs two white couples in the end. While local papers largely defended the novel, Cable's portrayal of Southern religious practice and brutality outraged some local readers. For instance, Grace King charged that Cable had "stabbed the city in the back in a dastardly way to please the Northern press."[9] Mark Twain praised Cable on the same grounds, however: "When a Southerner of genius writes modern

English, his book goes . . . upon wings; and they carry it swiftly all about America and England, and . . . Germany—as witness the experience of Mr. Cable and Uncle Remus, two of the very few Southern authors who do not write in the southern style." But the novel turns from its brilliant "winged" writing of Clemence's lynching and from Cable's self-described insistence that he "meant to make *The Grandissimes* as truly a political work as it ever has been called" into the marriage plot at its conclusion, a collapse that reproduces the very silence about race relations otherwise so powerfully attacked in the novel.[10] As in *The Scarlet Letter* the national past of *The Grandissimes* is reconstructed as a site of potential subversion only to be buried again. It is opened to our view so that we might see the interior of the national body as criminal, lust ridden, and layered with religious secrets. But as suggested by Dimmesdale's notorious "hush" bidding Hester be quiet, these narratives of national identity lead us from detection, revelation, and contrition back into suppression.

Reception of Cable's novel has always been embroiled in the very questions of regional, ethnic, and racial identity at the heart of the novel's focus on Louisiana's humiliating subordination to a hated American government. The novel portrays the white Creoles as outraged natives for whom any participation in the new colonial authority is, as the leading Creole of the community explains to the new American governor, "odious—disreputable—infamous" (101). Clemence's death, within this context of imperial transfer, is a colonial drama of scapegoating, of power infamously executed by the soon-to-be powerless against the most abject.

After Grandissime captures his "Voodoo," the sympathetic narrative voice fully accedes to Clemence's oscillating patois (colonial French, Afro-English, and standard English), the torture unleashing the celebrated polyglossic culture of colonial New Orleans into its horrific double, the heteroglossic near-gibberish of suffering: "'Qui ci ca?' asked the Captain, sternly, stooping and grasping her burden, which she had been trying to conceal under herself. 'Oh, Miché, don' trouble dat! Please jes tek dis-yeh trap offen me—da's all!'" (313). Clemence's escalating desperation is marked in the text by her alternations between French and English and typographically by the alternation between standard and italicized print: "*[O]h! fo' de love o' God, Miché Jean-Baptiste, don' open dat ah box! Y'en a erin du tout la-dans, Miché Jean-Baptiste; du tout, du tout!* . . . Oh! you git kill' if you open dat ah box, Mawse Jean-Baptiste! *Mo'parole d'honneur le plus sacré*—I'll kiss de cross!" (313). Jean-Baptiste's discovery of the waxen arm jettisons Clemence into a dizzying linguistic performance that splinters into a near chaos of dialects as she is strung up to be hung only to be let down and ordered to run so that she can be shot in the back. Illicit seeing triggers verbal virtuosity as the

pages of sadistic interrogation and lamentation that describe the death of
"the Voodoo" and of voudou break religious and racial otherness apart
into a vastness of competing languages. Clemence's oscillations between
dialects not only commemorate this death but visualize language itself:
the standard typography is invaded by italicizations and phoneticisms.
Clemence's verbal struggle to arrest her death pits the mute religious
icon against speech's mobility, transformative capacities, and multiple national identifications. Clemence's language soaks in the power of the unseen dimension, while its very materiality and visibility paradoxically register its impotence. Thus while the scene's various rhetorical devices of
amplification, repetition, and dialect alternation measure the absence of
language's communicative power, those same devices, in rendering language more visible, preserve (if only partially) the memorial power of the
iconic.

For the novel's implicitly Northern, Anglo-American readership, Cable's multilingual representation of New Orleans and the lynching in particular constructs a South at once bewildering in its racial, religious, and
linguistic complexities—a mysterious regional Other for the national
eye—and scaled down to the simplicity of the regional, translated into
the comprehensibility of the quaint. Representative of the ascendant
Anglo-American culture, the novel's protagonist, the German-American
immigrant Joseph Frowenfeld, must struggle to clarify these doubled realities of Southern life. Frowenfeld is alternately mystified and horrified
by the various colonial Others who people New Orleans and whose evident racial miscegenation figures in the mixture of languages that beset
him in the pharmacy he establishes: colonial French, "negro French"
(321), metropolitan French, patois, African English, and Creolized English. Frowenfeld's own Protestant German heritage rapidly becomes
synonymous with the novel's Americanness, an identity characterized by
semicomprehension, a cognitive emptiness whose political and religious
equivalents advertise themselves as forms of purity. Stranded in English,
Frowenfeld is both student and incipient master in all spheres—domestic, political, and religious. To decipher the languages of New Orleans is
implicitly to purify Southern miscegenation, to replace the regional with
the national, Catholicism with Protestantism, voudou with Frowenfeld's
apothecary. And finally, the novel replaces torture with the sentimental
domesticity of Frowenfeld's eventual marriage to a Creole woman.
Frowenfeld, who cannot understand the coded speech Clemence speaks
to him as she travels through the town square selling cakes, ultimately
deciphers Clemence precisely by not understanding her. Although at the
center of the novel, he does not witness her persecution or death and is
never shown assimilating its implications.

Clemence's outraged speech at her death is already familiar as the intercultural speech of the black, white, and mulatto communities—all of whom know how to speak the speech of the other and how to corrupt their own and others' languages depending upon the communicative urgencies of context. For instance, Cable's rendition of Clemence's pleading pronunciation of "acci*dent*" (313) fuses Afro-English and Afro-French pronunciations. The term's slippage into italics makes this fusion visible. We are continually confronted with the estranging effect of "seeing" the novel's language as we both read it and read the narrative voice's efforts to interpret it for us. Italics signal the transition from one language to another as a "descent" from the standard into the variant, from the naturalized imperial viewpoint into the marginalized speech of the Other. In this way italics function as typographical equivalents of the stereotype, of Palmyre viewed as a "woman of the quadroon caste, of superb stature and poise, severely handsome features, clear, tawny skin and large, passionate black eyes" (57).

The narrator's standard English—that "hated tongue prescribed by the new courts" (65)—sets up a doubled relation of conquest to its characters. Their French must be represented as "peculiar" (66) both aesthetically and politically—an exoticism whose other side is mastery of the racial Other. Frowenfeld, bewildered immigrant and suitor, stands in for Cable's postbellum, implicitly Northern reader: New Orleans as the South appears before him "in a strange tongue . . . a volume whose displaced leaves would have to be lifted tenderly . . . re-arranged, some torn fragments laid together again" (103). Both 1803 New Orleans and the postbellum South are "romantic" fragments whose decipherment depends upon our patient submission to a linguistic instruction that Frowenfeld avoids.

With the disclosure of the tiny coffin Cable produces race and religion in miniaturized form, jointly and horrifically compacted in the term "Voudou"—the essence to be caught, rendered visible, and ultimately "cured." The discovery of the coffin then instances the materialization of the colonized Other as both individual and alternative religious tradition. This materialization transgresses the propriety of the hidden or twilight region of the half-seen that harbors various figurations of the mulatto as uncanny by emerging into a flagrant visibility that must be rendered invisible again, murdered through an extended verbal representation. Voudou thus operates on dual levels of iconic representation, at once a fit subject for the nostalgic, miniaturizing perspective of "local color romance" and at the same time so blasphemous that it must be subjected to a ritualized death by torture. Miniaturization aggrandizes the very contexts that it excludes.[11] The horror of this double capture is summarized in the coffin's capture of the reader's gaze. As Bachelard observes of miniature houses, "false objects that possess a true psychological objectivity," Palmyre's miniaturized image of Bras-Coupé uses the hapless inadequacy of image fashioning—the necessarily fragmentary representation of divinity—to voice a new-world history of racial violence and mystification. The "inversion of perspective" achieved through miniaturization echoes that involved in slavery's radical diminution of personhood.[12] Similarly, in the scaled-down representation characteristic of regional fiction, the region is the "small" to the nation's greatness, materiality to the Union's immateriality.

The coming-into-sight of the coffin's contents figures the ultimate penetration of the recesses of the subordinated Other, the achieved access into the confines of superstition. Looking in on the coffin's contents recapitulates the fascinated investigation of monastic interiors so popular in anti-Catholic fiction while the discovery of a body part therein echoes Protestant horror at the various disassembled body parts at the heart of othered religious traditions, such as new-world cannibalist practices or old-world Roman Catholic dismemberments in the Inquisition or destruction of illegitimate offspring in convents.[13] And, as the revelation of Palmyre's vengeance, the sighting of the coffin's contents forges a link between the novel's fragmentary narrative (the whispered renditions of Bras-Coupé's story) and the culminating disclosure. It invites us to consider the imagistic renditions of the religious Other: as the duplicitous phantom and as the material object. Bras-Coupé's waxen arm is the "it" that locates, homogenizes, and finally arrests the linguistic heterogeneity of the text, grounds an otherwise anarchic word, and clarifies the speech of the Other.

But Palmyre's sculpture raises further questions about the reassemblage of the body of the religious Other, for, in providing a radical form that entraps the fragmentary retellings of Bras-Coupé's story, it reincorporates him into the national body. Cable's historical romance is a doubled detective narrative: we struggle both to find out the story of Bras-Coupé and the story of America's relationship to France, Spain, Germany, England, Africa, and the West Indies. We resist the knowledge that America has indeed a past whose regional truths are not cut off from the national one but intrinsic to it. Imperial formation and bodily dismemberment or disfigurement are linked narratives. Not only are the wages of imperialism violence, but also the imperial nation is formed through severing parts of the national body or history. The story of America, like *The Grandissimes* and *The Scarlet Letter*, is at base a crime story: Who is guilty of the murder of Bras-Coupé and Clemence? How did the nation become "white" in the face of all this nonwhiteness, innocent in the face of all this terror, and empty in the face of all these material traces? While Hester's cloth letter evokes a suppressed Catholic embodiment, Palmyre's arm, in its very rude fleshiness, doubly simulates the body, a repetitiveness that reveals a religious sensibility wholly other to Christianity. The religious Other is dependent upon a literal synecdoche for its voicing. Both the legend and its method of resurrection spill out when the coffin's contents are disclosed. If the scarlet *A* reveals the subversive art of needlework, Bras-Coupé's arm, clutching a knife, reveals another (but far more troubling) womanly art of revenge—voudou.

Bras-Coupé's fragmented body and story supply the enticement of the untold, the true history of the South's racial violence that will be reiterated in Clemence's death. As history it is the inner, contestatory truth of the romance, a truth of region that does battle with the nationalist ideology of plantation romance, which encloses it. Eventually restored to completed sequence, it is, ironically, suppressed when Bras-Coupé's body, reduced to a miniature arm, becomes a relic. Preserved in the form of the carefully molded waxen arm, Bras-Coupé's existence is resurrected from the apolitical, fragmented status of legend into the urgencies of political narrative, only to precipitate a release of vengeful violence against voudou. This captive/resistant body and its metaphoric name are literalized and commemorated by Palmyre's religious art, which forces it into sight as "voodoo." This viewing, like the Protestant Mary's viewing of the Madonna on her wall, moves ineluctably toward eclipse of the religious Other.

And yet this image suggests a curious semiotic relation, for it visualizes something that, literally speaking, never existed: the cut-off arm. The molded waxen arm does not portray a man's face (the man who called himself "Bras-Coupé") but a part of him that claimed only metaphoric existence, that is, a self likened to a cut-off arm. Palmyre's relic materializes an abstraction of slavery—its theft of personhood. But this political truth is a fiction, an imaginative illustration which she supplies to Bras-Coupé's conversion of himself into text. Even more paradoxically, Cable resupplied his heroic slave with the arm traditionally cut off or missing in local legends. Writing to his daughter after the novel's publication, Cable noted that some local opposition to *The Grandissimes* was provoked by his revision of the Bras-Coupé's legend. Cable made his hero whole-bodied. "They considered . . . that my version of it was faulty, because I had taken the liberty of saving Bras-Coupé's arm whole. The fact that he certainly did chop it off seemed to them to be a precious verity of history not to be trifled with, and I believe the insistence upon this point was a conscious tribute to the African's magnificent courage."[14] Cable's restoration of Bras-Coupé's arm is a bid for realism, an effort to demythologize the legend's critique of slavery in order to sharpen it. Yet Bras-Coupé's essentially allegorical status remained prominent in Cable's characterization of him, for after Bras-Coupé names himself, the narrative voice reports that he thus made himself into "a type of all Slavery, turning into

flesh and blood the truth that all Slavery is maiming" (171). Cable's metaphorical representation of the missing arm narrows the character into
near allegory. Ironically, Cable's view of Bras-Coupé as voluntarily rendering into bodily terms the abstractions of slavery is contradicted by the
name's significance, which marks the loss of the capacity to be useful, to
make meaning, and to signify. The two authors, Bras-Coupé and Cable,
are joined in rivalry. If, as one critic notes, Cable grafted "the 'fact' of
self-mutilation from his readings on Santo Domingo" (Stephens 405)
onto local legends of insurgent slaves who had been injured or punitively
maimed, his metaphorization of the "bras-coupé" lends a carefully pro-
scribed Haitian militancy to the figure of the American slave. Fully
"armed," Cable's Bras-Coupé suppresses the spectre of African violence;
the boundaries of the American slave body remain intact as do the
boundaries of the nation. The plot of *The Grandissimes* implies that Haitian revolutionary violence will be contained within a more powerful white
violence: the disclosure of the waxen limb now armed with a knife—
synecdoche of revolution—precipitates the catastrophic assault upon
Clemence and, ultimately, the banishment of Palmyre and her revolutionary iconography.

Cable's novel bids us reflect on how the religious Other is commemorated as figure of both the criminal and the quaint—a process of miniaturization essential to the construction of an expansionist national identity out of theological ruin and racial violence. If Stowe's historical
romance anticipates the transformation of religion entire into souvenir
and decorative accessory, Cable's exploration of the deviant religious icon
suggests another, more disturbing implication to Western iconoclasm.
The destruction of the icon liberates thought or in the terms of *The
Grandissimes*, the cut-off arm generates and is nobly commemorated by
the novel's masterful realism. But the destruction of the icon at the
novel's conclusion also forecloses further interpretation. Clemence drops
to the earth and no one knows who has fired the bullet. Nor does anyone
pick up the coffin, even as a souvenir. It is closed to view but not in the
way Clemence had prayed for.[15]

Notes

1. Accounts of Protestant iconoclasm that have shaped my understanding of
print culture's competition with the image include John Phillips, *The Reformation of Images: Destruction of Art in England* (Berkeley: University of California
Press, 1973) and Walter J. Ong, *The Presence of the Word: Some Prolegomena for
Cultural and Religious History* (New Haven: Yale University Press, 1967).

2. See Jesper Rosenmeier, "'With My Own Eyes': William Bradford's *Of Plym-*

outh Plantation" in Sacvan Bercovitch, ed., *Typology and Early American Literature* (Amherst: University of Massachusetts Press, 1972), pp. 69–106. Examples of the diasporic consciousness can be found in Homi K. Bhabha, *The Location of Culture* (London: Routledge, 1994), pp. 139–70; Theophus Harold Smith, *Conjuring Culture: Biblical Formations of Black America* (New York: Oxford University Press, 1994); and Paul Gilroy, *The Black Atlantic: Modernity and Double Consciousness* (Cambridge: Harvard University Press, 1993). For a penetrating meditation on the pleasures of minimalism at the heart of Reform sensibility, see Julia Kristeva, "Holbein's Dead Christ," in *Black Sun: Depression and Melancholia,* trans. Leon S. Roudiez (New York: Columbia University Press, 1989), pp. 105–38.

3. Bhabha's account of the construction of the colonial subject can be profitably applied to thinking about the construction of the religious subject and object. While Bhabha uses primarily racial and sexual terms in his account of the colonial Other as "fetish," I do not mean to fold religion in as one more category of difference within "the binding of a range of differences and discriminations that inform the discursive and political practices of racial and cultural hierarchization" (*Location of Culture*, p. 67) but rather to suggest how the entire field of religion qua religion has been constructed as a colonial domain within postmodern studies as indigenous, lost, and primitive. Indeed, colonialism and secularization are reciprocal processes of reification and reduction to the status of the "trinket." See also W. J. T. Mitchell's account of the fetish as the "antithesis of the scientific image, epitomizing irrationality in both its crudity of representational means and its use in superstitious rituals. It is a 'producer' of images, not by means of mechanical reproduction, but by organic 'breeding' of its own likeness"; in *Iconology: Images, Text, Ideology* (Chicago: University of Chicago Press, 1986), pp. 14–19, 162.

4. I borrow the phrase "inner language" from Susan Stewart, *On Longing: Narratives of the Miniature, the Gigantic, the Souvenir, the Collection* (Baltimore: Johns Hopkins University Press, 1984), p. 17.

5. For an account of Stowe's logic of affective ownership in *The Minister's Wooing*, see Lori Merish, "Sentimental Consumption: Harriet Beecher Stowe and the Aesthetics of Middle-Class Ownership," *American Literary History* 8 (1996): 1–33.

6. Pierre Nora situates contemporary practices of commemoration within larger cultural experience of the loss of tradition: "No society has ever produced archives as deliberately as our own, not only by volume, not only by new technological means of reproduction and preservation, but also by its superstitious esteem, by its veneration of the trace. Even as traditional memory disappears, we feel obliged assiduously to collect remains, testimonies, documents, images, speeches, any visible sign of what has been, as if this burgeoning dossier were to be called upon to furnish some proof to who knows what tribunal of history. The sacred is invested in the trace that is at the same time its negation." See "Between Memory and History: *Les Lieux de Memoir,*" *Representations* 26 (1989), p. 19, for quotation in the text. The quotation above is from pp. 14–15.

7. For classic accounts, see Albert J. Raboteau, *Slave Religion: The "Invisible Institution" in the Antebellum South* (New York: Oxford University Press, 1978); Robert Farris Thompson, *Flash of the Spirit: African and Afro-American Art and*

Philosophy (New York: Random House, 1983); and Karen McCarthy Brown, *Mama Lola: A Vodou Priestess in Brooklyn* (Berkeley: University of California Press, 1991). Also see Jessie Gaston Mulira, "The Case of Voodoo in New Orleans," *Africanisms in American Culture* (Bloomington: Indiana University Press, 1990), pp. xxii, 34–68.

8. See Arlin Turner, *George W. Cable: A Biography* (Durham, NC: Duke University Press, 1956), p. 102. Charles Swann argues that the novel's politics are in the service of the "bourgeois revolution" against the "stagnations of caste," among which, although Swann does not discuss them, are the practices of voudou. See "*The Grandissimes*: A Story-Shaped World," *Literature and History* 13 (1987): 257–77. The quotation above is from p. 260.

9. Alice Petrey Hall makes the nice point that it was ironically only the outraged white Southern reaction that correctly surmised the dark side of Cable's vision, precisely what we today appreciate as his greatness; it was Northern readers who were strangely blind to the terror in his writing, seeing more charm than scandal in his portrayals of religion. See "Native Outsider: George Washington Cable," in *Literary New Orleans: Essays and Meditations*, ed. Richard S. Kennedy (Baton Rouge: Louisiana State University Press, 1992), pp. 1–7 and Louis D. Rubin, Jr., *George W. Cable: The Life and Times of a Southern Heretic* (New York: Pegasus, 1969), p. 263.

10. See, Arnold Goldman, "Life and Death in New Orleans," in *The American City: Literary and Cultural Perspectives*, ed. Graham Clarke (New York: St. Martin's, 1988), p. 151; and George Washington Cable, "My Politics," in *The Negro Question: A Selection of Writings on Civil Rights in the South*, ed. Arlin Turner (New York: Doubleday, 1958), p. 14. Swann argues that, to the contrary, Cable's return to the relative trivialities of the white marriage plot invites us to "place that sentimentality" ("*The Grandissimes*," p. 273).

11. Stewart argues that the "miniature has the capacity to make its context remarkable; its fantastic qualities are related to what lies outside it in such a way as to transform the total context" (*On Longing*, p. 46).

12. Gaston Bachelard notes the "inversion of perspective" involved in fantasy tales of miniaturization as well as the freedom from imprisonment and implicit mastery of reality it provides (*The Poetics of Space*, trans. Maria Jolas [New York: Orion, 1964]), p. 149.

13. For account of European and Euro-American fears of cannibal dismemberment, see Greg Dening, *Mr. Bligh's Bad Language: Passion, Power, and Theatre on the Bounty* (Cambridge: Cambridge University Press, 1992); Michel de Certeau, "Montaigne's Cannibal's," in *The Writing of History*, trans. Tom Conley (New York: Columbia University Press, 1988); and Stephen J. Greenblatt, *Marvelous Possessions: The Wonder of the New World* (Chicago: University of Chicago Press, 1991). For accounts of Protestant legends about Catholic dismemberment, see Jenny Franchot, *Roads to Rome: The Antebellum Protestant Encounter with Catholicism* (Berkeley: University of California Press, 1994). Bhabha's discussion of "gathering" as the best available way to conceive of existence in the wake of diaspora attempts to find in fragmentation a source of political and intellectual strength, to convert the sign of a fragmented otherness into that of a redemptive postmodern consciousness. My awareness of these issues has been heightened by Caroline Walker Bynum's fine studies: *Fragmentation and Redemption: Essays on*

Gender and the Human Body in Medieval Religion (New York: Zone Books, 1992) and *The Resurrection of the Body in Western Christianity, 200–1336* (New York: Columbia University Press, 1995).

14. Robert O. Stephens supplies a useful account of the various source legends that fed into Cable's initial treatment of the Bras-Coupé legend in his short story "Bibi," a short story then modified into the story of Bras-Coupé that forms the crux of *The Grandissimes*. (As Stephens argues, Cable's reading of Mérimée exposed him to the "linkage of the African slave trade with Creole culture, the confrontation of African, Creole, and Anglo-American values, gothic action, and searching irony.") The internationally renowned pianist, Louis Moreau Gottschalk includes in his memoirs his childhood memories of a Bras-Coupé as a bogeyman haunting the woods around New Orleans—a figure whose legendary abilities at the "bamboula" dance Gottschalk later transcribed into his famous concert piece, "Bamboula: Danse des Nègres"—a piece whose revolutionary implications made it a favorite among audiences in the revolutionary year, 1848. See Robert O. Stephens, "Cable's Bras-Coupé and Mérimée's 'Tamango': The Case of the Missing Arm," *Mississippi Quarterly* 35 (1982): 387–405. The quotation above is from p. 398.

15. This essay has drawn on the following editions of novels by Cable, Stowe, and Hawthorne for quotations: Cable, *The Grandissimes: A Story of Creole Life* (Harmondsworth, England: Penguin, 1988); Stowe, *The Minister's Wooing* (New York: Derby and Jackson, 1989); Hawthorne, *The Scarlet Letter: An Authoritative Text, Essays in Criticism, and Scholarship,* ed. Seymour Gross et al., 3rd edition (New York: Norton, 1988).

4

The Place of Ritual in Our Time

SUSAN L. MIZRUCHI

RITUAL ACTS express an unbridgeable gap—a chasm—between what is sought or aspired to and the historical present. Ritual actors are always at a loss in relation to some prior moment of greater spiritual promise and communal coherence. In this sense, sacrifice is the quintessential ritual form, and its mark or signature is its articulation of nostalgia. I mean nostalgia in its most literal sense: *nostos* ("return to home") *algia* ("pain" or "sickness")—a longing to the point of sickness for return, for home. The idea of return is implicit in sacrifice, in its attempt to restore a lost relationship between humans and gods or to atone for some spiritual offense. Also integral to sacrifice is a certain wistfulness about the legitimacy of its appeal. Sacrifice has long been viewed as a precarious enterprise, its ritual identity deriving in part from the fact that it appears out of place, outmoded, an historical antique or remnant that is fast disappearing. Thus many of the sacrificial actors or witnesses I will be talking about worry about the authenticity of the ritual procedure, its infiltration by elements that are not supposed to be there. But the act itself of sacrifice, whether actual or alleged, becomes a token of authentic belief: where there is sacrifice, there is faith.

And where there is faith, there is interdisciplinary study. For religion is one of the points in our different disciplinary discussions of culture where overlap is inevitable and most productive. Because religion involves, by definition, the transcendence and reconstitution of boundary, it occupies borders between the imagined and real, the historical and universal, the known and unknown. Religion's own "borderline" position calls for an academic response that is necessarily interdisciplinary and richly aware of the productivity and authenticity of the "illusory" in culture.

To "place" ritual in our time will require some leaps and bounds. So I will be ranging from an American breakfast table, to a suburban backyard in the 1990s, to Kiev, Russia in the early decades of this century. All of these scenes will project us further back to an ancient era when sacrifice was a predominant social institution. This is because sacrifice, ritual, is an act of commemoration. It's a reminder of previous intensified events, of their ongoing vitality, and also of their anomalous character. However present this Judaeo-Christian legacy remains, we would do well to recognize its exceeding strangeness. I have deliberately chosen extreme examples in this analysis—the subliminal and the graphic, the extremes of trope and literalization—in order to highlight what lies between—the status of sacrifice as an ongoing norm.

I want to preface this essay with a note of warning: some of the cases that I will be describing are violent, offensively so. Violence is fundamental to sacrifice in its foundational form—think of the (near) Sacrifice of Issac or the Crucifixion of Christ. In what follows, I argue that the traces of sacrifice which we confront on a daily basis, which we would call "benign" and "normative," bear the residue, and exist on a continuum with more overtly violent examples of sacrifice, which are themselves ritually authentic. If sacrificial acts look extravagant to us, we might recall Jonathan Z. Smith's remark that religion "is not nice."[1]

I have said that sacrifice is nostalgic as a practice and interdisciplinary as an object of study. A third premise of my argument is that sacrifice is ordinary. It is not an act confined to extremists or extremes. One sign of this is the fact that sacrifice is grounded in eating, and I begin my analysis accordingly, with the most common of objects, a box of breakfast cereal. I will then turn to a domestic murder that looks aberrant, in order to show that it is far more familiar than we think. My final and fullest example comes from high culture: a novel, Bernard Malamud's *The Fixer*, based on a remote event, whose pertinence to our own time was rightly recognized by its author. Implicit in this emphasis on literature is my belief that literature can help to conceptualize other cultural events; it allows us to read incidents which are not textually bound. I want to make my case by demonstrating the reach of sacrifice at the present time: from a popular culture item to a way of expressing rage, worship, fear, of defining boundaries between kin and non-kin, those who eat what we eat and those who don't, to a mode of historical reflection and explanation. I will be arguing then for the reasonableness of ritual acts, and by implication, for the necessity of our ongoing scholarly attention to the commonplace extravagances that seem so safely displaced. My essay will be a plea for recognition of the continuum between intellectual work and ordinary life, for the continuity between esoteric and common practices.

Cereal Rites

The ad shown in figure 4.1 has appeared on the back of "Wheat Chex" cereal boxes for the past three years. Its significance for me lies in the way it brings together the acts of consumption and sacrifice with the impulse of nostalgia. Consider the four-word phrase that at once commands and

Figure 4.1

disclaims: "Eat Right, Sacrifice Nothing." The imperative—"Eat Right"—may register the extraordinary spiritual portent of consumption. Eating right, in conformity with the proper ritual requirements, is next to Godliness. As anthropologists have recognized, food is a language for expressing God's wisdom (when God himself is consumed especially); and food is a language for articulating boundaries, whether between individuals or nations (food is one of the most prominent commodities in international trade). Thus food articulates boundaries as it passes back and forth across the boundaries of bodies; as it delimits the very prospects of survival both for persons and for states; and as it distinguishes the spiritually pure from the impure.[2] This ad sanctions the alimentary appeal to goodness and bounty; but it repudiates the idea that a payment must be exacted as part of that appeal. What I want to call attention to, is the expectation itself. The expectation, which is presumably shared with the consumer audience to which it is addressed, is that virtue and plenitude require sacrifice. On what other grounds could it be a selling point of Wheat Chex that it nullifies this requisite exchange? This ad relies on the common wisdom that you pay for everything. It sells its product by promising that in the case of Wheat Chex—miraculously—you *don't* have to pay.

So the first thing to note about this ad is its logic. Something has to be given up if someone is to benefit. I would designate it a logic that is widespread in American culture. The second thing to note is that eating and sacrifice are presumed to be interdependent. The word "eat" and the word "sacrifice" are graphically contiguous here rather than opposed: "eat" may be said to rest upon "sacrifice." This contiguity or interdependence is confirmed by at least two major religions in the United States, Judaism and Christianity, where sacrifice is integral to the religion's foundational consumptive event—the Commensal Meal of the Early Semites, and the Last Supper of Christ. To partake in either of these ritual feasts is to forge ties of kinship. Food, in the words of the late-nineteenth-century interpreter of Early Semitic traditions, Robertson Smith, is a "sacred cement," uniting worshippers with one another and with their God as "flesh of the flesh and bone of the bone." The Last Supper is designed in part to destroy a certain narrow form of kinship ("separate categories of people tied tightly to their own kin") in order to make "one new creation in which there were no divisions and no favorites," with all things reconciled through Jesus.[3] Eating is tied to sacrifice in both of these rituals because it is believed traditionally that the God himself provides the substance of the meal. It is on this basis that scholars have traced the Last Supper to early forms of agricultural sacrifice: the common premise of "one man dying for the good of the community."[4]

How different is this ancient supposition—that perfection and Godliness had a material form that allowed them to be consumed and thereby

imparted to the believer—from the message of the "Wheat Chex" box—
that eating well is right, even righteous? The rhetoric of this ad—"whole
grain," "honest," "perfect," "down to earth"—would have us believe
that these small brown squares of wheat carry the prospect of goodness,
perfection, and even authenticity. To eat Wheat Chex is to absorb these
qualities. What I want to question, or rather complicate, is the repudiation itself. For I want to suggest that sacrifice in the classic sense is invoked here because it has been renovated, rather than displaced. The
contemporary cereal company holds the promise provided in ancient
times by the body of God: to unite the community, and, it may be in-
ferred from the dominant color scheme—red strawberries, white back-
ground, blueberries, the American community in particular. In keeping
with this, the ad promotes identifiably American ideals of health, physical
integrity, purity, and simplicity. On the whole, physical values—"tastes
great," "body needs," "without adding fat,"—are continuous with moral
values—"whole," "right," "goodness." We have come to a point in our
technological development where rightness can be attained without
suffering.

While the tone and scheme are triumphant, there is a prevailing inti-
mation of loss which is critical to the ad's evocation of sacrifice. I refer to
the nostalgia it implies for a close-knit, homogeneous society, the anxiety
it conveys about the impurity or inauthenticity of available forms of worship. From the earliest times, sacrificial actors were preoccupied with perceptions of God's distance, and even indifference, and this preoccupation
became integral to the rite. It's appropriate that this is an ad for food,
since food has so often been a vehicle of nostalgia. Consider in this case
the sunrise inset, the filmic fade-in that recalls so many Hollywood
scenes, and so many echoes of them in twentieth-century American
novels (as in the wrenching blueberry cobbler scene in *The Bluest Eye*).

As figured in the cereal box, nostalgia means recurrence as bounty and
bounty as the promise of recurrence, of replenishment anew every morning for the entire community of Wheat Chex eaters. The brushed edges
of the image, which blur the line between beginning and end (is this
sunrise or sunset?), source and outcome, cause and effect, confirm that
we are in the realm of mythology. In contrast, the other elements of the
ad, the fruit, wheat grains, and cereal, seem distinctly objectified. But it's
precisely the overt constructedness of this filmic promise of renewal and
abundance that defines the ritual work of sacrifice here. This is sacrificial
theatre, where a rift between the ritual appeal and the hoped for result is
presumed. In sacrifice, there are no guarantees. The classic model ensures
that no good comes without sacrifice, but fails to ensure the reverse: that
good is its inevitable issue. The Wheat Chex box puts both prospects into

question. But that doesn't make it any less beholden to sacrificial assumptions.[5]

My point is that there is a tension between the dominant declaration of this ad and the images that surround it, a tension that is standard to sacrificial convention. I want to keep in mind certain features of this cereal box—the image of blood-red strawberries; the ideal of redemption; the nostalgia for a purified, agriculturally based, social order—as we move from a scene of domestic harmony to a scene of domestic violence, where sacrifice mediates the annihilation of community, rather than the promise of one.

In the following section a phenomenon that I have characterized as a late-nineteenth-century recuperation of sacrifice in a largely American (but also European) interdisciplinary context will resonate profoundly. There were many reasons why sacrifice became a prominent category among intellectuals helping to shape the emergence of professional disciplines in the United States, as well as among realist writers, theologians, and amateurs participating in public debates on the major social questions of the day. The ritual held strong symbolic value for those struggling to reconcile faith with rationalism and communal coherence with capitalist expansion. Perhaps most significant of all was the role of sacrifice in mediating America's emergence as a "multicultural" society.

Indeed, sacrifice might be called a foundational script of our multicultural becoming.[6] Sacrifice was critical to modern reconceptualizations of kinship. What had been common knowledge since the time of the "Early Semites" was discovered anew: the recognition that absolute sanctions for defining communal and national boundaries were untenable. That recognition was growing in the late nineteenth century throughout the human sciences, as well as in religion and literature. Writers like DuBois and Durkheim, Henry James, F. H. Giddings, and Robertson Smith, distinguished the assurances of traditional kinship, where membership has a primal force issuing in a "common life . . . common religion . . . common social duties," from a modern situation, where "kinship has no absolute value, but is measured by degrees, and means much or little, or nothing at all."[7] Sacrifice is the practice that formalizes the fury occasioned by that gap. Through sacrifice, this gap is both expressed and suppressed. For sacrifice in this period was also a fervent staging of blood kinship, a melodramatic, even violent theatre of common bonds. We are not without our own dis-ease over kin. The violence of urban youth gangs, and the revenge plot that culminated in the catastrophic bombing of the Oklahoma City federal building, can be seen as different eruptions from a single postmodern crisis of kinship.

Last Rites

This essay is structured in three movements, from the most subliminal example, to the most disturbing example, to the most explanatory and analytical example. This allows me to deal first with what I view as cultural symptoms (an advertising image and a domestic murder), and then to move to a text, *The Fixer*, which helps me analyze those symptoms. It allows me, further, to move from a commonplace image that becomes increasingly meaningful and also disturbing on reflection, to an event whose seeming excesses are the key to its commonplaces, to a novel which provides a way of reading the peculiarly unsettling dynamics of both image and event.

On August 30th, 1995, *The Boston Globe* reported a chilling incident. Two nights earlier, in a middle-class section of Framingham, a northern suburb of Boston, Richard Rosenthal, a Jewish life insurance executive at John Hancock, and Laura Rosenthal, his Christian wife, who had recently converted to Judaism and had quit her job as a market trader at Hancock to care for their baby daughter, had gotten into an argument over their burned supper. The husband followed his wife out to the backyard, where he proceeded to beat her with a rock the size of a softball. After she was dead, he methodically carved out her heart and lungs with a butcher's knife, and impaled them on a wooden stake in an altar-like formation.[8]

Everything about this event is ordinary in secular terms, from battery to murder (the *Globe* is full of stories describing the death of a woman at the hands of her husband, ex-husband, or male lover), except for the final moments of mutilation. These were the details of course that were seized upon by the lawyers who formulated Rosenthal's unsuccessful insanity defense. (Rosenthal was convicted of first-degree murder "with extreme atrocity and cruelty," on November 8th, 1996.) These are also the details that seem most amenable to religious analysis.[9] Such details of ritual violence might be considered a "scandal" to enlightenment thinking, the thinking that has underwritten the 300-year-long effort to imagine religion with a mind of reason.[10] While one might argue, with the prosecution psychiatrist, that the outrageous elements of the case were contrived by the defendant to "cop a plea," the facts themselves remain suggestive.

Fact one: Rosenthal excised the very organs that were believed to have caused the 1994 death of their first-born son. The child died shortly after birth, presumably of a weak heart and lungs. Some biblical blame game—an eye for an eye, a tooth for a tooth—may have been orchestrating his violence. Fact two: according to witnesses from the local Jewish synagogue, Rosenthal, for at least a year before the murder, had become actively, even aggressively, observant. Fact three: the Rosenthals were an intermarried couple, a matter that weighed increasingly on Richard Rosenthal in the time following their infant son's death. On the night of the murder, police discovered in Rosenthal's car a skullcap and a Torah reader in addition to the bloody clothing. And a month before the murder, at temple services Rosenthal had marked a passage from the Book of Numbers designating the "circumstances [in which] vows of women can be annulled by the father or husband." The defense characterized the murder as "primitive," highlighting a moment on the Massachusetts Avenue Bridge when the defendant believed God spoke to him directly. As Rosenthal put it, his son had died because "he [Rosenthal] was not strictly observant." In his own bizarre way, Rosenthal may have been enacting a version of Old Testament justice.[11]

Indeed, I want to argue that his "extreme" and "cruel" murder of his wife can be read as a type of sacrifice. The traumatic loss—in his own estimation, "sacrifice"—of his first-born son is compensated by the death of a wife now resolutely imagined as an "alien" or non-kin. I need hardly say that this is neither to excuse the killer nor to abuse the memory of the victim. Rather, it is to understand the matter in precise ritual terms. To this end, I want to emphasize the representative quality of the event. This uniquely gruesome murder, apparently isolated to one man's lunacy (legal innocence) or evil (legal guilt), expresses anxieties, conflicts, and resolutions that are far more pervasive in our culture than we have recognized. It confronts us in incidents that we read about in our newspapers over morning coffee: for example, the brutal slaying of James Byrd, Jr., an African-American, by three members of the Aryan Nation in Jasper, Texas. In the words of that victim's friend, Ethel Parks, "As small as James seemed in life, he is powerful in death. Maybe it took this to force us all to find a way to heal." This was the headline in *The Boston Globe*, June 12th, 1998: "To force us all to find a way to heal." Redemption through force is the script of sacrifice—the mutability rite that enlarges the small, elevates the profane, and saves the community.[12]

I have already suggested how the Rosenthal case might be read as a sacrificial revenge plot—the husband's distorted construal of his wife's guilt for the death of their first-born son, who may in fact have been afflicted with a genetic disorder inherited from Rosenthal himself. This would make the murder an appeasement of his own projected guilt. Rosenthal was preoccupied with his son's death. For a person reportedly obsessed with control, the death of his son was a stunning sign of his helplessness. Following the death, Rosenthal barraged hospital authorities with requests for explanations, requests characterized as "repeated and increasingly demanding." On the day of Laura Rosenthal's murder, Richard wrote a letter to the chief executive officer of the hospital where his son had died, expressing dissatisfaction with the staff's unresponsiveness to his overtures.[13]

If the hospital was short on explanation, Rosenthal was not without his own. And prominent among them was Rosenthal's experience of what I have called "a contemporary crisis of kinship." Whether "staged" or sincere, Rosenthal in the period of the murder was prone to imagine encounters with aliens from outerspace, imaginings that were shaped by concerns with ethnic identity or kinship. In his pocket when he was arrested were notes about alien conspiracies, including one that depicted "Jews . . . sent from outer space to mate with earthlings and bring harmony." At his trial, the defense argued that Rosenthal thought his wife "was an alien, as he beat her in their Framingham backyard." These details, together with his renewed devotions, suggest that Rosenthal, over time, developed an increasingly unsettled and finally murderous attitude toward his interfaith marriage.[14] From this perspective, Rosenthal's act might be categorized, in the words of an anthropologist known for her work on the Dogon of Mali, as a sacrifice performed for the sake of "non-personalized ritual or spiritual power," whereby "one who has breached a prohibition finds himself at a *loss* of spiritual substance . . . [T]he effusion of sacrificial blood and the release of vital force that accompanies it have . . . the function of making good this loss."[15]

The Rosenthal murder seems to me an example of "sacrifice by the book." The Torah reader, or book of ancient Jewish law, found with Rosenthal when he was arrested, had bloody handprints on it, which suggests that he was holding it at some point during or after the murder. And Rosenthal's knowledge of Judaism so impressed both prosecutors and defense attorneys that an expert from Brandeis University was called in to verify its extent. The Brandeis professor concluded that Rosenthal's learning was vast, and also that there was nothing particularly unusual about it. His engagement with his religion appeared altogether appropriate, even conventional. The professor made note of two details: that the Torah reading for the Sabbath preceding the murder concerned the subject of sacrifice, and the Hebrew conversion name taken by Rosenthal's wife, presumably at Rosenthal's own bidding, was "Asherah," which translates as the stake (or tree branch) used on the sacrificial altar.[16] This last detail is especially significant because Rosenthal, according to his first testimony, after murdering his wife, went into the woods abutting their yard to select a tree branch stake upon which to mount her excised organs.[17]

Rosenthal's actions are readily classifiable as ritualized and methodical. The coroner testified that Rosenthal's excision of his wife's organs was clean and expert, a procedure that would have taken patience and time— over two hours. Rosenthal also took the time to drag his wife's body away from where he killed and carved her, to perform a surface burial with wood chips. To recall, his separate mounting of the organs on the tree stake had "the look of an altar." The case sparked a remarkable variety of responses which all shared a single question of control: did Rosenthal's act express his complete control over his wife, or lack of it, or some combination of the two? The courtroom minutes on the case reveal that it was precisely the question of control that alternately polarized and mystified the prosecution and defense.[18]

I believe that the best prospects for elucidation lie in a recognition of the centrality of Rosenthal's religious preoccupations. In the trial this was a gray area made use of by the defense because it seemed to bolster the case for insanity, and by the prosecution because it seemed not to. The defense characterization of Rosenthal's behavior as "frenzied" and "primitive," a strange sort of atavism, indicated psychosis. The prosecution countered that Rosenthal was narcissistic, and that his murderous actions, like the crime scene itself, were contrived, even theatrical. The prosecution psychiatrist cited as an example of this deliberateness the fact that Rosenthal took off his bloody socks before reentering the house, so as not to track up the floor, and then showered.[19] From the perspective I have been developing, both arguments, defense and prosecution, are supportable. Rosenthal's behavior, from the devoutness precipitated by mourning for his son to the murder itself, *were* "primitive." Yet the very same devoutness and murderous acts also looked highly controlled.

Rosenthal acted in ways that were both rational and irrational. His actions highlight why people use ritual: to put themselves in touch with the inhuman and transcendent, by way of minute attention to exacting prescriptions. Sometimes, there is special emphasis on the inhuman. Religion at its most rational can also be religion at its most violent. This is of course not to denounce religion. I understand any religion as a complex tissue of contradiction which is best illuminated, in both its benevolent and harmful aspects, by detailed attention to specific peoples and scenes. Judaism, in this particular case, helped to generate a sense of universal victimization, to fuel a thirst for blame and revenge, to revive an apparently submerged anxiety about kinship distinctions and their violation. And, most important, to an extremist like Rosenthal, Judaism could appear to supply the ritual form that would answer and repair this range of emotions.[20]

Blood Rites

Now I proceed to my third and final example. To move from the Rosenthal case to Bernard Malamud's *The Fixer* and the story of Mendel Beilis upon which it is based, is to move from a scene where sacrifice is viewed as a sign of fanaticism verging on insanity (thus requiring that the perpetrator be locked up for the good of society), to a scene where sacrifice is viewed as a standard ritual procedure of a pariah nation (thus requiring that a *representative* perpetrator be locked up for the good of society). *The Fixer*, which was awarded a Pulitzer Prize and a National Book Award when it was published in 1966, reflects upon in vivid and self-conscious terms, an individual, ethnic, and national experience of spiritual crisis. The problem of religion from the modern period, as Malamud conceives it, is a problem of memory: what we remember and what we don't, and what others choose to "remember" about us. A fictional retelling of the notorious prosecution of Mendel Beilis, a Russian Jew tried in Kiev in 1913 for killing a Christian boy and draining his blood for ritual purposes, the novel confronts in the most literal terms the place of ritual sacrifice in the twentieth century. By exhuming for Americans in 1966 an historical investigation of sacrifice, the novel highlights the ongoing imaginative power of this ancient practice.

What explains this haunting of the modern mind? At least one explanation provided in *The Fixer* is the role of sacrifice in expressing spiritual anxiety or ambivalence. In Malamud's novel, sacrifice becomes a ritual stage for the dilemma of belief. Through his first-hand experience of the "blood accusation," Malamud's protagonist, the disbelieving skeptic, Yakov Bok, discovers, according to the anti-Semitic priest who articulates the charge in fanatical detail, "how much truth remains despite our reluctance to believe."[21] Thus, *The Fixer* transforms the story of Mendel Beilis into the fictional history of Yakov Bok: detailing Bok's abandonment of his fragile ties to Judaism and the Jewish community of the Pale; his attempt to survive as an unidentified factory manager in Kiev; and his arrest and long imprisonment for ritual murder.

The facts of the Beilis case are well established. On March 19, 1911, the body of a thirteen-year-old Russian boy, Andrei Yushinsky, was found in a cave on the outskirts of Kiev. He had been stabbed forty-seven times, and the wounds convinced authorities of a deliberate intention to drain his blood. The boy's funeral was unusual, not only for its mass attendance, but for the leaflets strewn among the populace by members of the Black Hundreds and other nationalist groups, accusing the Jews of the murder. As one leaflet explained, "The Yids have tortured Andryusha Yushinsky to death! Every year, before their Passover, they torture to death several dozens of Christian children in order to get their blood to mix with their *matzos*."[22] Despite the fact that many Russians, from governmental officials to ordinary citizens, considered such accusations mythical; despite the mountain of evidence incriminating a gang of thieves who lived next door to the boy and his mother; and despite the questionable behavior of the mother herself following the child's disappearance; in July of that same year, Mendel Beilis, a Jew who managed a brick factory located near the cave where the body was found, was arrested and charged with the murder. The charge at first was simply murder, since the evidence for ritual murder was scanty. Over time, however, the prosecution was able to patch together a ritual charge, which was formally leveled in the summer of 1913, shortly before Beilis was brought to trial.

While influential newspaper editors and key investigators championed Beilis's innocence, making sure to publicize information critical to Beilis's eventual vindication, the indictment itself and its prolongation seemed inevitable in the ethnic climate of that time.[23] It was the culmination of a long campaign against Russian Jewry by right-wing extremists: a campaign which began with the ferocious pogroms of 1903–5 and ended with more literate forms of persecution. From 1905 to 1916, with the active encouragement of the czar's government, these extremists produced and distributed over 14 million anti-Semitic pamphlets and books. The blood accusation was a mainstay of these publications, as it had been of similar campaigns in other times and places. Dating back to the First Crusades, the blood accusation in its earliest incarnation was directed against the Christians by the Romans, but it became, over time, mainly identified with the Jews. Historians have remarked on the increased frequency of the blood accusation in the nineteenth century, throughout Europe, most notoriously in Greece, Hungary, and Russia. The Beilis trial was preceded by the renowned trial of Blondes, a Jewish barber in Vilna, who was also, eventually, acquitted. According to Herman Strack, who, as a professor of theology at Berlin University and author of the influential book *The Jew and Human Sacrifice*, was on the list of expert witnesses slated to testify on Beilis's behalf, the blood accusation stems from the "universal" belief in "the efficaciousness of blood." "The exceeding importance of blood in life," he declares at the start of his book, "has doubtless been evident to mankind from remotest times. Extraordinary effects are procured by blood, particularly the human, but also animal blood."[24]

The larger purpose of Strack's book—and this is obviously why he was sought out by Beilis's defense—is to absolve the Jew of a spiritual stake in blood. Strack points in his introduction to his success in shifting the vocabulary in the debate over Jewish culpability, from "Jewish ritual murder," to "Jewish blood murder." "Ritual" is the damning category. A ritual claim presumes a terrible compulsion—simultaneously ethnic and spiritual—while simple blood-lust is neutral, even human. To speak of "blood murder" rather than "ritual murder" is to secure an immunity for Judaism and Jews. But Strack was alert to the extraordinary staying power of the ritual charge in the Russian context.

There have been various explanations for the long life of medieval anti-Semitism in Russia, but the most persistent and compelling emphasize the demographic vitality of the Russian Jewish population in the latter half of the nineteenth century, and the identification of the Jewish community as a whole with the forces of modernization. From the 1880s on, the Russian "Jewish population appeared a rapidly growing, intractable, foreign, and increasingly hostile body . . . [M]ore and more the Jews came to symbolize for [Slavophiles] the threat of an alien and decadent West, of a destructive modernism, one that would undermine their hopes and dreams for Russia." This observation confirms the mythological character of the blood accusation in modern Russia. According to that mythology, modernism's frightful aspect is drawn Jewish (to resemble a select, high-profile class of secular Jewry); then distorted (to resemble the far more numerous class of traditional Jewish peasants in the Pale); and then given a final twist (to reveal the demonic ritual agent lusting for Christian blood). This final mythological variant is set against the modern forces associated with the first Jew. The Jew therefore becomes a Russian kaleidoscope, shifting between history and universalism (as represented by an unchanging ritual mode). The comforting message of the demonic Jew is: "Don't worry, nothing has changed; we're still up to the same old stuff."

The Jew engaged in these bloody transactions stands for spiritual authenticity. Blood ritual, paradoxically in light of its surrealism, is above all, real. This is sincere belief, and the Russian anti-Semite is thrilled to see it, though he's the self-conceived victim. From this perspective, we can understand Richard Rosenthal as a figure dreamed up by the Russian right. And we can understand the blood libel as having a multidenominational significance. For the obsession with the ritual aggressions of Jews in modern Russia, at least in the mind of Bernard Malamud, one of its ablest interpreters, expresses a general state of spiritual crisis. The medieval long-nosed bogeyman staring back in Russian mirrors in the early decades of the twentieth century reflected a social quest for spiritual authenticity.

Like Russians in 1911 drawing on a history of blood accusations, Malamud in 1966 believes that the subject has continuing relevance for his contemporaries. As one early reviewer remarked, "The moral overtones of this most famous of all 'blood libel' trials is very much a part of the contemporary sensibility. And, too, the sales of Malamud's fiction . . . hint that these concerns are shared by those in the marketplace as well as by those who write for it."[25] *The Fixer* can be thought of, most simply, as an attempt to preserve this historical incident so as not to forget. This explains Malamud's astonishing faithfulness to the details and the texture of the Russian environment of the case. That faithfulness is exemplified most obviously by the parallels between *The Fixer* and *The Story of My Sufferings*, the autobiography Mendel Beilis wrote in 1926 for the Jewish Publication Society of America. Beilis had become, predictably, a martyr for a cause, and his book is at once authentic and mythic: a personal martyrology designed to further international enlightenment on the Jewish question. Given its political purpose, *The Story of My Sufferings* is remarkable for its restraint, and invaluable for what it reveals about Malamud's absorption in the case.

Malamud's decision to preserve so much of the autobiography confirms his belief that the case, in its own terms, had much to teach his time, and he sought to fit the historical figure Beilis, now the fictional character Bok, into the richest possible context. Malamud invests Beilis's story with emotion and intellect, a framework, as it were, that includes a history of the Jews, and sustained reflection on the more general problem of spirituality in the modern and postmodern eras. Both retellings of the Beilis case, the autobiographical and the fictional, begin with an image of framing, as if to highlight that the narrative focus will be ritual understanding, not ritual per se, a given subject's apprehension of what counts and what doesn't count as meaning. Both protagonists look out the window upon a troubling scene of mass movement.

First, *The Story of My Sufferings*:

> The window which I faced while at my desk overlooked the street. As I looked through the window on that cold, dark morning, I saw people hurrying somewhere, all in one direction. It was the usual thing to see individual workers coming to the factory, at that time, or occasional passers-by. But now there were people in large groups walking rapidly, coming from various streets. I went out to find the cause of the commotion, and was told by one of the crowd that a body of a murdered child had been found in the vicinity.[26]

Now *The Fixer*:

> From the small crossed window of his room above the stable in the brickyard, Yakov Bok saw people in their long overcoats running somewhere early that morning, everybody in the same direction. *Vey iz mir*, he thought uneasily, something bad has happened. The Russians, coming from streets around the cemetery, were hurrying, singly or in groups, in the spring snow in the direction of the caves in the ravine, some running in the middle of the slushy cobblestone streets. Yakov hastily hid the small tin can in which he saved silver roubles, then rushed down to the yard to find out what the excitement was about. He asked Proshko, the foreman loitering near the smoky brickkilns, but Proshko spat and said nothing. Outside the yard a black-shawled, bony-faced peasant woman, thickly dressed, told him that the dead body of a child had been found nearby. (p. 7)

Notice what Malamud keeps: the window frame, and the sense of urgency and anxiety inspired by the mass movement. Both the history and the fiction introduce the protagonist through the details his looking takes in. The details in both cases are simple and sparse, the voices plain: the mounting sense of panic is generated by the events themselves. The onlookers are resigned, even phlegmatic: they've seen hordes of excited Russians before. The individual in each scene gazes down upon the crowd, hinting that Christian metaphors are in place from the start. As if to highlight the difference between his fiction and fact, Malamud crosses his window: the lattice does the work of crossing the "t" in metaphor, as it were, forcing the implicit Christian content into the light of common day. This will be a story of crosses borne and crosses abandoned, picturing the utter degradation of the body and subsequent ascent of the spirit. Malamud's revisions and additions work this way throughout: they declare themselves subtly and sometimes more overtly, in order to show what fiction can do to fact. For the depth of Malamud's engagement with the Beilis record serves to reveal, above all, the surreal quality of the actual events. *The Fixer* exposes, as no historical account can, the true character of the blood libel charge as a kind of aesthetic miracle: a fiction compelling enough to elicit faith in its own right.

Malamud adds Yiddish idiom, the ethnic tongue writ large in the eternal refrain: "*vey iz mir*," literally, "woe is me." Identity and doom, according to the *Mama Loshen*, are near equivalents; every historical calamity is a wish fulfillment. Malamud adds seasonal and sensual detail: the snow of the Russian winter now run to spring slush provides a natural supplement to the gray stream of humanity. The streets assume an aspect—they're "cobblestone"; the factory gains definition—it makes bricks and the kilns are smoking. Reading Malamud's novel beside Beilis's autobiography is like watching a photograph come into its own in a darkroom. The accumulation is gradual, the pleasure is visual, the sense of possibility momentous. With detail comes emotional complexity. The blank crowd becomes resistant, sinister: a "foreman" becomes an informant who has perhaps said too much (as we later learn, to the authorities) and now says too little (cloaking the valuable facts disdainfully in spit); an old woman, bony and foreboding, spells things out. The suspicion and gloom of these characters conveys the threatening tenor of the crowd toward the Jew among them, whose guilt is a *fait accompli*. To discover a Christian child's corpse during the Passover season is to know a Jewish ritual murderer is lurking nearby. And Malamud adds a literary tradition.

I would suggest that no novelistic forebear is more pronounced here than Nathaniel Hawthorne's *The Scarlet Letter*. To begin with, *The Fixer* shares *The Scarlet Letter*'s renowned method of historical layering. Like

Hawthorne's historicized fiction, which provides a Victorian re-creation of the Puritan past and draws on much in between, Malamud's novel invokes several time frames, from Beilis's modern Russia and the medieval ideology it absorbs, through the Holocaust, to Malamud's America. Both openings serve to set up the events that follow. There is the image of the crowd, grimly attired in "long overcoats," reminiscent of the "sad-colored garments" of Hawthorne's "throng of bearded men." There are the shared images of the cemetery, and the shared prospects of emprisonment: two universal methods for confining people, while still inside the community (prison), or somehow *kept* outside (cemetery). These are scenes of prosecution and persecution, whether promised or fulfilled, and each narrative initiates a search for a criminal. The crowd defined as "Russians" corresponds to the Puritan collectivity: in both novels the spectacle of transgression and its punishment—what it sensationalizes and censures—becomes a critical means of reinforcing the fragile borders of citizenship. Moreover, each community, Puritan and Russian, faces a spiritual turning point: can their traditional faith, rigorous and all-encompassing, withstand the challenges of a new era, the looming forces of modernity and social heterogeneity? The isolated protagonist in each novel—the marked female sex offender in a sea of male magistrates, the Jew in a sea of Christians clamoring for their Easter revenge—is different in kind and creed as well as in deed. Hester Prynne is as much an alien in the opening environment of *The Scarlet Letter* as Yakov Box in *The Fixer*, and the question for each narrative is whether the elaboration of events will make them more or less of one. Like the female, Hester Prynne, Yakov Bok is born under a cloud: he is bound to be a goat.

The whole opening sequence of *The Fixer* seems designed to confirm this destiny. Here we learn of Bok's early orphaning; his faithless wife and their childless marriage; and we meet his one remaining "relative," his father-in-law Shmuel, a devout and penniless peddler "who looked as if he had been assembled out of sticks and whipped air." "Bok," Russian for "goat," is drowning in goatness, a goat on all fronts. The world seems in conspiracy against him, and the rendition of the Russian Pale as a giant graveyard (in one particularly gruesome image, the body of a Jew left on the street after a pogrom becomes food for a pig) confirms the inescapable sense of Bok's fate. God, whether responsible for this landscape or a mere reflection of it, is, as Bok later puts it, "written off as a dead loss" (231).

This brings us to Malamud's most prominent contribution to the story of Mendel Beilis: the drama of skepticism, the struggle of the modern secular Jew against the ritual belief system of Jewish tradition and the Gentiles who want to tie it around his neck like a noose. Beilis is a more or less programmatic observant Jew, who prays with a tallis before marriage and without one afterward, who doesn't know the exact function of the *afikomen* at the Passover seder, who performs the rituals more in testimony of his membership in a community of believers than with a guiding sense of their purpose and meaning. Bok is the modern non-believer, estranged from the community and trying to assimilate: a struggle initiated by the symbolic gesture of tossing his phylacteries into the Dneiper River. Attempting to dissolve his connections to Judaism, Bok finds himself confronted with a culture in the throes of its own spiritual crisis, and made to reclaim his religious birthright in a monstrously revived form.

The ongoing irony of Bok's sufferings is his own enlightened intolerance for Judaism's ritualized aspects. It's clear that he's never had much patience with traditional Judaism, especially its superstitions, and after he leaves the Pale, he repudiates them altogether, so much so that when he encounters the old Hasid, the source of the damning matzoh found by police in his rooms, "it came as a surprise to the Fixer that it was Passover" (21). Such rituals in *The Fixer* are the preserve of traditional Jews, often mentioned but seldom seen; corrupt officials in league with charlatans, and looking to enflame a pogrom; or experts devoted to researching the role of ritual through the ages. Malamud, by way of his protagonist, can be considered one of a continuing line of such interpreters, beginning in the late nineteenth century with James Frazer and William Robertson Smith, who concerned themselves, respectively, with the genesis of scapegoating practices, and Semitic sacrifice.

The symbolism of the Dneiper River scene could not be more precise. Among the prayer things thrown overboard is the "bag . . . containing phylacteries," a gift from his father-in-law, who hands them over Polonious-style with words of wisdom: "we live in the middle of our enemies. The best way to take care is to stay under God's protection" (19). This is the ritual import of the phylacteries: bound on the arms and forehead of the devout Jew each morning, they recall God's dispensation in Exodus, a figurative reminder of the blood displayed on the doorposts of Jewish homes to ensure the lives of the firstborn sons within. The command to wear the phylacteries is a command to remember a sacrifice: specifically, the Passover sacrifice. All Jews from this time forward are enjoined to transmit this ritual obligation: "Therefore I sacrifice to the Lord all that openeth the womb, being males; but all the first-born of my sons I redeem. And it shall be for a sign upon they hand, and for frontlets between thine eyes; for by strength of hand the Lord brought us forth out of Egypt."[27]

The image of the Hasid in *The Fixer*, who binds his phylacteries "gently over the crusting wound" on his brow (the result of a rock attack by Russian boys, 63), resonates both backward and forward in time. The

Hasid's blood, the blood of Jewish victimization, anticipates another kind of Jewish victimization involving blood: Bok's arrest and imprisonment for his alleged sacrifice of another Russian boy. In each instance, actual blood meets symbolic blood to confirm Bok's haunting by history, and eventual incrimination. It is not incidental that the scene with the Hasid is a flashback, narratively speaking. It's a flashback that ripples with prior and subsequent contexts: from the most immediate (Bok on the Dneiper River tossing his phylacteries), to the most remote (the ancient commandment to wear them in the first place), to the most damaging (Bok's arrest and imprisonment as representative of his people's ritual need for blood). As Bok sputters at one point, "What was being a Jew but an everlasting curse? He was sick of their history, destiny, bloodguilt" (206). As if responding directly to its bitter protagonist, the plot moralizes, "what you don't know about your past, your spiritual history, is sure to get you."

The warning to the Jew who tries to assimilate is the nightmare of Jewish identity: you're force-fed your Judaism for breakfast, in the most abhorrent stereotypical terms. Bok's nightmare is captured in the quibbling over labels at his arrest, where Bok declares himself, "a Jew by birth and nationality . . . [but] not a religious man," and is told, "legally you are a Jew" (81). Repeatedly, Bok proclaims his estrangement in the voice of the wicked son at Passover, "But what has this got to do with me?" (91–92); repeatedly he is informed that for Jews it is not a matter of consent. What is being staged here, I would suggest, is a debate over the nature of ritual and identity. According to Bok's prosecutors, Jewish murder *is* ritual murder. Ritual comes naturally to Jews: it's in the blood. This Russian stereotype is implicit in the scene where Bok bakes "bread that did not rise" unknowingly during Passover, in helpless fulfillment of the ritual obligation. To the devout Jew, however, the situation is almost exactly reversed. According to the laws of Jewish observance, you have to act out your consent every day. A traditional Jew is not a "believer," but an "observer of the commandments," in other words, one who practices the proper rituals.[28]

At the center of Malamud's highly intellectual novel is the question of the complex affiliations of Judaism: Judaism as Identity (Essential) vs. Practice (A Way of Life or Thought). What kinds of practices constitute authentic ritual acts? Why is a lapsed Jew still a Jew? Malamud's portrait of Bok as Representative Jew is premised on a certain paradox. There's perpetual irony toward the irrelevance of Bok's own spiritual struggles. Bok's faith, or lack of it, is independent of *what happens* to him, how he's identified by anti-Semites. It's irrelevant to the workings of fate that lock him into an essential Jewish legacy. Bok's survival is imperiled as a Jew in essence. This may explain why Malamud sidesteps the "real" ending of the Beilis case—the acquittal—because he wants to emphasize the perilous circumstances of the Jew in this pre-Holocaust moment. But Malamud also brings that imperiling forward to his own historical time, through his portrait of Bok's struggle with faith. For we are to understand that Bok's survival as a Jew is as much imperiled by his secularism as it is by the Jewish identity affixed to him by the authorities in search of a scapegoat.

The question which comes to overshadow the survival of the particular Jew, Yakov Bok, is whether Judaism specifically and religion more generally can survive and be reconciled with skepticism, the estrangement from tradition. Does religion have a persistence that transcends ritual practice? Consider one further significance of the phylacteries. According to the commentary on Exodus, the phylacteries are worn "over against the brain," in order to "teach" the mind its subjection to "His service" (261). Bok, however, resists this type of subjection; in fact he regards it as indistinguishable from any other. Superstition, irrationalism, as portrayed in *The Fixer*, is multi-denominational: it's a terror shared by all religions, and sacrifice is its ongoing expression. In full historical dress, sacrifice is a ritual for the ages, ranging over time from creed to creed. As the fair-minded investigator, Bibikov puts it, "The blood mystique arose in a belief of a primitive people that there is a miraculous power in blood. It is, of course, a most dramatic substance in color and composition" (156). However multi-denominational in practice then, as a charge or attribute, sacrifice is always narrowed to a national vocation, a cultish affinity for violence.

From this recognition of sacrifice—ranging in ritual purpose yet specified and insular in attribution—comes the conceptualization of another type of spirituality—rational, humanistic, cosmopolitan. Functional as opposed to mystical and alienated, its aim is true exchange, not the shot in the dark that is sacrifice. This is the import of Bok's allegorical identity as "The Fixer." "I fix what's broken—except in the heart," he remarks early on, "In this shtetl everything is falling apart—who bothers with leaks in his roof if he's peeking through the cracks to spy on God?" (10). Traditional dealings with God, this suggests, are always a discrepant business. For one glimpse of his shining aspect, you endure years of wet and cold. The alternative spirituality of *The Fixer* is humanity centered, a blend of Spinoza and Emerson. The world here is thought through, "connected up." "A man's mind is part of God," and "you're free, if you're in" it (71). From this religious perspective, the Fixer finds pleasure in rare moments of tranquility. Awakening after a prison beating, for instance, to glimpse "a bit of horned moon at the small high beamed window . . . he watched for a while in peace" (99).

Yet how real, finally, is this alternative? For one of the most striking aspects of Bok's spiritual odyssey is the fact that his gradual abandonment of Jewish practice is countered by his growing preoccupation with ritual. This is in part necessity—he can't *afford* to concede this ground to the anti-Semites who control the case. Sometimes, he's an ethnographer: "everybody knows the Bible forbids us to eat blood . . . I've forgotten most of what I knew about the sacred books, but I've lived among the people and know their customs." Elsewhere he's an inspired reader in the grips of a powerful novel. Here, for example, is how he responds to Christ's characterization in the New Testament. "He was a strange Jew, humorless and fanatic, but the Fixer liked the teachings and read with pleasure of the healing of the lame, blind, and of the epileptics . . . Jesus cried out help to God but God gave no help . . . Christ died and they took him down. The Fixer wiped his eyes" (209). Likewise, he pores over scraps of the Old Testament, torn out of the phylacteries given him in prison (to make him look more authentic). "He read longer and faster, gripped by the narrative of the joyous and frenzied Hebrews, doing business, fighting wars, sinning and worshipping—whatever they were doing always engaged in talk with the huffing-puffing God" (216).

The point of Malamud's narrative is that Bok is drawn, over the course of it, more and more deeply into the particulars of blood worship, not as a reverential but as an aesthetic exercise. Bok's experiences seem to return him, with a dreamlike coerciveness, toward religion, rather than away from it. In the end, he's as haunted by ritual as he is by history. This haunting is captured in the scene where a jar of strawberry jam in his apartment is turned magically to blood by the prosecution. Struggling to keep things nailed down to fact, he cries, "Jam is not blood. Blood is not jam," which is true, of course, except in a certain spiritual light. For ritual thinking is always illuminating if not enlightening—a moral that might be drawn equally from the Wheat Chex cereal box, the Rosenthal murder, and Malamud's novel. Here, respectively, strawberries *are* blood; murder *is* conversing with God; and modern investigators hunt for witches in the night. And, blood worship, precisely for its terrible prospect of transformation, remains a powerful proposition.

The field of religion came into its own with the Enlightenment. Through its auspices, religion became exceedingly rational in its seeming irrationality, simultaneously individual and communal, interior and public, an elite as well as mass art. The interpreter of religion was the enlightened anthropologist, whose pursuit of "exotic" subjects was driven by the prospects of elucidation and of wonder. What was undersold was an altogether different spiritual subject: one that found expression in an alternative language of indeterminacy and horror. Hence the advantage of an interdisciplinary approach informed by the humanities. In confronting a cultural sea of religious signification whose extent is unbounded, whose importance is unquestioned, and whose meaning has only begun to be tapped, neither the human sciences nor the humane arts are sufficient unto themselves.

Notes

1. Jonathan Z. Smith, *Imagining Religion: From Babylon to Jonestown* (Chicago: University of Chicago Press, 1982), p. 110.

2. Gillian Feeley-Harnik, *The Lord's Table: The Meaning of Food in Early Judaism and Christianity* (Washington: Smithsonian Institute Press, 1982), pp. 165–68.

3. William Robertson Smith, *Lectures on the Religion of the Semites: The Fundamental Institutions* (1889; reprint, New York: Ktav, 1969), pp. 313 and passim, and Feeley-Harnik, *Lord's Table*, p. 149.

4. See Smith on the Commensal Meal as a feasting on the Totem or God, *Lectures*, pp. 29–30 and passim, and Grant Allen on the resemblances between Christian and agricultural sacrifice, *The Evolution of the Idea of God: An Inquiry into the Origins of Religion* (New York: Henry Holt, 1897), pp. 272–300.

5. Advertisers have a talent for normalizing the most terrible subjects, succeeding where psychotherapists and criminal correction officers often fail. Yet while this object honors its medium by keeping its gloom in check, latent, it is anything but trivial. Like the supermarket goods described in Don DeLillo's *White Noise*, this cereal box is portentous, its message " concealed in symbolism, hidden by veils of mystery and layers of cultural material." One could say that the "Wheat Chex" image confirms a key insight of *White Noise*: that consumer goods provide a means by which "the dead speak to the living." *White Noise* (New York: Penguin, 1984), pp. 37, 326.

6. Susan L. Mizruchi, *The Science of Sacrifice: American Literature and Modern Social Theory* (Princeton: Princeton University Press, 1998), p. 369.

7. Smith, *Lectures*, pp. 274–75.

8. Michael Grunwald and Tom Moroney, "Executive Held in Grisly Slaying," *Boston Globe* August 30, 1995: 1, 26.

9. Judy Rakowsky, "Jury Convicts Rosenthal in Grisly Murder," *Boston Globe* November 8, 1996: B1–B2.

10. Smith, *Imagining Religion*, p. 104.

11. Grunwald and Moroney, "Executive Held"; Michael Grunwald and Matt Bai, "Rosenthall Had Turned to Religion," *Boston Globe* September 1, 1995: 33–34; Ellen O'Brien, Michael Grunwald, and Tom Moroney, "Genetic Fixation May Be Behind Slaying," *Boston Globe* September 10, 1995: 1, 40; Rakowsky, "Crime Scene Staged, Psychiatrist Says," *Boston Globe*, November 1, 1996: B1, B7.

12. Bob Hohler, "Brutal Slaying Tears at a Texas Town," *Boston Globe*, June 12, 1998: 1, A24.

13. O'Brien, Grunwald, and Moroney, "Genetic Fixation," 40.

14. Rakowsky, "Rosenthal Jury Deliberates, Takes Recess," *Boston Globe* No-

vember 7, 1996, B1; Rakowsky, "Psychiatrist Rebuts Killer's 'alien' claim," *Boston Globe* November 6, 1996: B2.

15. Madame Dieterlen, quoted by J. H. M. Beattie in " On Understanding Sacrifice," in M. F. C. Bourdillon and Meyer Fortes, eds., *Sacrifice* (New York: Academic Press, 1980), p. 41.

16. See Henri Hubert and Marcel Mauss on the significance of the " ashera," in *Sacrifice: Its Nature and Functions*, trans. W. D. Halls (1898; reprint, Chicago: University of Chicago Press, Midway Reprint, 1981), p. 121, Note 143.

17. *Trial Transcripts*: Commonwealth of Massachusetts v Rosenthal, Richard H., Middlesex Superior Court, 10/15/96–11/7/96.

18. *Trial Transcripts*.

19. Rakowsky, "Crime Scene Staged," B1, B7.

20. I want to emphasize that the ritual prominence of sacrifice extends beyond the Judaeo-Christian traditions discussed here, to encompass other world religions, including Islam, Buddhism, Brahminism, and many others. Let me also emphasize that sacrifice is as often associated with positive and enobling religious emotions, as it is with violent or negative ones, as I have shown in my study, *The Science of Sacrifice*, of the ritual's ongoing significance for major spiritual, intellectual, and aesthetic traditions of the late-nineteenth and early-twentieth centuries. What interests me in particular about contemporary Jewish observance (in its Reform, Conservative, as well as Orthodox variants), is the extent to which the prominence of sacrifice in Ancient Judaism tends to be overlooked. Thus, a typical Conservative service during the High Holiday Ceremonies that include *Rosh Hashana*, the Jewish New Year, and *Yom Kippur*, the Day of Atonement, features extensive commentary on the *Akedah*, or Binding of Issac in Genesis, an event renowned for its symbolic testimony of Judaism's disavowal of human sacrifice, but attends minimally, if at all, to the equal centrality in the service of the mass animal sacrifices performed at the Ancient Temple, which are recounted in detail, in Leviticus. In keeping with this, a recent article in the *Forward*, by a Rabbi who visited a Nepal shrine to witness a weekly ceremony of animal sacrifice, recounts how the event recalled the Akedah, which served as a distant but admirably circumscribed emblem of a still instructive " spiritual value." What the author overlooked was how this "bizarre" ceremony resembled conventional Judaic practice: the procession of animal sacrifices performed at the Temple and recalled every year in the portion of Leviticus read on the Day of Atonement (Rabbi Niles Goldstein, "Father and Son Watch Animal Sacrifice: Gory Ancient Ritual in Nepal Is More Spiritual Than It Seems," *Forward*, July 17, 1998, p. 17). As confirmed by a history of biblical commentary extending from ancient times to Maimonides and beyond, the ritual of animal sacrifice was neither decorative nor dispensable to Judaism; it was integral. The prophets did not disavow sacrifice, as commonly assumed; rather they distinguished *pure* from *impure* sacrifice, defining proper Jewish sacrifices against "heathen" sacrifices. This was the import of the localizing of sacrifice in the precincts of the temple, which was designed to customize and set apart what had long been an integral practice.

21. *The Fixer* (New York: Penguin, 1966), p. 121; subsequent references to this edition will appear parenthetically in the text.

22. George Kennan reporting on " The 'Ritual Murder' Case in Kiev," for

Outlook, November 8, 1913, quoted in Maurice Samuel, *Blood Accusation: The Strange History of the Beilis Case* (Philadelphia: Jewish Publication Society of America, 1966), p. 17.

23. World reaction to the Beilis case ranged considerably, and it was possible to find supporters of the prosecution like Albert Monniot in France, who was inspired to write his own grizzly account published in Paris in 1914, *Le Crime ritual chez les Juifs*, a 374-page book which provided the Beilis case with an international lineage of Jewish ritual offenses, extending from 1154 through 1913. Declaring his "facts . . . guaranteed by testimony which had not yet come under the influence of the modern press," Monniot includes in his charge a modern Jewish conspiracy controlling world opinion and prohibiting widespread knowledge of these crimes. In a less inflammatory vein, there was the polite waffling of *The Oxford and Cambridge Review*, which concluded "it is absolutely certain that Orthodox Judaism—nay, Judaism as a whole—stands free from even the slightest suspicion of blood-guiltiness; but to say that is not to say that no Jewish sect exists which practices ritual murder." On the whole, however, the voice of protest and outrage was in the clear majority. As one commentator in *The New York Times* put it, "this case reminds me of the farmer who saw a camel and said: 'There ain't no such animal.'" The Monniot book, and the commentary from *the Oxford and Cambridge Review* and *The New York Times*, both of 1913, are cited in Samuel, *Blood Accusation*, pp. 236, 239, and 231, respectively. There were at least two appeals in the United States Senate and House requesting an official rebuke of the Russian government for prosecuting the case, as well as an official testimony of support for Beilis. Americans followed the case closely, and rallies were held across the country protesting Beilis's victimization in general, and, as they became known, aspects of the trial in particular. *The Boston Globe* from November 3, 1913, for instance, included three press releases on the case. One of these, a report from Kiev by a *Globe* correspondent on the scene, described the testimony of theological experts for the prosecution and defense, which included questions about the "type of animal" substituted for Isaac in the Akedah as well as questions about "the part of the body" "out of which the soul is mostly held [according to the Talmud and Cabbalah] to issue with the blood." There was ongoing concern over the composition of the jury, which was thought by many in America to be dominated by a benighted peasant element still dangerously susceptible to "the ritual murder legend." Testimonials like the following in *The Globe*, drawn from Mary Antin's *The Promised Land*, did not make for reassurance on this point. Antin's 1912 book, an autobiographical account of her own allegorical pilgrimage from a childhood in the Russian Pale to her education and professionalization as an American author in the Boston area, depicts a rather stark ascent from a region of darkness to one of light. The Russian blood accusation, in Antin's view, is merely one of the "barbarous persecutions by which professing Christians blacken the name of Christianity in Russia." Israel Zangwill, however, as quoted in *The New York Times*, November 1, 1913, was not so sure that such a clear demarcation was possible. Explaining his refusal to attend a London rally, he commented, "I would no sooner protest against an accusation of ritual murder than against one of cannibalism. . . . Medieval practices still abound," he goes on, "the American people lynches negroes, the British govern-

ment feeds forcibly and administers the 'Cat and Mouse' act—but we Jews have long passed such stages of civilization or barbarism." Zangwill denies the clean moral oppositions celebrated by Antin. The current Russian "nightmare" is not only compatible with "civilization" as we know it, but even necessary to it. In the grim light afforded by Zangwill's pessimism, barbaric spectacles like the Beilis case are expressions of nationalism. As long as nations exist, the show will go on. It's possible to see Malamud's *The Fixer* as a continuation of the literary debate initiated by Antin and Zangwill, which comes down on the side of the latter.

24. Herman L. Strack, *The Jew and Human Sacrifice. Human Blood and Jewish Ritual: An Historical and Sociological Inquiry*, trans. Henry Blanchamp (first pub.in German, 1891, London: Cope and Fenwick, 1909), p. 18.

25. Sanford Pinsker, " Bernard Malamud's Ironic Heroes," in *Bernard Malamud: A Collection of Critical Essays* (Englewood Cliffs, NJ: Prentice-Hall, 1975), p. 65.

26. Mendel Beilis, *The Story of My Sufferings* (Philadelphia: Jewish Publication Society of America, 1926), p. 26.

27. *The Pentateuch and Haftorahs: Hebrew Text, English Translation and Commentary*, 2nd ed, ed. Dr. J. H. Hertz, C.H. (London: Soncino Press, 5733–1972), p. 262.

28. See Michael A. Fishbane, *Judaism: Revelation and Traditions* (New York: HarperSanFrancisco, 1987), pp. 84–85 and passim.

5

Human Solidarity and the Problem of Otherness

GILES GUNN

IF THE notion of human solidarity has long functioned as one of the ways that in the West we have expressed our sense of shared humanity not only with ourselves but presumably with others, what happens, I want to ask, when so many of the languages in which that sense was expressed have in various ways become outworn or discredited? Those ways are not only empirical and political but also moral. If a fair number of physical anthropologists now maintain that there may be no such thing as universal human qualities, and we are everywhere confronted with the spectacle of the incommensurability of human perspectives in this, what Eric Hobsbawn calls, in *Age of Extremes*, the cruelest and most bestial century in the history of human records, there is also abundant evidence that identity, as the political theorist William E. Connolly has recently asserted, whether individual or collective, personal or cultural, can only establish itself by defining itself paradoxically in relation to a set of differences that it is constantly tempted to view not simply as "other" but also as inimical, hostile, offensive.[1]

There is a temptation to view those differences as "other," rather than simply as divergent or discrepant, because identity can best define and reinforce itself in terms of a series of oppositions whose operations are for the most part carried out beneath the levels of conscious reflection. And there is a corollary temptation to view "otherness" as antagonistic, even pernicious, because the sense of uncertainty already built into the need for identity itself is exacerbated in our late, modern era by a generalized feeling of resentment against all the globalized structures, disciplines, and practices that threaten to control, constrain, destabilize, or dismantle the self. Hence the risk that identity will be further dogmatized, difference further stigmatized, if we fail to develop genealogical modes of reflection that encourage the reconstitution of ethics around what Connolly calls the concern for difference.

This is a hope that depends on the institution of new genealogical modes of reflection on the relation between identity and difference, and that will need to draw on a democratic politics sensitive to the abundance of difference that exceeds any given political or personal identity. But in a world where questions of cultural as well as personal identity seem so often locked in destructive embrace with issues of cultural difference, where people not only seem to prefer their own values to the values of others but appear to be able to maintain their own values too often only at the expense of disparaging and frequently demonizing the values of others, is it actually possible to imagine that the forms of life that we traditionally encompass within the structure of "self" and "other" can any longer have a constructive impact on one another?

This is a question that can now no longer be begged, a question that indeed, it seems to me, has now cast a dark shadow, at least in the West, over our whole notion of the human. That notion of the human is linked to a sense of solidarity that has enjoyed a very long career in the history of human thought and that for at least the last century or two has been one of the Western world's, if not one of the rest of the world's, most significant "god-terms." Premised as it was (and, for many, still is) on the concept of a unitary humanity, the notion of human solidarity has historically offered a way of symbolizing the nature of the human bond not only within cultures but potentially across them, during a period when, in the West itself, formulations of a more orthodox kind, theological or otherwise, such as "imago dei," original sin, "divine spark," "the sacredness of the human spirit," or "inalienable human rights," could no longer be employed as easily, or at any rate as widely, as they once were to define our commonality as creatures. Not only in the master paradigms of some of those prominent nineteenth-century social thinkers who quickly became in the twentieth our secular theologians—Alexis de Tocqueville, Karl Marx, Max Weber, Ferdinand Tonnies, and Emile Durkheim—but also in the master narratives of many of those nineteenth-century writers who took upon themselves the task of supplying us with a new set of what Northrop Frye was rightly to call our "secular scriptures"—Jane Austen, Honoré de Balzac, Leo Tolstoy, George Eliot, Herman Melville, Joseph Conrad, and Virginia Woolf—the appeal to human solidarity has been at least one way, even if not the only way, that we have expressed, enacted, and critiqued our shared attributes as a species.

But now this notion of human solidarity is viewed with considerable suspicion, where it has not been discredited totally. Initially problematized and censured by social and political historians who have linked it so closely to the history of Western imperialism and the practices of European colonialism, the notion of human solidarity has now been subjected to renewed attack by the very science that imperialism begat, known as anthropology. Human beings, we are now told, instead of sharing a common nature, as was once assumed, now merely share a certain predisposition to define themselves by means of their practices, or, rather, by the connection, as Geertz puts it more exactly, between their generic capacities and their specific performances. Either way, human beings are no longer understood to be creatures possessing a universal nature to whose collective ethical center one can appeal, but rather are viewed as members of a species given to defining itself relentlessly in terms of the disparagement of human difference.

Ethnic and religious violence of the sort that sets Serbs against Albanians, Palestinians against Israelis, Tutsis against Hutus, Azerbaijanis against Armenians, and Poles against Gypsies may present only the most dramatic spectacle of this fact, but it is a fact nonetheless. And it is a fact the more disturbing simply because the appeal to blood loyalty so easily and sometimes inevitably legitimates the need for blood sacrifice. Nationalism has, of course, always been defined in relation to the conditions that permit a people to resort to force or violence in their own defense, but ethnic and religious nationalism all too readily transform a warrant for violence into a mandate for it. An essential ingredient in this process that connects blood loyalty with blood sacrifice is a psychology, as Michael Ignatieff has recently reminded us, that appeals to peoples' better instincts rather than their worst. In other words, the sanctions for violence derive not from what people hate but from what people cherish. This helps explain why ethnic and religious nationalists are so often, and without contradiction, sentimentalists. They are in the grip of a set of feelings stronger than enmity, stronger even than the desire for self-preservation. Hence, as Ignatieff observes, "there is no killer on either side of any check points that will not pause, between firing at his enemies, to sing some nostalgic song or even to recite a few lines of some ethnic poem."[2]

More disturbing still, this psychology that puts murder in the service of love helps illumine the logic of ethnic cleansing, which permits groups that have lived together on terms of the greatest intimacy and understanding, often for centuries, to become the targets of each other's most murderous rage. While all societies may practice a form of symbolic sacrifice that permits them to prevent their aggressive instincts from running unchecked and allows those instincts to be rechanneled and concentrated on the society's, or the group's, perceived enemies, ethnic and religious communities in particular respond to perceived threats to their identity with a ritualistic virulence that is without parallel. The more dire the imagined threat to the community's social being, the more important must be the victim sacrificed to preserve that social being. Under such circumstances, former neighbors, and even family members, offer themselves as the perfect vehicles of sacrificial mediation. The community of significant selves can be saved only by exterminating those "others" which were once so valuable to it.

Such rites of sacrifice, which prevent violence from spreading any further and function to keep vengeance in check, pose a moral, not to say political, challenge of enormous magnitude. At the most basic level, that moral challenge is simply to figure out how the self may be made more corrigible with respect to the "other." At a considerably more complex level legislated by global revolutions in communications, information, and representation, the question becomes how to make the self more corrigible with respect to the "other" without at the same time simply turning the "other" into a surrogate or simulacrum of the self. This question arises almost inevitably, I would argue, from one of the basic epistemological postulates of the West. This postulate states that if the primary condition for understanding virtually anything remains the self's willingness to place its own convictions and assumptions at risk for the sake of encountering that which is different, "it is only through an engaged encounter with the Other," as the pragmatist philosopher Richard J. Bernstein puts it, "with [indeed] the otherness of the Other, that one [also] comes to a more informed, textured understanding of the tradition to which 'we' belong."[3]

This postulate about how self-understanding is predicated on the understanding of, or at least the attempt to understand, the "Other" is now bound to activate a corollary question, much pondered, for example, by the Jewish philosopher and Talmudic scholar Emmanuel Levinas, as to whether the alterity of the "different" or the "Other," in such formulations, is thereby in danger of being reduced to what Levinas calls the "Same." If, for example, the self is ethically constituted, as Levinas has long argued that it is, by an encounter with that which is radically "other," how does the "Other," in this transaction, or even merely the "different," retain its alterity?[4]

This is a question that may well have been answered more cogently, according to Bernstein, by Levinas's old friend and sometimes critic Jacques Derrida than by Levinas himself. Against Levinas, for example, who is prepared to sacrifice any connection between self and "Other" for the sake of preserving the integrity of otherness itself, Derrida counters that the so-called "Other" can only maintain its alterity if in fact it actually remains part of the "Same." While "the other," Derrida writes, "is the other only if his alterity is absolutely irreducible, that is, infinitely irreducible," its otherness must be recognized as part of the ego, actually as a kind of *alter ego*, if that otherness is not to dissolve. Hence Derrida concludes: "the other as alter ego signifies the other as other, irreducible to *my* ego, precisely because [as Husserl maintained] it is an ego, because it has the form of the ego. . . . This is why, if you will, he is a face, can speak to me, understand me, and eventually command me." To put this in slightly different terms, only if the "Other" is represented as something which, because it possesses the form of an ego, our "I" must address can it remain that in relation to which our "I" must remain accountable, to which "we" are indeed answerable.[5]

For Bernstein, then, "self" and "Other" constitute a relationship of co-implication, even if that relation also contains within itself dimensions of estrangement, enmity, and violence, even of abjection and horror. Rather like Mikhail Bakhtin, Bernstein sides with Derrida (who is not usually thought of as siding with Bakhtin on this issue) in thinking that "self" and "other" are not absolutely opaque to one other, much less always reflective of mindsets or frames of reference that are utterly incommensurable. Indeed, if as Bakhtin holds, understanding is necessarily transgredient and exotopic, then the so-called "other" cannot be fully understood at all except from a point of view outside itself, which is to say within the terms of this binary formulation, from the point of view of the so-called "self." Bernstein therefore concludes, in conformity with Derrida but in disagreement with Sir Isaiah Berlin, like Bernstein another liberal, that the "other" cannot be totally incompatible, let alone fundamentally alien, to the "self," so long as the "self" feels some kind of ethical obligation, if not to understand the "other," then at least to understand itself in reference to the "other."[6]

But what if selves no longer feel this sense of ethical obligation? What if, along with the religious and social as well as epistemological transactions it once sponsored, this ethical sense has dissolved into thin air, or, more likely, has been reduced to ash by the furnace of hatred that has been set ablaze in this century by ideologies of race, ethnicity, class, nation, religion, and gender? This is the question raised most recently not only by the horrific spread of murderous violence, which is by turns ethnic, religious, and national, but also by the increasing normalization of that ancient religious practice that has accompanied it. To give that religious rite its proper name, I refer in particular to the sacrificial practice known as scapegoating where, as Kenneth Burke once noted, people cleanse themselves ritualistically by displacing onto others the burdens of their own undesired pollution and iniquity. The appeal of scapegoating, as we have learned in this latest round of ethnic and religious violence, is almost universal because of the opportunity it provides for what Burke describes as a kind of "vicarious atonement." The scapegoat presents itself as a "chosen vessel" whose function is to enable others to "ritualistically cleanse themselves by loading the burden of their own iniquities upon it."[7] And once this process of deprecatory displacement has been initiated, the scapegoat's therapeutic properties tend to increase in direct proportion to the violence by which its victims are attacked. In this ritualistic scenario, then, victimage, and the violence that accompanies it, are not merely instrumental to personal and social health but absolutely indispensable to it. Self-formation and cultural renewal are inextricably linked to a sacrificial procedure that enables those who feel threatened, inadequate, or guilty to find expiation and deliverance through the projection of their senses of vulnerability, deficiency, or corruption on some "other" who can then be vilified, shunned, or exterminated.

The question then becomes whether there is any conceptual way out of this cycle of deprecation and demonization when, as it happens, so many of our former constructions of human solidarity—frequently white, male, and Western—have been rendered problematic, ineffectual, innocuous, or worse. Global theorists like Anthony Tambiah and even Arjun Appadurai are inclined to explain the upsurge, really explosion, of ethnic and other forms of violence as products of contemporary world history, and more particularly, of the "incapacity of many deterritorialized groups," to quote Appadurai, "to think their way out of the imaginary of the nation-state." According to Appadurai, this forces "many movements of emancipation and identity, in their struggles against existing nation-states, to embrace the very imaginary they seek to escape."[8] Much as this observation has to commend it, it needs to be qualified by the realization that the problem of ethnic "belonging," as Michael Ignatieff has termed it, has also been exacerbated by the recent destabilization and collapse of so many nation-states in, say, the territorialities that once made up the borders of the former Soviet Union, or that remain as the legacy of colonialism throughout Africa, or that still mark the existence of people like the Kurds and the Palestinians, as well as those millions of deterritorialized guest workers and diasporans from the Middle East to Australia and from South Africa to Northern Europe. The problem they face is one of security. Who if not representatives of their own kind is to look out for them now that they have been deprived the shelter of larger political structures like the nation-state? Urging them to think their way out of the imaginary that supposedly blocks their route to emancipation and identity is a good deal more difficult when you cannot easily survive without either the protection or the recognition that, in Ignatieff's estimation, such imagined communities once routinely provided.

Burke himself may have suggested another way of responding to the question of how to break the cycle of the deprecation of difference when he urged us to consider the possibility of constructing human identity not only in terms of our sense of solidarity with our own kind but also in terms of what he called, only half-humorously, our "sense of fundamental kinship with the enemy."[9] By "enemy" Burke did not necessarily mean only our adversary, antagonist, or assailant but in fact anyone in opposition to whom—or constructed in opposition to whom—we find it necessary to define ourselves; in other words, the "Other." Constituting what he thought of as a "perspective by incongruity," this essentially comic recognition depends less on reversing the subject positions of "self" and "other," however much that maneuver might have to recommend it, than on using each as a kind of prismatic mirror to refract back to its opposite undetected aspects of itself.

In recommending such a stratagem, Burke was not foreshadowing the fashionable postmodernist view that we can only know others in ways that are always already forms of ourselves; nor was he implying, to the contrary, that there are no forms of ourselves that are also forms of others. He was merely asserting, with a contemporary of our own like Satya P. Mohanty, that even in our differences, whether lived or only imagined, we are still intertwined with them by virtue of the fact that we share histories that are not entirely separate, have suffered a fate that, however discrepant, is never entirely discrete.[10] Thus to turn the subject positions of "self" and "Other" into prisms that reflect is not simply to see elements of the "Other" within the "self" or elements of the "self" within the "other," nor even, much more difficult, to see elements of the "self" *as* "Other" and elements of the "Other" *as* potentialities of the self"; it is rather to see how, even in their opposition and, conceivably, total antagonism, "self and "Other" remain constructs that are at once implicated in one another's fabrication and necessary to each other's moral constitution. The kinship between "self" and "Other" is thus predicated less on any intrinsic qualities they may possibly share on any given occasion than on the pragmatic truth that neither can understand itself without reference to that which it is not, their notion of that which they are not most immediately and recurrently confirmed by their imagination of those whom they deem "Other."

To call that truth "pragmatic," however, is, in this intellectual environment, to invite the response that pragmatism isn't, in fact, political at all, since it possesses no way of appreciating how completely the relations between "self" and "Other" are always determined by distributions of power. Part of the responsibility for this view of pragmatism's indifference to politics has to be laid at the door of William James himself. In his well-known definition of the pragmatic method, James insisted that pragmatism stands for no particular results. Unlike other empirical philosophies with which it might be compared, pragmatism is a method only, lacking either dogmas or doctrines, but lying amidst all theories, to borrow a felicitous image from his fellow Italian pragmatist Giovanni Papini, like a kind of corridor in a hotel. Though many different doctrinal or dogmatic chambers open off of this corridor, the pragmatic method, James wanted to reassure his readers, makes no claim to them itself. It merely serves, or could and should serve, as the passageway which all must use if they are to obtain a practicable way of entering and exiting their rooms.[11]

Richard Rorty has since fastened on this disclaimer more than once to argue that pragmatism lacks a political consciousness. But this assertion at once disregards the limited point that James was initially trying to make about this new method of philosophical analysis—or, rather, as he phrased it, this "new name for some old ways of thinking"—and to discount what it quickly became in any case as a generalized intellectual perspective on experience. If the pragmatic method was designed to mediate the otherwise interminable disputes among rival metaphysical claims, it proposed to do so by in effect translating questions of meaning and truth into questions of practice and thus by deflecting attention away from "first principles, closed systems, and pretended absolutes and origins" and redirecting it—as he believed such predecessors as Socrates, Aristotle, Locke, Berkeley, and Hume had also done—"towards concreteness and adequacy, towards facts, towards action, and towards power."[12] The further claim, or at least imputation, that pragmatism lacks what, for want of a better term, I will call a political inclination or sensibility seems stranger still when applied to a philosophical orientation which accentuates not only the active but also the relational and unfinished character of existence; which insists that experience is plural, diverse, unpredictable, ambiguous, and messy; which maintains that all epistemological positions and philosophical standpoints are potentially unstable and thus susceptible to revision and correction; which holds that life presents us not with a hierarchy of answers but rather with a hierarchy of problems; which insists that all values are merely prejudices, or at least preferences, that need to be weighed and assessed against the preferences of others; which claims that culture needs to be democratized by dismantling the distinctions between high and low, between elite and ordinary; which assumes that the understanding of difference—and not just the difference that difference constitutes but the difference that difference makes—is the key to understanding itself; and which implies that one of the essential tasks of political life is to render such differences conversable so that the conflicts between them can, insofar as possible, become productive of human community rather than destructive of it.

Rorty would not dispute the fact that pragmatism has been so conceived; he merely denies that you can derive a ground for politics, or, for that matter, a ground for anything else, from a philosophy like pragmatism which is—and should be—antifoundational. If one is a pragmatist, therefore, one's politics are a matter of personal preference, not of philosophical persuasion. We choose the politics we do, Rorty maintains, not because we find better reasons for it but because it feels better to us.[13]

The feminist philosopher Nancy Fraser disagrees. In her estimation, for example, feminist politics will find stronger intellectual support from a discursive model that views languages as historically derived social practices rather than from one that views languages as symbolic systems or codes. Hence her preference for pragmatism over poststructuralism. Because it construes discourses not only as contingent but also as plural, and conceives of signification as a form of action rather than simply a mode of representation, pragmatism possesses distinct advantages as a discourse theory that none of the poststructuralisms do. It does not treat speaking subjects as products of immutable structures but rather as socially situated agents in emergent political processes, and it assumes that those processes need to be politically renegotiated constantly if society is to address such issues as power, inequality, and injustice. Fraser thus concludes that "the pragmatic approach has many of the features we need in order to understand the complexity of social identities, the formation of social groups, the securing and contesting of cultural hegemony, and the possibility and actuality of political practice."[14]

The recent recovery of some of pragmatism's political dimensions—which were first given their most extensive treatment in the series of books that John Dewey wrote between the 1920s and the outbreak of World War II—has more recently been reinforced by Chantal Mouffe in a book entitled *Deconstruction and Pragmatism*. A relationship that Rorty himself first explored in *Contingencies of Pragmatism*, its conjunction here allows the author of *The Return of the Political* and the co-author, with Ernesto Laclau, of *Hegemony and Socialist Strategy* to argue that pragmatism is not only saturated with political consequentiality but bears a special affinity for a democratic politics. This is a politics to which pragmatism can, and must, make a significant contribution, she feels, in light of its commitment to pluralism. But if this pluralism is to remain consistent with pragmatism it must also eschew the lyrical and unrealizable kind of democratic consensus that Rorty currently recommends in favor of more Derridian and Cavellian comprehension of the place of conflict, division, and undecidability in all democratic processes. In short, Mouffe maintains that democracy as reconceived and advanced by pragmatism brings us back to the epistemological proposition that originally launched this excursion into pragmatist theory by presupposing an unending, but not uninstructive, process of negotiation and renegotiation between "self" and "other" in which the moral constitution of each is determined by the way they both appropriate the tension, ambiguity, and inevitable contradiction between them.[15] The challenge is, as Burke put it, to discover one's sense of fundamental kinship with the enemy.

Such epistemological transactions are not, as it happens, all that unfamiliar to us. The best known in Western literature, perhaps, is the concession that Shakespeare wrings from Prospero in *The Tempest* when he says of Caliban, "this thing of darkness I acknowledge mine." This admission reflects some of the most troubling fantasies the European mind entertained about the wild man, but in no sense carries with it an assertion that Caliban now belongs to the human family; it merely registers Prospero's unsentimental realization, as Stephen Greenblatt notes, that Caliban is somehow part of him without, like Philoctetes' wound, entirely belonging to the being that Prospero is.[16]

Somewhat closer to us in time is the acknowledgment that Conrad's Marlow makes of a sense of "remote kinship with this wild and passionate uproar" that greets him as his steamer works its way up river in *Heart of Darkness*. Similarly sedimented, as in Shakespeare's play, with some of the West's darkest fantasies, in this instance nineteenth-century, connecting Africa and blackness with the primitive and the savage, Marlow is nonetheless unwilling to brand this outburst of the "Other" as inhuman, because he dimly senses within it something that not only elicits from him "the faintest trace of a response" but that will eventually permit him to recognize in images of this same "Other" what is lacking in virtually all Europeans, and most notably in Kurtz. Marlow refers to this something by various names—"inborn strength," "deliberate belief,"—and accounts it wholly responsible for restraining the African boatsmen, who practice cannibalism and are now near delirium from hunger, from making a meal of the whites. Speculating on the possible sources of such restraint—"superstition, disgust, patience, fear—or some kind of primitive honour"—Marlow rejects all but the last:

> No fear can stand up to hunger, no patience can wear it out, disgust simply does not exist where hunger is; and as to superstition, belief, and what you may call principles, they are less than chaff in a breeze. Don't you know the devilry of lingering starvation, its exasperating torment, its black thoughts, its sombre and brooding ferocity? Well, I do. It takes a man all his inborn strength to fight hunger properly. It's really easier to face bereavement, dishonour, and the perdition of one's soul–than this kind of prolonged hunger. Sad, but true. And these chaps too had no earthly reason for any kind of scruple. Restraint! I would just as soon have expected restraint from a hyena prowling amongst the corpses of a battlefield.[17]

This restraint remains for Marlow a mystery he cannot penetrate, an enigma that remains unfathomable, but the resonance of that "sense of primitive honour" on which it is based deepens as the book progresses and the reader witnesses the extent of its utter collapse in Kurtz. As the quintessential representative of those ideals that are supposed to redeem the depredations of imperialism, Kurtz's eventual depravity stands in starkest possible contrast to the restraint of the natives. Along with Kurtz's "The horror, the horror," it also constitutes the only reliable moral light in a world where so much else is shrouded in the darkness of colonial malevolence.

Nonetheless, as much as Conrad's evocation moves to transcend conventional understandings of human solidarity, his treatment of its opera-

tions in *Heart of Darkness* does not entirely escape usages that are Euro-
centric and racist. Therefore I want to turn to several other, more cred-
ible attempts to move, as it were, beyond solidarity through a recognition of one's sense of kinship not with the friend but with the enemy.
The first is represented by the literature and thought, and particularly the
folk art and folk thinking, of African American slaves and their descendants, who, having first been subjugated by the ideological domination
of the slave system and then by the system of institutionalized racism that
replaced it, managed to survive both by refusing either to accept or simply to reverse the Manichean regime of racial polarities that oppressed
them. What they did instead was to create out of its gaps and ruptures a
series of imaginative spaces located, so to speak, between the white world
and the black where, as the historian Lawrence Levine once put it, "legal
slavery [and its successors] could be prevented from becoming spiritual
slavery."[18] And nowhere was this more effective or dramatic than in slave
religion and the various forms of verbal and performative expression to
which it gave rise.

As numerous commentators from W. E. B. DuBois to Eugene Genovese, Eric Lincoln, Albert Raboteau, and Jon Butler have demonstrated,
African Americans and their descendants neither rejected white Christianity out of hand as evil nor simply grafted African meanings onto
white forms.[19] Instead they adapted the forms of white religion to the
needs, meanings, and structures of their own experiences as blacks. But
this entailed nothing short of a religious revolution in which African
Americans, instead of allowing themselves to be converted to the God of
white Southern Christians, converted that God, so to speak, to themselves. "There was no other safety," Paul Radin once wrote, "for people
faced on all sides by doubt and the threat of personal disintegration, by
the thwarting of instincts and the annihilation of values"[20]

The chief instrument of this conversation were ritual reenactments of
the divine acts of creation and salvation in song, oratory, narrative, prayer,
and dance, which were able not only to extend the boundaries of their
own world backward until it fused, as it were, with the Old Testament
narratives of deliverance, but also project their own world upward until it
merged with the New Testament narratives of beatitude and fulfillment.
The Negro spirituals thus constitute a move beyond solidarity. They are
the testimonial of a people whose sense of fundamental kinship with the
enemy, however attenuated, enabled them to find, as Levine puts it, "the
status, the harmony, the values, the order they needed to survive by internally creating an expanded universe, by literally willing themselves
reborn."[21]

Another sense of "fundamental kinship with the enemy" may be said
to have precipitated a similar move beyond solidarity in at least some of

the literature we call "postcolonial." To invoke the names of several of the figures who currently dominate its criticism, such as Edward Said, Homi Bhabha, and Gayatri Spivak, along with several of their shrewdest critics like Ajaz Ahmed and Benita Parry, is, of course, to be reminded that postcolonial literature is far from easily classified or summarized, but there still seems some agreement among the experts that this is a literature committed to resisting, if not subverting and supplanting, all those formal and informal discourses that seek to naturalize colonial power and to legitimate the perspectives that support it.[22] Such discourses are resisted in this literature through a process that is at least twofold. If the colonized "self" is to avoid the surrender of its identity to the terms dictated by the colonizing "other," it must not only forego the temptation to demonize that "other" but also contrive, at least at some moments, to transcend the discursive oppositions that presently define their relationship.

Such a maneuver is brilliantly accomplished in a text like J. M. Coetzee's *Waiting for the Barbarians* or, even better, his *Foe*, where the discursive terms that define the relation between, in the first instance, torturer and victim or, in the second, colonialist and colonized, are converted upward without necessarily either viewing as diabolical the first of the terms in each pair or inevitably denigrating the second. Friday's amputated tongue, and the resultant muteness it creates, enacts one version of the problem that the colonized typically confront: the problem of making meaning at all when others control the technology as well as the materials of its production. Yet the responses that Friday makes to his own muteness—dancing in a circle, playing a single note on his flute, writing and rewriting the letter "O"—all dramatize far more than his exclusion from the circles of interpretation that shut him out. They also comprise a counter-representational mode designed to escape the force of the discursive polarities still operative in his resistance to, and rebellion against, the practices which prevent his participation. By in effect turning those practices against each other, Friday succeeds in transforming the signs of his own silencing into symbols by which to signify it and thereby achieves, indeed enacts, a political agency that his former status as a colonized subject purportedly denied him.[23]

Still a third literary location where one may find evidence of a move beyond solidarity, as I term it, precipitated by some sense of fundamental kinship with the enemy is to be found in the literature that has been created in response to the Holocaust. Such literature—I am thinking, say, of the fiction of Primo Levi or the poetry of Paul Celan—which strives to make us believe, as Paul Celan says in his poem "Threadsuns," that "there are / still songs to be sung beyond humankind," positions itself like that tenuous light referred to in Celan's poem, which hangs over the waste and void before (or is it after?) creation, and yields, as in Celan's more famous poem "Death Fugue," images composed out of the words of the victims themselves and the language of his own memories. These are images—milk that is black, graves dug in air, hair of ash, dances fiddled for gravediggers—that simultaneously render the abomination in all its horror and, as John Felstiner says in his wonderful new book, find a voice to detail what happened in the language of the executioners.[24]

Part of the miracle of this poetry, then, is that its voice is created out of the language of those who sought to silence the kind of self responsible for its writing. Language must "pass through"—Celan's words—"its own answerlessness, pass through a frightful falling mute, pass through the thousand darknesses of death-bringing speech" to find the reality by which it is stricken, the shelterlessness that is both its condition and its possibility.[25] The poems thus enunciate in the tongue of their oppressor and nemesis a relation, at once cognitive and affective as well as linguistic, of strange and terrible consanguinity.

Here, in these poems of spare, most elemental, speech, alterity is not one element of identity among others, nor is it merely that over against which identity supposedly constitutes itself. Alterity is rather represented as that in relation to which identity must somehow, even at the risk of its very existence and often under the most inhuman of imagined conditions, still hold itself in tension and, to that degree, accountable. While this involves in Celan, as in some of the other writing associated with the Holocaust, a moral discipline of almost superhuman proportions, its expressions may nonetheless contain clues not easily reducible to paraphrase, much less translatable into political programs, for how to reverse, or at least to interrupt and deflect, those symbolic processes that associate the formation of human identity with the denigration of human difference. In addition, though this may merely be a utopian hope, I believe that such negotiations beyond solidarity may suggest some ways of re-conceptualizing, if not the substance of a common human nature, then at least the nature of a common, or in any event a sharable, human world, a world, that is, where the relations between self and "other," rather than being suffered as discursively deforming, can be experienced as dialogically, even ethically, enhancing.

Notes

1. See Eric Hobsbawm, *The Age of Extremes: A History of the World, 1914–1991* (New York: Pantheon, 1994), and William E. Connolly, *Identity/Difference:*

Democratic Negotiations of Political Paradox (Ithaca: Cornell University Press, 1991).

2. Michael Ignatieff, *Blood and Belonging: Journeys into the Now Nationalism* (New York: Noonday Press, 1995), p. 10.

3. Richard J. Bernstein, *The New Constellation: The Ethical-Political Horizons of Modernity/Postmodernity* (Cambridge: M.I.T. Press, 1992), p. 66.

4. Emmanuel Levinas, *Totality and Infinity*, trans. Alphonso Lingis (Pittsburgh: Duquesne University Press, 1969).

5. Jacques Derrida, *Writing and Difference* (Chicago: University of Chicago Press, 1978), pp. 104, 125.

6. See Mikhail Bakhtin, *The Dialogic Imagination: Four Essays* (Austin: University of Texas Press, 1981); Isaiah Berlin, *The Crooked Timber of Humanity: Chapters in the History of Ideas* (New York: Knopf, 1990); and Bernstein, *New Constellation*.

7. Kenneth Burke, *A Grammar of Motives* (Berkeley: University of California Press, 1969), p. 406.

8. Arjun Appadurai, "Patriotism and Its Futures," *Public Culture* 5 (3): 411–30; this quotation is from p. 418. See also Appadurai, *Modernity at Large: Cultural Dimensions of Globalization* (Minneapolis: University of Minnesota Press, 1996), and Anthony Tambiah, "Ethnic Conflict in the World Today," *American Ethnologist* 16 (1989): 335–49.

9. Quoted in Stanley Edgar Hyman, *The Armed Vision* (New York: Vintage, 1995), p. 380.

10. Satya P. Mohanty, *Literary Theory and the Claims of History: Postmodernism. Objectivity, Multicultural Politics* (Ithaca: Cornell University Press, 1997).

11. William James, "What Pragmatism Means," *Pragmatism and the Meaning of Truth* (Cambridge: Harvard University Press, 1975).

12. James, "What Pragmatism Means," p. 31.

13. Richard Rorty, *Contingency, Irony, Solidarity* (New York: Cambridge University Press, 1989).

14. Nancy Fraser, "The Uses and Abuses of French Discourse Theories for Feminist Politics," *Boundary 2* 17 (1990): 82–101. This quotation is from p. 94.

15. See Chantal Mouffe, *Deconstruction and Pragmatism* (London: Routledge, 1996) and *The Return of the Political* (New York: Routledge and Kegan Paul, 1979); and Ernesto Laclau and Chantal Mouffe, *Hegemony and Socialist Strategy: Towards a Radical Democratic Politics* (London: Verso, 1985).

16. Stephen Greenblatt, *Learning to Curse: Essays in Early Modern Culture* (New York: Routledge, 1990).

17. Joseph Conrad, *Heart of Darkness and The Secret Sharer* (New York: Signet, 1950), p. 113.

18. Lawrence Levine, *Black Culture and Black Consciousness: Afro-American Folk Thought from Slavery to Freedom* (New York: Oxford University Press, 1977), p. 80.

19. W. E. B. Du Bois, *The Souls of Black Folk* (New York: The Modern Library, 1966); Eugene Genovese, *Roll, Jordan. Roll: The World the Slaves Made* (New York: Pantheon, 1974); Eric C. Lincoln, *The Black Church in the African American Experience* (Durham: Duke University Press, 1990); Albert Raboteau, *Slave*

Religion: The 'Invisible Institution' in the Antebellum South (New York: Oxford University Press, 1978), and Jon Butler, *Awash in a Sea of Faith* (Cambridge: Harvard University Press, 1990).

20. Quoted in Levine, *Black Culture and Black Consciousness*, p. 33.

21. Levine, *Black Culture and Black Consciousness*, p. 33.

22. See, Edward Said, *Culture and Imperialism* (New York: Knopf, 1993); Homi Bhabha, The *Location of Culture* (London: Routledge, 1994); Gayatri Spivak, *In Other Words: Essays in Cultural Politics* (New York: Methuen, 1987); Ajaz Ahmed, *In Theory: Classes, Nations, Literatures* (London: Verso, 1992) and Benita Parry, *Conrad and Imperialism: Ideological Boundaries and Visionary Frontiers* (London: Macmillan Press, 1983).

23. J.M. Coetzee, *Waiting for the Babarians* (New York: Penguin, 1982), and *Foe* (New York: Penguin, 1987).

24. John Felstiner, *Paul Celan: Poet, Survivor, Jew* (New Haven: Yale University Press, 1995).

25. John Felstiner, "Translating Celan's Last Poem," *The American Poetry Review* July/August (1982): 23.

6

Ascetics, Aesthetics, and the Management of Desire

GEOFFREY GALT HARPHAM

THE WINDS of academia today are blowing against religion but in the direction of dogma and piety. Many positions, whether interpretive, evaluative, or theoretical, have the status of articles of faith. Faith itself, on the other hand, is the one position it is impossible to profess without careful qualification or even irony. When, in the late 1980s, the prestigious journal *Critical Inquiry* announced a special issue on "God," the project languished for some years. No scholar, it seemed, wanted to write on the subject, and when at last the project came to fruition, "God" had shrunk to a mere three articles, a "section" rather than an "issue." And yet credulity is everywhere; it is just attached to secular objects: the culture of advanced scholarship today is dominated by a spirit of *belief* without the *sacred*.

In its magnified way, the culture abroad also expresses a certain quasi-religious devotion, even reverence, for a number of concepts and principles currently in favor in the academy, including embodiment, performance, sexuality, and desire. In the larger as well as the smaller culture, there is a general displacement of *desert* by *dessert*; or, if *desert*, by the notion of deservingness, with the emphasis on the second syllable. Still, there may be a possible reunification of religious sentiment with religious concepts in the domain of art. For one unquestioned value in both general and academic culture today is the notion of freedom—freedom from determination by biology, by history, by authority, by ideology. And one way of envisioning and enacting freedom is, as Hegel said, through art. The aesthetic representation liberates the mind from the tyranny of the real and sets it loose in the domain of symbol, with its indeterminate significations, so different and so distant from the mundane world we normally occupy. So different and distant, in fact, that the free realm of art may be one plausible way of imagining the kind of absolute alienation that was in another time and place imaged by the desert itself. The modern aesthetic may, in other words, constitute one possible version of the ancient ascetic.

In order to grasp these two concepts together, we will need to set aside or bracket a whole set of associations of the aesthetic with concepts of repletion, fullness, monumentality, sensuousness, excitation, and the satisfying union of form and concept. But we will also have to disengage the desert, the scene of ascesis, from concepts of separation, emptiness, evacuation, nullity, denial. We will, that is, have to liberate art and asceticism from their conventional attributes; but we will, perhaps, be rewarded by a far more complex understanding of the deep relationship between the two, the indirect but effective ways in which each performs some necessary functions, captures some vital quality, that the other cannot.

We need a point of entry into this tangled region, and we have one, I believe, with the notion of desire. "Be like Daniel," Saint Bonaventure counsels, "a man of desires. . . . Ask grace not instruction, desire not understanding." Now it must be admitted that Bonaventure adduces objects of desire that have few partisans today, and those not conspicuous for their religious feelings: "*My soul chooses hanging and my bones death.*"[1] But the point is that, if soul and bones get what they want, desire will have been gratified, if at considerable cost. Like all objects of desire, hanging and death will have been converted into something *more and other than themselves*; their fatality will have been reconfigured as keys to eternal life. Asceticism deploys the fundamental mechanism of desire, the conversion or translation of things into other things. This is also one way to conceive of the fundamental mechanism of the work of art. For art is, in its classic formulations, a compensation for an insufficiently satisfying world, a "*promesse de bonheure,*" a refiguration of tragic existence into a consoling form, a mystified form of ideological antagonisms, an unproblematic source of pleasure and delight—in all ways, an expression or a fulfillment of desire, and this despite the superficial indifference, even antipathy, of both asceticism and aesthetics to worldly or fleshly desire as such.

The fact that asceticism and the aesthetic hold this complex relation to desire in common helps explain why, within the broad range of practices that can be called ascetical, the creation and reception of art has been so instrumental. Historically, art has played a major role in what has been called "self-fashioning" (Greenblatt) or "self-forming" (Foucault). The contemporary emphasis on "performance" in contemporary ethnography, gender studies, drama, and literary theory also characteristically suggests an ascetic genealogy. For the performing subject is a disciplined subject, one trained, often by long and tedious practice, to produce a certain kind of display. So while performance sounds more like a hobby and less like a necessity—more like a choice or preference and less like a blood passion—its capacity to hone itself through discipline reflects its ideological and historical affiliation with those practices of self-denial, or self-fashioning, that arose as testimonials of grace and faith within early Christian asceticism. Within those ascetic practices, the task of converting oneself from the flawed, fallible, failing, and flailing thing that one is, to the rigid monument to the Way that one would like to be, requires a practice of framing, planning, and construction—a practice that fulfills the requirements for what we have, since Kant, learned to call aesthetic creation. Surprisingly, perhaps, the ancient violences of desert Christianity turn out to accord pretty well with the distinctively modern category of art.

Two premises emerge into view. The first is that aesthetics is not merely a modern name for an aspect of asceticism, but constitutes asceticism's specifically modern form, its modernity. The second is that asceticism brings pressure to bear upon the very concept of art precisely insofar as art is modern.

Taking the last first, we could point to the manifestly ascetic quality of that touchstone of the modern conception of the aesthetic, disinterestedness. In addition to being one name for a general quality of detachment that characterizes the relation of the artifact to the world and to the perceiver, disinterestedness also characterizes the mode of being of the creative artist, especially the modern creative artist. For modern art is often said to emerge at the expense of the artist, who suffers privation in order to prepare himself for creation; who mutilates himself in the act of creation; who surrenders himself in the execution; and who cuts himself off from selfhood in sending the work out into the world. Nietzsche was not alone in seeing castration at the core of art's modernity; others, including Flaubert, Mallarmé, Conrad, Gide, and Kafka, made the connection as well. In the discourse of the aesthetic, modernity rearticulates, in a secular vocabulary, the traditional religious concern with self-negation, self-overcoming, self-alienation, self-transcendence as ways of achieving a pure presentness, an openness to being. As Donald Kuspit writes, modernity can be seen as "that point of view which sees art as the mastery of purity," purity being the ascetic virtue *par excellence*.[2] Moreover, within the ascetic aesthetic, practices and concepts that originally emerged within an intensely religious context, as its most extreme expression, survive essentially undisturbed the utter loss of that context—survive, indeed, precisely because modernity marks the loss of that context. The modern religion of art institutes an ascetic devotion not to religion, but to a kind of anti-religion. The practice is primary, surviving and sustaining any set of meanings that may be attached to it.

To see art as an instance of ascetic practices of self-formation is to clarify the sheer violence of the modern work of art. To see asceticism on the model of art is, however, to awaken to the genuine freedom of ascetic discipline, a freedom that converges on the blank page, the empty canvas, the conductor's upraised baton, the next (undiscovered, improvised) step—the freedom to make what one will out of what one has, or is.

For early Christian ascetics, the imitability of their practices was crucial. An ascetic performance was wasted if it did not possess some display value, and, thus, some conversional power to inspire others to similar performances. One modern form of this power is realized, I believe, in aesthetic criticism. While in *The Ascetic Imperative in Culture and Criticism* I rehearsed the versions of asceticism instantiated by every school of criticism I could think of as though they were all substantially individuated, I now believe that criticism can be divided into two essential forms, which we could call "cenobitic" and "eremitic" (to recall the two basic forms of asceticism, the collective monastic institution and the solitary hermit), based upon the fundamental relation established between critic and primary text.[3] For simplicity's sake, I will begin by referring to a single text, Terry Eagleton's *Criticism and Ideology*. At the end of his first chapter, Eagleton outlines two options for criticism. In an older model, criticism acts as midwife to the text, a humbly self-effacing practice that represents itself as smoothing the passage from text to reader. Such a practice invariably winds up becoming authoritarian, acting as "repressive father, who cuts short the erotic sport of sense between text and reading, binding with the briars of its metasystem the joyfully pluralist intercourse of meanings between them." This account invokes, all unconsciously to be sure, certain aspects of cenobitism, which are redoubled in the protocols of scholarship itself: those elaborate conventions of citation, close reading, research, and attention to evidence that are collectively designed to neutralize, regulate, or castrate the subjective reader by promoting the claims of the Other—the other author, the other reader, the other scholar, the textual other, the historical other.

In the second, preferred (eremitic) sense, however, criticism does not claim humbly to "redouble the text's self-understanding" or seek to "collude with its object in a conspiracy of eloquence. Its task," Eagleton writes, "is to show the text as it cannot know itself, to manifest those conditions of its making . . . about which it is necessarily silent. . . . To achieve such a showing, criticism must break with its ideological prehistory, situating itself outside the space of the text on the alternative terrain of scientific knowledge."[4] This empowering break, in which criticism ascends the pillar in the glaring desert sun of science—displaying a truth of the text that, without such a gesture of wild self-denial on the part of the critic, would remain invisible in a world of ideology and tradition—is still castration; for, once again, it is a heroic leap to knowledge because it is a leap away from the critic's self-interest.

If Eagleton's first critical option entails a spirit of collective humility, the second is a practice of solitude and austerity. Eagleton would, I imagine, vigorously resist this assimilation of science with asceticism, since science for him means a rejection of religion and its manifold idealities, myths, and ideological fantasies. But he might be chastened by reading the third essay of *On the Genealogy of Morals*, in which Nietzsche begins by establishing science as modernity's best hope of stamping out asceticism altogether and ends by conceding that science is the purest form of asceticism yet discovered. Indeed, the way Eagleton casts the problem, it is ascetic through and through, for it urges that we choose not what we might want—the feminine gratifications of midwifery, conspiracy, eloquence, and repetition—but rather what is necessary, the sterner task of breaking with history, the task of scientific knowledge. But Eagleton is not alone here. Others—the libertines and libertarians of literary theory, whether operating according to the Rule of Roland, the Rule of Jacques, or the Rule of Julia—urge a break with a tradition they depict as ascetic, involving self-effacement, humility, and anonymity, in favor of values and practices of self-fulfillment, *jouissance*, dissemination, play, sport, and a general renunciation of renunciation.

In the newer discipline of cultural studies, the model of initiation is not close reading, but ethnographic fieldwork, with its intense personal involvement in the subject, as opposed to the remote, removed perspective of the scholar. The anti-ascetic point, as practitioners such as Dwight Conquergood, Clifford Geertz, and Renato Rosaldo insist, is that cultural studies is an embodied practice rather than a practice of alienation and distance. The larger point I would make in response to this is that whatever the choice, something is renounced and something embraced; and therefore desire is always both gratified and negated. In the case of cultural studies, scholarly authority is earned by what anthropologists call "time in the field"—by the surrender of the comforts and pleasure of the library, the office, the study; and the immersion in the ethnographic site, with its exposure, bad food, disease, and boredom, not to mention the hostility of the invaded subjects. It is always possible to depict a scholarly practice as either pleasurable or unpleasurable, fulfilling or castrating, because all such practices operate by the law of compensation—denial of something, gratification of something else. Scholarly practices, in particular, provide a conspicuous instance of an ascetic imperative that simply cannot be avoided, any more than it can be perfectly realized. Scholars and critics in particular seem to prefer, out of professional obligation, castration's compensations to the pleasures of pleasure.

Not coincidentally, what unites aesthetic works and their critics is, I believe, precisely this ascetic law of denial and compensation. As I indicated earlier, aceticism is a structure of compensation, in which something is granted—"treasure in heaven"—in return for something being given up—"all that thou hast" (Luke 18.22). Peter Brown and Carolyn

Walker Bynum have argued that what is literally, and most painfully, being given up in early Christian asceticism is food rather than a more
obvious candidate, sex.[5] Call me a traditionalist, but I want to insist—
especially with respect to the modern form of asceticism, aesthetics and
its criticism—on the primacy of sex. I begin by suggesting that both art
and criticism compensate for the surrender of physical sexuality by providing imaginative gratifications that have their own attractiveness. Freud
argued that beauty (by which I would understand both its creation and
its reception) represents a sublimation of sexuality, a rerouting of transgressive energies along socially acceptable lines; and while this seems a
decidedly modern view of the matter, I would argue that we can in fact
locate the germ of sublimation, the beginnings of a modern understanding, in ascetic art and its cultural interpretation.

As one among countless examples, I want to focus on a picture by
Sassetta (c.1440–50), one of a series depicting the life of St. Anthony
(fig. 6.1). In this image, the meeting between Anthony and Paul the
Hermit (died c. 347), sometimes called Paul of Thebes, is efficiently depicted, using the spatial narrative style common to the time. The compensation I am hunting for does not withhold itself, for the meeting
between the two saints represents a momentary relief from the intense
solitude suffered by each; their holy embrace provides, in fact, not only
an affirmation of the worthiness of the ascetic life, but an astonishing
interval of sensation, an unrepeatable break amid the unrelieved decades
of self, or rather of denial of self. The image represents an especially holy
moment in the lives of wholly holy men.

I want to dwell on, or in, the peculiar arch formed by Paul and Anthony's embrace. Perhaps its most immediate formal function is to repeat
the arch of the cave immediately behind them, Paul the Hermit's home.
Doing so, they manage to suggest in human form the rock rolled back
from the tomb, and thus the Resurrection, and thus the compensatory
treasure in heaven that will be enjoyed by those who deny the flesh and
live in the spirit. There is a certain formal precedent for such embraces,
which generally carry the same message of compensation. A late twelfth-
century Flemish painting of Mary and Elizabeth, for example, stages an
even more elaborate display of symmetry, indicated not only by the loving embrace of the two women, pregnant with Jesus and John the Baptist, but by such incidental features as the crossing of the feet, a feature
this painting holds in common with the Sassetta.

But to the viewer suffering the trials of life the embrace may have (and
has had) different meanings than for Anthony and Paul, or for Elizabeth
and Mary. The case for giving up all, for living in the world but not of it,
may seem, from some points of view, less than persuasive. One recalls
Huck Finn's description of *Pilgrim's Progress* as a book "about a man

Figure 6.1 *The Meeting of Saint Anthony and Saint Paul,* c. 1440, tempera on panel. *(Samuel H. Kress Collection, National Gallery of Art, Washington, DC, reproduced with permission.)*

that left his family, it didn't say why." The surrender of food, sex, and the metaphorical extensions thereof may seem a harsh price to pay even for heaven's booty, distant and immaterial. For most people struggling to commit themselves to a life of abstinence, the most salient and purely attractive element of the story of Anthony may be not the decades of fasting and solitude that preceded and followed the embrace, but the embrace itself, which suggests the principle of reward, of human contact not as transgression of the principle of sacrifice, but enfolded within the sacrifice itself.

A closer look at Sassetta's painting discloses that this enfolding, and the careful negotiation of intervals, serve as a structural principle of the composition as a whole. The dominant form of the painting is, surely, the arch; and it is replicated everywhere—not only in Paul's cave, but in the route of the road, the forms of the mountains, the shapes of the trees, the very clusters of leaves—as if their embrace were not merely an instance of affection and fellow feeling, but also a human enactment of a principle of natural form. Even the colors of Anthony's and Paul's robes repeat the colors found in the right and left sides of the cave. The feeling is thus thoroughly naturalized. Still, one cannot help noticing that the position of the embrace itself is highly unnatural in the sense that it is clumsy, almost impossibly awkward, bad for aging backs. Why do they assume this queer posture?

Is it only in order to create an arch? Or might there be some other, negative motivation? In the case of Elizabeth and Mary, the interval between the bodies leaves room for pregnant bellies to swell, and thus foregrounds the fertility of the two women. There may be something of that convention in this composition—with fertility being applied metaphorically to men who bear the Word within them. But I see another possibility in addition to this: that the unnatural posture, depicted by an artist manifestly grappling with the rigors of pictorial realism, is motivated by the necessity of creating a gap or space between bodies, a gap that would preserve, in the face of a certain transgressive threat, the interval, and so maintain the holy character of the embrace. The law of the holy embrace is clear: the genitals cannot touch, for such a touch would represent not just compensation but overcompensation. The very avoidance of genital contact through an unnatural posture permits the equally unnatural placement of the hands on the buttocks. And so, in representing a natural embrace as an amplification and reinforcement of a natural principle, and a natural principle of form, the artist has created two forms of the unnatural, the physical posture and the homosexual embrace.

The unnatural act hinted at by the holy embrace would, I have no doubt, have been almost perfectly invisible to the anticipated audience for the painting. It may, for all I know, have remained invisible to everyone who had ever seen the painting until I did a few months ago, after years of looking at it on my office wall. So heavily coded as orthodox and natural is the image that the possibility of an unnatural act occurring, or about to occur, before our eyes seems more monstrous than . . . than a centaur. The efficient resolution with which the mind censors, screens, and represses has, however, the effect of permitting a transgressive desire for human, bodily contact—which might have seemed to a prospective ascetic not unnatural but perfectly natural, given the radical deprivation of the ascetic life—to thrive on the margins, in the corners, unchecked by the vigilant eye. Repressed instincts, Freud tells us, flourish in the dark, "ramifying like a fungus."

The status of nature in the composition is, I think one would have to admit, a bit wobbly. What can we make of the centaur, colored like nothing else in the painting? The centaur represents a compromise between the human and the animal, and this one in particular provides a formal completion of the wedge in the center of the picture created by the grove of trees; in fact, two of the tree trunks seem to represent his hind legs. The central, centering centaur is still, however, radically out of place in any natural, or naturalistic, setting. The human (the centaur suggests) is both natural and unnatural. In an ascetic context, this possibly means that the human is bound to the flesh but may, through the grace of God, transcend its animal nature. Asceticism thus embraces both a principle of affection that is entirely in keeping with nature, and a counter-principle of deprivation that entails a repudiation of nature. The unnaturalness of ascetic practices and ideology may thus license a view of discipline itself as unnatural. And this would mean, for those still following, that ascetic restraint falls into the category of an unnatural act—precisely the implication I am drawing from the human arch in Sassetta's painting.

Now if we turn to Paul, we note that, like the entrance to his cave, he is halo-colored, implying through the medium of color a perfect sanctity both in himself and in his domicile. Especially in light of the pictorial convention we saw in the painting of Elizabeth and Mary, this cave might represent the source of Paul's fertility, the confinement that issues in holiness, a metaphorical womb as well (as noted earlier) as a tomb. This would confirm, for modern skeptics, what might seem to be the hidden agenda of the ascetic *fuite du monde*, a return to prenatal wholeness. But, more pertinently in the present context, we must note that it is precisely the refusal of the womb that constitutes the demand for compensation, and thus drives the entire ascetic program. The womb must be denied, or converted, before one can honorably return to it.

But no conversion converts without remainder, without creating fresh opportunities and needs for further conversion. This truism is borne out, I believe, by the deep grooves on the top of the cave entrance, which mark it not as feminine-vaginal but rather as masculine-anal. The womb is converted by being naturalized. But it is naturalized by being masculinized, which is to say, unnaturalized. The natural form of the cave is made available for human purposes by being routed through the masculine, a two-stage conversion that renders the cave an object of desire, an object to desire instead of the womb: one lives in a cave instead of with a woman. This is, to the ascetic, a natural desire that takes natural form, the form of the cave, repeated in the embrace of the two men. But life in a cave also represents a renunciation of natural desire, a will to desire the nonnatural, the unnatural, to have an unnatural desire, the very type of which is anal intercourse. The cave—or anus—is the natural and human site of gender conversion or transformation. (Here I am reminded that the phrases "to use a woman like a man" and "to use a man like a woman" both designate the same act.) Let me explain, if I can. Anthony sets out for his object of desire, Paul, a feminized man associated with the cave, a cave man. But on achieving his destination, Anthony himself is feminized, his identity almost literally eclipsed by Paul, his head disappearing. Paul is also transformed: from a position of subordination to the greater and dominant Anthony, he becomes a dominant figure, masculinizing the cave. In the holy embrace, it is Anthony who is the midwife to holiness, rather than a flamboyant, charismatic eremite, while Paul emerges into a startling visibility. In terms used by Patricia Cox Miller, Anthony represents, at the culminating moment, the "dim body," while Paul suggests a dazzling "glorified body."[6] The suggestively pinkish robe carried by Anthony, a gift of his future biographer Athanasius, enigmatically contains the entire drama in its folds. Increasingly tumescent in each stage of his pilgrimage, the phallic robe nearly envelops Anthony at the end, but envelops him—is it too scandalous to suggest this? Can we still speak of scandal here?—as a womb, as the sign of Anthony's completed gender transformation. Fittingly, this robe will serve, as Jerome informs us in his *Life of Paul*, as Paul's shroud, the terminus of his short but complicated journey as well.

Here I confess that I have arrived at the navel of my dream, where my own analysis plunges into the unknown, and I feel powerless fully to reclaim the logic that constituted this representation, to abstract the architecture, the theory, from the image, which is also the un-imageable, even the unimaginable. I wonder, in fact, if the cave, the structural and conceptual center of the painting, might not indicate in its depths the essence not only of asceticism, but, as a form to which no concept could be fully answerable or adequate, of the aesthetic itself, the formless origin of form. Here I sense a kind of theoretical nausea in the presence, or absence, of something I can neither assimilate nor reject. And with this nausea comes a nostalgia for simpler messages, more legible images.

One such image was thoughtfully provided by the organizers of a conference on asceticism held at the Union School of Theology in 1994. The cover of the conference program featured an image painted in 1990 by a master of contemporary Coptic art, Dr. Isaac Fanous Youssef, for the Coptic Orthodox Church in Los Angeles (fig. 6.2). Dr. Youssef represents Anthony the Great in splendid, centered isolation, holding a scroll to express his devotion to the Word. The unfurled scroll extends all the way to Anthony's center, stopping at precisely the point where the bottom of the scroll might plausibly suggest an erect penis. The life of the

Figure 6.2 *Saint Anthony the Great*,
egg tempera on gesso. *(Reproduced
with permission of Father Antonious
L. Heinen.)*

Word, I infer, is fulfilling in ways all men can understand, with the Word
standing in, or standing up, for desire, arousal, expectation. Whether the
bottom of the scroll represents a Lacanian phallic signifier or something
else, perhaps a phallic signified, I cannot determine, but the coincidence
of Word with phallus seems incontestable. Anthony's centrality is, moreover, established by pictorial elements to his right and left that echo the
same general idea. On his right, he greets Paul, his hands flung back in
surprise or delight, while Paul reaches forward—why? toward what? On
Anthony's left, a pair of lions, an icon of the peaceability and solidarity of
asceticism, lie down not with lambs, but with each other—two strictly
symmetrical male lions, soon to bury Paul in Anthony's robe, cheek to
jowl, buttressing—again, in the natural world—the otherwise unnatural

homoerotic element already indicated on the other side. The lake behind them reinforces the theme of mirroring. If symmetry and mirroring are themselves at least potentially homoerotic in import, then even the very word "abba" participates, weirdly enough, in this message of brotherly compensations. The raven, whose function in the narrative of Paul and Anthony is simply to bring some bread, seems involved in a more ambiguous and aggressive mission here, diving like a kamikaze pilot into the trumpet of some extraordinary, Daliesque plant.

The primary function of such homosexual signals is, I want to emphasize, not to inject a missing principle into asceticism so as to make it attractive or bearable; nor is it to disclose a secret, traumatic kernel that lies at the heart of ascetic piety. They may in fact do both these, but their primary function is to make clear what would otherwise be terribly unclear, the conundrum of how desire, the guilty party in transgression, may be turned on itself, enlisted in the service of the Other and directed not to self-gratification but to self-denial. Desire must fold back upon itself in a spirit of apparent antagonism and actual realization; it must choose objects of desire that are not, in the old sense, desirable at all, and find its fulfillment there. But how? How are we to understand this essential negation, this negation of the essence of desire, which is the essence of ourselves—much less this desire for negation, a desire that seems so infernally complex, so unnatural? Gregory Collins's paper at the asceticism conference provided a rapid series of illustrations of the way this desire is managed. Collins employs three phrases—quoted, sanctioned, official phrases—that illustrate the effective indirection of ascetic rhetoric: asceticism, he says, is "a Spartan kind of straitness"; "asceticism must be penetrated by humility"; and "Christ is buried in us as in a tomb . . . and rises again, and raises us with himself."[7] These sentences raise mystery to sublimity, so that my understanding rests in a state of quiet apprehension of something beyond my powers to decipher. But insofar as I seek to understand, I attend to, and am bewildered by, the meaning. I cannot comprehend the literal sense of this Spartan straitness, this penetration, this burial of one man in another, this rising, this transfiguration. I am confused, I do not understand . . . unless—I do. But if I do, I perform a rapid, even instantaneous gesture of cancellation, because the conjunction between the mysteries of faith and the groaning, heaving process of homosexual fornication is so grotesque, impossible, ridiculous, that it could not be admitted. Thus, the homoerotic serves as an explanatory model in the material world of desire for faith, one that illuminates without defiling because it is so altogether defiled that its function is never actually admitted.

It cannot be admitted, at least, within the ideology of asceticism. For one of the main points of that ideology concerns the distinction between the spirit and the flesh, a distinction that actually *permits* the homosexual embrace to serve as a model for piety. I am not using ideology here in the older Marxist sense of false consciousness, but rather in the more contemporary sense of a structurally unconscious and flexible armature of concepts that govern not only attitudes and ideas, but perception itself. The Slovenian philosopher Slavoj Zizek insists on the unconsciousness of ideology as the feature that enables its functioning. Ideology, he says, is a form of knowledge whose form is not knowledge; we "do it but don't know it," it is "in us more than ourselves."[8] In this understanding of ideology, we can actually grasp the true importance of the homoerotic as the form in desire of ideology itself. For within what theoreticians of gender have called the psycho-social regime of compulsory heterosexuality—the silent premise that normal sexuality is and ought to be hetero—the homosexual Other within stands as a primary and primordial form of something in us more than ourselves, something we do, if we do, without knowing it.

I seem to have strayed far from the original subject of the spirit of asceticism in the modernity of art. But not really. For, as I have just indicated, there are excellent reasons why homosexuality in ascetic art goes unrecognized, and even why this nonrecognition should confirm its status as art. For if art, in the post-Kantian world, is defined by the disinterestedness that attends its reception, then a representation of a banished form of sexuality is preeminently something to be "disinterested" in. As the love that dare not speak its name, homosexuality bears the burden of love generally in an ascetic context, the burden of nonrecognition, invisibility, denial. The banished form of a banished category, a form whose banishment could be generally understood and endorsed, a structurally banished form, a form to which banishment is proper, homosexuality represents the banishment of human sexuality *per se*, a banishment not the least bit less effective for its literal nonappearance—since that is what banishment is all about.

Even modern critics interested in the body promote a restriction of erotic possibilities that reinforces this banishment. I am thinking here chiefly of Bynum, who argues throughout *Fragmentation and Redemption* that, in the Middle Ages, "bodiliness" as such was associated with woman, who thus entered into an especially intimate relation with the incarnate Christ. Bynum's admirable sensitivity to the fluidity of gender distinctions during this time casts a very bright light on what seem to us to be aberrant attributions of female characteristics to men and vice versa. But when she discusses Jesus as mother, Jesus as the issue of a female genealogy, Bynum begins to close off rather than to open up possibilities of identification a desire. And when, in an historicist spirit, she cautions against importing contemporary notions of sexuality into a medieval context in which other concerns (such as food) may have been more determining, then I begin to sense what Eagleton called a conspiracy of eloquence. That is, by cautioning that medieval people did not define themselves in terms of sexual orientation, and worried more about whether their desires came from God or from Satan than about what kind of desires they had, Bynum, perhaps inadvertently, limits one of the primary kinds of imitation of Christ, the kind we would today call homosexual.

I am, of course, all too aware of the controversial character of such readings, especially in a climate of extreme sensitivity concerning clerical homosexual pedophilia, a sensitivity stoked as well as described by such books as Jason Berry's *Lead Us Not into Temptation: Catholic Priests and the Sexual Abuse of Children*. It is not, I believe, altogether beside the point that, by Mr. Berry's estimate, 20 percent of American Catholic clergy are gay.[9] For what this means is that a life of sacrifice and renunciation (of sexual intercourse) continues to appeal to those who might be most responsive to the necessarily indirect and coded signals of homoeroticism—or to indirection and code generally. In the face of Mr. Berry's statistic, I must insist that the compensations I am speaking of are aesthetic, which is to say imaginary, but also, and more importantly, unconscious. There is, if not a decisive theoretical difference, a world of worldly *ethical* difference between a conscious, bodily act and an inarticulate, unconscious imaginative sensation.

I realize that I am perhaps working here with a somewhat less definite and restrictive account of asceticism than that employed by many (especially religious) people. But one of my own implicit points is that history repeats itself, above all in the illusion of doing something new; and that asceticism is one name for that repetition. Although predicated on repetition, asceticism yet stands for the new, the perpetually modern, the break. Historians, inclined to be immersed in the specificity of their materials, can easily lose track of, or sympathy with, such concepts. Out of an ascetic imperative to be faithful to "the facts," they can blind themselves to the possibility of an ongoing, self-renewing, self-discovering asceticism—just as theoreticians, wary of relapsing into a pretheoretical and therefore deluded empiricism, can deny themselves the wealth of riches embedded in what they might regard as the dark prehistory of modernity. My argument here about the survival of asceticism in art and criticism presumes that asceticism is not a transcendental event but an historical constant; it is the most comprehensive name for the ways in which we understand and refashion ourselves, the ways in which we formulate our ideal conceptions while accommodating our all too human needs.

Lastly, I would like to caution against the meliorism that might be thought a natural accompaniment of such universalizing. To see asceticism everywhere, including in the relatively gentle and moderate mode of aesthetic representation, is not to restrict asceticism to gentleness and culture. For if moderate forms of asceticism have any transfiguring function at all, it is because they summon up and borrow from the spectacle and violence of those other, more radical modes of self-overcoming— those documented so lavishly and compellingly in hagiography that the ancient stories are read and repeated even today by people struck with wonder at the principles of human behavior that might be exemplified by such mysterious forms. A disintoxicated asceticism represents a castration of castration, a repression of repression. As scholars, we are repressed enough already; we cannot afford to repress the truth that our repression is supposed to enable us to divine.

Notes

1. Bonaventure, *The Soul's Journey into God* in *Bonaventure*, trans. Ewert Cousins (New York, Ramsey, Toronto: Paulist Press, 1978), pp. 51–116. These quotations are from pp. 55 and 115, respectively.

2. Donald Kuspit, "The Unhappy Consciousness of Modernism," in Ingeborg Hosterey, ed., *Zeitgeist in Babel* (Bloomington: University of Indiana Press, 1988), p. 50.

3. Geoffrey Galt Harpham, *The Ascetic Imperative in Culture and Criticism* (Chicago: University of Chicago Press, 1987).

4. Terry Eagleton, *Criticism and Ideology: A Study in Marxist Literary Theory* (Chicago: University of Chicago Press, 1987).

5. See Peter Brown, *The Body and Society: Men, Women, and Sexual Renunciation in Early Christianity*, Lectures on the History of Religions 13 (New York: Columbia University Press, 1988); and Carolyn Walker Bynum, *Fragmentation and Renunciation: Essays on Gender and the Body in Medieval Religion* (New York: Zone Books, 1991).

6. See Patricia Cox Miller, *Dreams in Late Antiquity: Studies in the Imagination of a Culture* (Princeton: Princeton University Press, 1994).

7. Gregory Collins, "Simeon the New Theologian: An Ascetical Theology for Middle-Byzantine Monks," in Vincent Winbush and Richard Valantasis eds. *Asceticism* (New York: Oxford University Press, 1995), pp. 343–56.

8. Slavoj Zizek, *The Sublime Object of Ideology* (London: Verso, 1991), p. 76 and passim.

9. Jason Berry, *Lead Us Not into Temptation: Catholic Priests and the Sexual Abuse of Children* (New York: Doubleday, 1993).

7

New Baptized: The Culture of Love in America, 1830s to 1950s

RICHARD WIGHTMAN FOX

The Problem of Love in American History and Thought

In recent years historians of the United States have had a lot to say about sexuality, but comparatively little to say about love. They have taken to heart Lionel Trilling's coy comment, in his 1970 volume *Sincerity and Authenticity*, that love is "one of those words . . . best not talked about if they are to retain any force of meaning." Trilling quipped that "other such words are sincerity and authenticity"—ideas he proceeded to explicate historically with his usual insight and grace. He knew it was risky to speak of such grand and slippery notions as sincerity, authenticity, or love, but he knew that avoiding them was even worse, since they are so basic to the history of our culture. I want to suggest some of the ways American historians might examine love as an idea and an experience. Reviewing a long stretch of time, schematically and episodically, I alternate large brush strokes with finer detail. I argue explicitly that studying love historically means analyzing individual experiences of it. And I argue implicitly that historians of love must ponder not just what past writers have said about love, but the full range of phenomena to which the word "love" points, today and yesterday. That is the only way—in this arena of the deepest human feelings, longings, and duties—to be clear about what past writers meant to say when they spoke of love, and to derive what moral illumination we can from their reflections.[1]

Love, this simple, elegant Old English word perfectly shaped for soft whispering in the ear of one's lover, or in prayer to one's God, has carried an unimaginably weighty load of meanings across the expanse of centuries. It has stood valiantly and alone for a daunting string of Greek terms—especially *eros* (love as desire), *agape* (love as sacrifice), *philia* (love as friendship)—that encompass an evolving set of classical, Judaic, and Christian usages. The *Oxford English Dictionary* traces sixteen uses of the noun "love," and eight uses of the verb, going back to the ninth century. If we are to understand ourselves or our ancestors in the slightest degree, we must try to unpack the meanings of this historically encrusted word. This is not only an exercise in etymology. We must try to grasp the powerful personal experiences this word has tried to express, and fathom the social uses to which it has been put. And we must be culturally specific: American love has been distinctively religious as well as secular, a duality that must always be kept in view as it evolves over the centuries.[2]

The problem Trilling faced in studying sincerity and authenticity, he said, is that their scope is "virtually coextensive" with the entire European high culture of the last four centuries. Imagine, then, the problem of love, a term so pivotal and so pliable that it has for many more than four centuries stood at the heart of high-cultural reflection and representation in the West. Not to mention the further problem that it is no longer intellectually defensible to limit ourselves arbitrarily to high-cultural debate. Historically significant cultural production takes place in all corners of society, and the idea and practice of love has been at the center of lived experience through wide swaths of American and European society for at least a couple of centuries.[3]

The problem of studying love is magnified many times over when we realize that love is not only a cross-class experience, but a cross-gender, cross-religious, cross-ethnic, cross-age-group, and cross-regional phenomenon too. Any generalization we make about the "American" experience of love (not to mention the "Western" experience of it) is liable to be unsupportable, an instance of the "higher guesswork" at best. Even if we try to leave the other variables aside and stick to class, the interpretive complexity remains benumbing, for class always ends up interweaving with region, age, ethnicity, religion, and gender. And love has been at the heart of at least two different, overlapping cross-class experiences.

By the nineteenth century working-class populations were picking up genteel tastes in romance (and in Britain, contrary to our retrospective intuition, property-less individuals may have been free to marry "for love" a century or two before that—since their parents had no social position to protect). At the same time, in both America and Britain, a romanticized Christian evangelicalism was bringing a militant "love-talk"—love of God and neighbor as well as proper passion for one's companion—to masses of the previously unchurched. Love spread its intersecting meanings through the American middle class (and through the ranks of those aspiring to *be* middle class) as men and women curled up by the fireside with romantic novels and as they sat on wooden benches entranced by preachers on the stump. The student of American love must take to heart the intermingling of secular romantic and Christian sacrificial loves. "Call me but love," Romeo appealed to Juliet on the balcony, "and I'll be new baptized." Americans have followed his path of sanctifying the secular even while they secularized the sacred. Religiosity and secularity have not been zero-sum combattants in the United States. They have deepened one another's hold.[4]

Doubtless throughout the history of the West eros, agape, and philia have blended into one another in actual life much more than they have in philosophical reflection. But nineteenth-century America may have been an unusual instance of their explosive interpenetration. "Love" took on a distinctively American range of meanings as it was put to use in a northern Protestant culture paradoxically obsessed with both "freedom" and "community"—with liberating individuals from community while at the same time shoring community up. "Love" in its very amplitude suggested a way of bridging liberation and stability, openness and boundedness. It connoted an enduring web of fellowship and nurture, yet signaled a power to lift individuals beyond the routine or the mundane into the sheer transcendence of a lover's or God's embrace. Love was so potent a social and historical force because it promised to do what, on any rational accounting, was impossible: to bolster personal and public order while transporting people beyond the well-worn ruts of cultural expectation.

Love in Industrializing America

Love was, and is, an experience and an idea in the lives of individuals (and the experience itself often comprises ideas—reflections upon love—as well as raw sensations and feelings). Yet love was, and is, a social force standing apart from individuals—an ideology and set of ritual practices that offered legitimacy (but also socially legitimate challenge) to established habits and institutions. Love as a lived experience could be a harmonizer of personal tensions and a mitigator of social conflicts, but it could prompt and justify transgressive assaults on respectable conventions.

By the early nineteenth century Americans of the middle class were putting enormous intellectual and emotional energy into the cultivation of love, a commitment that paralleled their idolization of entrepreneurial callings. The *culture* of love was literally a matter of sowing and reaping, making it grow ("husbandry"). Building up a sphere of protected, "private" love was essential support for the erection of a sphere of territorial expansion and business mastery. In the middle-class United States love was preached as a united state of domestic virtue. By joining individual men and women, love offered tangible evidence that the inevitable brutalities and compromises of the political and economic jungle could be transcended. Liberalism trumped republicanism most completely, perhaps, by getting the so-called "best men" to take politics not as "virtue" (the republicans' view of politics) but as "corruption" (the republicans' view of commerce). Business entrepreneurship could then be seen as at least no worse than politics, and probably better, since it produced the progress that, for all its undeniable inequities, fostered civilization and the wherewithal for more men to improve themselves.[5]

Love was pivotal in this scheme: it could be seen as surpassing not only the morass of the market and the pit of politics, but the transitoriness of history itself. Love was a permanent thing, in the face of which even death, as John Donne famously put it, could not be proud. We get an important clue to the history of a culture when we attend to what that culture considers beyond history. For middle-class Americans in the industrial era, love was beyond history. And for the increasingly pious Protestant-American majority of the nineteenth century, "love" merged with "God" in the realm within and beyond history. The equation of love and God, brought to its fullest development in liberal Protestantism (the informal religious "Establishment" of Victorian America), was a central cultural pillar of the industrial era. Love was a marvelously ideological force because it could camouflage the fact that its promised states of union were always implicated in a system of power and division—a system of male dominance that despite many challenges and adjustments over the entire industrial era has always deserved the name of "patriarchy." But love would not have worked as ideology if it had not been more than ideology. Anyone who has been in love knows that for at least a time love *is* a state of union, and that it seems to point beyond history to a vitality that springs from some deep source, whether biological, cultural, spiritual, or some mixture of all of them. *Omnia vincit amor*, Virgil wrote, *et nos cedamus amori*: love conquers all things, let us too give in to love.

American thinkers, religious and secular, were preoccupied by love in the century of industrialization from the 1830s to the 1920s, and in this obsession they reflected a fixation of the wider culture, as masses of working-class and middle-class Protestants deepened their piety and distinguished themselves from Catholic and Jewish immigrants by stressing their devotion to Jesus as the companionate God of love. Victorian culture in Britain as well as America was marked by a profound commitment to the ideal and practice of love, and in both countries the secular and religious (primarily Protestant) sources of love-talk flowed together in a single stream. But in the United States evangelicalism and secular romanticism interacted potently with a broad cultural allegiance to "freedom"—freedom from traditional customs, and freedom to create an approximation of God's kingdom on earth. One by-product of this distinctively American secular-religious millennialism was the "free love" agitation of the mid-nineteenth century—a movement that petered out by the 1880s but left its traces in the thinking of turn-of-the-century figures such as William James, who continued to struggle with this prototypically American problem of reconciling freedom and community. Love could be grasped as the fundamental tie between the two, although many thinkers knew it was a fragile one. Love was the answer: it brought individual freedom to its highest fulfillment and anchored a community of cooperating selves. Yet love reintroduced the problems it ostensibly solved: it imposed new constraints on individuals and unsettled the communities it was supposed to solidify.

The idea that love is or should be "free," that it is an abundance to be given, is of course a traditional Christian notion. The Calvinists of Puritan America understood *God*'s love as the paradigmatic "free" love—his grace flowed abundantly to whomsoever he chose as its recipient. What a radically democratic doctrine at the heart of the Gospel: God might touch the soul of a woman, or a slave. What a radically undemocratic doctrine at the heart of the Gospel: God does all the deciding. His love is abundant but he is mercurial and often holds it back; one can do nothing to earn it, although those who have it are liable to perform visible good works. Christian thinkers over the centuries came to razor-sharp acuity on the apparent contradictions of freedom, human and divine. One's own efforts to attain salvation were unavailing, one's freedom to do good was seriously impaired by self-seeking and self-delusion, but one was always free to love God, to recognize one's sinfulness and accept a proper relation of obedience, submission, and repentance. However ground down one was by the devil's taunts, God always provided the means for a person to recognize God's sovereign power—the power to give his love freely. God told Satan he could do whatever he wished with Job except lay his hand on him. However dire his situation, Job would always have access to God's ultimate help, the help that persisted even in the face of God's apparent indifference.

The story of early nineteenth-century northern Protestant American culture is perhaps above all the story of rising impatience with the maddening paradox that God's love was free but it wasn't *free*, and of the ultimate breaking of the Puritan frame: the flow of God's love was undammed by upscale Unitarians, downscale Universalists, and circuit-riding Methodists. It was made freely available to all who chose to drink from the brimming divine cup. Yet even when God's love flowed like waters, paradox remained: if divine love was so abundant, its *gift*edness might be obscured, its spontaneity might be lost, freedom in the spirit might come to be a run-of-the-mill state of pious sincerity rather than an at-the-brink condition of raw authenticity. Whence the emergence of revivalistic evangelists such as Charles Grandison Finney who specialized in engineering urgency for those sincere, liberal Christians who sat back sunning themselves in the assumption that God's provision of grace was never in doubt. Whence too the emergence of more radical dissenters, secular and religious, from Henry James, Sr. and Horace Greeley to Stephen Pearl Andrews, John Humphrey Noyes, and Mary Gove Nichols, who noticed the contradiction that love made freely available had become love saddled to sanctimonious bourgeois prescription.

This dissenting spirit pushed deep into mainstream northern Protestant culture in the nineteenth century. Karen Halttunen's 1982 volume *Confidence Men and Painted Women* helps explain why. Nineteenth-century bourgeois culture created its own peculiar tension by trying to codify the self-determined behavior it cherished—behavior that was supposed to be spontaneously self-controlled and therefore could not be codified without severe damage to its essentially free character. Many commentators at the time were conscious of this dynamic, aware of the danger that love—which, to be itself, had to be freely given—would be adulterated by its status as an ideal for solid burghers. Many liberal Protestants followed the religious renegade Ralph Waldo Emerson in calling for authentic selfhood, real love, love freed from enslavement to culture. "Truth is handsomer than the affectation of love," he wrote in "Self-Reliance." "Your goodness must have some edge to it, else it is none. The doctrine of hatred must be preached, as the counteraction of the doctrine of love, when that pules and whines."[6]

Emerson's project, in simple terms, was to seed evangelicalism with romanticism: push beyond the arbitrary limits of bourgeois respectability, secure the radical insights of the Gospel by attacking its domestication by genteel culture. Meanwhile, the cleverest Christian thinkers, preachers such as Horace Bushnell and Henry Ward Beecher, adopted the risky strategy of first welcoming romanticism in order to revivify evangelicalism, and then trying to circumscribe romantic energies by reasserting the moral primacy of Gospel truths. Christian faith propelled itself forward in the nineteenth century by alternating between undamming and redamming the romantic impulse. Historians have recently paid little attention to this crucial American cultural dialectic. They have debated the nineteenth-century fortunes of "republicanism" and "liberalism" without bringing out the romantic and evangelical context in which actual republicans and liberals contended.[7]

"Free Love" in Victorian America

The most radical dissenters on love—the "free-lovers" as they sometimes called themselves, and as they were always labeled by opponents—

emerged in a northern Protestant industrializing culture that could not get enough of freedom. The slogans of the day are relentless: "free labor," "free soil," "free trade," "free grace," "free thought." In a world where individuals defended themselves against what they considered arbitrary communal authority, it was natural for some reformers to question the shape of marriage, the subordination of women, the constriction of feeling. Why should the state rule over family formation, or men rule over women, or the community impose conformity on individuals? In the 1850s free-love ideas prompted many respectable citizens, such as Henry James, Sr., to push for divorce reform: marriage would be strengthened if poor matches could be annulled, if marriage could be made safe for true love. But more uncompromising reformers, those we typically term "utopians," men and women such as John Humphrey Noyes, Stephen Pearl Andrews, and Mary Gove Nichols, asked deeper questions about love and freedom.

In its essence, they believed, love was free, spontaneous, uncoerced. Love allowed the free individual to attain a fullness of freedom by overcoming isolation, uniting with another to form a bond of mutuality. But that interpenetration of two selves also posed a prospective threat to a person's autonomy, a threat resistible only so long as the connection remained voluntary. Individuals, like states, needed the right of secession, the right to declare independence. Government regulation of love through the marriage contract was a direct assault upon love, not because it gave husbands property rights in their wives (an outrage in its own right) but because it constrained the freedom of husbands and wives alike to embrace a new "affinity." Marital and divorce reform—giving women equal property rights and easing divorce requirements—might be necessary, but they also made matters worse by diverting attention from the real issue: getting the state out of the business of sanctioning relationships of love in the first place. The goals and assumptions of these mid-nineteenth-century free-lovers were various: some, like Stephen Pearl Andrews, were anarchists enamored of the idea of individual sovereignty, and others, like John Humphrey Noyes, were collectivists devoted to overcoming merely individualist passions and jealousies. But all of them agreed that legal controls should go and that individuals had to be free to form and dissolve love relationships as they saw fit. All of them shared a zeal to broadcast the essential freedom of love in the face of a bourgeois society that left love, they thought, everywhere in chains.

John Humphrey Noyes, graduate of Yale Divinity School and the founder and patriarch of the Oneida community from the 1830s to the 1870s, was especially inventive in confronting those issues. Here is a man who believed, in the face of a brick wall of cultural opposition to his views, that mature adults benefited from multiple intimate relationships with persons of the opposite sex. Orthodox marriage was therefore out of the question. The romantic, companionate nineteenth-century form of marriage was an advance over earlier practices in its emphasis on spiritual and physical intimacy, but it too was objectionable, since it arbitrarily limited the intimate life to the spousal pair. The spirit of love blew where it may; one could never rule out future affinities.

But human nature presented a deep obstacle to fruitful intimacy, according to Noyes, even when marriage was avoided: individuals were prone to imperial possessiveness, on the one hand, and submissive surrender on the other. They were liable either to infringe upon the freedom of the loved one or, conversely, to give up their own freedom to a possessive lover. At Oneida Noyes developed what he called "free love," and later "universal love" or "complex marriage," to solve this problem. Individuals would have multiple intimates: no one was permitted to pair off into an exclusive relationship. Sexual relations were multiple too, but the sex was strictly monitored by Noyes and his close associates, who included his sister and other female leaders. Men were required to practice *coitus reservatus*, sex without orgasm, except in those few cases designated for reproduction; women, by contrast, were permitted, and encouraged by their lovers, to achieve climax. The point of all this sexual management was not just to control conception, but to ensure that while intimate, soulful ties were cultivated, jealousy and possessiveness were blocked. The goal was stable union with the community and with God, not the chimera of passionate union with a single true lover—the kind of union that in Noyes's view destroyed individual autonomy along with community solidarity. Love was a united state, but on the model of the United States of America: love was a federation of independent selves accepting some limits on their sovereignty for the purpose of greater freedom. Individual selfhood was revitalized by a plurality of intimate friendships, and it was protected against the romantic self-aggrandizement or self-erasure that accompanied passionate attachment.

Of course there was some majestic sleight-of-hand going on here, since individual freedom was being protected by taking it from individuals and giving it to John Humphrey Noyes and his central committee. Individual freedom was so precious that it could not be left to individuals. Noyes shared with the social conservatives of his day a profound belief in the power of unruly passion to destroy social order, and he shared with them an implicit understanding that freedom required self-discipline, including physical and spiritual continence. Conservatives and liberals and anarchists all agreed on this overriding need for the protection, indeed the hoarding, of vital resources; they disagreed on how far individuals could be trusted to acquire self-discipline on their own. This basic nineteenth-century consensus on promoting internalized self-control is hard for us to fathom, since we associate the idea of freedom with images of release and abandon rather than restraint and control. Nineteenth-century reformers, whether anarchists like Stephen Pearl Andrews and Mary Nichols, collectivists like Noyes, or liberals like *New York Tribune* editor Horace Greeley, were trying to ground social order in the voluntary self-limiting of individuals rather than the discredited communal controls of the unenlightened past.

What is so interesting about Noyes is his impatience with the liberal faith in the beneficence of individual desire, individual growth, individual self-possession. He laughed off Fourierist proposals for "associated" living offered by liberals such as Greeley, according to which monogamous couples would live in close proximity to other couples, sharing food preparation and other chores as well as social intercourse. In the absence of a rigid collective discipline, Noyes believed, this free social intercourse would certainly lead to adultery, hypocrisy, and family destruction. As a student of the Bible he believed that individuals were self-enlarging, liable to extinguish the freedom of others in their quest to magnify themselves. The collectivist Noyes concurred with conservatives in bewailing the excesses of liberal individualism; indeed, he surpassed many conservatives in his readiness to rule by patriarchal fiat. But he diverged from them in his belief that a new social order was ready to be born—one in which the pleasure and vitality of multiple intimacies was obtained by building a collective shield against possessiveness. Free love was disciplined, ordered, bounded love; it depended upon an elaborate defense against the false freedom of unbridled passion.[8]

The Civil War put an end to the much publicized free-love idealism of the 1840s and 1850s. The Oneida community limped into the postwar era and closed down for good in 1879. Stephen Pearl Andrews, the one remaining militant activist from the 1850s, soldiered on by attaching himself to radical free-lover Victoria Woodhull's retinue. But the public discussion of free love was dominated by the career-making rhetoric of conservative reformer Anthony Comstock, who rose to prominence, as historian Taylor Stoehr has put it, by kicking the dead horse of free love back to life. Free love was transformed, thanks to the symbiotic grandstanding of Comstock and Woodhull, from a small but voluble antebellum movement for social transformation into a free-speech issue—a shift that allows us to account for the arrival in the public eye of the astonishing Emma Goldman at the turn of the century. The media called her first "the anarchist queen" and later "Red Emma," and she pushed the free-speech issue as much as she did free love as such. But she also had much to say, sometimes in public, but mostly in her countless letters, about the conundrums of love and freedom. Like Noyes, Goldman made an original contribution in thinking through the complexities of love, freedom, and community. She was unusual in her clarity, but typical of a wide swath of American opinion—Jewish and Christian, religious and secular—in her insistence that love is the key to personal and social fulfillment.[9]

Goldman emigrated from Russia as a 16-year-old in 1885, and after the hanging of the Haymarket martyrs in 1887 she attached herself to the anarchist cause and joined Alexander Bergman's entourage in New York—just in time to help him plan the quixotic assassination attempt on Henry Clay Frick, chairman of Carnegie Steel, at Homestead in 1892. After that debacle she labored for another 25 years in the anarchist movement before being deported to Russia by Attorney General A. Mitchell Palmer in 1919. Historians have long noted Goldman's role in American political and labor history, but it was not until feminists of the last generation rediscovered her that her experience of (and thinking about) love came fully to light.

Goldman harks back to the anarchist free-lovers of the 1850s in her blanket indictment of modern society for trampling on the rights of individuals. The state has no business policing personal life. Freedom will only be realized when the government leaves individuals alone and when the wider culture respects individual differences. But Goldman's militant cultural libertarianism—her defense of what we might call "negative" or "laissez-faire" freedom—was joined to two other basic ideas. First, she held that individuals were free only when they passed from the freedom of being left alone to the freedom of mutuality—either the solidarity of a group of producers or the union of a pair of lovers. And second, she believed that women were especially at risk in this quest for (what we might call) "positive" freedom, since the men with whom most of them wished to become united were stuck in a pattern of primitively possessive yearning. Goldman is strikingly contemporary in her self-consciousness about the quandaries of women seeking freedom in love, and in her overall conviction that there can be no genuine freedom in love when women are not equal to men in other domains. Yet she was decidedly Victorian in her quest for romantic union with a man, for the high and passionate drama of a love that was always spiritually as well as sexually intimate.

Her intense relationship in the 1900s and 1910s with Ben Reitman, Chicago's famous Hobo Doctor, presented complexities in experience that played havoc with the consistency of thought that she publicly championed. Being in love with Reitman was a quest for union that lay always beyond reach. "You are like anarchism to me," she wrote to him, "the more I struggle for it, the further away it gets." In principle she knew that love was true only if it was freely given and received. Either partner should therefore be free to pull out at any time, to pursue love with whomever he or she chose. Yet she craved Reitman's undivided attention, and longed for it all the more whenever he did pursue another love, which was often. She came to feel that love was freest, "highest," when supported by a free choice to renounce other loves. That renunciation was paradoxically an integral component of love's freedom. Reitman was incapable of such renunciation, a fact that drove Goldman to distraction but threw her all the more at his mercy. She saw herself as the sincere civilizing mother taming the authentic wild young man (he was ten years her junior), and therefore found his free, untamed sexuality irresistible even as she condemned it. "Love stands over me," she wrote, "like a mighty spectre, and . . . has both life and death for me. . . . I have no right to speak of freedom when I myself have become an abject slave in my love." She had literally *fallen* in love: love was now free only in the sense that it was having its own unobstructed way with her. She was tossed about by her passions, out of control and miserable, drawn inexorably to love's enlivening yet destructive force. Love, she wrote, "is robbing me of all my well ordered ideas and ideals."

Goldman was in such deep turmoil because she had come to see that to be free, the passion between two lovers required the mutual, voluntary renunciation of other loves. Yet in her own life with Reitman, the renunciation came only from her, and even her renunciation was partially vitiated, in her view, since it was not so much voluntary as culturally induced. Having as a woman been programmed by culture to adopt the renunciatory position, she was undermined as a free individual from the start. The free love she preached was unrealizable by her. That awareness caused her to careen into a self-destructive attraction to Reitman's wildness, the only "freedom" uncontrolled enough to compensate for her own imposed renunciation. Goldman came to see this endlessly recurring personal struggle as a sign of the social dislocation in the larger world, but unlike Noyes she never saw it as evidence of a universal dislocation within the human spirit. Her own experience was "tragic," she believed, but she remained a thoroughgoing progressive: human experience was not tragic at its core. She traced her own "dramatic emotional swings" to her capacity to feel "the terrible agony of the human family," whose psychic pains and brutal circumstances could be overcome once governments and ruling classes ceased their suppressions and exploitations. She thought her own pain was social in origin, not psychological alone. She disparaged Freud, who in her view had missed the real source of psychic distress: irrational social configurations. Love was blocked institutionally and historically, not individually and for all time.[10]

Goldman's experience with Reitman made her throw herself all the more into political work—as an escape from all the personal turmoil, but also as a way of putting the turmoil in perspective. Since there was no line of division between the personal and political, the political might save her from the personal. She could look at politics as a means of salvation from the disappointments of personal love, because like the other anarchists and socialists around her she could still imagine politics as a terrain for love, love of "the people." For Goldman the personal and the political were always interlaced and mutually permeable realms of opportunity; love was never confined to the personal arena. She saw her life as full of pain and unhappiness, but she did not give up on the quest for love as a higher state—a state of union with a lover and a state of fellowship with other free individuals.

The free-lovers of the nineteenth century, people like John Humphrey Noyes and Emma Goldman, spoke incessantly of freedom, and spent their lives building new institutions for the practice of love (like Noyes) or attacking laws and social conventions that put arbitrary limits on love (like Goldman). But they were not advocates of boundless release. They were sure that free love depended upon freely accepted constraints. Free love was bounded love, freest when most certain of its limits. John Humphrey Noyes's free love depended on the geographical boundedness of his Oneida Community, and on the elaborate regulations that governed life inside its perimeter. Emma Goldman's free love was circumscribed by the obligations and dependencies that grew up in each of her love relations—obligations and dependencies that she could escape for a time in political work, where her love broadened to encompass "the people." Noyes was more conscious of the tragic limits to freedom within human nature itself, Goldman more aware of the gendered social and social-psychological barriers that warped desire and wracked love. The most striking thing about them both is that their realism about obstacles only strengthened their craving for a transformation of individual and social life. Goldman was especially remarkable. Noyes was used to getting his way in the world, through charisma and male privilege; he could keep faith in blazing a path through the forest of convention because he was in command, at least among his own followers. Goldman suffered one disappointment after another in love and politics, and believed she had been dealt an unequal hand when she was born female. Yet as she trudged from one cheap hotel to the next on her lonely lecture tours, writing a dozen letters or so each evening before retiring, she kept voicing her faith in bridging freedom and community through love—a big, romantic, harmonizing love, love as sexual and spiritual higher union, the kind of love lost increasingly to experience and aspiration, if not to nostalgia, by the 1920s.[11]

William and Henry James on Love

The work of the James brothers at the end of the nineteenth century is a telling indicator of the lingering but waning power of the grand ideal of love. Each of the brothers sensed the ideal was dying, and sought to bury the dying version and to revive a vital one—in art or in thought if not precisely in lived experience. Neither of them could countenance the kind of rhapsodic love talk that animated their father, Henry Senior, as it did Noyes and Goldman and a whole succession of thinkers and activists stretched out across the century. William assailed all "tenderminded" proclamations about the power of love and reason to remake the world, while Henry cast a derisive eye on the moralizing fictions of sentimental authors and their high-mindedly respectable critics. Yet both William and Henry, formed by their father's worldview even as they were repelled by it, thought the "toughminded" "naturalists" (or "materialists" or "empiricists") were as bad as their "intellectualist" and "rationalist" opponents. In search of a middle ground, of what William called the "ideally real," they could not avoid putting love at the heart of their work.[12]

And in the conceptually harmonizing practice of the "pragmatism" that William developed and to which Henry, as he put it, "unconsciously" subscribed—a pragmatism that systematically dismantled such dualisms as subjectivity and objectivity, reason and imagination, the factual and the moral—the brothers challenged the impulse of philosophers and theologians to separate "eros" from "agape." Eros was traditionally seen as desire, self-gratification, possession, while agape was viewed as the renunciation of desire, self-denial, sacrificial subordination of the self to others. Those fascinated, like the Jameses, with the lived experience of love had a hard time distinguishing eros from agape, or even from "philia" (friendship). Of course they granted that there were differences between eros and agape, most obviously because eros is often a sexual desire, and agape is not. And the intimacy of philia is cooler, more even-tempered in its steady amiability than either eros or agape, both of which tend toward a high pitch of passion. But the Jameses, reflecting on the concrete phenomenon of love, framed eros in a way that returns it to the orbit of agape and philia. Love was unitary. Whether it was eros, agape, or philia, the experience of love contained a fierce wonder at the blessed reality of some other being or group of beings—a lover, a God, a child or parent, a friend, perhaps a stranger. Eros implies a romantic aspiration or attachment, agape implies a sacrificial obedience, philia implies a friendship of mutual support, but all three express a devotion to some cherished other, and imply a celebration of the whole created world—a world that exhibits a stunning array of such enthralling others.

In his 1898 essay "What Makes a Life Significant," William James gave memorable voice to this intense wonder beating at the heart of love, whether it is love as eros, agape, or philia. Love is a marveling at the irreplaceable, exuberant reality of other lives. James is intrigued by the limits we blindly place upon this love, our habit of focussing our passionate energies on a particular person to the exclusion of everyone else. If the big question for a contemporary liberal pluralist like Richard Rorty is "how wide the circle of the 'we,'" of those who prompt us to fellow feeling, the big question for the more romantic, turn-of-the-century liberal pluralist William James was in effect "how wide the circle of the beloved, of those who will prompt us to passionate wonder."

"Every Jack," James writes in "What Makes a Life Significant," "sees in his own particular Jill charms and perfections to the enchantment of which we stolid onlookers are stone-cold."

> Which has the more vital insight into the nature of Jill's existence[, he or we]? Is he in excess, being in this matter a maniac? Or are we in defect, being victims of a pathological anesthesia as regards Jill's magical importance? . . . Surely to Jack are the profounder truths revealed; surely poor Jill's palpitating little life-throbs *are* among the wonders of creation, *are* worthy of this sympathetic interest; and it is to our shame that the rest of us cannot feel like Jack. . . . He struggles toward a union with her inner life, divining her feelings, anticipating her desires, understanding her limits. . . . whilst we, dead clods that we are, do not even seek after these things, but are contented that that portion of eternal fact named Jill should be for us as if it were not. Jill, who knows her inner life, knows that Jack's way of taking it—so importantly—is the true and serious way; and she responds to the truth in him by taking him truly and seriously, too. . . . Where would any of *us* be, were there no one willing to know us as we really are or ready to repay us for *our* insight by making recognizant return?

But James is not going to limit this united state of love to a single pair of intimates. "We ought all of us to realize each other in this intense . . . and important way. If you say that this is absurd, and that we cannot be in love with everyone at once, I merely point out to you that, as a matter of fact, certain persons do exist with an enormous capacity for friendship and for taking delight in other people's lives; and that such persons know more of truth than if their hearts were not so big." Read one way, James retreats here from eros to philia: having raised the prospect of *love* for "everyone at once," he pulls back to the safer ground of multiple *friendships*. But read another way, he is suggesting that love and friendship are continuous, and that the passionate life consists in the making of pleasurable, intimate connections to more and more of the people around us.[13]

William James would scarcely have chosen the term "free love" to describe his views, since a century ago the phrase connoted to most people, as it still does, an endorsement of promiscuity. But his plea for extending the vitality of love to many significant others bears a certain kinship to the free-love doctrines of the mid-nineteenth century. For the free-lovers love was a fulfillment and a threat: it supplied images of a freedom as yet unachieved, or unimagined, but it meant joining oneself to another, or to a group, a joining that might well curtail one's freedom. William James coped with these tensions by conceiving of love as a state of union but not of stasis. Love was the passion, the heightened feeling, available to people who reveled in the plural universe of particular beloved others. It was observational—preserving distance and autonomy—but it was intimate: a spark of affection leapt across the distance and ignited a mutual knowing. Freedom and community: William James was still, at the end of the century, deliberating about the fundamental Protestant middle-class dilemma that disturbed and challenged his father's generation. But he had given up the metaphysical assurances that Henry Senior had found indispensable, assurances that both of his famous sons now judged irredeemably tender-minded.

Henry, Jr. may well have thought, however, that his brother William's perspective on love was too complacent regarding the power of thought to encompass the experience of love. Despite all his talk of love as the passionate wonder we feel at the vital existence of concrete others, William the philosopher was reaching for a universal contemplative standpoint from which love could be grasped. From Henry's vantage point, such intellectual satisfaction came at the cost of smoothing out the tensions that proliferate in actual as opposed to theorized states of love. For Henry James, as for Noyes or Goldman, love is inevitably an individuated experience—an experience modulated by age, gender, class, region, historical moment, and many other variables, including the intrusion of contingent, one-time events. The intensity of love's pain and joy, obvious to everyone at one time or another in their actual lives, may be impossible to render in the generalizing reflections of the philosopher, even a philosopher as literary and evocative and pluralistic as William James. He talked about particularity, but he did not do enough to particularize his own viewpoint.

Henry's fiction may do a better job than William's essays at communicating these fundamental facts of individuation and contingency—a contingency that extends even to the standpoint of the writer himself. Henry gives us characters like Isabel Archer in *Portrait of a Lady*, Olive Chancellor in *The Bostonians*, and Lambert Strether in *The Ambassadors* who cannot rise above the trajectory of their particular moral circumstances to a position of contemplative distance. They remain, like Emma Goldman, lodged in loves of decisive and devastating particularity, in which eros, agape, and philia not only intersect, but collide and career out of control. Strether, Chancellor, and Archer know not what they do as love or desire take possession of them—until they awaken finally, and partially, to their delusions. James's narrative voice does appear at first to offer the

deliverance of distance, of a perspective universal and detached, but especially in his late fiction he closes off that escape route by implicating the
narrative voice in the historically contingent world of his characters. Like
William he is a moral analyst of love in relation to freedom, but he suggests in effect that William's vision is limited by an uncritical faith in our
ability to transcend our circumstances in actual life, as opposed to art.

It is in fiction that Henry transcends those circumstances in language
of breathtaking beauty as well as intricacy. Here is Henry on one kind of
love in *The Ambassadors*, in a passage on Lambert Strether's rendezvous
with his new friend Maria Gostrey: "He was extraordinarily glad to see
her, expressing to her frankly what she most showed him, that one might
live for years without a blessing unsuspected, but that to know it at last
for no more than three days was to need it or miss it for ever. She was the
blessing that had now become his need." "Expressing to her frankly what
she most showed him"—James tells us of the unity between them by
building it into the sentence structure, effecting a tender rhetorical equation between *his* expression and *her* showing. Then he extends the con-
course between them into the sheer music that follows, a rhythm marked
by the beautiful inversion of word order: the "blessing unsuspected."
Henry James may be a more thoroughgoing pragmatist than his brother
in tracing the *meaning* of love to the actual experience of it. We always
think about love, according to Henry, from a position of immersion in it.
Love exists in thought as well as action, but it is always embodied in
webs of power, influence, and desire among actual persons. For Henry
James, what we talk about when we talk about love is people's real lives.[14]

Henry James's standpoint resembles John Humphrey Noyes's in its
attentiveness to the contradictions between freedom and love. Embracing love means embracing submission or deception (including self-
deception), with all the tragic consequences that may entail for an Archer, a Chancellor, or a Strether. William James continues to aspire to a
love beyond submission. His famous "will to believe" takes him beyond
his brother's tragic sensibility in the realm of love. The admittedly abstract free love he proposes rejects the metaphor of submission. James
was as upset by images of self-surrender as his contemporary Friedrich
Nietzsche was. But James's idea of love does depend on the metaphor of
gifting. The essence of Jack's and Jill's love, according to James, is the
gift of their knowing, a gift they bestow effortlessly, freely. They give
nothing up; every act of giving brings reciprocal return, and each lover is
refreshed. Each lover lingers in wonder at the magical reality of the other.
Each sees the other truly, so each is delivered from the impossible burden
of knowing himself *by* himself. Each gets to be herself in the extended act
of being known. And for James, in his gesture of solidarity with nine-

teenth-century free-love doctrine, this life of passionate knowing was open-endedly possible. It could, indeed it should, carry a person into a multiplicity of loves and friendships.

Love for Goldman and Noyes and the James brothers was always free and bounded, open-ended and limited, in varying degrees and proportions, according to their divergent viewpoints and to the many slippages inherent in the terms "free" and "bounded." What united all of these Victorian thinkers and lovers was their sense of the intense passion of love, the overwhelming gratitude the lover felt at the very existence of another being, or of other beings, or, as Jonathan Edwards put it a century and a half before the Jameses, of "being-in-general." For Edwards, "true virtue" consisted in gratitude for "being-in-general," for the gift of life that promised not happiness, but a bounded love between self and Creator. William James pointed repeatedly to Walt Whitman's nineteenth-century secularization of Edwards's worship of being-in-general. Whitman's poem "Crossing Brooklyn Ferry," which James quotes at length in his essay "On a Certain Blindness in Human Beings," is one of the most exquisite expressions of Whitman's love of being-in-general. Whitman is crossing the sun-splashed East River and he experiences a flood-tide of connections, not just with "crowds of men and women attired in the usual costumes," but with those who will pass here "fifty years hence," "a hundred years hence, or ever so many hundred years hence," who "will enjoy the sunset, the pouring in of the flood-tide, the falling back to the sea of the ebb-tide."

> It avails not, neither time or place—distance avails not.
> Just as you feel when you look on the river and sky, so I felt;
> Just as any of you is one of a living crowd, I was one of a crowd:
> Just as you are refresh'd by the gladness of the river and the bright
>   flow, I was refresh'd; . . .
> I too, many and many a time cross'd the river, the sun half an hour
>   high;
> I watched the twelfth-month sea-gulls—I saw them high in the air,
>   with motionless wings, oscillating their bodies,
> I saw how the glistening yellow lit up parts of their bodies, and left the
>   rest in strong shadow,
> I saw the slow-wheeling circles, and the gradual edging toward the
>   south . . .
> These, and all else, were to me the same as they are to you.

Whitman seems to mean this literally: "these were to me the same as they are to you." There is one experience, only, of these things. This is the united state of love for Whitman, this passionate wonder in the full spectrum of created things. We can all feel the same flood-tide of desire and satisfaction at the rushing human drama, especially as it is embodied in those beings, thousands upon thousands of them if we are Whitman, with whom we are in love.[15]

The Twentieth-Century Assault on Harmonizing Love

Henry James's second thoughts about the romantic ideal of love as a united state—about Whitman's and his brother William's vision—had much in common with the tragic sense of human limitations that became widespread among American intellectuals by the mid-1920s. The romantic ideals that had still animated the radicalism of Greenwich Village in the early 1910s—when Emma Goldman rubbed shoulders with Max Eastman, Floyd Dell, and John Reed—gave way to widespread scoffing about the social or personal viability of life-transforming romantic union. We tend to associate this waning faith in grand, harmonizing love with such secular anti-bourgeois whistle-blowers as H. L. Mencken, Sinclair Lewis, Margaret Mead, or Robert and Helen Lynd. They built on late nineteenth-century assaults on sentimentalism offered by naturalist writers, and instructed Americans to stop being saps about highfalutin ideals in a world controlled by behind-the-scenes powers—from the sex drive itself to the hard-boiled politicians or businessmen who actually got things done.[16]

But religious thinkers also had a great deal to do with discrediting the romantic aspiration to the perfect privacy of virtuous love. They were indispensable to the work of undermining the nineteenth-century bourgeois system, in which freedom and community were bridged, in part, by the doctrine and experience of unifying love. Just as historians need to pay more attention to the religious and not just the secular meanings of love in the era of bourgeois infatuation with it, so they need to examine the religious as well as secular forces that put love, in the twentieth century, in a far more circumscribed cultural place.

Joseph Wood Krutch's *The Modern Temper* (1929) is the classic secular statement on the fate of love in the twentieth century. According to him, love was "exposed" by the moderns, who ripped away the elegant draperies with which the Victorians had rightly shrouded it. Modern Americans imagined love could be delivered from the oppressive weight of dialectical niceties: the boundedness of free love, the tragic potential of all high aspiration. Krutch lamented the loss of love as the high romantic ideal for which individuals would willingly sacrifice themselves. Just as the heights and depths of Elizabethan tragedy made no sense in the modern era, the dramatic passions of self-transforming love could no longer be cultivated or even grasped in an emotional world "freed" from the supposed inhibitions and obfuscations of Victorian society. Modern Americans were "in despair," he wrote, "because, though [they] are more completely absorbed in the pursuit of love than in anything else, [they have] lost the sense of any ultimate importance inherent in the experience. . . . Love is becoming gradually so accessible, so unmysterious, so free that its value is trivial. . . . Many other things we have [also] come to doubt—patriotism, self-sacrifice, respectability, honor—but in the general wreck the wreck of love is conspicuous." Cultural authority now passed to those writers who adopted the posture of exposing unpleasant realities. There was purity now in the stance of detachment from community, autonomy both from the corrupt dealings of the world and the false promises of idealized deliverance from it.[17]

Late nineteenth-century secular and liberal Protestant apostles of love had already understood their role to be that of critics of phony middle-class love-talk. Trying to free love from the old cultural bounds of Calvinism, they were also attentive to the new chains imposed on love by bourgeois complacency. Victoria Woodhull was the most sensational of the secular critics, so sensational in her outlandish attacks on marriage in the 1870s (all in the name of love) that she was hounded out of the public arena. The more mainstream liberal Protestants also beheld a new cultural threat closing in on love, and they took two basic tacks in resisting it: the Social Gospel associated with names like Washington Gladden and Walter Rauschenbusch, and the gospel of personal transformation linked especially to the name Henry Ward Beecher. But individual liberals stood astride both camps. Rauschenbusch pushed personal piety as much as social justice. Beecher and other opponents of social meddling nevertheless held that the law of love could eventually, through an accumulation of individual conversions, suffuse the whole society. Love for the liberal Protestants was an irresistible power in public as well as personal life. For the most romantic preachers like Beecher, there could be no separation between public and private spheres. The wider social world as well as the domestic arena was poised for takeover by love.[18]

One might think that twentieth-century Protestant thinkers would have shared Krutch's (admittedly nostalgic) yearning for a world that put love at the center of things, but the greatest American Protestant thinker of them all, Reinhold Niebuhr, was in fact one of those "moderns" for whom "love" needed to be exposed—as the ideological workhorse of foolish and flighty sentimentalists who whistled of love while the industrial world burned first in pitched class warfare and then in mechanized international savagery. These liberal dreamers could not grasp the perennial place of power in human affairs because they thought love was itself the power to trump all others. Love for them was also a final state of harmony that would render calculations of justice superfluous. Love was dangerous, Niebuhr thought, because it was more liable to lead people astray by offering the chimera of passionate union than it was to prompt them to self-denying generosity.[19]

Early in his career, Reinhold Niebuhr was himself a liberal missionary of love—he understood God's love as a personal force transforming selves, and a social force harmonizing relations among the classes. But international and domestic events of the 1920s turned him against love-talk. Like many secular cultural critics of the 1920s, he could not condemn "sentimentality" often or harshly enough. He was revolted by what he considered his liberal Protestant forbears' adherence to mere ideals, their evasion of realities. William James's middle-ground formulation, in which one sought out the indispensable vitality of the "ideally real," now struck Niebuhr as hopelessly tender-minded in its own right. He was so determined to discredit vacuous hopes for social peace through love, good will, education, and scientific advance, so attached to the tough-minded use of power to promote justice, that he either had to banish love-talk altogether, or relocate it outside the path of real social advance. He made the latter choice: love became the "impossible possibility," a behind-the-scenes if ever-hovering ethical standard by which human efforts to do good were found wanting, but by which human beings were also prophetically challenged to seek justice.

What was gained in Niebuhr's formulation was a dialectical view of love that brought judgment back into relation with goodness, and hence a so-called "neo-orthodox" view of God as a sovereign power, not just a loving companion. God removed himself to a transcendent sphere from which he lambasted his creatures even as he forgave them their failings. This vision of love in relation to justice—true love, the self-sacrificial agape of Jesus, is located beyond everyday human life, but it sparks people to labor for justice—had enormous influence in liberal Protestant culture beginning in the late 1920s. But what was lost in Niebuhr's formulation was the sense that love—either the love of God, of neighbor, or of one's lover—was an intense emotional engagement. The idea of love still had real social and political weight as a principle of judgment and a goad to action, but love was no longer the "religious affection," as Jonathan Edwards had called it, that filled the heart "in very high degree."[20]

Niebuhr did in his later work find a place for what he called "mutual love" (philia) in the life of society. But he never developed the notion of love as social *and* personal transformation, the still evangelical view that Walter Rauschenbusch had espoused in the Progressive period: love as ethical ardor joined to intense feeling. Religious feelings for the modernist Niebuhr were as bad as ideals; they were too often paper-thin, merely intentional, lacking the tough substance of action. By the 1920s Niebuhr regarded talk of growth in personal love as smug self-indulgence at a time of social crisis. Niebuhr's onslaught against liberal Protestant love-talk was a decisive contribution to the 1920s assault on Victorian love-romanticism that Joseph Wood Krutch announced, and denounced, in *The Modern Temper*.

Niebuhr's scoffing at Victorian Protestant love-talk resembles earlier attacks on Noyes or Goldman, who were also dismissed for being sentimental, utopian, preoccupied with personal growth, ignoring the limits around human striving. But the love advocates, I have argued, knew a good deal about limits. A more compelling critique than Niebuhr's of secular and religious love boosters came from writers who agreed with the Noyes and Goldmans, the Beechers and Rauschenbusches, that the good life *was* the life of love—of deepening personal intimacy and passion—but who followed Krutch in arguing that contemporary secular and religious practices of love were irretrievably *un*intimate, *un*passionate. H. Richard Niebuhr, Reinhold's younger brother, and Dorothy Day, leader of the Catholic Worker movement, are good examples of thinkers who were fed up with liberal love-talk not because it substituted ideals for realities, not because it diverted people from serious matters into a self-absorbed quest for heightened feeling—the reasons Reinhold Niebuhr objected to it—but because it failed to deliver on its promise of high ideals and heightened feeling. It didn't deliver passion. Like Joseph Wood Krutch, they wanted love to be big, a quest for an intense union. Liberal culture had abandoned such quests, they concluded, and they turned to Christian orthodoxy for an alternative path to them.

It is easy to miss the originality of their course by calling it, correctly, a return to tradition in religion, or a rejection of liberalism in politics. It is more revealing to see their work as a cultural campaign to rekindle passion and to free love from its dependence on the modern, humanistic understanding of freedom. In *The Kingdom of God in America* (1937), Richard Niebuhr noted that it was the "*humanism*" of the liberals' faith that distinguished them from their evangelical forbears and opponents. Human standards, not God's own mysterious ways, were the liberals' final seat of authority. If original sin or infant damnation or the substitutionary atonement made no human sense, they could be jettisoned. Conversely, if selfless goodness was the highest human virtue, then it was the highest divine virtue too. The liberals, in Niebuhr's view, made the mistake of "defining love of neighbor as the essence of Christianity, as though men could practice this love without . . . apprehension of the divine sovereignty or without revolutionary change from natural to divine affection." They then further erred by "confusing love with amiable sentiment."[21]

Richard Niebuhr gets to the heart of the liberal Protestant mindset by emphasizing not, as Reinhold did, its well-meaning campaign for future human fellowship, for what it called the Kingdom of God on Earth, but its perennial insistence on human standards. By conceiving of God as their loving, not their sovereign Father, liberals reconceived love as the fluid medium in which divine and human differences were largely overcome. From the liberals' point of view it made no sense to speak of separation between God and humanity. They would certainly concede to Niebuhr that the divine was higher and the human was lower, but there was one fluid spectrum, one warm bath of spirit. God was love and love was God. *Love* was sovereign, human and divine. From Richard Niebuhr's point of view, the liberals had given up the whole game by putting human and divine realities on a single continuum. Human love had become the standard for judging divine love, and as a consequence the full scope and intensity of the human drama had been surrendered.

In a talk he gave in 1958 on Jonathan Edwards, one of his theological heroes, Richard Niebuhr pointed out that the old liberal objection to Edwards—that he demeaned humanity by making God large and humanity small—could be turned against the liberals: "what Edwards knew," he wrote, ". . . was that man was made to stand in the presence of eternal, unending absolute glory, to . . . rejoice in the service of the stupendous artist who flung universes of stars on his canvas, sculptured the forms of angelic powers, etched with loving care miniature worlds within worlds. . . . Man who had been made to be great in the service of greatness, had made himself small by refusing the loving service of the only Great One; and in his smallness he had become . . . covetous of the pleasures that would soon be taken from him."

Ironically, Niebuhr noted, twentieth-century catastrophes had led many people to question old liberal certainties about the goodness of humanity, yet newfound doubts about human prospects did not make people any more receptive to Edwards's overall framework. The stumbling block was no longer so much his idea of hell, of human aspirations coming to grief: that was all too plausible for mid-century Americans obsessed with the threat of nuclear destruction. What they really couldn't stand, according to Niebuhr, was Edwards's view of the power of God's love and the severe boundedness of human freedom. The twentieth-century American God, Niebuhr wrote, "is someone we . . . use for solving our personal problems, for assuring us that we are beloved." This God was a human construct. Edwards's God was "eternal, immortal, invisible." He was a God of "holy love" with "the power that can set us free to be free indeed"—free, indeed, Niebuhr argued, of the American assumption that we are most free when pursuing our self-interest.

Americans had it backwards: they thought freedom was about choosing who they would be, and in their freedom to choose they picked a convenient religion with a God of sweet love. But they did not truly love

their *God*, they loved themselves. They were not "free to love God" because they were "bound to love" themselves even in religion. Real freedom was not a condition that preceded the choice of who you wished to
be; it was a state that followed the recognition of who you really were. It
followed upon the acceptance of your relation to your Creator, who had
etched you into life with loving care. In Niebuhr's view, Edwards pointed
the way toward liberating love from its cultural captivity to a warped
notion of human freedom. Love at its most profound was not the outcome of a free search, but the gift of the holy lover who at his own
pleasure gave a person life and held a person in being. The boundaries
around that love were firm and unyielding, but they encompassed a vast
territory for experiencing the travails of life and the joy and celebration
that accompanied repentance.[22]

Niebuhr's contemporary Dorothy Day came from an American back-
ground as different from his as one could imagine—he grew up in
church, a cleric's son in the midwestern cornbelt and a diligent teenage
seminarian and then minister; she grew up an urban agnostic, and gravi-
tated to the experimental life in Greenwich Village by the time she was
20. Day actually tasted the life of avant-garde American freedom and
found it unpalatable—not only the ideology of economic freedom, which
she bashed along with her radical friends around *The Masses* magazine,
but the practice of sexual freedom which many of them endorsed. Her
experience of it taught her that American freedom diminished love instead of deepening it, exactly the conclusion H. Richard Niebuhr reached
through reflection.

As she reports in her autobiography, *The Long Loneliness*, she had her
"own groping for the love of others, [her] own desires for freedom and
for pleasure," but she never grasped the physical and spiritual power of
love, she said, until she had her daughter, Tamar, by her common-law
husband. Her state of union with Tamar led her to God and the Catholic
Church, a course that seemed to her radical friends, and to her husband,
whom she soon left, an incomprehensible surrender of freedom. She later
recalled that "when I became a Catholic, it never occurred to me to
question how much freedom I had or how much authority the Church
had to limit that freedom. . . . I had reached the point where I wanted to
obey. . . . I was tired of following the devices and desires of my own
heart, of doing what I wanted to do, what my desires told me I wanted
to do, which always seemed to lead me astray." Her religious experience
was an extension of her maternal experience: discovering a fuller love in
obedience to an obligation. Love was not about fulfilling a desire but
accepting a responsibility from God and obeying his commandment to
love him along with one's neighbor.[23]

Day understood that believers who claimed to be obeying a command
rather than fulfilling a desire might be deluding themselves. She knew

that her own love of the poor was quite possibly laced with hypocrisy—
she might be in love with her own goodness, or secretly enjoying her
exposure to the dissolute habits of the down-and-out. One never knew
the real state of one's own soul. That was God's business. Love could not
be securely grounded on the idea of human freedom, which in its humanist version ignored the vagaries of self-love and self-deception. Day's
critique of freedom, like Richard Niebuhr's, was at bottom a critique of
humanism, of human standards for love and human standards for freedom. It was a firm rejection of Emma Goldman's orientation—not just
her free-love advocacy, which Day considered "promiscuous," but her
basic assumption that freedom and love rose or fell together. Real love
could only happen, for Goldman, in a world rid of oppressive institutions. For Day it could happen whenever God chose.[24]

Looking at Day and Goldman together one is first tempted to see
them as opposites—the fiery atheist rebel and the saintly Catholic charity
worker—and then one begins to register a deeper continuity: each
woman gained public prominence as a "maternal" advocate of the poor,
each quite consciously sublimated her desire for personal, sexual love into
love for the people. Each woman brought the personal together with the
political by dramatizing the one really *free* love that women can un-
answerably claim in a public world run mostly by men: the love of a
mother for her actual or figurative children. Both women pursued the
traditionally shrewd path of female reformers who justified their public
activity by tying it to their maternal responsibilities, to which in principle
there could be no objection.

But this accord between Day and Goldman can obscure a still deeper
opposition, one that helps illuminate the whole long history of thinking
about free and bounded love. They disagreed profoundly about the character and significance of freedom itself, and disagreed therefore about
what the free experience of love would be like. For Goldman freedom
was a state in which fruitful growth of the self took place. The personal
was political because oppressive structures imprisoned individual psyches
as well as social groups, prevented people from realizing themselves as
fully cultured beings. Goldman was as Victorian as Jane Addams in her
conviction that a world of civilized achievement had been built up brick
by brick and must be made available to everyone, not just the privileged.
Free love between individuals depended on this ever-expanding social
freedom: the love she sought for herself and for everyone else was a
united state of physical pleasure and impassioned conversation. Sexual
communion would reach its peak when it was intertwined with high
ideals, ideals she called spiritual.

Dorothy Day's idea of freedom was utterly different not just because it
lacked Goldman's focus on sexual pleasure, but because it lacked Goldman's notion of cultured conversation—and of a politics determined to

expand the social reach of that conversation. One might say that while for Goldman the personal was political, for Day the political was personal: true political activity was direct service, spiritual and physical, to individual persons in need. She had no sense of a politics linked to the expansion of a civilized culture, one to which all human beings should be granted access. She thought the whole idea of civilization was elitist, a diversion from *agape*, from passionate service. The Catholic Church appealed to her especially because it was the church of the untutored masses. She had inherited no culture she wished to transmit to them. On the contrary, it was *their* simple faith and love for which *she* yearned. Love was not a function of social freedom, as it was for Goldman, but of the freedom to confess one's creaturely boundaries. The passionate life was not the life of conversation but the life of surrender, in which the full, ancient meaning of passion was rediscovered. Free love for Goldman was one component of a fully realized social and intellectual condition, that of the cosmopolitan individual. Free love for Day was the choice of a "passion" in which individual growth was replaced by dying to self. Goldman and Day take us deeply into the lived experience, respectively, of eros and agape.

Today we hear the word "passion" and think of "sex," or "romance." But the first four meanings of passion listed in the *Oxford English Dictionary*, dating from the twelfth century, are "the suffering of pain," "the sufferings of a martyr," "suffering or affliction generally," and "a painful affliction or disorder of the body." It was only in the sixteenth century that Shakespeare, Spenser, and others began to use "passion" to mean "amorous feeling," and in the seventeenth century that it started to mean "sexual impulse" or "an eager outreaching of the mind towards something, an overmastering zeal or enthusiasm for a special object." Dorothy Day's calling was to make love passionate by linking it once again to suffering, indeed, to death. "Love," she wrote, "is a rehearsal for death." This love is agape, not eros, selfless love, not sexual love. But in Day's conception it is nonetheless passionate—indeed, bodily—love. She does not envision suffering love as a withdrawal from people or a renunciation of intimate emotional encounter. In her autobiography she tells the story of having to evict a slovenly and obstreperous woman from her New York hospitality house. She did kick her out, but not before taking her in her arms, kissing her, and telling her she loved her, loved the real person she was, the one obscured temporarily by atrocious behavior.

The passion of Dorothy Day, like that of her French contemporary Simone Weil, was a self-conscious quest to rekindle love in a time of social breakdown and cultural atrophy. The foundation for love could not be culture or politics, they thought, not the freedom produced by culture or defended by politics, but the free gift of God's love. "Love is the exchange of gifts," Day wrote, quoting St. Ignatius. Love for Day is a unified state of gift-giving and forgiving: God gives the original gift of life; the believer receives that gift with a return act of loving God, passes on gifts of her own to her neighbors, and asks forgiveness, of God and neighbor, for all of her inevitable trespasses. This web of reciprocal obligation and repentance was certainly "free love" in the sense that it rested on spontaneous giving, not coercion, but it was a freedom based on voluntary submission to a commandment, not the freedom to pursue a desire or develop a self.

The notion that love involves submission is not an idea liable to fly very far in our time, although anyone who is a parent quickly discovers the reality, and the pleasure, of such starkly bounded love. We would so gladly and instantly surrender our lives for our children that the whole idea of feeling free, having freedom, to love them is rather nonsensical. It is this sort of starkly bounded love that Day has in mind when she speaks of the love of God, a love that came to her only when she felt the extravagant power of the tightly, umbilically united love she felt for her newborn daughter. "No human creature could receive or contain so vast a flood of love and joy as I often felt after the birth of my child," she wrote. "With this came the need to worship, to adore." This is the highest gift for Day, this bounded state of union with the Creator who let a new creation wriggle through her body.[25]

American thinkers and writers reflecting on love, and on their experience of it, have been decisively shaped by the fundamentally American dilemma that became evident in the nineteenth century: the taxing battle to reconcile individual freedom with community. From John Humphrey Noyes and Emma Goldman to Dorothy Day and Richard Niebuhr, they have illuminated the hopes and contradictions faced by a (largely Protestant) culture premised on pushing freedom to its limit while preserving social order—a conservation effort often defined not as traditional but as a "new order of the ages." Yet in responding to specifically American preoccupations, these thinkers find themselves returning to traditional classical and Christian debates about the nature of freedom. The American story becomes, for many of them, a retelling of the human story. Telling the story of the history of love in America means attending to the dialectical interchange between secular and religious beliefs, and it means opening up a wider Western history of thought and experience that puts the paradoxes of bounded freedom and selfless self-realization at the heart of the drama.

Notes

Earlier versions of this essay were delivered as lectures in 1997 at Indiana University and the École des Hautes Études en Sciences Sociales in Paris. My thanks to the respondents on both occasions who helped me clarify my ideas.

1. Lionel Trilling, *Sincerity and Authenticity* (Cambridge: Harvard University Press, 1972), p. 120. Robert Westbrook and I examine history as "moral inquiry" (as well as factual inquiry) in the Introduction to *In Face of the Facts: Moral Inquiry in American Scholarship* (New York: Cambridge University Press, 1997). Two vital works on the history of Western reflection about love are Jean H. Hagstrum, *Esteem Enlivened by Desire: The Couple from Homer to Shakespeare* (Chicago: University of Chicago Press, 1992) and Allan Bloom, *Love and Friendship* (New York: Simon and Schuster, 1993), a profound work for which those acquainted only with Bloom's polemical and slapdash *The Closing of the American Mind* (New York: Simon and Schuster, 1989) will be wholly unprepared. Raymond Carver's story "What We Talk About When We Talk About Love," in his collection of that title (New York: Knopf, 1981), is essential reading for those, like me, who claim that love can be analyzed historically or philosophically. One way of reading the story suggests that when we talk about love we are actually talking about something else—like possessiveness, domination, pain, or dislocation. Another way of reading it suggests that we do know what love is when we see or hear about people (like Carver's aged couple in the hospital) who are living it. Historians need to be as sensitive to the lived experience of love as fiction writers like Carver are, and as alert to the chance that in thinking and writing about love we may be diverting our attention from the real thing.

2. The literature on love in American historical scholarship might be summarized briefly by identifying a number of interrelated pockets of research. (1) Surveys of what thinkers and writers have said about love. Among many other indispensable works are Leslie Fiedler, *Love and Death in the American Novel* (New York: Stein and Day, 1960, with two later revisions), and the "American" sections of both Peter Gay, *The Bourgeois Experience*, vols. 1 and 2 (New York: Oxford University Press, 1984, 1986) and Stephen Kern, *The Culture of Love: Victorians to Moderns* (Cambridge: Harvard University Press, 1992). (2) Surveys of popular attitudes toward and experiences of love, such as Beth Bailey, *From Front Porch to Back Seat: Courtship in Twentieth-Century America* (Baltimore: Johns Hopkins University Press, 1988); Ellen K. Rothman, *Hands and Hearts: A History of Courtship in America* (New York: Basic Books, 1984); Janice Radway, *Reading the Romance: Women, Patriarchy, and Popular Literature* (Chapel Hill: University of North Carolina Press, 1984); Stanley Cavell, *Pursuits of Happiness: The Hollywood Comedy of Remarriage* (Cambridge: Harvard University Press, 1981); and Pamela S. Haag, "In Search of 'The Real Thing': Ideologies of Love, Modern Romance, and Women's Sexual Subjectivity in the United States, 1920–40," *Journal of the History of Sexuality* 2 (1992), 547–77.

(3) Histories of religious discourse and experience. Most of these works are about religious thought, not experience. They include books by "general" intellectual historians such as Henry May, *Protestant Churches and Industrial America*, (New York: Harper and Row, 1949), and Donald B. Meyer, *The Protestant Search for Political Realism, 1919–1941* (1960; Middletown: Wesleyan University Press, 1988), and students of the history of religious thought, such as Harlan Beckley, *Passion for Justice: Retrieving the Legacies of Walter Rauschenbusch, John A. Ryan, and Reinhold Niebuhr* (Philadelphia: Westminster Press, 1992). I have tried to write a history of the experience of religious and secular love (including

the "thought" that was always part of that experience) in *Trials of Intimacy: Love and Loss in the Beecher-Tilton Scandal* (Chicago: University of Chicago Press, 1999).

These histories of religious thinking and experience blend into (4) books on American reform movements, which often document the Protestant bent, and overwhelmingly female makeup, of such movements. This vast literature going back to the turn of the century includes such works as William Leach, *True Love and Perfect Union* (New York: Basic Books, 1980); Lori Ginzburg, *Women and the Work of Benevolence* (New Haven: Yale University Press, 1990); and Robyn Muncy, *Creating a Female Dominion in American Reform, 1890–1935* (New York: Oxford University Press, 1991). Books in this fourth group come the closest to treating the interpenetration of religion and secularity in American culture, but they tend to see "reform" as the issue of primary importance, and hence grasp "religion" as significant to the extent that it promotes "secular" advances in social welfare or political equality.

Mid-twentieth-century studies of nineteenth-century female reform groups by scholars such as Carroll Smith-Rosenberg led by the late 1970s to (5) feminist explorations of love-bonds among women (Smith-Rosenberg took the lead with her pathbreaking essay "The Female World of Love and Ritual," the centerpiece of her collection *Disorderly Conduct* [New York: Oxford University Press, 1985]), and then to revisionist works that contested Smith-Rosenberg by stressing love-bonds between men and women (Karen Lystra, *Searching the Heart* [New York: Oxford University Press, 1989]) or, more subtly, by configuring women's lives as a totality of experiences of love and work in interlocking gendered and cross-gendered domains (Laurel Ulrich, *A Midwife's Tale* [New York: Knopf, 1990]).

(6) Histories of sexuality and the body, sparked by the broad cultural re-examination of gender roles and sexual identity-making. Foucault has been instrumental here, but the "American" reading of him has had the unfortunate effect, in my view, of pushing scholarship away from "love" as such to apparently wider but actually narrower (and thinner) ruminations on power and the cultural construction of all meaning. Some studies of sexuality do remain interested in the history of love: Steven Seidman, *Romantic Longings: Love in America, 1830–1980* (New York: Routledge, 1991) and George Chauncey, *Gay New York* (New York: Basic Books, 1994) are two important examples.

3. Trilling, *Sincerity and Authenticity*, Preface.

4. *Romeo and Juliet* act II, scene II, line 50; Lawrence Stone, "Passionate Attachments in the West in Historical Perspective," in Willard Gaylin and Ethel Person, eds., *Passionate Attachments: Thinking About Love* (New York: Free Press, 1988), 15–26.

5. On "privacy" and "virtue," see the excellent historical assessments of those terms by Nancy Cott and Joan Williams in Richard Wightman Fox and James T. Kloppenberg, eds., *A Companion to American Thought* (Cambridge: Blackwell, 1995).

6. Ralph Waldo Emerson, "Self-Reliance," in Irwin Edman, ed., *Emerson's Essays* (1926; New York: Thomas Y. Crowell, 1961), p. 36.

7. I treat Beecher in relation to Bushnell in "The Culture of Liberal Protestant Progressivism, 1875–1925," *Journal of Interdisciplinary History* 23 (Winter,

1993): 639–60, and I give further attention to Beecher's evangelical romanticism in relation to both liberalism and republicanism in *Trials of Intimacy*. Henry May's excellent *The Enlightenment in America* (New York: Oxford, 1976) shows how liberal, republican, and evangelical ideas interpenetrated in eighteenth- and early nineteenth-century America. We need an account that extends his analysis by adding antebellum romanticism to the mix.

8. The best treatment of Oneida and of Noyes himself is Spencer Klaw, *Without Sin: The Life and Death of the Oneida Community* (New York: Allen Lane, 1993), but Noyes's authoritarian approach to individual freedom still needs to be put in its full religious, cultural, and intellectual context.

9. Taylor Stoehr, ed., *Free Love in America* (New York: AMS Press, 1979), p. 45.

10. Goldman quoted in Candace Falk, *Love, Anarchy, and Emma Goldman* (New York: Holt, Rinehart, and Winston, 1984), pp. 89, 113, 130, 155, 461.

11. Joseph Wood Krutch's *The Modern Temper* (New York: Harcourt, Brace, and Co., 1929) is the key text in linking the rise of modernity to the erosion of the ideal of deep, life-altering love.

12. William James's 1906 lectures published as *Pragmatism* (New York: Longmans, Green, 1907) were framed as a search for the middle ground between realism and idealism. Pragmatism, as he put it at the end of the lecture on "Pragmatism and Humanism," was the "mediator between tough-mindedness [empiricism] and tender-mindedness [intellectualism]." Pragmatism preserved the immediacy and vitality of "experience" and promoted the open-endedly adaptive search for meaning ("truth"). As he wrote in his 1899 essay "On a Certain Blindness in Human Beings," the fruit of heightened experience was the realization that "there is life; and there, a step away, is death. There is the only kind of beauty there ever was. There is the old human struggle and its fruits together. There is the text and the sermon, the real and the ideal in one." Pragmatism is often equated with instrumentalism, with practicality, but as James asserts, it is only "in some pitiful dreamer . . . , or when the common practical man becomes a lover" that "the hard externality give[s] way, and a gleam of insight into . . . the vast world of inner life beyond us, so different from that of outer seeming, illuminate[s] our mind." ("On a Certain Blindness in Human Beings," in James, *Writings 1878–1899* [New York: Library of America, 1992], pp. 847, 854). Jamesian pragmatism is fundamentally a philosophy and practice of love, and a well-developed justification of religious belief. It is other things as well, including a theory that highlights practical problem-solving, but no account of it that leaves out love and religion does even minimal justice to James's own conception of it. It is not surprising that Henry James, a great thinker as well as storyteller about love, should have found himself "lost in wonder," as he wrote to his brother after reading *Pragmatism*, at "the extent to which all my life I have. . . . unconsciously pragmatised" (quoted in F. O. Matthiessen, *The James Family: A Group Biography* [1947; New York: Vintage Books, 1980], p. 343). Cf. Richard A. Hocks, *Henry James and Pragmatistic Thought: A Study of the Relationship between the Philosophy of William James and the Literary Art of Henry James* (Chapel Hill: University of North Carolina Press, 1974). On love in Henry James's fiction there are many significant studies, including Martha Nussbaum, *Love's Knowledge: Es-*

says on Philosophy and Literature (New York: Oxford University Press, 1990), David McWhirter, *Desire and Love in Henry James: A Study of the Late Novels* (Cambridge: Cambridge University Press, 1989), Philip Sicker, *Love and the Quest for Identity in the Fiction of Henry James* (Princeton: Princeton University Press, 1986), and Naomi Lebowitz, *The Imagination of Loving: Henry James's Legacy to the Novel* (Detroit: Wayne State University Press, 1965).

13. David A. Hollinger, "How Wide the Circle of the 'We'? American Intellectuals and the Problem of the Ethnos since World War II," *American Historical Review* 98 (Apr. 1993): 317–37; William James, "What Makes a Life Significant," *Writings 1878–1899*, pp. 861–62. This 1898 essay suggests that as a social philosophy Jamesian pragmatism, contrary to the popular stereotype that judges it a doctrine of progress, seeks yet another middle ground: that between the recognition and validation of "progress" ("that strange union of reality with ideal novelty") and the stoic realization that "the world is a standing thing, with no progress, no real history" (pp. 876, 879).

14. Henry James, *The Ambassadors*, Book Third, Chapter 2, end of first paragraph.

15. Walt Whitman, "Crossing Brooklyn Ferry" (1856), *Leaves of Grass* (New York: Library of America, 1991), pp. 308–9.

16. Margaret Mead's *Coming of Age in Samoa* (New York: William Morrow, 1928) is a crucial document in the spread of the "realistic" approach to sex, and the dismantling of love as a high passion—developments that Joseph Wood Krutch bemoans in *The Modern Temper*. Robert and Helen Lynd's *Middletown* (New York: Harcourt, Brace, 1929) should also be seen as a dismissal of romantic love-talk, which in their view diverts people from methodically assessing their life course and placing themselves appropriately in the social body.

17. Krutch, *The Modern Temper*, pp. 67, 69, 73. I put Krutch in relation to other intellectuals who discovered "the tragic sense of life" in the second quarter of the twentieth century in "Tragedy, Responsibility, and the American Intellectual, 1925–1950," in Thomas P. Hughes and Agatha C. Hughes, *Lewis Mumford: Public Intellectual* (New York: Oxford University Press, 1990).

18. I discuss Woodhull's and Beecher's ideas about love in *Trials of Intimacy*.

19. This treatment of Niebuhr draws on my *Reinhold Niebuhr: A Biography* (1985; Ithaca: Cornell University Press, 1997, with new Afterword).

20. Jonathan Edwards, *Treatise on Religious Affections*, quoted in John E. Smith, Harry S. Stout, Kenneth P. Minkema, eds., *A Jonathan Edwards Reader* (New Haven: Yale University Press, 1995), p. 150.

21. H. Richard Niebuhr, *The Kingdom of God in America* (1937; New York: Harper, 1959), p. 113.

22. H. Richard Niebuhr, "The Anachronism of Jonathan Edwards," in his *Theology, History, and Culture*, ed. William Stacy Johnson (New Haven: Yale University Press, 1996), pp. 127–30, 132.

23. Dorothy Day, *The Long Loneliness* (1952; New York: Image, 1959), p. 60; Day, *By Little and By Little* (New York: Orbis, 1992), p. 168.

24. Day calls Goldman's free love doctrine and practice "promiscuous" in *The Long Loneliness*, p. 60.

25. Day, *The Long Loneliness*, pp. 139, 225, 256.

8

"The Mystery of Life in All Its Forms": Religious Dimensions of Culture in Early American Anthropology

GILLIAN FEELEY-HARNIK

OUR COMMON subject in this volume is "religion and cultural studies." As an anthropologist employed in an American university and now caught in the controversies about the epistemological status of "culture" in anthropology, as well as in cultural studies, I suggest our subject might also be: culture in an era of persisting debates about whether social theory is religion or science. The ways that scholars in America argue about "culture" make it difficult ethnographically to keep "culture" separate from "religion" as a neutral analytic term through which the workings of religious faith and practice in and "*beyond* culture" might be understood. I have therefore taken the subject of "religion and cultural studies" as an opportunity to explore historically how the concept of "culture" in American anthropology emerged out of debates over the separation of "science" from "religion" beginning in the 1840s. These debates contributed in turn to the formation of separate natural and social sciences in which we are still involved. Here I focus on the efforts of Lewis Henry Morgan, one of the founders of anthropology, to solve what he called "the mystery of life in all its forms" by research on the human family worldwide, and the American beaver in northern Michigan, during the mid-nineteenth century. By taking an ethnographic approach to the historical creation of "culture" in American anthropology, we may achieve greater clarity in the use of our analytic terms. By subjecting our own scholarly assumptions and practices to the same ethnographic scrutiny we would apply to others, we may create a more open comparative perspective, rather than unwittingly assimilating the works of others to our still unresolved controversies.

What Is Culture?

Culture is a notoriously elusive notion. Yet here I want to argue that, beyond the disputes about its definition, the term as it has come to be used in anthropology reproduces older debates about religion in relation to science. Like religion, culture has become ever more ideational by opposition to an ever more materialist understanding of science, without helping us to understand or resolve many of the dilemmas about ethics originally involved in those debates. By the 1960s, the focus on culture as a system of meanings was so clearly developed that Geertz's essay on "religion as a cultural system," published in 1966, could almost be understood as a tautology.[1] Yet the same trend toward ideational definitions is evident even in those proposing, like Edward Burnett Tylor in 1871, a "science of culture."

Tylor defined "Culture or Civilization, taken in its wide ethnographic sense," as "that complex whole which includes knowledge, belief, art, morals, law, custom, and any other capabilities and habits acquired by man as a member of society." By approaching "the general study of human life as a branch of natural science," he intended to "carry out, in a large sense, the poet's injunction, to 'Account for moral as for natural things'" in the same analytic terms. He hoped "to escape from the regions of transcendental philosophy and theology, to start on a more hopeful journey over more practicable ground."[2]

In America by the early 1950s, "culture, in the technical anthropological sense," which Kroeber and Kluckhohn attributed to Tylor, had become, in their view, "one of the key notions of contemporary American thought . . . comparable to such categories as gravity in physics, disease in medicine, evolution in biology." Like Tylor, Kroeber and Kluckhohn undertook their famous survey, *Culture: A Critical Review of Concepts and Definitions* (1952), in the name of "science."[3] They examined the "terminological matrix" from which "culture" emerged historically, covering almost 300 definitions, including 164 in detail. They acknowledged that "the idea of betterment, of improvement toward perfection" still clung to the terms "culture" and "civilization" in both scholarly and popular usage. They also discussed several common preoccupations among scholars—"Integration, Historicity, Uniformity, Causality, Significance and Values, and Relativism"—of which Significance and Values "seem most distinctive of it [culture] and most important."[4] Yet from these considerations, they deduced that "in science as of 1952, the word culture has acquired also a new and specific sense (sometimes shared with civilization), which can fairly be described as the one scientific denotation that it possesses. This meaning is that of a set of attributes and products of human societies, and therewith of mankind, which are extrasomatic and transmissible by mechanisms other than biological heredity, and are as essentially lacking in sub-human species as they are characteristic of the human species as it is aggregated in its societies."[5] Indeed, they argue that this "ethnographic and modern scientific sense of the word . . .

sometimes described as extraorganic or superorganic" is what Tylor originally had in mind, because it originated with Gustav E. Klemm, in the
first volume of his *Allgemeine Culturgeschichte des Menschheit*, published
in 1843, "from whom Tylor appears to have introduced the meaning
into English."[6]

A generation later, and from a different philosophical and national perspective, Raymond Williams refused to discern a single scientific denotation in the complexity of "culture," which he considered "one of the two
or three most complicated words in the English language."[7] He noted
Herder's "decisive innovation," in *Ideas on the Philosophy of the History of
Mankind* (1784–91), "to speak of 'cultures' in the plural: the specific
and variable cultures of different nations and periods." Yet, in keeping
with Herder's own stress on the "indeterminate" use of the term, Williams emphasized that "the complex of senses indicates a complex argument about the relations between general human development and a particular way of life, and between both and the works and practices of art
and intelligence, [including] fundamentally opposed as well as effectively
overlapping positions; there are also, understandably, many unresolved
questions and confused answers." In short, the complexity "is not finally
in the word but in the problems which its variations of use significantly
indicate," an argument to which we will return later.

Definitions of culture have proliferated since then, not only in anthropology, but in many other fields. Probably few scholars would still advocate using terms like "extraorganic" or "superorganic" to describe their
cultural subjects. Yet at least in anthropology in the United States, scholars once dedicated to the study of human beings in all their aspects, are
now increasingly divided between cultural and biological specialties, despite the fact that "the body," for example, has become a subject of great
interest for both. Keesing's review of "culture" in 1974 found a distinction between a growing plethora of "ideationalists, " including "materialists," and a dwindling minority of "adaptationalists." In studies published
in the mid-1990s, Kahn, Kuper, and Keesing, in his own reassessment,
discuss only scholars whom Keesing would earlier have called "ideationalists."[8] Polarizing debates about the culture of science have since contributed to splitting anthropology departments along cultural and biological
lines.[9] While scholars in cultural studies, who would be unlikely to call
themselves "scientists," nevertheless use "culture" as if it were an epis-
temologically neutral term, defenders of the objectivity of "science" dis-
miss cultural analysis as if it were a kind of neo-creationism based on
faith, not facts.

In American anthropology, during and after the first and second world
wars, Franz Boas and Alfred Kroeber developed the now dominant ide-
ationalist view of culture as a way of countering scientific racism. Yet, as

Mukhopadhyay and Moses have recently pointed out, their radical separation between culture and biology makes it difficult to explain how the deadly effects of racist ideologies and practices, persisting despite their efforts, may extend far beyond overt forms of violence. How are "races" so created in the United States that they could become realized in differential mother and infant mortality rates, for example? Current divisions between culture and biology make it difficult to understand many other phenomena lying across organic-inorganic lines, including not only life and death processes in human social relationships, but the very environmental processes for which Boas argued so strongly.[10]

Still lying at the heart of these debates about organic and inorganic phenomena, especially as they are realized in birthing and dying, are questions about ethical and moral dilemmas. These concerns are most clearly evident in E. Valentine Daniel's ethnographic work on violence between and among Sinhalas, Tamils, and the Sri Lankan state in 1983–94.[11] Daniel argues that violence is "a counterpoint to culture," because even the most open-ended, processual, dialogic approaches to culture still assume some sense of connections or relations that could ultimately, if not immediately, constitute a "complex whole," as Tylor called it. Violence "will and should remain outside of all (C/c)ulture" in order to remind us in our scholarship and in our daily lives "to be humble in the face of its magnitude . . . and vigilan[t] . . . so as never to stray towards it and be swallowed by its vortex into its unaccountable abyss." Yet violence itself entails connection; violent acts originate in the very cultural relations they are intended to destroy. Whether we understand the "complex whole" in Tylor's, Williams's, or Daniel's terms, inherent in the connections, however minimal and fragmentary, must also lie humans' culturally developed capacities for annihilating others and thus themselves.

How we might create a concept of culture that could comprehend these contradictions is not obvious. Whereas some scholars, like Steedly, would give up on the term altogether, others, like Kuper, advocate what Kuper calls, following D'Andrade, a "particulate theory of culture." Taking a sociological, rather than D'Andrade's psychological, approach, Kuper suggests that "It would still make sense to break it up into parts, and then to see whether elements in the complex mix of culture may have their own specific (though not fixed) 'relations to other things'." But having made this suggestion, Kuper nevertheless concludes his study as if he were approaching Daniel's sense of the limits of "culture" from another angle: "Finally, there is a moral objection to culture theory. It tends to draw attention away from what we have in common instead of encouraging us to communicate across national, ethnic, and religious boundaries, and to venture between them."[12]

Here I have tried to get a critical perspective on "culture" by understanding the ethical or moral implications that seem to be deeply embedded in the most diverse conceptions of culture, yet without providing the analytic tools allowing scholars to comprehend the violence that Daniel describes so clearly. I too will propose an historical approach. Yet as Kroeber and Kluckhohn noted, "The history of the word 'culture' presents many interesting problems in the application of culture theory itself."[13] Perhaps predictably, given the increasingly ideational tone of the concept of culture, most scholars have focused on the history of ideas, as the work cited above indicates. Perhaps because anthropologists have generally accepted Tylor's intent "to escape from the regions of transcendental philosophy and theology," if not his "science of culture," they have not explored how controversies about religion and science might have contributed to scholarly and popular ideas about culture in Tylor's lifetime, or later, when they were supposed to be resolved in a secularized social science. Yet the pioneering work of Beidelman on William Robertson Smith, and more recently Goldberg on historical relations between Jewish Studies and Anthropology, have shown the fruitfulness of such an approach in ethnographic studies of religion, where questions about religious sectarianism have arisen.[14] The work of sociologists like Vidich, Lyman, and Wolfe, historians like Hollinger, and scholars working across disciplinary boundaries, like Hyman and Mizruchi, show how such questions are relevant to our understanding of the historical formation of the disciplines of history, literature, and the social sciences more broadly, including anthropology.[15]

Here, I want to return to the epistemological debates over religion and science that prompted Tylor and his contemporaries to see how they could "account for moral as for natural things" free of metaphysics and theology. My hypothesis is that anthropologists' conceptions of culture derived historically from debates about science and religion as competing modes of explanation, and that our current conceptions of culture are still caught, if less obviously, in those same debates. In the United States, as most evident in controversies over the teaching of creation and evolution in public schools, these debates, while changing in form and content, have been continuous for almost 140 years. In his recent study of scientific creationism, Ronald Numbers emphasizes the need for a fully historical analysis of these debates in the United States.[16] Given what I surmise to be the continuing involvement in these debates of scholars living and working in the United States, whether or not they are directly involved in high school teaching, I advocate an ethnographic approach as well.

I suggest that we take the same ethnographic approach to the analysis of anthropological modes of understanding that we would adopt in studying "the range of what people 'mean by meaning'" elsewhere.[17] In keeping with the approach of Fernandez and Herzfeld, I argue that we can get a better grip on the definition and relevance of our analytic terms if we get some understanding of the complexities of the historical-material circumstances in which they achieved their social generality, thus their capacities, but also possible limits to their broader application. Thus, this inquiry into the sectarian religious roots of the concept of "culture" in American anthropology focuses not on the history of ideas, but on the life and times of "the father of American anthropology," Lewis Henry Morgan (1818–1881), and his contemporaries, especially Ely S. Parker, the Seneca Indian who worked so closely with Morgan on the research resulting in *League of the Ho-de'-no-sau-nee, or Iroquois* (1851).[18] As Major John Wesley Powell, founder of the Bureau of American Ethnology, explained when Morgan became president of the American Association for the Advancement of Science in 1879, Morgan gave the world "its first scientific account of an Indian tribe."[19]

Based on continuing archival and ethnographic research, I will argue that Morgan and Parker were also dealing with questions about the capacities of theological and scientific approaches to discerning and explaining "relations," the very notion of a "complex whole," then understood as the problem of design.[20] Morgan's and Parker's vision of the Iroquois in the *League* was first a humanist vision explicitly connected to American circumstances, a kind of American classicism. They concurred in arguing that the "Indian nations whose ancient seats were within the limits of our republic" (p. 3), in particular the Iroquois, should be recognized as constituting the classicical foundations of the republic in this new world, just as the Greeks and Romans provided the historical foundations of civil society in Europe. Yet this political vision was also, for both, a vision of the Iroquois transformed by adoption of Christianity, though not without contradictions in that their vision entailed a social critique of the practices of settlers who called themselves Christians, but who acted like "savages" and "barbarians."

I will argue that the social practice of "interpretation," cross-cutting differences in their humanist, political, scientific, and sectarian concerns, persisted in the methods and conception of Morgan's later work on kinship and animal behavior and, through his work on kinship in particular, persisted into later anthropological conceptions of culture. Morgan and Parker were critical in creating many elements of the ideational paradigm of culture in which we are still caught, so through their work we might begin to understand how it came to envelop us. Yet, working almost a generation earlier than Tylor, for example, and—especially in the case of Parker—drawing on different life experiences, they were still sufficiently outside that paradigm that, through them, we too might be able to get outside enough to transform it.

"Morgan's Attitude toward Religion and Science" Revisited

We owe our understanding of Morgan as a man "for Science" not only to his contemporaries, but also to later assessments of his work, notably an essay on "Morgan's Attitude Toward Religion and Science," written by anthropologist Leslie White, and published in 1944, during World War Two.[21] Morgan clearly fostered this understanding of his work, as we shall see. Yet the papers he saved, the common library he kept with his wife, together with other historical data, suggest that Morgan was more concerned about certain complexities in relations between religion and science than White's categorical assessment would allow, and that his concerns contributed directly to the work that proved to be so influential in anthropology later. A brief sketch of Morgan's life will help to introduce some of these concerns.

Morgan was born on November 21, 1818, on his father's farm south of the village of Aurora on Lake Cayuga in western New York State. His grandfather had migrated to this area from Connecticut in 1792, when the American government offered former Iroquois land to soldiers who had fought in the Revolutionary War. His father, Jedediah, had expanded from farming wheat to raising merino sheep. When Jedediah Morgan began ailing in 1822, he left the farm to one of his older sons by a first marriage and moved into Aurora, then the capital of Ledyard County and its main transit point for grain, wool, and lumber. Jedediah died there in 1826, leaving his second wife, Harriet Steele Morgan, with the means to give their household's eleven minor children "a common English education" at Cayuga Lake Academy, a block north of them and across from the Presbyterian church where they attended services. Morgan transferred to Union College in Schenectady for his last two years (1838–40).[22]

At Cayuga Lake Academy, Morgan, his siblings, and his cousin studied Greek and Latin languages and literature. At Union College (founded in 1795 as the first nonsectarian college in the country, then under the presidency of the Presbyterian Reverend Eliphalet Nott) he took, in addition to such courses as Graeca Majora and Rhetoric, several mathematics and science courses, including Trigonometry, Algebra, Optics, Mechanics, Hydrostatics, Physiology, and probably Geology.[23] Returning to Aurora after graduation, Morgan wrote essays in 1841 "On Geology" and "On the History and Genius of the Grecian Race" while reading for the bar, to which he was admitted in 1842. Morgan's essay on the Greeks was probably written for "The Gordion Knot," the secret society he had formed on New Year's Day of 1841 with teachers and students at Cayuga Lake Academy to study the classics.[24]

In 1843, Morgan proposed to his fellow members that they reorganize themselves on the principles of America's ancient peoples, specifically the Iroquois who had once occupied the northeast, some of whom were still living in reservations in western New York State. By February 1844, they had received permission from Aurora's former Freemasons to meet in the lodge of their temple, already occupied on the ground floor by St. Paul's Episcopal Church. Morgan wrote the first by-laws for "The Grand Order of the Iroquois," as they first called themselves publicly, and later an account of the secret rites of "inindianation," by which new members were initiated. The efforts of Morgan and fellow members to gather accurate information about the social organization of the Iroquois led to Morgan's meeting with Ely S. Parker in a bookstore in Albany in spring 1844. Parker, then sixteen, was a Seneca from the Tonawanda Reservation northeast of Buffalo, serving as interpreter for elders from Tonawanda who were lobbying state politicians for the return of reservation land.[25] Morgan's research with Parker from 1844 through 1850 was the basis of *League of the Ho-de'-no-sau-nee, or Iroquois*, published in 1851 and dedicated to Parker, a collaborative work to which we will return shortly.

In late winter of 1844, Morgan moved to Rochester, where he began practicing law. In August 1851, a few months after the publication of *League*, he married his first cousin, his mother's brother's daughter, Mary Elizabeth Steele, from Albany. Mary Elizabeth Steele inherited money which, following the passage of the Married Women's Property Act in 1848, she was able to use to buy half of a duplex in Rochester's elegant Third Ward. The Morgans' three children were born there: Lemuel Steele in August 1853, Mary Elizabeth in December 1855, and Helen King in March 1860. Both girls died of scarlet fever within three weeks of each other in May and June 1862, at the ages of six and two. Lewis Henry Morgan died on December 17, 1881, a month after his sixty-third birthday; Mary Elizabeth Steele Morgan died two years later on December 1, 1883. Lemuel lived in the Morgan house for another twenty-two years until his death on July 29, 1905 at the age of fifty-one, following which the house was sold and most of the Morgans' property given to the University of Rochester, including Lewis's papers and collections, the books from their common library, the bookcases, and money from the sale of their house, stocks, and bonds to support the education of women.[26]

Morgan's contemporaries named him "the father of anthropology" not only for the *League*, but also for later works on a larger geographical and historical scale, notably *Systems of Consanguinity and Affinity of the Human Family* (1871) and *Ancient Society* (1877). He was also recognized as a scientist for *The American Beaver and His Works* (1868), a study of beaver communities in northern Michigan.[27] With *Systems*, Morgan virtually invented the study of kinship in anthropology, as Thomas Trautmann has argued.[28] Morgan's *Systems* was foundational in anthropology because, in the midst of controversies about polygenism and monogenism, his work assumed and confirmed the unity of "the Human Family," a unified human subject of inquiry within which the similarities and diversities among people could be explored and explained. Morgan's work was foundational of anthropology as a "science" precisely because, in contrast to theological arguments drawn from the Bible, for example the Quakers' *ab uno sanguine* (from Acts 17:26), Morgan's "Science of the Families of Mankind" (as he described his subject in dedicating *Systems* to his dead daughters) was based on data that came directly from the families themselves.[29]

Morgan's work as the progressive founder of the new science of anthropology is commonly contrasted to the lifelong religious devotion of his wife, Mary Elizabeth Steele Morgan, who was studying to be a missionary when they married.[30] Besides reproducing worn-out stereotypes about male and female interests, such a contrast suggests that "religion" dwindled into a backwater of superstitious ignorance while "science" flourished. Morgan himself contributed to these stereotypes in creating an archive of his life's work that includes almost nothing from Mary Morgan. In the one critical exception, a bookish analogue to the practice of sleeping in the same bed—for Morgan, an "American" practice that "tends to increased friendship and mutuality of life, and is one of the reasons why American husbands are better than German or French husbands, and why a woman's position in the United States is higher than in any part of the earth"—the Morgans kept a common library list. The list begins with the books that "L H Morgan & Wife" brought to their marriage in 1851 and ends with the books that "L. H. & M. E. Morgan" acquired in the year of Lewis Morgan's death in 1881 (although Mary Elizabeth Morgan died two years later).[31]

In their catalogue of the Morgans' library, Trautmann and Kabelac note that the collection of books Mary Elizabeth Steele brought to her marriage is "surprisingly large for a young woman of her time and place."[32] The number of study Bibles, monographs on biblical books, collections of sermons, and studies of particular theological and ethical issues in the list as a whole is staggering. The consistent presence of these books over the years of the Morgans' marriage is a reminder that the revolution in science was matched by a revolution in theology. While Lewis Henry Morgan was researching radical transformations of American social relations, Mary Elizabeth Steele Morgan was researching no less radical transformations in American theology, and they might well have been discussing these issues with each other. To be sure, "friendship and mutuality of life" in marriage does not entail intellectual unanimity. Yet the Morgans' unusual common inventory suggests that we need to know both what was going on in Morgan's "science," and in the "religion" he shared in some way with Mary Morgan and perhaps more generally with his contemporaries.

In earlier work, I have argued that Lewis Morgan's anthropological work on kinship derived from efforts to rethink Divine Creation as a social, material process in historical time, while retaining an ethical perspective on social relations. A closer look at the research he did on *The American Beaver and His Works* (1868), concurrently with his research and publication of *Systems* (1871), shows that Morgan's interests in "consanguinity and affinity" were grounded more deeply in questions about the very nature of life itself, the "mystery" of "life in all its forms," as he called it in the Beaver book.[33] *Systems* is famous among anthropologists, while *The American Beaver* is scarcely known; *The American Beaver* is a classic in the natural history of North America for biologists, who are completely unaware of Morgan's work on the Human Family.[34] Abstracting Morgan's work on kinship from its larger context contributed to the division between "religion" and "science," now perpetuated in the division between "culture" and "biology." So a deeper understanding of the "life" issues he was trying to solve in both may help us get a broader sense of Morgan's contributions to our understanding of "culture" in American anthropology.

While Morgan speaks often of "life," and occasionally of "civilization," he nowhere uses the term "culture." Indeed, as we shall see, he did not know at first what to call the "relics" of Indian life that he and others were collecting in the 1840s. Here I have followed the paths in Morgan's methods of inquiry and, through his paths, his growing and changing sense about "relations" that seems to emerge. Fernandez and Herzfeld warn us that just as "field methods must provide a clear account of the field paths followed to obtain the data out of which the local knowledge and the eventual ethnography built upon it are constructed . . . similarly . . . historical method must be critically aware of its path dependency, and, at the same time, of the degree to which it may be overly influenced by a teleological dynamic which overcommits it to final causes and a priori endpoints of pathlike reasoning."[35]

Indeed this is a issue in Morgan's case. Morgan was clearly trying to open new paths of understanding in the broadest sense. Unlike several of his brothers and sisters, he did not migrate away from western New York State. Yet except for his brother Alfred Gray, who had left for Kentucky in 1836, and then for California in 1850, he traveled farther afield than any of them, as far west as the Rockies, as far east as Europe, and many points between.[36] Yet precisely these issues of randomness and contingency were among his main concerns: not simply as one of the new scientists of his day, but as one whose science could not be separated from spiritual questions about the very existence of a grand design. Morgan's paths of knowing took many directions, related to his work as a lawyer and investor, as well as his scholarly research. The farthest reaching of these was unquestionably the path of eschatology dealing with death, morality, and judgment.

"Life in All Its Forms Is a Mystery"

In *Systems* (1871), Morgan tried to cover the full range of ways in which the Human Family reckoned kinship, from "primitive promiscuity" to "monogamy," and his "conjectural history" of how these might have evolved from each other if the world's peoples had but one origin. Morgan researched and wrote *The American Beaver* (1868) concurrently, from the mid-1850s to the late 1860s. Later he commemorated their common creation by saving the pen with which he had done his writing, sewed to a little card where he noted its use and goodness.[37] In the *Beaver* book, Morgan identifies his subject as the "mystery" of "life in all its forms" (p. 258). Perhaps anthropologists, in contrast to biologists, have generally ignored this work, because "Culture or Civilization" in Tylor's *Primitive Culture* (1871), published shortly after *The American Beaver*, was already limited to human beings: "acquired by man as a member of society." Indeed, Tylor was making the common argument in defining human beings by "culture," in contrast to "inferior animals," which had only "instinct." Morgan was unusual even among his scholarly contemporaries in arguing against this notion. His research on the beaver communities in Michigan's northern peninsula was intended to demonstrate that animals were like human beings in possessing "Mind." "The Mutes," as he eventually called all nonhuman creatures, differed mainly in how they expressed themselves. Morgan's view of animals' capacities for remembering, reasoning, and imagining contributed to how he understood the capacities of human beings, as we shall see. But first, his conception of his overall subject warrants closer attention.

Morgan identified "Mind" with the very "Life" of a creature. His chapter on "Animal Psychology," following his detailed exposition of the beavers' works, is the context in which he is finally forced to say that "life in all its forms is a mystery." What does he mean by this? By the time that Morgan wrote these words in 1868, Darwin had also introduced his subject in *On the Origin of Species* in the same terms: "the origin of species—that mystery of mysteries, as it has been called by one of our greatest philosophers."[38] Like Darwin, Morgan was also concerned with how to understand creation, Divine and otherwise. But as with Darwin, so I think for Morgan also, these questions about life processes entailed further mysteries about death that were, if anything, even more difficult to answer.

In popular usage—for example, Dickens's *The Mystery of Edwin Drood* (1870), Dickens being one of the Morgans' favorite novelists—mystery refers to a puzzle that can be solved, and once solved is no longer a mystery.[39] Morgan's description of the mystery of "life in all its forms" seems to suggest that he is dealing with such a soluable problem:

> *The Principle of Life.* Life in all its forms is a mystery. As a formative power, it builds up the infantile body from weakness into maturity and strength. It maintains a perpetual conflict with the elements of disorder and decay until the organism in which it dwells breaks up, or wears itself out. Is death the destruction of this principle? or is it immaterial, and expelled, like the spirit from the body? If it be a principle, and, therefore, immaterial, it would be difficult to show that the living and thinking principles are separate and distinct entities. It seems to be more than surmisable that the two are identical. It is I—the spirit—which lives, and not the body, which is material. If life comes of the union of body and spirit, then it is not an entity, but a result; and all there is of life is the life of the spiritual essence, or of the principle of intelligence.[40]

Morgan's purpose in detailing the beavers' works manifest in their dams and lodges, and the humans' works—their systems of consanguinity and affinity—manifest in their kinship terminologies and marriage practices, is to show that this "formative power" is a "principle" and thus equivalent to "life." As we shall see, these works are to be understood as evidence of inhering principles that form and structure life as much as if they were rib bones and, paradoxically, more enduring. This mystery is difficult enough. Yet perhaps here, and certainly throughout his work, Morgan was also dealing with mysteries of a more intractable sort, having a long history in Christian theology, referring back to passages in the New Testament, especially in the letters of Paul.

What Christians count as a mystery, especially *the* mystery, varies historically. For example, some theologians now suggest that for Paul, *the* mystery was the inclusion of Gentiles as well as Jews in the promise of universal salvation (Rom. 16.26; Col. 1.27; Eph. 3.3–6). For the gospel-writers the mystery was the kingdom of God (Mark 4.11; Matt. 13.11; Luke 8.10). What the mysteries were to Morgan, and possibly his contemporaries, we might learn by looking to the work of the Presbyterian minister who became one of his closest lifelong friends, the Reverend Joshua Hall McIlvaine. Trautmann has argued that McIlvaine's intellectual interests in language may have contributed to the kinds of philological reasoning that Morgan used in his research.[41] Here, I will suggest that McIlvaine's

theology—his conception of the mysteries from a Christian point of view
and his arguments about how to interpret them—may have contributed
to Morgan's understanding of "the Word" in ways that complemented
and perhaps complicated his philology.

McIlvaine's conception of the central mystery of Christianity is plainly
stated in the book he published just before he arrived in Rochester in
1848 to take over the First Presbyterian Church where Morgan, and later
Mary Morgan, attended services: *The Tree of the Knowledge of Good and
Evil* (1847).[42] McIlvaine had written this book because he had found that
"some of the mysteries of the Word of God" can present "sincere people" with great difficulties, "difficulties from which the writer himself has
greatly suffered, and from which so many suffer in this age of rationalistic
and infidel philosophy" (p. iv). He starts with puzzles that seem ridiculous, then plunges into the terrifying heart of the matter: "If it has ever
occurred to [the reader] that the account of a 'talking snake' in the
temptation of man is an improbable story; if the blasphemy of the infidel
sneering at the account which God has given of the sin and fall of man,
has ever disturbed him; if the mystery of the atonement made by the
sacrifice of the Innocent for the guilty, has caused him to offend;—perhaps upon these and other points he may find some relief from the following pages."[43]

McIlvaine claims that Christian mysteries are incomprehensible by ordinary human reason. I think Morgan questioned that view, and so too
did some of his contemporaries. Here I will argue that Morgan and Parker's research on the Iroquois, later published in *League of the Ho-de'-no-
sau-nee, or Iroquois* (1851), was motivated in part by a concern to solve
these persistent mysteries, in particular "the mystery of the atonement
made by the sacrifice of the Innocent for the guilty," a motivation that
Morgan and Parker shared in different ways. In the early 1800s, the Iroquois were seen as a dying people. Because of the newly completed Erie
Canal, stretching across the state from Albany to Buffalo, Rochester in
the 1820s was the fastest growing city in the entire country. According
to Eastman's *History of the State of New York* (1832), settlers, mainly
from Holland, Great Britain, France, and Germany, had increased from
586,000 in 1800 to 1,616,000 in 1825, while the "remains" of the Iroquois were estimated at 5000.[44]

A graphic image of the vacant wilderness that most New Yorkers saw
themselves entering, and how they saw the place of their works as integral to the "Works of God," is presented in the frontispiece to *A Gazetteer of the State of New-York*, published in 1843 (fig. 8.1). The engraving shows the mountains of the state, arranged according to their relative
heights, above its rivers, lakes, and canals, arranged according to their
lengths. The portrait of the mountains, what Eastman calls "The Face of

Figure 8.1. "Comparative Height of Mountains &c—Comparative Length of Rivers,
Lakes, Canals." Frontispiece to J. Disturnell,
A Gazetteer of the State of New-York (Albany,
1843). Reproduced with the permission of
the Department of Rare Books and Special
Collections, University of Rochester Library.

the Country," celebrates the first geological survey of the state (1836–
41), documented in the facts that J. Disturnell had compiled in the
Gazetteer and prompting him to observe in the preface, written in Albany
in 1842:

The State Geologists, appointed pursuant to an act of the Legislature of 1836,
have also greatly aided in disclosing the mineral wealth, and other natural resources of the state. They have made extensive researches, discovered many

new localities of these resources, given names to Mountains, Lakes and Rivers, heretofore unnamed, and almost unknown; and have thus, altogether, furnished a very large amount of most valuable, interesting and correct information, much of which is embodied in this Gazetteer.

Though her admirable system of Internal Improvements has doubtless been the chief means of the remarkably rapid growth of New-York, . . . yet, after all, her geographical position, features and relations, must be regarded both as the original groundwork of her permanent greatness, and as the true explanation of the extraordinary *productiveness* of her public works . . .—with the noble Hudson reaching northward through a fertile, populous and interesting district, more than one hundred and fifty miles, as if consciously seeking to become connected, by means of the Erie and Champlain canals, with the great northern and western lakes, and through them, with the vast and fertile regions beyond.[45]

The research that Morgan and Parker did on Iroquois life, culminating in the *League*, was an effort to put the Iroquois back into that vacant wilderness and to set down the unwritten history and social organization of the Iroquois before they disappeared. Morgan and Parker were determined to show, as Morgan states several times in the *League*, that the "American wilderness" was not some "savage solitude until the white man entered its borders, [but that it] had long been vocal in its deepest seclusions, with the gladness of happy human hearts," and that those hearts still spoke through the place-names that Iroquois had long ago given to the mountains, lakes, and rivers of the state, many of which still lived on in contemporary use.[46] In addition, Morgan and Parker's research was perhaps also an effort to reveal the answer to the mystery of their dying, namely, how could it be just, or even comprehensible, that the innocent should die to atone for the wicked? With this work on the Iroquois, I think Morgan and Parker dedicated themselves to revelation as a human practice, and that Morgan, and later generations of Parkers, especially Arthur C. Parker, Ely's brother Nicholson's grandson, returned again and again to the analytical problems that they felt to be involved in fathoming this mystery. I will discuss Morgan and Parker's research on the Iroquois first, then return to the questions of documentation and analysis that this research involved and how these might have contributed to later understandings of "culture" generally.[47]

Morgan's and Parker's Research on the League of the Ho-de'-no-sau-nee, or Iroquois

Morgan's and Parker's *League of the Ho-de'-no-sau-nee, or Iroquois* is explicitly dedicated to giving the Iroquois a written history and a place in contemporary life that both Parker and Morgan felt they did not have. Although I cannot substantiate this point properly here, I think their first purpose was to establish this soon to be "ancient" people as the classical foundation of the American republic, more appropriate to the new world than the Greeks and Romans who then dominated the "Classics" at such schools as Cayuga Academy, Union College, and Yates Academy (where Parker went for a couple of years). The Iroquois might have appeared already "ancient" to Morgan, if not Parker, because his interests in the Iroquois were originally prompted not by his close acquaintance with living Iroquois, but with what former inhabitants had left behind when forced to leave the area where Morgan was now living. The Cayuga sold the last of their reservation land close to Aurora in 1807, some ten years before Morgan was born in 1818. What he first saw were artifacts—and the very bones of the Cayuga—turned up by the plows of people like his grandfather and father, who were now farming the land the Cayuga once occupied.

Evidently Morgan collected these artifacts in his youth, as did many of his contemporaries. So when the Regents of the state's new university sent out a call for Indian antiquities, he responded, and volunteered the names of others. New York State had created a Cabinet of Natural History in 1843 for the collections resulting from the state's geological survey in 1836–41, and in 1845 the state placed it in the hands of the Regents, who got state funds to expand into antiquities. As Morgan later explained to Parker in a letter of October 30, 1848, they would "make it a department of the Geological Collection. It is a good idea and ought to be encouraged."[48] In short, the artifacts were to be incorporated with the rocks and fossils.

When Morgan went searching for artifacts outside his own neighborhood in 1845 and 1846, he seems to have established with far more certainty that these objects were grave goods. These excerpts from his journals convey some of the circumstances in which he found them:

> The Indians for the past fifty years until quite recently have made annual visits to this Indian burial place. . . . Even last year one solitary Indian was seen kneeling upon the mound, and apparently engaged in the performance of some religious ceremony. In the fields adjacent, bodies are frequently ploughed up and the kettle and other ornaments buried with the dead. One of these brass kettles which would hold about 2 quarts I purchased. [Journal 1:20, Canasateago near Geneva, November 1845.]

> Captain Frost at Onondaga informed me recently that the Iroquois were never buried sitting; herein he must have been mistaken. Mr. Brown found three in a triangle, all in a sitting posture, with the feet crossed at the ankle and the hands

upon the viscera, their heads were within two feet square. All ever taken out in this section were found in a sitting position. [Journal 1:6, Onondaga, December 1845.]

On my way home . . . stopped at Mr. Sheldon's . . . to make some inquiries. Found that there were two Indian burying grounds upon his farm, and the traces of an old fortification. Made an agreement to go out in the spring and dig up a grave (almost too outrageous) to see the position of the skeleton as all those interviewed in the valley of the Genesee and in Monroe County are in a sitting posture.

    Mr. Wheeler of Honeoye Falls has some relics. [Journal 1:6, Valley of Genesee, January 1846.]

They found in this hill many graves. The skeletons are all in a sitting position with their faces to the east, (I think he said) beside them they found pipes of various kinds of men's heads and animal heads figured on the bowls, the same as those I found at Lima. None of the skeletons were in a horizontal posture. [Journal 1:7, Fort Hill, February 1846.][49]

In responding to the Regents' call to the citizens of New York for antiquities, Morgan's argument was that "such a collection . . . would enable the Red Race to speak for itself through these silent memorials."[50] Anthropologists now call these objects "material culture," but as I mentioned earlier, Morgan did not know exactly what to call them besides "relics," "antiquities," "Indian curiosities," or "vestiges of our Indian predecessors," the common terms among English-speakers. He had to ask Ely S. Parker what to call them. In his letter to Parker of October 30, 1848, having written about how the Regents' plan to incorporate the objects as "a department of the Geology Collection . . . is a good idea and ought to be encouraged," he went on to add:

I wish to attach correct Indian names to all of mine as it would be in better taste, and I must turn to you of course for the names themselves. I enclose a list which I wish you would go over and place the Indian name opposite and return it; giving me an explanation of each in your answer if any should be necessary. . . .

    What would be a pretty name for a "Collection of Indian Antiques" or "Indian relics," or "Aboriginal Curiosities," or "Cabinet of Indian History," or "Indian Museum." If you can give me a fine name for the new collection, which is to be confined to our State principally [?], I will suggest it to the Regents. You know what I want. Think it over, and send me what would be your choice, with the translation. *One word* is to be preferred. It must all be in one word. Send me a number of names, with their meanings. This will be questions enough for you to answer, as I shall expect an answer for each.[51]

Morgan eventually enlisted the aid of the whole Parker family in these efforts. They helped him to collect objects, and when he or they could not find them among their things or those of their neighbors, the Parkers made them according to their personal knowledge of Seneca practices past and present, which Morgan and Ely S. Parker also wrote down. Thus, in the course of this work, Morgan and Parker were also working together gathering information about social organization and other matters. While Morgan was putting together his reports for the New York State Museum, he was also writing essays on the Iroquois, presented as if they were essays from "Schenandoah" (as he was called in the Grand Order of the Iroquois), to Albert Gallatin, one of the current experts on Indian people. These essays, combined with some material on the objects, formed the basis of the *League*, which Morgan dedicated to Ely S. Parker. In effect, Ely S. Parker's names and the names that Morgan got, through him and his siblings, from their parents, their other relatives, their neighbors, the Iroquois from other reservations, and everything else they told Parker and Morgan, began to speak for the silent memorials, now with the voices of living people.

Elsewhere, I have argued that Morgan and Parker together identified the Iroquois with the land, as if they were speaking for voices of the dead emanating from the land. Here I will argue that the work that Morgan and the Parkers did together bears comparison with another activity in which the Iroquois were deeply involved during these years, namely, the "New Religion" of Handsome Lake. Handsome Lake, a Seneca council member (*sachem*) in the League of the Iroquois, was around sixty-five years old in 1799, when he began to have visions of messengers from "the Creator" that compelled him to travel among the several nations of the League, advocating a return to Iroquois ways through temperance and other reforms. Some ten years after his death in 1815, Seneca at Tonawanda, where the Parkers lived, took the initiative in reviving Handsome Lake's teachings by asking Jemmy Johnson, his grandson, to recall Handsome Lake's "good message" in public gatherings and later at council meetings.[52]

Research and Revitalization

Among anthropologists, Handsome Lake's New Religion is one of the best known examples of a "revitalization" movement, as Anthony Wallace called it.[53] Ely S. Parker's notes on the teachings of Handsome Lake's grandson, Jemmy Johnson, at the Seneca's Tonawanda reservation in 1845 and 1848, some of which are reproduced in the *League*, are the main written source of information on Handsome Lake's message. As Parker's notes show, Handsome Lake had many vital concerns quite similar to those among the settlers who had begun to surround the reservations in his lifetime. Besides temperance and spiritual guidance, these included, especially, concerns about familial relations. Handsome Lake exhorted the Iroquois not to consort with "pale faces," not to cohabit with them, not to marry them. He urged spouses to stay together, young women not to use abortifacients, and young parents not to quarrel, lest their quarrels drive their babies back to the Spirit Land from which they came. I do not agree with Wallace's psychological theory of cultural revival, that visionaries like Handsome Lake work by transforming frustrating "cultural distortions" into coherent patterns better adapted to satisfying their followers' emotional and physical needs. Yet Handsome Lake and Jemmy Johnson were clearly concerned about ways of bringing the Iroquois back from death, and more specifically, as Tooker has shown, restoring land.[54]

We would benefit from seeing Morgan and Parker's *League of the Ho-de'-no-sau-nee, or Iroquois* not simply as the world's "first scientific account of an Indian tribe," but comparable to Handsome Lake's "New Religion" as well. Like the teachings of Handsome Lake and Jemmy Johnson, their work is a revitalization movement in an incipiently anthropological form, differing from the "New Religion" mainly in their philosophy and religious aspirations. As Arthur Parker, the grandson of Ely S. Parker's brother Nicholson, later wrote in his biography of his great uncle, "The Parker home was in a measure the spot where a new American science was born."[55]

The Parkers had many diverse interests and relations.[56] Ely S. Parker was related to Jemmy Johnson and Handsome Lake through his mother. Ely's brother Levi's daughter, Laura Parker Doctor, who inherited the homestead where the Parkers lived at Tonawanda, still held the right to nominate the successor to Handsome Lake's title as *sachem*, which she gave to her brother Otto, until he died in 1914.[57] Through these familial ties, Ely S. Parker could speak to Jemmy Johnson in ways that Morgan could not. As Jemmy Johnson said plainly in one of his remembrances, Handsome Lake explicitly disavowed the sanctity of Jesus Christ. As Ely S. Parker wrote, in reporting for the *Batavia Times* in October 1847 on the Council of the Six Nations held at Tonawanda: "The doctrine laid down was not much adverse to universalism, although the preacher rejected, in toto, the idea of the Indians being saved by means of the Saviour." He concluded with these words: "Such is a condensed report . . . and heaven only knows whether the place where the chiefs and wise men of the Six Nations have so often met to counsel, will continue to be preserved to them, or whether that, to them sacred ground, is to be desecrated by land speculators."[58]

On at least one occasion, Jemmy Johnson had challenged Morgan's purposes. Having met "by agreement at 9 AM. Newton Parker as Interpreter assisted by Dr. Sanford," Morgan's notes begin:

> Jemmy Johnson says . . . that he wishes to know why I wish to get these words out of him when we know how important a thing it is that the religion of us and of him do not agree. And he wishes to know why I want to get their Religion & what use I intend to make of it. ["I replied that", deleted] that their religion was designed for them alone & he supposed I wishes [sic] to expose it to the whites. I replied that I had great respect for him. I had no intention to make an improper use of the information he gave me, that I supposed he knew more about the religious beliefs of the race than any other person & therefore I came to him. That he need have no concern on that account. It seems the old man has some scruples about telling. He also himself refuses to talk on religious subjects after noon. The old man being satisfied at length began.[59]

Ely S. Parker was able to speak to Jemmy Johnson. Yet the Parkers were also variously involved in precisely the Christianity that Handsome Lake (and other Iroquois leaders like Red Jacket) so vehemently opposed, through their studies at the schools of Christian missionaries on Seneca reservations and through their work as interpreters and translators. Ely's brother Nicholson eventually married Martha Hoyt, the niece of Asher and Laura Wright, the Baptist missionaries at the Cattauragus Reservation. His grandson, Arthur, studied in a Christian seminary for four years, before finally deciding against the ministry and going into anthropology. Laura Parker Doctor was "always an ardent church worker," and Otto Parker a "preach[er] in the Seneca tongue," when Arthur interviewed them in 1912–19.

The *League* has an explicitly Christian message. This is evident in the description of Handsome Lake's "New Religion," suggesting that his is a "professed" revelation."[60] The Christian message is also stated in the conclusion, where the focus is on "the question of his ['the Indian'] reclamation, certainly, in itself, a more interesting, and far more important subject than any which have before been considered." In one sense, the Iroquois' "reclamation," or "saving," is to be their reclamation as citizens of the Republic, and thus their saving from extirpation as a people. In another sense, their reclamation unquestionably entails their "quicken[ing] . . . with the light of religion and of knowledge."

> To these establishments among the Iroquois ["the schools of the missionaries"], from the days of the Jesuit fathers down to the present time, they are principally indebted for all the progress they have made, and for whatever prospect of ultimate reclamation their condition is beginning to inspire. . . . [T]he

Iroquois, if eventually reclaimed, must ascribe their preservation to the perse-
vering and devoted efforts of those missionaries, who labored for their welfare
when they were injured and defrauded by the unscrupulous. . . . The schools of
the missionaries, established as they have been, and are, in the heart of our
Indian communities, have reached the people directly, and laid the only true
and solid foundation of their permanent improvement. . . . In fact they have
gathered together the better elements of Indian society, and quickened them
with the light of religion and of knowledge.

Indeed, Morgan goes to the point of saying that "the education and
christianization of the Iroquois is a subject of too much importance, in a
civil aspect, to be left exclusively to the limited and fluctuating means of
religious societies." The "State" should place "a portion of the public
money . . . at the disposal of the local missionary."[61]

The *League of the Ho-de'-no-sau-nee, or Iroquois* might be understood
as a reformist effort to create a more Christian form of Christianity, exemplified in the missionaries who saw themselves as truer Christians than the
alleged Christians around them. This comes out even more clearly in
Minnie Myrtle's retelling of Iroquois history in *The Iroquois, or the Bright
Side of Indian Character*, published in 1855.[62] Minnie Myrtle's work
draws on the *League* and the personal assistance of Morgan and several
members of the Parker family. Her account is far more outspoken about
the distinctions some people then saw between settlers and their forebears who called themselves Christians, on the one hand, and the missionaries working on the reservations and the Iroquois families with
whom they were associated, on the other. For example: "It is said the
Indian was cruel to the captive . . . [but] we know very little of the secrets of the Inquisition, and this little chills our blood with horror; yet
these things were done in the name of Christ, the Saviour of the world—
the Prince of Peace; and not savage, but civilized, *Christian* men looked
on, not coldly, but rejoicingly, while women and children writhed in
flames and weltered in blood!"[63]

These kinds of hypocrisies, raised again and again in Minnie Myrtle's
work, going from the Inquisition to the Pequot Massacre to current
"land-stealing," raised questions about the Christianness or barbarism of
the allegedly Christian settlers so severe that Ely S. Parker, toward the
end of his life, completely disavowed any adherence to Christianity (this
in correspondence with Harriet Converse, with whom he often discussed
the issue). Arthur Parker, the grandchild of Nicholson Parker and Martha
Hoyt, while documenting the contributions of his devoutly Christian relatives, no less carefully documents their doubts and the observations of
injustice on which they were based.

Thus, as expressed in Morgan's dedication of the *League* to "Hä-sano-an'-da (Ely S. Parker), A Seneca Indian, This Work, The Materials of Which Are The Fruit Of Our Joint Researches, Is Inscribed: In Acknowlegment Of The Obligations And In Testimony Of The Friendship Of The Author," the research that Morgan and Parker carried out together was intended to be redemptive for Indians and English-speakers alike. As Morgan concludes in the words of Cicero: "without the highest justice a republic cannot be governed" (461). The *League* was to be not simply a new kind of classicism and a new testament for the Iroquois, but also a new, more humanistically and scientifically based testament for American civil society,

Social Practices of "Interpretation"

Following Fernandez and Herzfeld, we need to understand these analytical practices in historical and ethnographic terms. Here I will argue that social practices of "interpretation" created an important crossroads, perhaps even some common ground, among divergent social, political, religious, and scientific interests. In the case of the Iroquois, this might seem obvious, but that very supposition bears closer scrutiny. At the time that Morgan and Ely S. Parker were collecting objects they considered distinctive of the "ancient Iroquois," the contemporary Iroquois were becoming ever more like the settlers of English, Dutch, German, and French origins around them. Yet most still spoke "Indian," as the English-speaking settlers called the several Iroquoian languages, and Seneca-speakers in later years were still criticizing the linguistic correctness of "interpreters who Anglicize their Indian too much."[64]

Ely S. Parker later recorded that the Baptist missionaries at the reservation school he attended as a child in the 1830s forbid the students to speak Seneca, but he and others did anyway. According to a story that Laura Parker Doctor later told Arthur Parker, when Ely was required as a child to interpret for a Baptist missionary in a church service at Tonawanda, he fell down in a faint. By his own account, he did not decide to learn English until a year later, returning from Canada, when he found himself the butt of jokes from English soldiers who thought he could not understand what they were saying. He then became an expert not only in speaking and writing English (including penmanship, as his contemporaries repeatedly observed), but also a skilled translator between Seneca- and English-speakers, as did his brother Nicholson, who became an interpreter for the federal government. Nicholson Parker also worked with Asher Wright on translations of the New Testament gospels and other religious works into Seneca, published under Wright's name, including the journal that Wright called *The Mental Elevator*.

Both brothers became renowned for their oratory, Nicholson in particular, who gave several speeches around western New York in the early
1850s. A common subject was "Indian character," of which their very
oratorical skill was a demonstration, contributing to the arguments that
Morgan and Parker made in the *League* that the Iroquois should be recognized as the Greeks of this new American republic.[65] Morgan's sensitivity to language and its interpretation is evident in the fact that he
almost always noted who was working as interpreter in his visits to Tonawanda and other Seneca communities; in his frequent questions to Ely
S. Parker concerning Seneca terms; his use of these in the *League* and in
other writing; and in his numerous short commentaries on language and
linguistic practices, especially naming practices, in the journals, in the
League, and in several papers. Perhaps for different reasons, both Morgan
and Ely S. Parker were especially sensitive to the ways in which the Iroquois, dead and living, spoke through the land.[66]

Following the pioneering work of Mary Black-Rogers, scholars of Native American history have become increasingly interested in the ethnose-
mantics of archival texts.[67] The sociolinguistic dimensions of relations
among settlers in western New York during the lifetime of Handsome
Lake and in the 1840s and '50s, when Jemmy Johnson, Ely S. Parker,
and Morgan were working together, raise many questions that deserve
further research. How did these social practices of "interpretation"
among different social worlds, frequently related to adoption, fosterage,
and intermarriage, relate to the ways that participants understood those
worlds for themselves as well as others? How might these interpretive
practices have been taken up in what Morgan later called "instruments,"
new methods of understanding in religion and science, as well as politics?
And how, through their use in common contexts, might these new practices of mutual understanding or disagreement have been related to each
other? Interpretation was a marked event in encounters between Iroquois
and their English-speaking neighbors. What is perhaps less obvious is that
interpretation was no less critical among the English-speakers, the subject
to which we now turn.

I have argued so far that Morgan's and Parker's research among then
dwindling numbers of Iroquois was dedicated to revelation as a human
practice, to understanding an enduring Christian mystery: How could it
be just that the innocent should die to atone for the wicked? How might
their suffering possibly redeem the republic, as well as themselves? Interpretation was critical to the analytical problems they encountered in pursuing this mystery, not only interpretation between Iroquoian and English ways of speaking, but also interpretation between these forms of
speech and forms of imagery and action, ways of making things, ways of
living. While these forms of interpretation might seem self-evident to us

now, I will argue that they were then embroiled in fierce debates about the connections within God's Word (for example, interpreting the New Testament between English and Seneca), and between God's Word and what some would call God's Works, but others would not.

The debates about how to grasp the revelation of the Word and Works represented in the Bible were inseparable from the debates about how to interpret the connections between the Bible itself—ever-increasing quantities of Bibles—and the world. Most obviously, these were debates about the Christian doctrine of incarnation—long-standing questions about the revelations of God's Word in human and humanly apprehensible forms. In western New York State at this time, these questions were also intensely political. Protestants' convictions about everyone's right to decide such matters for themselves were federally supported in the post-Revolutionary United States by their First Amendment rights to the free exercise of religion. Battles to extend these rights continued to be fought out in the states until the passage in 1868 of the Fourteenth Amendment prohibited the states from abridging the "privileges or immunities" of any citizen. For people like Morgan, these questions were also about what he and others were beginning to call "science." For Morgan, this included knowledge and means of knowing and understanding that were public in the political sense, as when he had sought to open to all interested parties the investigations of the Grand Order of the Iroquois; and that were material in being incarnate in human beings and humanly apprehensible phenomena, yet without resolving how one might grasp this incarnation and in what forms.

The forms of God's Works were evidently not identical to linguistic patterns, even to the extent that God's Word could be understood as such. So how might God's Works be patterned? How structurally might they be connected to the forms of God's Word? How might these forms or patterns endure or unfold over time? Were these forms and patterns accessible to ordinary human beings? And how, in their multiple and shifting incarnations, at once in and yet seemingly beyond history, were they to be apprehended? Or was it so, as many Christians argued, that God alone could reveal them to human beings? And if so, did God reveal them to all people, or only to some, completely, or only partly, leaving some ineluctable mysteries to be revealed only in the fullness of Eternity, but if so, which and why? These I will argue posed critical problems of interpretation for Morgan and his contemporaries. They could draw analytical insights from how they interpreted between varieties of speaking in their polyglot social, political, and religious communities, but had to go beyond them to understand these forms beyond speech.

Given the roots of so many of these problems in struggles over the Christian mysteries of incarnation, I will begin by examining how the

Morgans' close friend, Reverend McIlvaine, sought to interpret God's Word and Works for his parishioners and teach them how to interpret for themselves; then turn to Morgan and the research he did after his collaboration with Ely S. Parker. I will argue that McIlvaine's notion of "historical symbols" uniting Words and Works may have helped Morgan to create what he eventually called "instruments" for interpreting links among humans from Adam and Eve to the present day. As we shall see, Morgan took these inquiries, and the ethical questions about suffering and death that they entailed, much farther than McIlvaine, into the realm of other living creatures who were indubitably among God's Works, but seemingly not incarnations in quite the same ways as humans. Morgan eventually called them "the Mutes," because he, like some of his contemporaries (but not McIlvaine, for example) considered these other creatures to be very like humans, yet communicating without speech. I will argue that Morgan saw the interpretation of the works of the Mutes as illuminating the interpretation of God's Works in ways that the interpretation of words alone could not.

Interpreting God's Works: "Truths Afterwards to Be Declared in Words"

In the years between 1842, when he was ordained by the Presbytery of Albany, and 1848, when he became the minister of the First Presbyterian Church in Rochester, where he stayed for the next twelve years, Reverend Joshua Hall McIlvaine was serving as pastor in small-town churches in western New York State: in Little Falls (1842–43) and Utica (1843–47). According to the *Gazetteer* for New York, published in 1843, Aurora (to which Morgan had just returned after graduating from Union) had 80 houses, 500 residents, and three churches (Presbyterian, Episcopal, and Methodist); Little Falls had some 2500 residents and five churches; Utica had 12,810 residents and one to four churches for nine denominations. All these places were located in the midst of the "Burned-over District," in which Presbyterian, Congregational, Methodist, Baptist, Episcopalian, and other religious groups were swept by reforms so scorching that New Yorkers compared them to the fires they used to clear forest land.[68]

Besides the sectarian competition, McIlvaine would also have been contending with the practice that Captain Basil Hall of the British Royal Navy noted with interest when he traveled across western New York State in 1827: "In America, the clergymen, are chosen by their congregations, and may be dismissed at pleasure."[69] Basil Hall suggested that the constitutional disestablishment of religion in America fostered a distinctly independent attitude toward religious practices. Although Protestant Christianity persisted so many decades into the twentieth century as to belie this political claim, one can still detect, in what Basil Hall described, a distinct prickliness in the convictions of the people he met in western New York. Precisely as Americans, they had the right to whatever beliefs and practices they chose, including the right to fire the preacher who did not suit them. One of the strongest arguments of Iroquois leaders against Christianity was that the political support for freedom of religion, and doctrinal support for tolerance, were not applied to Iroquois religious practices.[70]

To these circumstances should be added the proliferation of Bibles and Bible commentaries since the 1820s, evident in the Morgans' own library. The Morgans' collection included one of the most popular of these (besides John Brown's *Self-Interpreting Bible*): the five-volume *Holy Bible*, popularly known as the "Scott's Family Bible," including "original notes, practical observations, and copious marginal references." "Scott's" was the family Bible of Harriet Steele, Lewis's mother, Mary's father's sister, which they inherited in August 1854 after Harriet's death.[71] Besides other Bibles and Testaments, they also kept acquiring numerous commentaries on specific biblical books throughout their lifetimes. Peter Wosh argues that the phenomenal growth in the printing and distribution of religious literature in the United States during the nineteenth century was part of a deliberate effort of some sectarians to create a Christian American culture. He attributes the growth of the American Bible Society in particular to the Society's innovations in capitalist business practices that eventually put them at a much greater social distance not only from their own workers, but also from their buyers.[72] McDannell argues further that "what prompted the extraordinary growth in the Bible industry was the development of an ideology that stressed the importance of the Bible in the home," a "parallel rise in America of affectionate religion and domestic sentimentality."[73]

The intimacy of these relations, virtually fusing biblical and contemporary figures, is powerfully expressed in the love poem that Mary Morgan sent Lewis Henry Morgan for Valentine's Day, February 14, 1848, based on Genesis 1.1–3. Lewis himself seems to be the very "One Who changed the darkest chaos into light" (fig. 8.2). The Morgans also bought Bibles and Testaments in order to give them as gifts. The personal nature of their Bibles and Testaments may be evident in the fact that most of those listed in the Morgans' library list seem to have been kept by family members and never made it into Rochester University's library. Yet I would argue that here too the huge growth in Christian literature—the proliferation of big family Bibles, including commentaries, as well as the ever-growing number of studies of specific biblical

Thy thoughts are haunting me!
O, there are words of low-toned eloquence,
That sound within the heart more thrillingly
Than the most joyous peals of music-choirs!
We would hush horn & lute & singer's voices,
To list to melody that fills the soul.
We would listen on for ever. Listen,
Unmindful of the crowd that hovers round,
Of noisy mirth, of careless badinage;
Thoughtless alike of flying wings of time,
Of the moon hastening in her onward path,
Of stars that burn to ashes in the sky—
Thy thoughts are moving through my spirit now,
Like as on 'face of waters' moved the One
Who changed the darkest chaos into light.

V.

[Mrs Mary Elizabeth (Steele) Morgan]

Feb. 14, 1848

Figure 8.2. Poem based on Genesis 1.1–3, given to Lewis Morgan on Valentine's Day, February 14, 1848. Based on the handwriting, the poem is attributed to Mary Elizabeth Steele. It was pasted with other correspondence into the scrapbooks of letters Morgan kept in his study (Morgan Papers, Box 1:12). Reproduced with the permission of the Department of Rare Books and Special Collections, University of Rochester Library.

books and Bible dictionaries—was also an expression of the fiercely defended right of people to decide religious matters for themselves, including the interpretation of the Bible, and to tell others, through these exchanges, how they might do the same.

McIlvaine's *The Tree of the Knowledge of Good and Evil*, which he had published in 1847 just before coming to the First Presbyterian Church in Rochester in 1848, suggests that he had his hands full trying to explain to his parishioners how they should read their Bibles. His *Tree* is not limited to elucidating the mystery of the talking snake, or even the mystery of why innocent people should be sacrificed to atone for the evils of others, although he keeps returning to these matters. McIlvaine's main concern was to explain the very principles of "interpretation" that would allow his readers to read their Bibles for themselves, even if only God could grant them revelation. McIlvaine's key to interpreting the Bible lay in his emphasis on the unity of God's Words and Works as represented in the events of the Bible. His *Tree* would show that "most of these events have a symbolical and significant character . . . [,] justify upon acknowledged principles this way of viewing those events; and at the same time to vindicate their claim to be facts which actually occurred as they are recorded."

McIlvaine felt compelled to offer this common ground for interpretation because of a growing divide between advocates of "literal" and "spiritual" interpretations of God's Word:

> Not infrequently they [the literalists] are suspicious of every attempt to show a meaning in any part of its narratives, deeper than that which appears upon the surface. They are afraid lest they should find their Bible explained away into myths and allegories, such as the fables of the heathen. Therefore they constantly affirm the literal sense of what is recorded, and deny what they call a spiritual sense.
>
> Another class of readers and students of the Word are always seeking to pierce through the literal sense after something more profound and spiritual. These are often unwilling to regard a given narrative as a record of facts and events. For them it must be left free to convey an allegorical sense which is often inconsistent with the literal one.

His argument is that the Word is both literal and spiritual: "each of these views, exclusive of the other, is narrow, incomplete, and fraught with manifest evil consequences. . . . The histories of the Old Testament do record facts and events which occurred as they are narrated and described, and . . . these facts and events are to be taken as types or symbols of spiritual truth." The ritual laws described in the Old Testament exemplify "truths afterwards to be declared in words." The account of Jonah, who was three nights and three days in the belly of the whale, is another example of an historical event which is also a truth—the truth of the crucifixion and resurrection of Jesus Christ—that was only afterwards declared in words. Jonah's story exemplifies "an historical event which occurred as it is described. But it is not barren. It is pregnant. It is full of divine significance. It sets forth as in a living picture the universal truth. . . . [The] power [of such stories] is to be felt by gazing upon them rather than by reasoning about them. . . . Mere enunciations in words can never attain to the life and power of such symbols as these." The person who denies "the life and power of these historical symbols" must beware: "[He] turns away from the only door into the Holy of Holies, and seeks to climb up some other way. . . . If he should discover order it may be but the order of his own mind. . . . He casts himself loose upon a wide and dangerous sea without chart, or compass, or rudder. He is liable to be continually driven and tossed upon an infinite chaos of his own imaginations, over which the Spirit of God has never brooded."

McIlvaine goes on to argue against Christians who believe that only some people will be saved. This was a common attitude toward the Iroquois, as Minnie Myrtle noted.[74] McIlvaine uses this to make a more general point about biblical interpretation, analogous to his general reasoning about "historical symbols": in the Bible, particulars have their specific historical validity, but they are also general truths. Thus, God's Word was given "through a chosen and peculiar people, for humanity."[75]

Morgan's views in the *League* suggest that, although he did not share McIlvaine's convictions about revelation, he did assume the existence of these truths in historical forms, and that people anywhere, even without God's Word, might discern them through their interpretations of God's Works. Thus, in discussing "the faith of the Iroquois," he states that "Man, shut out from the light of revelation, and left to construct his own theology, will discover some part of the truth, as shadowed forth by the works of nature." For example, the immortality of the soul is "another of those truths, written, as it were, by the Deity, in the mind of man, and one easily to be deciphered from the page of nature by unperverted reason."[76]

The Morgans' own Family Bible exemplifies one of the most crucial forms in which they and their contemporaries might have confronted such matters in their everyday lives, and the questions such matters might have raised for them. When Lewis Morgan and Mary Steele married, they got a new Family Bible, with which they began their Library List. As was commonly done, they incorporated their own family history into the Bible, keeping written records of births, marriages, and deaths, as well as other documents, at the back of the book. Some time, perhaps in 1862, around the time of the deaths of their two young daughters, they set into the inside front cover of the Bible, a composite portrait of their family, including daguerreotypes of themselves and their three children (fig. 8.3). Just as the frontispiece to Disturnell's *Gazetteer of New-York* (1843) includes not only the mountains, rivers, and lakes of God's Works, but also the canals that rival the rivers in length, so the Morgans' Family Bible includes not only the posterity of Adam, Eve, and Noah, but also themselves and their own descendants. As their Scott's Family Bible stated, "all mankind are of one family, and nearly related in Adam and Noah."[77] The Morgans' reckoning of their near and far relations was no less numerical than the heights and lengths of the "face of the country," including full and half siblings and first and second cousins who could be at various removes. Yet here too, the nature of these apparently precise relations, compounded by their intimate yet distant connections to biblical figures, was far from obvious, especially as they were repeatedly broken by death. In the deaths of their daughters, the Morgans faced "the great catastrophe of humanity," as Lewis called it in the *League*.[78]

For Morgan interpretation was not only a mode of biblical inquiry, but also scientific inquiry, following William Whewell's Aphorism 17, "Man is the interpreter of nature, science is the right interpretation" in his *Philosophy of the Inductive Sciences* (1840), elaborated in Whewell's *The Plurality of Worlds*, the new American edition of which Morgan bought shortly after it came out in 1855.[79] In retrospect, as Morgan himself later emphasized in his introduction to *Systems of Consanguinity and Affinity of the Human Family* (1871), these years, from the mid-1850s into the 1860s (which happened to be when he and Mary Morgan were raising their three children and burying two of them), were critical to his future research on familial relations, which gradually spread from the Iroquois to all humanity. In 1857, he returned again to his study of the Iroquois, focusing on their unusual system of descent through the mother, their particular system of "Family Relationships," and how "their celebrated League was but an elaboration of these relationships into a complex, and even stupendous system of civil polity."[80] In summer 1858, business interests took him to the iron-mining country around Marquette, Michigan, on the southern shore of Lake Superior. There, in speaking to local Ojibwa Indians about their paternal system of descent, he discovered an astounding phenomenon. Although the Iroquoian and Algonquian languages of the Iroquois and the Ojibwa were entirely different, and likewise their methods of calculating descent, yet structural patterns of their family relationships were virtually identical, suggesting to Morgan that they might have been related in the far distant past. In August 1859, he presented his discovery of the "System of Consanguinity of the Red Race in Its Relations to Ethnology" at the annual meetings of the American Association for the Advancement of Science.

Figure 8.3. Daguerreotypes of Lewis H. Morgan and Mary Elizabeth Steele Morgan (married in 1851), and their three children, Lemuel Steele Morgan (born in 1853), Mary Elizabeth Morgan (born in 1855), and Helen King Morgan (born in 1860), set into the inside front cover of *The Holy Bible* (New York, American Bible Society, 1848). Each child's portrait seems to have been made at about the same age (around two years old?) in the same dress, perhaps their christening dress. The symmetry suggests that the composite portrait in the Family Bible was made at one time, whether before or after the girls' deaths in May and June 1862 is not known. Reproduced with the permission of the Department of Rare Books and Special Collections, University of Rochester Library.

From a particular people, the Iroquois, and a particular "code of descent," he moved to the Indians of North America and "the elaborate and special character of the system itself." Almost immediately he began sending out inquiries around the world, to business people and government representatives, but especially to missionaries, asking them to question the people around them about their family relationships to see if semantic patterns common to these relationships might prove powerful enough to substantiate the unity of the Human Family overall. Already in

"System of Consanguinity of the Red Race," he envisioned "*the fountain of descent*," (his emphasis), which is simultaneously "the footsteps of migrations, long since buried in the gloom of departed ages . . . the pathway of the generations . . . marked with epochs of migration from age to age."[81]

These common patterns, semantic and perhaps geographic, hidden within disparate ways of speaking, as if they were silent memorials of the historical events long past, are not unlike McIlvaine's "historical symbols" that would only "afterwards . . . be declared in words." Yet Morgan's emphasis is different, and he himself felt that he had discovered in these patterns a "new instrumentality" that could replace conventional philology as the foundation of ethnological research.

> The argument is not, as before stated, in the identity of the words used to describe the relationships, but in the ideas which are embedded in the system; and which are constant and unvarying. It may thus be found that a system of relationship endured with the constancy of ideas standing in definite relations to each other and with the immortality of an idea, will reach farther back upon the covered footsteps of the human race, than language itself; and resolve questions of the genealogical connection of races, which philology cannot compass; thereby opening to ethnology a *new instrumentality* with which to press forward her great inquiry concerning the original genealogical connections of the nations of the earth. . . . It is within the possible; nay more, there is some encouragement, that with a thread as delicate, almost invisible as a system of relationship, we may yet reascend the several lines of the outflow of the generations, and search and identify that parent nation from which we are, we believe, all alike descended.[82]

Trautmann argues that Morgan's "System of Consanguinity of the Red Race" presents us in embryo with the argument of his great work on the *Systems of Consanguinity and Affinity of the Human Family*. He shows in detail how Morgan's discovery derived from the philological approaches to the study of history and society in his time and yet how Morgan completely revolutionized it.[83] Here I have suggested that Morgan's theological assumptions about the interpretation of God's Works might have contributed to the way he conceptualized his "new instrument for ethnology." Now I want to explore how Morgan's longtime interest in animals, prompted by his larger concerns about "the mystery of life in all its forms," might also have contributed to that discovery, and how he pursued these concerns not only in his global investigations of the systems of blood and marriage of the Human Family, but also in the research he did concurrently on the riverine beaver communities in northern Michigan.

Interpreting "The Mutes": The American Beaver and His Works

Morgan's papers show that while he was writing essays and giving papers on geology, the Greeks, the Iroquois, and the Human Family, he was also interested in the question of "Mind vs. Instinct" in animals. In 1843, he published two papers on this subject for *The Knickerbocker*, one of his mother's favorite periodicals.[84] He returned to this subject again in a paper he called "Animal Psychology," delivered to the other members of his "Club" on April 7, 1857 (the same year he had started working again on Iroquois family relationships), then again in a paper on "Beaver Dams and Lodges," presented to them on October 16, 1860, when he had begun to inquire about family relations around the globe.

Morgan's antipathy for the concept of "instinct" was already evident in his earlier essays for *The Knickerbocker* (1843) on the "lower animals," as he then called them; in his later (1857) account of "Animal Psychology," he speaks of "the Mutes," or "the Mutae." Of instinct, he says bluntly: "We have here a system of philosophy in a definition; we have an installation of the supernatural, which silences at once all inquiry into the facts."[85] His language might serve as a reminder that "instinct" was as much a subject of theology and the epistemology of science, as of philosophy, psychology, and zoology. According to the view of the day, in contrast to "the brutes," who lived by instinct, human beings lived by reason and moral obligation and thus they advanced spiritually, as well as scientifically. Asa Mahan's *A System of Intellectual Philosophy*, published a few years earlier in 1854, was typical in illustrating this claim with the beaver and its works: "With all his observations, the brute has never advanced a single step. He is now just where he was six thousand years ago. The beaver builds his dam, lives and dies, just as did the first that ever appeared on earth. The same is true of the action of every brute race."[86]

When Morgan returned to "Animal Psychology," he had visited Marquette once in the summer of 1855, as one of several business men from Rochester investing in the new railroad enterprises of the Ely family, formerly Rochester's leading flour-millers. Morgan had not yet started to do research on the beavers around Marquette. This research began in July and August 1860, right after he had launched his worldwide investigations of human consanguinity and affinity. But clearly, judging from little comments in "Animal Psychology," he had been talking and making observations, for example, about the Ely family's pets. He stayed with the family of Samuel P. Ely, to whom he dedicated *The American Beaver and His Works*. Interspersed with accounts of marmosets, quails, beavers, rats, elephants, dogs, insects, cranes, and wild goats in Crete, drawn from natural histories, and popular and scholarly magazines, are stories about Hervey Ely's impressions of local lizards and Mrs. Ely's cats.[87]

His examples, drawn from such disparate sources, are a clue to the generality of the convictions he was trying to explore. Based on the parallels between the physiological structures of human beings and other creatures, especially the sensory organs, which he regards as "the inlets and the instruments of all objective knowledge . . . a condition of life," Morgan argues that "the thinking principle is the same throughout the realm of animated nature. . . . It is precisely here, as it seems to be, that God has revealed to us a feature in the plan of creation scarcely less wonderful, than the creation of mind itself." To understand the thinking principle, scientists should study all creatures, because it dwells in living creatures in their entirety, including "the lost, as well as existing species, and rendering possible [the existence of] intelligences higher than man endowed with the same principle."

The key to his argument is in his view of the many forms, not limited to speech, in which the thinking principle may be expressed, and the extent of our consciousness of how they structure our lives. In Morgan's view, scholars like William Hamilton, who argue that "An instinct is an agent which performs blindly and ignorantly a work of intelligence and knowledge," make a mistake in assuming that

> the mind is necessarily conscious of all of its own processes and that it is at all times percipient of itself. The mind is capable of operating with electrical rapidity. We teach the mind to think in human language, to cloth its thoughts in a dress of words. These words are material, so to speak, and the use of every syllable requires a particle of time. Hence our mental processes which are deliberate require time for their evolution. But once place the mind under the pressure of excitement, or sudden peril, and away in an instant goes your cumbrous machinery of human words; and the mind flies along a line of images or short hand symbols all perfectly intelligible hieroglyphics at a rate of velocity which defies the tardy speed of consciousness. It is reasonable to believe that all those acts of ours which we cannot account for in any rational manner, are the work in some way we cannot fully understand, of that great and marvellous endowment: the thinking principle. For that class of phenomena of the human mind usually called instinctive we have a corresponding class of phenomena among the inferior animals but beyond these the acts of the Mutae are as explainable as those of the human race."[88]

In fact, Morgan suggests that such "line[s] of images or short hand symbols" are a more basic form of thought than words, truths only later to be clothed in words. Thus:

Although the Mutae have not articulate speech, it does not follow that they have no mode of communication with each other. Thought is anterior to all language, and not necessarily dependent upon it. Every man must be conscious of mental processes, and of reasoning from premises to conclusions without the use of words. From facts within our knowledge it would not be difficult to prove, I think, that the Mutae are able to communicate their thoughts to each other, independent of the great fact that all social life would be impossible without it [communication].

The corollary of these observations for Morgan is that "man alone is not a progressive animal." "Modern man" is not "one shade beyond" the greats of ancient times like Homer, Euclid, and Archimedes in the profundity of his intellect. On the contrary, unlike the Greeks and Romans who believed that animals could reason and remember, "we deny them all rights and savage them with wanton and unmerciful cruelty . . . the habitats of many species would contract until they would be finally extirpated." He concludes that the ancient philosophy of the transmigration of souls provided "a shield for the protection of the inferior animals against the rapacity of man. . . . Great is the pity then, that like the shield of Achilles, it now exists only in poetry."[89]

Thus I think it is possible that Morgan adopted the structural framework of McIlvaine's arguments about "truths afterwards to be declared in words," without adopting McIlvaine's convictions about revelation. Abstracted from its doctrinal, but not its ethical, entailments, this is Morgan's new instrument for ethnology. Not only did Morgan's later research on the beavers document their myriad works, clear evidence, as he saw it, of the ways they learn to adapt to different environments and pass on this learning to the next generation; his research also led him to conclude that their works provide proof of the capacities of these creatures to imagine, experiment, adapt and improve themselves over centuries, until now finally they are being destroyed or driven out by humankind.

Morgan makes his points through direct research on the beavers' works, drawing and measuring their dams, lodges, and canals. As I have argued elsewhere, he also brings in as evidence the observations of the "Indian trappers" who are his guides, for example, Paul Pine, Jack LaPete, William Cameron, and William Bass, among others. With their help, Morgan encountered not the movements of souls of "that ancient philosopher, whoever he was, who first promulgated the doctrine of the transmigration of souls," but ideas and practices based on the capacities of animals, humans, and spirits to shift their shapes into one another. These derived from the intimate interrelations of animals and humans, considered to be akin to one another. Animals served as critical intermediaries between human beings and spirits of various kinds, working through their powers of interpretation. The people who worked with Morgan, many of them descendants of unions of affinity made across the social lines separating Indians and Europeans, were themselves experts at interpretation. Much like the shape shifters in their stories, they were fluent in several language, typically including more than one Indian language, as well as French and English, and often, like Ely S. Parker and his brothers, they worked as interpreters.[90]

The prevalence of arguments based on animal behavior in making theological, as well as social and zoological arguments, and the unusualness of Morgan's research, premises, and conclusions in this intellectual environment, is evident once again from the concurrent work of his close friend McIlvaine. While Morgan went on to do firsthand research on his theories of "instinct," focusing on the beaver communities around Marquette, McIlvaine continued to affirm: "Human reason is a nobler endowment than the instinct of the beaver."[91] Even after Morgan's years of research and the publication of *The American Beaver and His Works*, McIlvaine still held the same view, now contributing to his arguments about social organization in *Organization of the Fundamental Principles of Social Science*, published in 1876:

> It is true, however, that in some species of insects we find striking semblance of organization. . . . But even in this case, the individuals of each class are mere repetitions of each other, and are engaged in the same operations, to which they are confined by a distinct and peculiar physical constitution. We can discover nothing here of the nature of voluntary division or organization of labor. . . . Even here . . . as in so many other cases, the operations of instinct counterfeit those of reason. Among animals in general there is not even this semblance. Those of the same species are all confined to means and operations which are precisely or nearly the same. Birds of the same species build their nests in the same manner, and there is no part in the work of a beaver-dam which one beaver cannot perform as well as another. Mere animals are incapable of specializing.[92]

Reconsidering Providence in Human Progress: Balance and Accident

When he wrote "Animal Psychology" in 1857, Morgan was still hopeful that a divinely ordained "balance" in the design of mutual relations among living creatures would prevent human progress, apparently inextricable from the massive slaughter of other animals, from extirpating entire species.

If the human race should maintain its present attitude towards the mutae and progress in numbers and civilization for several centuries, the habitats of many species would contract until they would be finally extirpated. But this will never happen. God created every creature primarily for the creature himself. The gift of life was designed for him alone who received it at His hand, subject to the law of relation established between the species. He has adjusted a balance between these races, and given to each the vital and vegetative power necessary for its perpetuity. Every species is surrounded alike with the means of life, and the means of enjoyment; and no one is made dependent upon the will of another.[93]

By the time he rewrote this paper for the conclusion of *The American Beaver*, published in 1868, both "progress" and "balance" had taken on new significance:

If the human family maintains its present hostile attitude toward the mutes, and increases in numbers and in civilization at the present ratio, for several centuries to come, it is plain to be seen that many species of animals must be extirpated from the earth. An arrest of the progress of the human race can alone prevent the dismemberment and destruction of a large portion of the animal kingdom. Domestication or extermination is the alternative already offered not only to species, but to families and orders of animals. It may be that this result was never intended in the councils of Providence. It is not unlikely that God has adjusted a balance among the several orders of animals which cannot be overthrown except at the peril of the aggressor; and that in some mysterious way this balance is destined to be preserved. . . . The annual sacrifice of animal life to maintain human life is frightful.[94]

By the time Morgan completed *Ancient Society* a decade later, he was suggesting that the "property career" which dominated his stage of "civilization" cannot be "the final destiny of mankind, if progress is to be the law of the future as it has been of the past," because "The dissolution of society bids fair to become the termination of a career of which property is the end and aim; because such a career contains the elements of self-destruction."[95] Here there is no balance. Although *Ancient Society* is based on whatever evidence of "progress" he can bring together, and dedicated to his friend, Joshua Hall McIlvaine still convinced of a God-given capacity for moral betterment unique to human beings, Morgan is now confronting too much counterevidence to claim anything certain but chance, accident, and an ever more inscrutable Providence:

It must be regarded as a marvelous fact that a portion of mankind five thousand years ago, less or more, attained to civilization . . . yet civilization must be regarded as an accident of circumstances . . . civilization might as naturally have been delayed for several thousand years in the future, as to have occurred when it did in the good providence of God. We are forced to the conclusion that it was the result, as to the time of its achievement, of a series of fortuitous circumstances. It may well serve to remind us that we owe our present condition, with its multiplied means of safety and of happiness, to the struggles, the sufferings, the heroic exertions and the patient toil of our barbarous, and more remotely, of our savage ancestors. Their labors, their trials and their successes were a part of the plan of the Supreme Intelligence to develop a barbarian out of a savage, and a civilized man out of this barbarian.[96]

Peculiarly "Historical Symbols" and Culture

Examining Morgan's life and his work with Ely S. Parker and others, it is possible to see many areas worth further study in which religious issues may have contributed to popular and scholarly understandings of what was later called "culture." These include the ways that the Bible was associated with culture, in the sense of "civilization," through the commercial proliferation of Bibles during the nineteenth century; the association of the Bible with culture in interpersonal relations through gift-giving and inheritance; the ways that people drew on biblical language and imagery to express their most intimate feelings for one another; and the close association of religious with political liberties in the post-Revolutionary United States. Anthropologists, motivated by the same ideal that motivated Morgan—open inquiry, unfettered by "supernatural" reasoning—have striven to shrive their discipline of doctrinal ties. Yet I think some roots of Protestant Christianity still remain in anthropologists' conceptions of culture—in the "types" and "symbols" of structural, historical reasoning and in the persistence of Morgan's questions, if not his answers, about the design of which these were part.

Judging from his writings, Morgan seems to have remained committed to some notion of design, which he calls "Providence," until his death. But now it is worth clarifying what he might have meant by that and just what relevance his concerns might have to us now. Clearly, his conception of Providence did not entail blind adherence to dogma. He emphatically objected to the popular notion of "instinct" in marking the "installation of the supernatural, which silences at once all inquiry into the facts." His main concern consistently throughout his life was ethics. I believe he questioned the very premise of McIlvaine's theology, that Christ's "blood cleanseth us from all sin." And he questioned its entailments, as McIlvaine described them in *The Tree of the Knowledge of Good and Evil*: "that the chastisements of labor, sorrow and death are holy things, to be submitted to in penitence and in faith; that the atonement of Christ is the only salvation for him; that he must be crucified with Christ in order to live and reign with him; that his own strength, or the obedience of his own agency, is utterly in vain to save him from the curse and power of sin; that the agency and obedience of Christ in and for him are all-sufficient to restore and perfect his spiritual life, and to bring into him an 'everlasting righteousness.' "[97]

Morgan kept questioning whether such sorrows and deaths could be divinely ordained as chastisements, whether it could be supposed that humans must blindly reproduce these mysteries of slaughter in their everyday lives and in their generations. I think "instinct" was the counterpart of the earth without form and void, the face of the deep before creation, that he was dedicated to revealing. Indeed, he widened the problem, extending the capacity for "revelation" to all living creatures, thus magnifying the question of how it could be possible for creatures knowingly to slaughter each other, others who could not be regarded as living stones. As he expanded his knowledge of the consciousness of creatures, so too, he was forced to expand his understanding of its social complexities, having to revise his conception of the hidden life of instinct to encompass the relations of creatures who had consciously to hide to protect themselves from slaughter by others. This included the rampant slaughter of the American beaver, who "with his life, has contributed in no small degree to the colonization and settlement of the British provinces and the United States," but also the Iroquois (in *League*), our "savage" and "barbarian" forebears (at the end of *Ancient Society*), and finally his own children, for whose deaths he held himself to blame.[98] He presents us not with the conventional historical irony of the Protestant ethic: that abstemious dedication to hard work should produce luxury; but rather that this work, which is intended to be so fruitful, could ultimately be so destructive of all that one values.

"Culture" may be "one of the two or three most complicated words in the English language," as Raymond Williams claims, because it still entails some consideration of the "mystery of life in all its forms," with which Morgan was also struggling. The complexity, as Williams states, "is not finally in the word but in the problems which its variations of use significantly indicate." Kroeber and Kluckhohn comment that "The history of the word 'culture' presents many interesting problems in the application of culture theory itself." Yet they clearly equate their own approach to "scientific definition" with how culture operates in history: "In the operation of definition one may see in microcosm the essence of the cultural process: the imposition of a conventional form upon the flux of experience. . . . [S]cientific definition represents a sharpening of the same process that occurs more slowly and less rationally in culture generally."[99] Williams, by contrast, sees culture in history as a kind of political argument. Morgan's focus was on those peculiarly "historical symbols" that might disclose the very source of life, suffering, and death, not simply how life is first created from chaos, as in Genesis, but how new life can be brought out of death and killing, again and again.

Morgan fell back on "sacrifice," as if suffering might still be redemptive. There are echoes of this biblical understanding of human history in Boas's later writings on eugenics—the social management of death—in 1916. As Degler points out, Boas argued against eugenics, not on the grounds one might have expected, that such practices could be turned against particular groups of people, but rather because of the cultural importance of suffering:

'The wish for the elimination of unnecessary suffering [the stated goal of eugenics]', [Boas] contended 'is divided by a narrow margin from the wish for the elimination of all suffering.' Such a goal 'may be a beautiful ideal [but] it is unattainable. . . . ' The work of human beings will always require suffering and 'men must be willing to bear' that suffering. Besides, [Boas] continued, many of the world's great works of beauty 'are the precious fruit of mental agony; and we should be poor indeed if the willingness of man to suffer should disappear. . . . We are clearly drifting toward the danger-line where the individual will no longer bear discomfort or pain for the sake of the continuance of the race, and where our emotional life is so strongly repressed by the desire for self-perfection—or by self-indulgence—that the coming generation is sacrificed to the selfishness of the living.' To the extent that the 'eugenic ideals of the elimination of suffering and self-develoment' are fostered . . . the sooner human beings will drift 'towards the destruction of the race.'[100]

As Carol Delaney and Susan Mizruchi have shown in different ways, the generations of scholars who created the professions of the social sciences in the late nineteenth and early twentieth centuries put sacrifice, what Mizruchi calls a "science of sacrifice," at the foundations of theories of social order that persist into scholarly and popular understandings about social life to the present day.[101] Although we are no longer using the language of Morgan and Boas, we are still faced with the same problems, with even greater capacities for the social manipulation of life and death processes. Morgan's work suggests that our definition of culture is critically connected to our humanity, not only in the sense of how we work these out, but also in our assumptions about who deserves to live and who to die. We need to find ways to make explicit these existential assumptions about the "mystery" of "life in all its forms" still hidden in conceptions of culture, so that they are open to discussion and debate.

Notes

1. See Clifford Geertz, "Religion as a Cultural System," in *Anthropological Approaches to the Study of Religion*, ed. Michael Banton (London: Tavistock, 1966), pp. 1–46.

2. See Edward Burnett Tylor, "The Science of Culture," in *Primitive Culture* (London: John Murray, 1871), vol. 1, pp. 1–22, especially pp. 1, 3.

3. See Alfred Kroeber and Clyde Kluckhohn, "Introduction," in *Culture: A Critical Review of Concepts and Definitions* (New York: Vintage, n.d.), p. 3. This work was originally published in the *Papers of the Peabody Museum of American Archaeology and Ethnology*, Harvard University, vol. 47, no. 1, 1952.

4. Kroeber and Kluckhohn, *Culture*, pp. 291, 311–54, 338.

5. Ibid., pp. 283–84.

6. Ibid., p. 14, drawing on the assessment of Klemm's work in Robert Lowie's *The History of Ethnological Theory* (New York: Farrar and Rinehart 1937), pp. 11–16.

7. See Raymond Williams, "Culture," in *Keywords: A Vocabulary of Culture and Society* (New York: Oxford University Press, 1976), pp. 76–82, especially pp. 76, 79.

8. See Roger M. Keesing, "Theories of Culture," *Annual Review of Anthropology* 3 (1974): 73–97 and Sidney W. Mintz, "Culture: An Anthropological View," *The Yale Review* 71 (1981/82): 499–512. For recent reassessments of "culture," see, for example: Roger M. Keesing, "Theories of Culture Revisited," in *Assessing Cultural Anthropology*, ed. Robert Borofsky, (New York: McGraw Hill, 1994), pp. 301–10; Joel S. Kahn, *Culture, Multiculture, Postculture* (London: Sage, 1995); Adam Kuper, *Culture: The Anthropologists' Account* (Cambridge, MA: Harvard University Press, 1999).

9. For example, see articles by Sylvia Yanagisako, William H. Durham, and James Lowell Gibbs, Jr., in "News of the Academy," *Anthropology Newsletter* October 1998: 21–22, on the division of the Anthropology Department at Stanford University into the Department of Cultural and Social Anthropology and the Department of Anthropological Sciences.

10. See Carl N. Degler, *Culture Versus Biology in the Thought of Franz Boas and Alfred L. Kroeber* (New York: Berg, 1989), which includes reponses by Marshall Hyatt and Barbara Duden. See also Carol C. Mukhopadhyay and Yolanda T. Moses, "Reestablishing 'Race' in Anthropological Discourse," *American Anthropologist* 99, no. 3 (1998): 517–33, especially their discussions of the current controversies between "classifiers" and "clinalists"; their sense of the likelihood that "races, although social constructions, do have a material reality and are in some sense and in some contexts biological groupings, although perhaps not by the criteria of physical anthropologists" (pp. 523–24); and their argument for new integrative frameworks for viewing "race" by "situat[ing] human biodiversity *within* a sociocultural framework, in effect reuniting culture and biology by embedding biology in society and culture" (p. 526, their emphasis).

11. E. Valentine Daniel, "Crushed Glass: A Counterpoint to Culture," in *Charred Lullabies: Chapters in an Anthropography of Violence* (Princeton, NJ: Princeton University Press, 1996), pp. 194–212, especially p. 210.

12. See Mary Margaret Steedly, "What Is Culture? Does It Matter?" in *Field Work: Sites in Literary and Cultural Studies*, ed. Marjorie Garber, Paul B. Franklin, and Rebecca L. Walkowitz (New York/London: Routledge, 1996), pp. 18–25; and Kuper in *Culture*, pp. 246–47. Arguing that "complicating or fragmenting the totality" simply reproduces the problems in "culture," while weakening

its analytical utility, Steedly advocates "writing around it" (p. 23). Like Kuper, but for different reasons, Ingold argues that the concept of culture common to social constructionist accounts "operates as a distancing device, setting up a radical disjunction between *ourselves*, rational observers of the human condition, and those *other people*, enmeshed in their traditional patterns of belief and practice, whom we profess to observe and study." Drawing especially on Gibson's "ecological psychology," Ingold emphasizes instead "people's *engagement* with the world" (his emphasis), involving enskilment, not enculturation, and the "education of attention." See Tim Ingold, "The Art of Translation in a Continuous World," in *Beyond Boundaries: Understanding, Translation and Anthropological Discourse*, ed. Gísli Pálsson (Oxford: Berg, 1993), pp. 210–35, especially pp. 213, 221.

13. Kroeber and Kluckhohn in *Culture: A Critical Review*, p. 68. They exemplify the problem in these questions: "Why did the concept 'Kultur' evolve and play such an important part in the German intellectual setting? Why has the concept of 'culture' had such difficulty in breaking through into public consciousness in France and England? Why has it rather suddenly become popular in the United States, to the point that such phrases as 'Eskimo culture' appear even in the comic strips?" Later (p. 78) they state plainly that they regard the scientific process of definition, in which they are involved, as exemplifying in microcosm how culture works historically.

Raymond Williams's observation (in *Keywords*, p. 76) that the complexity of "culture" in the English language derives in part from "its intricate historical development, in several European languages" suggests the need to combine approaches to the concept of "culture" based on the history of ideas with ethnographic analysis of the processes of state-formation through which "nations," unified around common languages and cultures, were created. Kuper's introductory remarks (in *Culture*, pp. xi–xv), drawing on his experiences as an undergraduate in South Africa in the 1950s, show how fruitful such an approach could be. Although Kuper returns to the history of ideas in the remainder of his study, Kahn (in *Culture, Multiculture*) takes precisely this approach.

14. See Thomas O. Beidelman, *W. Robertson Smith and the Sociological Study of Religion* (University of Chicago Press, 1974), and Harvey E. Goldberg, "The Voice of Jacob: Jewish Perspectives on Anthropology and the Bible," *Jewish Social Studies*, n.s., 2 (1995): 36–71.

15. See Arthur J. Vidich and Stanford M. Lyman, *American Sociology: Worldly Rejections of Religion and Their Directions* (New Haven, CT: Yale University Press, 1985); Alan Wolfe, *Whose Keeper: Social Science and Moral Obligation* (Berkeley, CA: University of California Press, 1989); David A. Hollinger, *Science, Jews, and Secular Culture: Studies in Mid-Twentieth-Century American Intellectual History* (Princeton, NJ: Princeton University Press, 1996); Stanley Edgar Hyman, *The Tangled Bank: Darwin, Marx, Frazer and Freud as Imaginative Writers* (New York: Atheneum, 1962); and Susan L. Mizruchi, *The Science of Sacrifice: American Literature and Modern Social Theory* (Princeton, NJ: Princeton University Press, 1998).

16. See Ronald L. Numbers, *The Creationists* (New York: A. A. Knopf, 1992). Numbers argues that "one of the best ways to learn about the history of 'science'

is to explore how interested parties have contested its boundaries. Many books in recent years have sought to discredit creationism scientifically or theologically, but only a few have examined the movement historically, and then primarily from a legal or pedagogical perspective. None has looked carefully at the intellectual origins of scientific creationism" (p. xiv). Numbers's own experiences growing up in "a fundamentalist Seventh-day Adventist family of ministers," which he outlines briefly (pp. xv–xvii), clearly contribute to his efforts to treat the creationists whom he interviewed "with the same respect I might accord evolutionists." Christopher P. Toumey's pioneering ethnography of contemporary scientific creationism in the United States, *God's Own Scientists: Creationists in a Secular World* (New Brunswick: Rutgers University Press, 1994), is based on a similar philosophy. In *Science, Jews, and Secular Culture: Studies in Mid-Twentieth-Century American Intellectual History* (Princeton, NJ: Princeton University Press, 1996), Hollinger also tries to understand the changing interactions of religion and other aspects of intellectual life in the United States as an historical (if not also ethnographic) problem, independently from partisanship or bigotry.

17. James W. Fernandez and Michael Herzfeld, "In Search of Meaningful Methods, " in *Handbook of Methods in Cultural Anthropology*, ed. H. Russell Bernard (Walnut Creek, CA: AltaMira, 1998), pp. 89–129, p. 93.

18. Lewis Henry Morgan, *The League of the Ho-de'-no-sau-nee, or Iroquois* (Rochester, NY: Sage and Brothers, 1851); dedicated to Ely S. Parker.

19. John Wesley Powell, "Sketch of Lewis H. Morgan, President of the American Association for the Advancement of Science," *The Popular Science Monthly* 18 (1880): 114–21; p. 115.

20. This paper is based on continuing research in the archives of Morgan's papers and related materials in the Department of Rare Books and Manuscripts, Rush Rhees Library, Rochester University, Rochester, New York in October 1994, July 1996, and June 1998; the historical archives at the John M. Longyear Research Library, Marquette County Historical Society, Marquette, Michigan in July 1997; the Special Collections of Schaffer Library, Union College in August 1998; and on ethnographic research on iron-mining in northern Michigan in July 1997. I thank Karl Kabelac and Amy Burnam, curators of the Morgan Archives; Linda Panian, librarian at the John M. Longyear Research Library; and Ellen Fladger and Betty Allen, archivists at Union College. I have also benefited from correspondence with Faye Swanberg at the Alger County Historical Society, Munising, Michigan. References to archival material will be handled as follows:

In the Lewis Henry Morgan Papers (A. M85), Department of Rare Books and Manuscripts, Rush Rhees Library, University of Rochester, New York. Morgan's unpublished essays and addresses, archived as "manuscripts," are referenced by the manuscript's number, then the page number(s). The unpublished journals of Morgan's trips (sometimes including notes on his reading), which he had bound in several series, are referenced by name ("Journal," for most of his logs and notes, or "Journal of a Visit to Europe"), volume number (sometimes followed by the section number within the volume), and page number(s). Morgan numbered a later insert by adding "1/2" or "a" to the number of the page it followed. All other material is referenced as archived in the University of Rochester's Rush Rhees Library, by its box number, followed by the number of its file within the box.

In Special Collections, Schaffer Library, Union College, Schenectady, New York, documents are referenced by title or file name.

21. Leslie A. White, "Morgan's Attitude Toward Religion and Science," *American Anthropologist*, n.s., 46; no. 2 (1944): 218–30. White advocated a new "science of culture," or "culturology," based on social evolutionary principles, which he traced back to Morgan. See White's *The Science of Culture: A Study of Man and Civilization* (New York: Farrar, Straus, 1949). White's concerns during and after World War Two about the need for "Science" in opposition to "Religion" should be seen in relation to the wider debates about science and democracy in America at this time. See Hollinger, *Science* (pp. 121–54 and passim), especially his analysis of the debates at the University of Michigan, where White was then teaching. See also William J. Peace, "Bernhard Stern, Leslie A. White, and an Anthropological Appraisal of the Russian Revolution," *American Anthropologist* 100 (1998): 84–93.

22. Jedediah Morgan's will, probated April 28, 1827 (Morgan Papers, ms. 108). The minor children included one son from Jedediah's first marriage; Jedediah and Harriet's eight children, of which Morgan, then eight years old, was the fourth; Harriet's son from her first marriage; and Harriet's niece. See Nathaniel Harris Morgan, *Morgan Genealogy. A History of James Morgan, of New London, Conn. and His Descendants; From 1607 to 1869. (13 Illustrative Portraits.), with an Appendix, Containing the History of His Brother, Miles Morgan, of Springfield, Mass.; and Some of His Descendants* (Hartford, CT: Case, Lockwood & Brainard, 1869); especially pp. 118–19 on Jedediah Morgan.

23. See the Union College *Merit Roles* available for some semesters in 1839 and 1840 (Schaffer Library, Union College). The "Union" referred to the ecumenical basis of the school, embodied in the diverse faiths of its board of trustees; the majority at any one time could not be drawn from the same sect. The name of the college was intended to express the ideals of the federal union. At that time most other colleges were denominational, concerned mainly with educating ministers in Christianity. Reverend Eliphalet Nott was a pastor of the First Presbyterian Church of Albany when he assumed the presidency of Union College in 1804. In 1828, Nott instituted a revolutionary parallel curriculum that included a Scientific Course as well as a Classical Course. Students could get the B.A. degree through either or through a combination of both. In 1842, Union College was the second, after Yale, among thirteen northeastern colleges in the number of its graduates. See V. Ennis Pilcher, *Early Science and the First Century of Physics at Union College, 1795–1895* (Glens Falls, New York: Coneco Litho Graphics, 1994), pp. 2, 41, and 31–55 passim.

24. Morgan Papers, mss. 2 and 3.

25. See Morgan's addresses, given as "Schenandoah," on April 17, 1844, in which he describes his meeting with Ely S. Parker, and on August 9, 1844, in which he describes the "form of Inindianation adopted" (Morgan Papers, mss. 9, 10).

26. See N. H. Morgan's *Morgan Genealogy*, pp. 176–79. According to Lewis Morgan's and Mary Morgan's wills drawn up in 1878 and 1880, their property was to be dispersed, mainly to the University of Rochester, only after the deaths of the surviving spouse and their son. By some agreement, nowhere preserved in the Morgan Papers, the Morgans arranged for Charles Rayner Morgan, the son of Lewis Morgan's deceased brother, Charles D. Morgan, to move with his wife and son from Waterloo, N.Y., to their house in Rochester's Third Ward, to care for Lemuel, who was not capable of caring for himself (Karl Kabelac, personal communication, October 1995). When Lemuel died in 1905, without a will and without issue, Walter Harry Morgan, Charles Rayner Morgan's younger brother, then working for what he called in court a "horse business" in Rochester, challenged the will, but he lost the case on multiple grounds in 1907. For the original wills and related material, see "Matter of Lewis H. Morgan Will . . ." (Morgan Papers, bound volume).

27. Morgan completed his research and writing on the beaver and kinship books at about the same time in the mid-1860s, but they were published in this order: *The American Beaver and His Works* (Philadelphia: J. B. Lippincott, 1868; reprinted with an introduction by Robert J. Naiman, Mineola, New York: Dover, 1996); *Systems of Consanguinity and Affinity of the Human Family*, Smithsonian "Contributions to Knowledge," XVII (Washington, DC: Smithsonian Institution, 1871; reprinted with an introduction by Elisabeth Tooker, Lincoln, NB: University of Nebraska Press, 1997); and *Ancient Society, or Researches in the Lines of Human Progress from Savagery through Barbarism to Civilization* (New York: Henry Holt, 1877; reprinted with an introduction by Eleanor Burke Leacock, Cleveland and New York: World, 1963).

Morgan joined the American Association for the Advancement of Science in 1856, nine years after it was founded in 1847. He gave several papers in annual meetings from 1857 to 1878, and organized and led a "Permanent Sub-Section of Anthropology" in 1875, before being elected President of the AAAS in 1879. He tried to found a Rochester Academy of Science in 1860, just before the Civil War. He was elected to the American Academy of Arts and Sciences in Boston in 1868, and the National Academy of Sciences in 1875. See Morgan Papers, ms. 46; Carl Resek, *Lewis Henry Morgan: American Scholar* (University of Chicago Press, 1960), pp. 68, 97–98, 133, 150–51.

28. Thomas R. Trautmann, *Lewis Henry Morgan and the Invention of Kinship* (Berkeley, CA: University of California Press, 1987).

29. Morgan Papers, Box 12:2.

30. White himself uses this contrast: "we know that Morgan's wife, to whom he was much devoted, was a very narrow, devout, and strict Presbyterian" (in "Morgan's Attitude," p. 226).

31. Morgan Papers, ms. 85 ("Inventory of books of L. H. Morgan and wife. 1851–[1881]") and 85a ("Library, as given to the U of R, 1910–1911"). The books were first dispersed in the University's library collections. After reuniting them in the University's Department of Rare Books and Special Collections, Trautmann and Kabelac wrote an annotated account of the Morgans' library. See Thomas R. Trautmann and Karl Sanford Kabelac, *The Library of Lewis Henry*

Morgan and Mary Elizabeth Morgan (Philadelphia: American Philosophical Society, Transactions vol. 84, Parts 6 and 7, 1994).

Morgan made his observations on American marriage when traveling with Mary Morgan and Lemuel in Europe in 1870–71. See Morgan Papers, "Journal of a Visit to Europe," volume 2:62.

32. Trautmann and Kabelac, *Library*, p. 33.

33. Gillian Feeley-Harnik, "'Communities of Blood': The Natural History of Kinship in Nineteenth-Century America," *Comparative Studies in Society and History* 41, no. 2 (1999): 215–68.

34. See Naiman's introduction to the Dover reprint of *The American Beaver*, pp. v–viii.

35. Fernandez and Herzfeld, "In Search," pp. 89, 93.

36. See "Capt. Alfred G." in N. H. Morgan's *Morgan Genealogy* (1869), p. 176. Morgan's journeys are documented in manuscript journals that he bound and kept in his library. They included four trips to the western frontier between 1859 and 1862, and at least ten documented trips to the Marquette area of Michigan's northern peninsula between 1855 and 1866. Lewis, Mary, and Lemuel toured through Germany, Italy, France, and Great Britain in 1870–71, a trip that both Lewis and Mary recorded in bound manuscript journals, now in the Morgan Papers.

37. Morgan Papers, Box 27:6.

38. Charles Darwin, *On the Origin of Species by Means of Natural Selection, or the Preservation of Favoured Races in the Struggle for Life*, facsimile of the first edition [1859], with an introduction by Ernst Mayr (Cambridge, MA: Harvard University Press, 1964), p. 1. Like J.F.W. Herschel (his "philosopher" here), Darwin may also refer to Sir Walter Scott's poem in *The Monastery* (1820) beginning, "Within that awful volume lies the mystery of mysteries!" Scott (who was one of the Morgans' favorite authors) was depicting sectarian disputes between Catholics and Protestants about laypeople's capacities to read and interpret the Bible for themselves. As in this poem, Scott clearly favored the "Happiest they of human race, / To whom God has granted grace / To read, to fear, to hope, to pray / To lift the latch, and force the way," as did Darwin and Morgan, who extended this approach to include their scientific investigations.

39. According to the *Oxford Universal Dictionary on Historical Principles*, 3rd ed., revised and edited by C. T. Onians (Oxford: Clarendon Press, 1955), "mystery" in the 1600s began to include secrets personal, political, diplomatic, and economic; and by 1738, the secrets of the Freemasons.

40. Morgan, *American Beaver*, p. 256.

41. See Trautmann, *Invention*, pp. 61–74, especially pp. 73–74.

42. Joshua Hall McIlvaine, *The Tree of the Knowledge of Good and Evil* (New York: M. W. Dodd, 1847).

43. McIlvaine, *Tree*, p. iv.

44. See Basil Hall, *Travels in North America, in the Years 1827 and 1828* (Edinburgh: Cadell and Co.; London: Simpkin and Marshall, 1829), v. 1, 155–56, and Francis Smith Eastman, *A History of the State of New York, from the first discovery of the country to the present time: with a geographical account of the coun-*

try, and a view of its original inhabitants, new edition (New York: A. K. White, 1832 [1831]), pp. 366–67.

45. In J. Disturnell, compiler, *A Gazetteer of the State of New-York: comprising its topography, geology, mineralological resources, civil divisions, canals, railroads and public institutions; together with general statistics: the whole alphabetically arranged. Also, Statistical tables, including the census of 1840; and tables of distances*, 2cd edition, with additions and corrections (Albany: C. Van Benthusysen & Co., 1843); frontispiece and preface, pp. iii–iv, his emphasis. See also Eastman, *History*, p. 14.

46. Morgan, *League*, p. 312, see 329.

47. Although I cannot pursue this argument properly here, I think Morgan's dedication to revelation as a human practice is evident in his changing attitudes toward the secret societies to which he belonged. Excerpts from *Kappa Alpha in Union College, 1825–1913* (for Lewis), and from the *Kappa Alpha Catalogue* for 1841 (p. 1852 on Hamilton) and for 1941 (item 160 on Lewis) in each brother's "Alumni File" (Schaffer Library, Union College) show that Morgan and his younger brother, Hamilton, had already joined the Kappa Alpha fraternity, the first and most prestigious of Union's fraternities, when they were students there. Although Nott tried in 1832–33 to ban Union's fraternities as "secret societies," they continued to thrive. Union College later described itself as the "Mother of Fraternities," based on Kappa Alpha's founding there in 1825. Although fraternities in America generally started in rural colleges, Wayne Somers suggests that Union's nonsectarian philosophy might have favored their development because they would have encountered less opposition on religious grounds. Although other colleges were farther west in 1825, Union was located at the threshold of the frontier on one of the major westward routes. Thus, "the 'elitist' fraternity system may have thrived at Union precisely because Union had such a preponderance of 'barbarians' from whom the 'Greeks' wished to distinguish themselves." See Wayne Somers, "Fraternities," in *Dictionary of Union College History* (ms., n.d.), pp. 126–28; p. 125. My thanks to Wayne Somers for allowing me to quote from this manuscript.

According to Morgan's brother-in-law, Charles Talbot Porter, "The Gordion Knot" was a secret society; its members broke into the then unused Freemasons' Temple in Aurora and wore their robes in their ceremonies. See Charles Talbot Porter, "Personal Reminiscences" ("Montclair, N.J., 6th February, 1901"), in *League of the Ho-de'-no-sau-nee or Iroquois* by Lewis H. Morgan, ed. Herbert M. Lloyd, "New edition, two volumes in one" (New York: Dodd, Mead and Company, 1904 [1901]), vol. 2, pp. 153–54.

"The Grand Order of the Iroquois," as it became known publically, also started out as a secret society, known to its members as *We-yo-ha-yo-de-za-de,-Na-ho-de'-no-sau-nee*, or "They who live in the home of the dwellers in the long house." Porter (in "Personal Reminiscences," p. 155) still remembered, over sixty years later, how the name should be pronounced. Morgan's correspondence in the late 1840s shows that disagreement over whether the Order should remain secret was one of the main reasons for its beginning to break up in 1847–48. In keeping with his growing interest in research on the Iroquois, which he saw as contributing to public knowledge and understanding, and later as a "science," Morgan was among those who advocated that the Order's methods and purposes should be public (Morgan Papers, Correspondence, 1839–51, Box 1: 1–16).

48. See Elisabeth Tooker, *Lewis H. Morgan on Iroquois Material Culture* (Tucson: University of Arizona Press, 1994), pp. 41–43, 53. Morgan saved some accounts of his collecting, including the work he did with Ely S. Parker and other members of the Parker family, in his bound fieldwork journals (Morgan Papers, Journals 1 and 2) and in his correspondence from 1847–51 (Morgan Papers, Box 1:11–16). Tooker's study reproduces most of these, together with correspondence from Parker and others, now in other archives, as well as the texts and images from Morgan's reports, published in the annual *Reports of the Regents of the University* in 1849, 1850, and 1852.

49. Reproduced in Tooker, *Iroquois Material Culture*, pp. 27, 30, 32, 296, n. 5 (chap. 3). Fort Hill was the only one of these sites to be turned into a cemetery (in 1852).

50. Tooker, *Iroquois Material Culture*, p. 45, from Morgan's letter of October 31, 1848 to the Regents, published in their annual report for 1848.

51. Tooker, *Iroquois Material Culture*, pp. 53, 56, from a letter now in the Parker Papers of the American Philosophical Society. The emphasis is Morgan's. Indications of [?] are Tooker's, signifying problems in transcribing the journals.

52. See Tooker, "On the Development of the Handsome Lake Religion" (1989), p. 37. Tooker argues that Handsome Lake's followers among Seneca at Tonawanda began reviving his teachings not in the 1840s, when Morgan happened along, as A. C. Wallace has argued, but about twenty years earlier, as indeed Iroquois tradition states. The spread of the revival from Tonawanda to the other Six Nations, and creation of the "Good Message," as it is now called, was accomplished not in Jemmy Johnson's time around 1850, as Wallace has argued. Rather, the revival took place gradually over almost fifty years, culminating in 1862, when a council of speakers met and decided upon a common form. Tooker's arguments would suggest that Morgan and Parker's research in the 1840s may have contributed to, and perhaps for Parker, may have been inspired by, a revival of Iroquois ways generally associated with the revival of Handsome Lake's teachings, but their research did not initiate that revival.

53. Anthony Wallace, "Revitalization Movements: Some Theoretical Considerations for Their Comparative Study," *American Anthropologist* 58 (1956): 264–81. For the notes of Ely S. Parker and Morgan, see Morgan Papers, Journal 1, *League*, pp. 226–59. See also Elisabeth Tooker, "On the Development of the Handsome Lake Religion," *Proceedings of the American Philosophical Society* 133, no. 1 (1989): 35–50.

54. See Tooker, "On the Development," passim.

55. Arthur C. Parker, *The Life of General Ely S. Parker, Last Grand Sachem of the Iroquois and General Grant's Military Secretary* (Buffalo, NY: Buffalo Historical Society, 1919), p. 89. Parker's observation is a far more accurate assessment of the relationships from which the *League* was created than William Fenton's half-joking aside in his introduction to the third reprinting of the *League* (1962, p. x) that "those who argue whether Albany is a cultural center are reminded how American ethnology was born in a hotel room" (where Morgan talked with Ely S. Parker and the Seneca elders from Tonawanda), or the observation of Morgan's

brother-in-law, Charles Talbot Porter, that these "ethnological investigations . . . all had their genesis in the old Masonic Hall in Aurora (in "Personal," p. 156).

56. Besides Arthur C. Parker's *Life of General Ely S. Parker*, see: Karl Sanford Kabelac, "Manuscript Materials at Rush Rhees Library, The University of Rochester, for the Study of Iroquois Indians: The Lewis Henry Morgan Papers, The Ely Samuel Parker Papers, The Arthur Caswell Parker Papers," in Russell A. Judkins, ed., *Iroquois Studies: A Guide to Documentary and Ethnographic Resources from Western New York and the Genesee Valley* (Geneseo, NY: Department of Anthropology, SUNY and The Geneseo Foundation, 1987), pp. 41–45; Ely S. Parker, "Writings of General Parker: Extracts from his Letters, and an Autobiographical Memoir of Historical Interest," *Proceedings of the Buffalo Historical Society* 8 (1905): 520–36; Elisabeth Tooker, "Ely S. Parker, Seneca, ca. 1828–1895," in *American Indian Intellectuals*, Margot Liberty, ed. (St. Paul, MN: West Publishing Co., 1978), pp. 14–30; and Hazel W. Hertzberg, "Arthur C. Parker, Seneca, 1881–1955," in *American Indian Intellectuals*, pp. 128–38.

57. Arthur C. Parker, *Life*, p. 231.

58. Morgan saved this clipping in his journals (Morgan Papers, Journal 1:2a. "Council of the Six Nations, Oct. 1847").

59. Morgan Papers, Journal 2:4:149 ("Tonawanda, November 30, 1949, at William Parker's.")

60. In *League*, p. 226, but this may be Morgan's editorializing, not Ely S. Parker's.

61. *League*, pp. 445, 446–47, 449, 452–53.

62. See Minnie Myrtle, *The Iroquois, or the Bright Side of Indian Character* (New York: D. Appleton & Co., 1855). As indicated in her other works, including a study of the German peasantry based on a two-year visit to Germany, Minnie Myrtle is the pseudonym of Anna Cummings Johnson (1818–92). Minnie Myrtle explains in the preface to *Iroquois* that she got to know the "Iriquois" through the "little Indian girl" whom missionaries on one of the reservations in western New York had sent to her parents to be Minnie's "pupil and companion" (p. 13). Like Morgan, she was adopted by the Seneca, receiving a Seneca name, and was later remembered by Arthur C. Parker (in *Life*, p. 89–90) as one of the chroniclers of Iroquois life most closely associated with Nicholson's family.

63. Myrtle, *Iroquois*, pp. 20–21, her emphasis.

64. The five original members of the Iroquois League—the nations of the Mohawk, Oneida, Onondaga, Cayuga, and Seneca—spoke "related but not mutually intelligible languages." By the mid-nineteenth century, the Iroquois were living in "ethnic enclaves," based on reservations. The Seneca at Tonawanda, where the Parkers lived, spoke Seneca; "only a few were fluent in English, and for this reason, interpreters were a necessity when dealing with whites." See Tooker, *Lewis H. Morgan on Iroquois Material Culture*, pp. 3–4. See also James Constantine Pilling, *Bibliography of the Iroquoian Languages* (Washington, DC: Government Printing Office, 1888), p. 177, who cites a marginal note in an undated edition of tracts in the Seneca language. The note refers to a sermon at Cattaraugus in February 1845, interpreted by William Jones, whose style "the old people regard as far more correct than that of our present interpreters."

65. See Arthur Parker, *Life*, pp. 263–87, who reproduces three of these and a

poster in which Nicholson's audience is promised that he will appear "in full Indian costume."

66. See Feeley-Harnik, "Communities," pp. 223–36. For Morgan, this may have derived from related interests in natural theology and geology. For Parker, this may also have been related to his upbringing, in which, as he recorded, his parents took care to ensure that he acquired "forest lore" (see E. S. Parker, "Writing"). Porter (in "Personal," pp. 157–58), writing over sixty years after he and Morgan were adopted into the Seneca Nation, had to acknowledge that he remembered "feeling deeply interested" in the "Indian traditions" he was hearing every night, but could recall not a word. Yet he still had a vivid impression of the mornings when Morgan was "obtaining geographical names, Parker, as always, acting as interpreter." He says: "I was full of admiration of these old men, who in their youth had hunted all over western New York, and who showed such a wonderful acquaintance with the location and course of every river and stream. In fact, the whole map appeared to exist in their minds. They seemed to have developed another sense, which we, who depend upon books and maps, and do not live in life-long familiarity with nature, do not possess." Porter's romantic memories of the Seneca as "men of the woods" nevertheless convey a relationship between people, language and landscape that warrants further study from a comparative perspective. See Keith H. Basso, *Wisdom Sits in Places: Landscape and Language among the Western Apache* (Albuquerque: University of New Mexico Press, 1996) and Keith H. Basso and Steven Feld, eds., *Senses of Place* (Santa Fe: School of American Research Press, 1996).

67. See Mary Black-Rogers, "Varieties of 'Starving': Semantics and Survival in the Subarctic Fur Trade, 1750–1850." *Ethnohistory* 33 (1986): 353–83; Bruce White, "Give Us a Little Milk," *Minnesota History* 48 (1982): 60–71; Bruce Trigger, "Ethnohistory: The Unfinished Edifice," *Ethnohistory* 33 (1986): 253–67, p. 262; David Murray, *Forked Tongues: Speech, Writing and Representation in North American Indian Texts* (London: Pinter, 1991); and Jennifer S. H. Brown and Elizabeth Vibert, eds., *Reading Beyond Words: Contexts for Native History* (Peterborough, Ontario: Broadview Press, 1996).

68. J. Disturnell, *A Gazetteer of the State of New-York* (1843), pp. 376, 480, 571. See also Whitney R. Cross, *The Burned-Over District: The Social and Intellectual History of Enthusiastic Religion in Western New York, 1800–1850* (Ithaca, NY: Cornell University Press, 1950).

69. See Basil Hall, *Travels*, v. 1, p. 149. Similarly, in his *History of the State of New York* (1832 [1831], p. 366), Eastman explains, as if to future immigrants, "In New York, the institutions of the *Christian Religion* are very generally regarded. The constitution makes no provision for its support, but secures to every man the free use and enjoyment of religious profession and worship, according to the dictates of his own conscience. The clergy are supported by the voluntary contributions of the people, and are excluded from holding offices under the government [his emphasis]."

70. Similarly, as Basil Hall observed, the practice of the New York legislature, of having "different clergymen, without any distinction of sects," give the prayer at the start of their daily proceedings, could not include "a black preacher [who] gave in his name as wishing to officiate," but withdrew after "vehement debate," before any vote was taken. See Hall, *Travels*, vol. 1, p. 140.

71. Thomas Scott, *The Holy Bible, containing the Old and New Testaments, with original notes, practical observations, and copious marginal references*, 5 vols. (6th American ed., from 2nd London ed., improved and enlarged; Hartford, CT: Sheldon & Goodrich, and Simeon L. Loomis). American publishers of the Scott's Family Bible sold 25,250 copies between 1808 and 1819. See Margaret T. Hills, ed., *The English Bible in America: A Bibliography of Editions of the Bible and the New Testament Published in America, 1777–1957* (New York: American Bible Society and The New York Public Library, 1961), pp. xxiii, 8–9, 20–21, 49; Trautman and Kabelac, *Library*, p. 117.

72. Peter J. Wosh, *Spreading the Word: The Bible Business in Nineteenth-Century America* (Ithaca, NY: Cornell University Press, 1994).

73. Colleen McDannell, *Material Christianity: Religion and Popular Culture in America* (New Haven, CT, Yale University Press, 1995), p. 72–73.

74. Myrtle, *The Iroquois*, pp. 284 ff.

75. McIlvaine, *Tree*, pp. 10–22.

76. Morgan, *League*, pp. 150, 168.

77. *Scott's Family Bible*, 6th American edition (1816–18), v. 1, p. 58.

78. Morgan, *League*, p. 172.

79. Published in Boston by Gould and Lincoln in 1854.

80. Lewis Henry Morgan, "Laws of Descent of the Iroquois," *Proceedings of the American Association for the Advancement of Science* 11 [1857]: 132–48.

81. Morgan Papers, "System of Consanguinity of the Red Race, in its Relations to Ethnology," ms. 45 [1859], p. 22.

82. Morgan Papers, ms. 45 [1859], pp. 9, 22.

83. Trautmann, *Invention*, pp. 58–114. See also Trautmann, "India and the Study of Kinship Terminologies," *L'Homme* 154 [2000], special issue on "Parenté, début de siècle."

84. Lewis Henry Morgan [Signed: "Aquarius. October, 1843"], "Mind or Instinct. An Inquiry Concerning the Manifestation of Mind by the Lower Orders of Animals," *The Knickerbocker* 22 (5) (1843): 414–20; 22 (6) [1843]: 507–15. See Feeley-Harnik, "Communities," pp. 228–30 for further discussion.

85. Morgan Papers, "Animal Psychology," ms. 41 [1857], p. 1.

86. Asa Mahan, *A System of Intellectual Philosophy* (New York: A.S. Barnes; Cincinnati: H. W. Derby), p. 423.

87. Morgan Papers, "Animal Psychology," ms. 41 [1857], pp. 18–18 1/2.

88. Morgan Papers, "Animal Psychology," ms. 41, 1857, pp. 4–14.

89. Morgan Papers, "Animal Psychology," ms. 41, 1857, pp. 23–25.

90. Morgan does not refer to Henry R. Schoolcraft's *The Indian in His Wigwam, or Characteristics of the Red Race of America from Original Notes and Manuscripts* (Buffalo: Derby & Hewson, Auburn, NY: Derby, Miller & Co., 1848), based in part on Schoolcraft's research among Chippewa (also called Ojibwa) around Sault Ste. Marie near Marquette. Nevertheless, it is noteworthy that Schoolcraft makes this observation: "They ['the Algonquins'] believe not only that every man, but also *that every animal, has a soul*; and as might be expected under this belief, they make no distinction between *instinct* and *reason*. Every animal is supposed to be endowed with a reasoning faculty. The movements of birds and other animals are deemed to be the result, not of mere instinc-

tive animal powers implanted and limited by the creation, without inherent power to *exceed* or *enlarge* them, but of a process of ratiocination. They go a step farther, and believe that animals, particularly birds, can look into, and are familiar with the vast operations of the world above" (p. 212, his emphasis).

91. Joshua Hall McIlvaine, *"A Nation's Right to Worship God, an address before the American Whig and Cliosophic Societies of the College of New Jersey* [later Princeton University], delivered June 28, 1859 (Trenton, NJ: Murphey & Bechtel, 1859), p. 6.

92. Joshua Hall McIlvaine, *Organization of the Fundamental Principles of Social Science* (New York: G. & C. Carvill, 1876), p. 631.

93. Morgan Papers, "Animal Psychology" [April 7, 1857], ms. 41, p. 25.

94. Morgan, *The American Beaver*, pp. 282–83.

95. Morgan, *Ancient Society*, p. 561.

96. Morgan, *Ancient Society*, pp. 562–63.

97. McIlvaine, *Tree*, p. v.

98. Morgan, *American Beaver*, p. 246; see Feeley-Harnik, "Communities," pp. 253–56, for further discussion about Morgan's response to his daughters' deaths.

99. Williams, *Keywords*, p. 76; Kroeber and Kluckhohn, *Culture*, pp. 68, 78.

100. Degler citing Boas, "Culture versus Biology," p. 11.

101. Carol Delaney, *Abraham on Trial: The Social Legacy of Biblical Myth* (Princeton, NJ: Princeton University Press, 1998); Susan L. Mizruchi, *The Science of Sacrifice: American Literature and Modern Social Theory* (Princeton: Princeton University Press, 1998).

9

Global Requiem: The Apocalyptic Moment in Religion, Science, and Art

JACK MILES

THE TITLE of Ernest Hemingway's first novel, *The Sun Also Rises*, published in 1926, came from the King James version of the Bible, more exactly, from the opening of the Book of Ecclesiastes (2:1–9):

> The words of the Preacher, the son of David, king in Jerusalem.
>> Vanity of vanities, saith the Preacher, vanity of vanities; all is vanity.
>> What profit hath a man of all his labour which he taketh under the sun?
>> One generation passeth away, and another generation cometh: but the earth abideth for ever.
>> The sun also ariseth, and the sun goeth down, and hasteth to his place where he arose. . . .
>> The thing that hath been, it is that which shall be; and that which is done is that which shall be done; and there is no new thing under the sun.

The Book of Ecclesiastes is an example of the wisdom literature of the Old Testament or Tanakh. Biblical wisdom differs from biblical prophecy in that God, who sometimes promises through his prophets that he will indeed do something new under the sun, is expected in wisdom literature to do no such thing. Unlike prophecy, wisdom envisions the future of the natural world as the continuation without change of the past. Vain illusion is overcome and relative peace achieved when the striving of human beings, each with just a brief lifetime to live, is seen against this backdrop of natural eternity: "One generation passeth away, and another generation cometh: but the earth abideth for ever."

The title that Hemingway borrowed from Ecclesiastes for his novel was well borrowed, for *The Sun Also Rises* does indeed present a picture of hectic, hedonistic striving. Its characters, a "lost generation" of expatriate Americans and Englishmen in the Paris of the 1920s, do not achieve resignation but only, on a few wistful occasions, aspire to it. The novel's title is not a description of its contents but, by allusion, the author's judgment on the vanity he is portraying. The central character, Jake Barnes, has been rendered sexually impotent by a war wound. It is he who comes closest to the inner peace that can only come, Hemingway suggests, in accepting the larger impotence of the human being pitted against nature in the cruel and unequal contest that he sees best ritualized in the Spanish bull ring.

Not all great literature and by no means all major religious traditions teach a wisdom that entails this kind of resignation to death as a part of the human condition. There are religious traditions, especially in the West, that promise victory over death, and there are works of imaginative literature that celebrate a reckless defiance of death that verges on outright denial of its reality. Within the Bible, the voice of prophecy—exulting with St. Paul "O death, where is thy sting? O grave, where is thy victory?" (I Corinthians 15:55)—is much louder than the voice of wisdom, and even secular art in the West often aspires to immortality through the undying fame of the artist or through the durability of the art itself. Thus, death can be defeated if, as Shakespeare's sixty-fifth sonnet conventionally puts it,

> . . . this miracle have might,
> That in black ink my love may still shine bright.

Even in the Bible, however, and even in secular Western tradition, the voice of resignation to death is never entirely silenced; and particularly if we recall that the wisdom that links the Book of Ecclesiastes to *The Sun Also Rises* also links it to the Four Noble Truths of Buddhism, this tradition may be regarded as a virtually perennial, virtually universal wisdom.

Within this universal wisdom, the typical function of the imagination has been to find ever more telling ways to contrast the brevity and vulnerability of human life and therefore the folly of human desire with the immemorial indifference of nature. You and I may grieve at our own passing or the passing of a loved one. We may ask, like King Lear with the dead Cordelia in his arms,

> Why should a dog, a horse, a rat have life
> And thou no breath at all?

Yet we may be consoled that, though we pass away, the sun rises, and the sun sets, and the earth abides forever. We may bring ourselves, by a spiritual discipline, into harmony with this whole. There are different paths to this harmony, some more ancient, some more modern, but the essential psychological mechanism at work here is older than Ecclesiastes, older than the Epic of Gilgamesh, as old, perhaps, as fully human speech.

In our own day, however, this ancient wisdom, this primeval therapy, is being undercut by processes that are both spiritual and physical. We have been in possession since Charles Lyell and Charles Darwin of a disturbing new awareness that nature too has a history. It does not abide forever. This alone is enough to undercut the age-old contrast between the temporality of humankind and the eternity of nature. But more recently that disruption has acquired a corollary. If the first generations that assimilated Darwin's thought were concerned with the origin of species, our own is concerned in an unprecedented way with the extinction of species and, above all, with the threat of extinction that faces the human species. During the 1850s, while Darwin was concluding *The Origin of Species*, the rate of extinction of species is believed to have been one every five years. Today, the rate of extinction is estimated at one every nine minutes.

Will the human species be extinguished in its turn? The statistical question, perhaps the statistical likelihood, is complicated, morally, by the probability that human extinction, if it comes about soon, will prove to have been species suicide. "Human reproduction," veteran foreign correspondent Malcolm W. Browne wrote in his 1993 memoir *Muddy Boots and Red Socks*,

> has some disturbing similarities to cancer. In an analysis published in 1990 in the journal *Population and Environment*, Warren M. Hem, an anthropologist at the University of Colorado, noted some striking clinical parallels between a typical urban community and a malignant neoplasm, a cancerous tumor. They share rapid uncontrolled growth, they invade and destroy adjacent tissues, and cells (or people) lose their differentiation, the concerted specialties and skills needed to sustain a society or a multicelled animal.
>
> In his monograph, Dr. Hem included photographs taken from space satellites showing the growth of Baltimore and the colonization of the Amazon basin, side by side with photomicrographs of cancers of the lung and brain. They were hard to tell apart.
>
> "The human species," Dr. Hem wrote, "is a rapacious, predatory, omni-ecophagic [devouring its entire environment] species" that exhibits all the pathological features of cancerous tissue. He grimly concluded that the human "cancer" will most likely destroy its planetary host before dying out itself.

"Many would disagree with that assessment," Browne concludes, "but for what it's worth, my own experience as a journalist bears it out" (p. 284).

As voices like Browne's are increasingly heard, the cause that until now has been presented as the defense of the environment, as if the environment were an importunate relative whom long-suffering humankind was being asked to support, is beginning to be presented as the self-defense of the human species itself. The environment is, after all, the human habitat, and time after time extinction has followed on loss of habitat when the species at risk was not able to adapt in time. Despite our large numbers, we are an endangered species.

As this paradigm shift takes place in the realm of politics and activist science, another change looms in the realm of the imagination and, perhaps also, in the practice of religion. If the earth is failing as a viable habitat for our species, then we can no longer imagine our individual deaths, as we have so long been accustomed to do, against a backdrop of continuing life. As we cease to do so, as we recontextualize our personal deaths in the emerging prospect of species death, can there, should there be a religious wisdom that will accept species death as if it were personal death? Can a new William Cullen Bryant write a new "Thanatopsis" in which "The paths of glory lead but to the grave" not just for each man and woman but for the human species as a whole? Beyond even that, can we resign ourselves in advance not just to extinction of our species but to the extinction of the terrestrial biosphere as we know it, consoling ourselves perhaps that the planets will still orbit the sun even when the one planet that for some few millions of years supported life no longer does so? Or should we, instead, repudiate this ancient wisdom as unwisdom and turn instead to the prophetic option, the path of protest and refusal rather than the path of acquiescence and acceptance? Do we prepare to die with dignity, or do we shed all dignity and prepare to fight to the death? The religions of the world have resources for either option; but whether we consider religion or art, the choice we face is an historic one, for step by step, the earth, which once seemed to abide forever, now seems to be dying around us.

In each part of the world the omens of this death are different. I grew up in Chicago, on the shore of Lake Michigan, and found a kind of peace, at different seasons of the year and of my early life, walking along the lakefront. A moment of ecological truth came for me when in 1987 I read William Ashworth's somber, brilliant book *The Late Great Lakes: An Environmental History*. Lake Michigan, which had seemed so timeless, was dying faster than I was. Before my own life was over, it might become a vast vat of chemicals, as devoid of life as ashes in a funerary urn. The ancient lake and my still young self seemed almost to be exchanging places. Unsettlingly, it was I who seemed to have the longer life expectancy.

But who in today's world is without some such experience to report? In Beijing, China, Liang Conjie, the president of a local environmental group, told a reporter: "When I was a little boy, the blue sky was really impressive. I can still remember that. Nowadays it's so hard for you to see the blue." Liang lives in a city in which citizens who can afford it patronize "oxygen bars" to escape air so polluted that breathing it is equal to smoking three packs of unfiltered cigarettes per day (*Los Angeles Times*, May 4, 1997). Residents of Shenyang, China, the most polluted major city in Asia, breathe in "up to ten times the limit of sulfur dioxide and particulate matter" set by the Chinese authorities themselves (*Los*

Angeles Times, April 27, 1997). Sulfur dioxide emissions in China may well be the cause of acid rain over Japan and of a huge cloud of smog often visible over the western Pacific Ocean.

Belatedly, the Chinese are coming to the defense of their own environment, but China faces in a particularly acute form the choice that the whole world faces between waging war on pollution and waging war on poverty. Given the fact that the per capita energy consumption in the United States, with roughly one quarter China's population, is more than four times the per capita consumption in China, a one-child policy in the United States country might do more in the short run to halt global warming than the same policy in China. But the United States is no more likely to adopt a one-child policy than China is likely to adopt American-style restrictions on the burning of soft coal.

I offer merely representative examples. The question I want to pursue, however, does not entail duplicating *State of the World*, the Worldwatch Institute's annual report on "Progress Toward a Sustainable Society." I want to ask, instead, what the consequences for religion and for the arts, especially literature, will be if and when we conclude that the effort to produce a sustainable society has definitively failed. Long before the human species is extinct, we may know that we are irreversibly en route to extinction. Just as any of us may discover tomorrow that he is not just mortal but actually dying of an incurable disease, so we may discover as a species that we are not just endangered but actually doomed, and that within a foreseeable, measurable time span. Such a prognosis, if it comes, surely will not come as it does in the disaster movies that are now so strangely popular; namely, with a warning that unless a given action is taken within ten days or ten hours, the world will end. No, it will come rather as an accumulation of ignored warnings from scientists and science journalists and an ensuing consensus that the opportunity to take the action that would have saved the species has come and gone. At that scientifically apocalyptic moment, should it be reached, and we can certainly imagine it being reached, actual extinction may still be far enough in the future that there will be time for a new kind of religion and a new kind of art to develop. These will be, no doubt, a religion and an art born of despair, but religion and art—far more than politics or commerce or science—are precisely those products of the human spirit to which we turn in times of despair. The last days of the human race may be, not to speak at all flippantly, our finest hour.

Apocalyptic warnings have been so frequent in the past and so invariably wrong that I hope I may be forgiven if I multiply the sober, unfanatic voices that seem to be joining the chorus that delivers science's version of the Book of Revelations. Among representative book-length warnings on what could be a much longer list, I note:

The Heat Is On: The High Stakes Battle Over Earth's Threatened Climate by Ross Gelbspan (Addison-Wesley)

The Last Harvest: The Genetic Gamble That Threatens to Destroy American Agriculture by Paul Raeburn (University of Nebraska Press)

Noah's Choice: The Future of Endangered Species by Charles C. Mann and Mark L. Plummer (Knopf)

The Sixth Extinction: Patterns of Life and the Future of Humankind by Richard Leakey and Roger Lewin (Doubleday).

There are also warnings that do not come as reports but, more impressively and alarmingly, as manifestos, urgent calls to political action. A mailing from the organization Zero Population Growth cries out in huge red letters: " 'Why aren't you as scared as I am? Global population growth should be second in importance only to avoiding nuclear war.'— Paul R. Ehrlich." If that seems a bit shrill, the "World Scientists' Warning to Humanity," sponsored by the Union of Concerned Scientists, does not. As sober in its style as it is sobering in its substance, this warning comes signed (as of April 1993) by more than 1670 scientists, including 104 Nobel laureates—a majority of the living recipients of the prize. The introduction to the Warning reads:

> Human beings and the natural world are on a collision course. Human activities inflict harsh and often irreversible damage on the environment and on critical resources. If not checked, many of our current practices put at serious risk the future that we wish for human society and the plant and animal kingdoms, and may so alter the living world that it will be unable to sustain life in the manner that we know. Fundamental changes are urgent if we are to avoid the collision our present course will bring about.

After summarizing threats to the environment under the headings "The Atmosphere," "Water Resources," "Oceans," "Soil," "Forests," and "Living Species," the signatories come to their collective point:

> WARNING We the undersigned, senior members of the world's scientific community, hereby warn all humanity of what lies ahead. A great change in our stewardship of the earth and the life on it is required, if vast human misery is to be avoided and our global home on this planet is not to be irretrievably mutilated.

There follow five exhortations:

1. We must bring environmentally damaging activities under control to restore and protect the integrity of the earth's systems we depend on.
2. We must manage resources crucial to human welfare more effectively.

3. We must stabilize population. This will be possible only if all nations recognize that it requires improved social and economic conditions, and the adoption of effective, voluntary family planning.
4. We must reduce and eventually eliminate poverty.
5. We must ensure sexual equality, and guarantee women control over their own reproductive decisions.

The scientists conclude their warning:

> We require the help of the world community of scientists—natural, social, economic, political;
> We require the help of the world's business and industrial leaders;
> We require the help of the world's religious leaders; and
> We require the help of the world's peoples.
> We call on all to join us in this task.

I can testify from personal experience that some of the signatories to this warning have lent more than just their names to it. The late Henry Kendall, a Nobel Prize winner from MIT, came to the *Los Angeles Times* in 1994 when I was a member of its editorial board and spoke with eloquent urgency of how high the stakes were and how potentially short the time: no more than a few decades and perhaps as little as a single decade.

Recalling the Warning's virtually unprecedented overture to organized religion, I was interested to read an advertisement in the *New York Times* by the National Religious Partnership for the Environment, a partnership uniting the United States Catholic Conference, the National Council of Churches of Christ, the Evangelical Environmental Network, and the Coalition on Environment and Jewish Life. Under the headline "Care for God's Earth Requires Justice for the Poor," the Partnership's statement opens as follows:

> Americans have reaffirmed their commitment to environmental protection. And across the spectrum of faith groups, care for God's creation is increasingly at the heart of what it means to *be religious*.
>
> We are working to protect the planet's air, seas, forests, and species. But, as we reflect on the state of the union and the many communities we serve, we see a need for far greater moral resolve to address the impact of environmental destruction on poor and vulnerable people, most particular people of color.

An observer innately more optimistic than I might perhaps take the World Scientists' Warning to Humanity and the Religious Partnership's exhortation to the readers of the New York Times as hopeful signs. I confess that my own sad conclusion is that if the human habitat can only be saved by "stabiliz[ing] population," "reduc[ing] and eventually eliminat[ing] poverty," and "ensur[ing] sexual equality," and if we have no more than a few and perhaps no more than one decade in which to bring about these changes, then we are lost.

I cannot offer this prospect as demonstrable, only as conceivable. Even as merely conceivable, however, it changes everything. A majority of living recipients of the Nobel Prize in the sciences would not lightly say that life as we know it could end, but this is what they have said. They speak of a "collision course," which is another metaphor for the one I used when I imagined our species receiving the same diagnosis of incurable illness that an individual man or woman might receive. Perhaps the diagnosis is wrong; but if it is correct, then perhaps, like many an incurably ill patient, we are simply refusing to accept the diagnosis. One wants to avoid foolish alarmism but also foolish complacency. Perhaps, if the diagnosis is correct, a remedy will be applied in time. But what if no remedy is applied in time? What if, as other warnings and warning signs accumulate, the view suddenly takes hold, spreading like a virus through the Internet, that humankind is doomed? Then what?

I am reminded here of an image from an earlier such warning, the infamous 1972 "Club of Rome" report entitled *The Limits to Growth*. To illustrate the character of exponential growth, the writers of that report said that if an algae plume were doubling in size each day on the surface of a pond, then two days before the pond was completely covered, it would still be three-quarters clear. The exponential processes that are deleteriously affecting the human habitat do not have a twenty-four-hour doubling time, but we may yet find the health of the planet going from pretty good to desperately bad with terrifying suddenness. The "Club of Rome" report has been mocked because some of its near-term quasi-predictions—more exactly, its extrapolations from then-available data—did not come to pass. But global modeling is a branch of science that was then only taking its first steps. A generation later, the World Scientists' Warning has occasioned rather less alarm and less notice than the "Club of Rome" report did a generation earlier, but if the doubling time shrinks noticeably for even one or two key parameters, that calm could vanish in a hurry.

Take the world grain situation. In a very unalarmist review essay for *The New York Review of Books* (February 20, 1997), Daniel J. Kevles reported that "throughout the world, since 1972, some 500 million acres have been turned into deserts; and farmers have lost 480 million tons of topsoil, more than all of the topsoil on all US farmland. In recent years, growth in grain yields has not been making up for losses in grain-growing land." An earlier, equally cautious and qualified article entitled "Shortfall in the Grain Fields" in the *New York Times* (November 19, 1995) concluded: ". . . the stresses [on the world food supply] could easily rise to the level where the Malthusians once again get a more respectful hearing." We must all hope that Dennis Avery, head of the Center for Global Food Issues at the Hudson Institute, who was quoted in this article, was correct when he said: "The world has more food security than at any time in history." But if Avery is mistaken, he is mistaken about an issue with potentially staggering consequences.

The issue, to repeat, is not change as such but the acceleration of change, the issue that first struck me when I read *The Late Great Lakes*. After summarizing a number of recent studies in global warming, Bill McKibben wrote in *The New York Times* (May 3, 1997): "Understand this about these changes: They are enormous. They do not represent small shifts at the margin, the slow evolution that has always occurred on earth. Spring a week earlier; 20 percent more storms, 10 percent more vegetation since 1980. These studies are like suddenly discovering that most Americans are 7 feet tall. If we were looking through a telescope and seeing the same things happen on some other planet, we would find it bizarre and fascinating. If someone's watching us, they're doubtless bewildered." I venture to say that few in the global modeling community would go so far as to join McKibben in equating the newest studies with a discovery that most Americans are 7 feet tall. But we do seem to be moving toward rather than away from some such state of alarm. McKibben concludes his article: "All those things that people said would happen if we didn't clean up our act? They're happening. This is a new planet, not the earth we were born on."

Nearly two years later, on January 28, 1999, the American Geophysical Union published an official policy statement saying that there was a "compelling basis for legitimate public concern" about human-induced climate change. Writing in the *New York Times* (January 29, 1999), William K. Stevens characterized this report as "the latest in a long list of statements on global warming over the last two decades by prestigious scientific groups that have reached similar conclusions."

If McKibben is right and we are indeed living on "a new planet, not the earth we were born on," then the religions and arts that served us well enough on the old planet may no longer be serving us so well. On this new planet, the title *The Sun Also Rises* carries other connotations than those Hemingway intended, and the somber vision of Ecclesiastes no longer quiets the soul. How can we take up the question of how we might expect or wish art and religion to change in response to such drastically changed circumstances?

As a preliminary response, I should like to review the career, especially the late career, of John Cage, a man who has been honored as an artistic and perhaps even as a religious visionary. Cage, who died in 1992, achieved world fame and lasting influence in 1952 when his epoch-making anti-composition *4′ 33″* was first performed. George J. Leonard, in a brilliant study entitled *Into the Light of Things: The Art of the Commonplace from Wordsworth to John Cage*, quotes from a firsthand report of the second-ever performance of *4′33″*, which took place at Carnegie Recital Hall:

It was a hall that you could hire, quickly, and it would seat a modest number of people—seventy-five at most. A small, beautiful little hall. It was in the summertime, and the windows were open, either in the hall or in the hallway outside. We heard the traffic sounds. David Tudor, then very young, came out and sat at the piano, and I believe he had a somewhat formal outfit on, as befitting a performer. He adjusted, in the usual manner, his seat—I remember this very vividly—because he made a pointed activity out of it. He kept pushing it up, and pushing it down. He had a stopwatch, which was the usual way of John's things—being timed. And he opened up the piano lid and put his hands on the keys as if he was going to play some music. What we expected. We were waiting. And nothing happened. Pretty soon you began to hear chairs creaking, people coughing, rustling of clothes, then giggles. And then a police car came by with its siren running, down below. Then I began to hear the elevator in the building. Then the air conditioning going through the ducts. Until one by one all of us, every one of that audience there—and I think they must have been all of our kind [artists], began to say "Oh. We get it. Ain't no such thing as silence. If you just listen, you'll hear a lot." I was very struck by *4′33″*. I intuited that it was his most philosophically and radically *instrumental* piece. *Instrumental* in the sense that it made available to a number of us not just the sounds in the world but all phenomena. Then the question is, now that everything's available, what do you do? (*page 189*)

Though John Cage published several manifestos about music over his long life, the statement that has come to be taken as the canonical expression of his own interpretation of *4′33″* came in 1956 as a remark to a midwestern student audience about to watch a performance by the Merce Cunningham dance company. On that occasion, Cage said: "Our intention is to affirm this life, not to bring order out of chaos nor to suggest improvements in creation, but simply to wake up to the very life we're living, which is so excellent once one gets one's mind and one's desires out of its way and lets it act on its own accord" (Leonard, 174).

If this much-quoted statement sounds vaguely Buddhist, there is an explanation ready to hand. In an interview with Leonard, Cage said: "Since the forties and through study with D. T. Suzuki of the philosophy of Zen Buddhism, I've thought of music as a means of changing the mind . . . an activity of sounds in which the artist found a way to let the sounds be themselves. John Cage, in short, was one of the many American artists of his day who were deeply influenced by the daring Japanese émigré who, consciously modeling himself on St. Paul, made himself into

Zen Buddhism's apostle to the gentiles. Leonard explains Suzuki's sudden and seemingly inexplicable success by showing how it built on a preexisting Western artistic movement that had been gathering strength since the time of William Wordsworth and that sought beauty and indeed a kind of religious experience by seeing anew what the great romantic poet had called "the simple produce of the common day." In each successive generation between Wordsworth and Cage, this movement enlarged the boundaries of what could be considered art until, at length, there was no difference between art and reality itself. For those with eyes to see, anything could be art.

Suzuki, who had acquainted himself with this Western movement by reading Ralph Waldo Emerson while still in Japan, seems to have recognized Emerson's ideal as analogous to the satori sought by the Rinzai Zen sect to which he belonged. Among American artists, this school of Zen—which Americans initially equated with the whole of Zen—provided an artistic evolution that was already under way with a new rationale and a thrilling acceleration. "Suzuki's satori," Leonard writes,

> is largely identical to transfiguration of the commonplace. "Satori finds a meaning hither-to hidden in our daily concrete particular experiences," Suzuki explains, regarding the world from the "religious aesthetical angle of observation. . . ." The "artist's world," therefore "coincides" with that of the Zen-man except that the Zen-man, Suzuki was teaching by 1938, has freed himself of art objects. "While the artists have to resort to the canvas or brush or mechanical instruments or some other mediums to express themselves, Zen has no need of things external. . . . The Zen-man is an artist," but he "transforms his own life into a work of creation!" (*page 161*)

The path from Suzuki's classroom to Cage's silent recital hall is extraordinarily well marked. Cage's *4' 33"* announced the end of art, the ne plus ultra of a hundred-fifty-year process, more radically and years earlier than did the Brillo boxes of Andy Warhol, who indeed frankly acknowledged his debt to Cage. And though Cage came decades later than Marcel Duchamp and his famous urinal, Duchamp was celebrated for epitomizing what at the time he intended to satirize. The French artist eventually came to accept his artistic destiny, but in 1917, when he first displayed the urinal, the gesture bespoke not Zen but Dada.

4' 33" is aleatory music inasmuch as chance determines what real-world sounds will fill the silence. During the first performance of the work at Woodstock, New York, a rainstorm broke out, and the silence was filled by the sound of raindrops on the roof of the concert shed. Cage has written other kinds of aleatory music, but he and everyone else regards *4' 33"* as his most important and most visionary work. For that reason, it is interesting and much to the point of today's investigation to learn, as one does in Leonard's book, of the degree to which he later turned against his own vision.

To speak poetically, what John Cage eventually heard in the silence he had created was the sound of the world dying, and he could not bear to hear it. During the last thirty years of his life, he was what George Leonard sees fit to call an ecology activist, though Cage's activism seems to have consisted mainly of writing fragmentary poetry in defense of the environment. This was, in effect if not by intent, the composer's response to his critics, and he did have his critics. In 1969 the Harvard theologian and culture critic Harvey Cox in a book entitled *The Feast of Fools* faulted him sharply for "assum[ing] a creation that is not only good but perfect." To Cox, though he astutely recognized the theological dimension in Cage's work, the composer's stance risked becoming "a supine acceptance of the world as it is." And there were artists and art critics who had similar objections. Rather than awaken her audience to "this excellent life," one performance artist said in 1981 she wanted to awaken it to "the ways in which we have been led to *believe* that this life is so excellent." And as late as 1989, performance art critic Henry Sayre faulted Cage for being "so vastly apolitical, so vastly unconscious of social and political reality" (Leonard, 175–76).

These critics were, if you will, the reassertion of classic Western prophecy against Cage's fusion of a form of Western aestheticism with a form of Eastern mysticism, but by the late 1960s Cage had begun to find his own way back toward prophecy and, in principle, toward activism. His was, however, a halting retreat. His 1968 collected essays, *A Year from Monday*, began with the sweeping proclamation, much in the spirit of that revolutionary year: "Our proper work now if we love mankind and the world we live in is revolution." But the first long poem in the collection was entitled: "Diary: How to Improve the World (You Will Only Make Matters Worse)." Obviously, the activism of "How to Improve the World" and the passivism of "You Will Only Make Matters Worse" contradicted each other. To judge from Leonard's extended report, enriched by long interviews with the composer, Cage never resolved this contradiction. On the one hand, he could write in this diary-poem:

We've
poisoned our food, polluted our air
and water, killed birds and cattle,
eliminated forest, impoverished,
eroded the earth [. . .]

What would you call it?
Nirvana?

On the other, he stopped short of following the example of Newton Harrison, an award-winning sculptor who destroyed all his sculptures and, with his wife, dedicated himself to reclaiming rivers and waterways. Cage admired the Harrisons. If they were not doing this, Cage told Leonard, he would be doing it himself, but one doubts his resolve. The first John Cage, the monk of music, lived on too powerfully within the second, just as the second had survived hidden within the first.

I am drawn to Cage's struggle because it seems so much to be our own, only the more acutely ours as the ecological crisis worsens. The pre-crisis Cage, asked on one occasion if there was too much suffering in the world, said that, no, there was just the right amount. Consistent with that view, the early Cage, contemplating the prospect of the death of Mother Earth and all her children with her, might have said, as we say when one of our own mothers dies, "It's sad, but then she had a rich and full life." In other words, the early Cage, rewording his famous interpretation of *4′ 33″*, might have exhorted us to awaken to species death as "excellent once one gets one's mind and one's desires out of its way and lets it act on its own accord." If resignation to death is good counsel for the individual, why would it be bad counsel for the species?

The post-crisis Cage, however, the composer turned ecological poet, could only counsel other artists to follow the example of the Harrisons, even though he himself could not do so. Once it became clear that the sound wafting through the window of the concert-less concert hall was indeed the voice of Mother Earth crying murder, the concert would have to be canceled—not canceled in favor of some more prophetic or political performance, something that would necessarily keep the artists employed as artists, but canceled in favor of direct, urgent action—a general mobilization as in wartime with guarantees for nobody.

The hope was once entertained for art—perhaps, above all, for poetry—that it could become a secular substitute for religion, but in our day that hope has been dashed by the termination of the very process that initially raised it. Natural supernaturalism, to borrow M. H. Abrams's famous phrase, began in the belief that artistic attention could bless ordinary reality and make it holy. But at the end of that process, when there is nothing left that is not art, and therefore nothing that is not holy, nothing toward which we cannot take Suzuki's "religious aesthetical angle of observation," then even the death of the human species will seem just the last produce of the last day: nothing to do but watch it happen. Perhaps if the planet could be returned to and kept in the condition in which it stood during the lifetime of Matthew Arnold, then art in the condition in which it stands today might be a passable substitute for religion. Art as we have known it scarcely seems able to play that role on the eve of human extinction.

And yet the activism with which the late Cage flirted cannot substitute for religion either. What matters is not the merit or even the eloquence of an ecological poet's words but the likelihood that enough people will read them and take them to heart. When results are the criterion, as they are for activism, then the size of the audience is critical. If a grave warning from a majority of the world's Nobel scientists can go largely ignored, surely no body of poetry is likely to be heeded.

For some, I realize, science itself has seemed to be the answer. I once thought to contrast the trajectory of John Cage with that of David Friedrich Strauss, the nineteenth-century German Bible scholar whose last book, *The Old Faith and the New*, was a repudiation of Christianity in favor of Darwinian biology. But the specter of the Soviet Union—so rich in scientific knowledge but so poor in everything else—must haunt anyone still clinging to the hope that science can save the world. And I note again that the Nobel scientists have stated explicitly that they cannot meet the current crisis without the help of the world's religious leaders.

In what may be the last years of the human race, the role of the imagination, I am driven to conclude, lies not in supplanting religion but in imagining how existing organized religious traditions might adapt their old resources to meet this new challenge. Most artists and writers, called upon to imagine such a thing, would reply "That's not my job." So much the worse for human survival if a few cannot escape this suffocating secular orthodoxy.

Worldwide, the time when religious traditions of all kinds most often make an appearance is the time of death. When a memorial service is held for a man or woman who practiced no religion, the mourners—in this country, typically, of widely varying beliefs—have to organize themselves into a kind of ad hoc congregation. I recall, in my own recent experience, the memorial service for poet Joseph Brodsky at St. John the Divine in New York, and a much humbler service for Benjamin Pinkel, a deceased RAND Corporation physicist in Santa Monica. On both occasions, traditional religious elements were combined with a set of secular readings that took on an inescapably religious coloration.

So we may find ourselves doing if we come to believe that we are in the last days of the human species. Whether or not we believe in the existence of any transcendent reality, we may find ourselves forming ad hoc congregations that combine secular and religious elements in a mood that, in such a somber moment, will surely seem more religious than secular. The religious traditions of the world do have major resources to draw on. All of them speak of death and of such violent actions as slaughter and war in two senses, one of which, as I might put it, corresponds to the early Cage and the other to the late Cage.

All of them prepare the individual man or woman to accept physical death as the human lot. If the death of the human species truly cannot be avoided, we can at least hope to dignify this passing with decent grief and try by our resignation to prevent the last years of the human species from being a battle of all against all. However, all of the major religious traditions of the world also celebrate sacrifice to the point of martyrdom and even (in the West, I maintain, as well as in the East) self-martyrdom. And all—short of that extreme—teach disciplines variously described as the slaying of desire, inner jihad, or self-mortification. If the death of the human species can be averted at all, it surely cannot be averted without enormous sacrifice. In *Losing Ground: American Environmentalism at the Close of the Twentieth Century*, science journalist Mark Dowie speaks depressingly of the spread of the "Wise Use" movement, an ecological counter-movement that, as he sees it, refuses to accept the possibility— for Dowie it is a virtual certainty—that profits must be sacrificed to save the human habitat. When profits go down for the rich, wages, contrary to the hopes of the National Religious Partnership for the Environment, invariably go down even faster for the poor. So long as it is possible to do well while doing good, so long as what is best for the bottom line can be sold as good enough for the environment, then no recourse to the ideologies of religious self-sacrifice will be required. Enlightened self-interest will suffice.

But I doubt, personally, that enlightened self-interest will in fact suffice. Enlightened self-interest is no basis on which to exhort a man who does not wish to do so to place the interests of posterity above his own. The objection "What has posterity ever done for me?" is unanswerable on that basis—that is, with respect to that demand for reciprocity. Nationalism or patriotism once mobilized self-sacrificial behavior to an extraordinary degree, but patriotism may have seen its day. The dedication John Cage affixed to his *A Year from Monday* was: "To us and all those who hate us, that the U.S.A. may become just another part of the world, no more, no less." When one's own country is just another part of the world, a leader who commands as John F. Kennedy did, "Ask not what your country can do for you, ask what you can do for your country," becomes a laughingstock. Many breathe easier as patriotism fades, having seen the horrors that patriotism-become-fascism can perpetrate. As Arthur Koestler once said, the altruism of the individual is the egoism of the group. We are right to fear it.

And yet can we possibly save the human species without it? And whither, if not to the religious traditions of the world, can we turn in search of a benign form of altruism? Speaking very personally, I shrink from the challenge of religious leadership. It is not by accident that I am an ex-Jesuit rather than a Jesuit. But the survival of the species seems likely to require a degree of self-sacrifice rarely seen beyond the family.

The evolution of our species to this point in time has not required that degree of self-sacrifice. Unfortunately for us, our environment has now changed. In his 1998 book *Becoming Human: Evolution and Human Uniqueness*, palaeontologist Ian Tattersall writes: "Environments may be relatively stable or they may not; but when they change, they usually do so pretty rapidly, at rates with which adaptation by natural selection would be hard put to keep up. When such change occurs, the quality of your adaptation to your old habitat is irrelevant, and any competitive advantage you might have had may be eliminated at a stroke" (p. 102). Self-sacrifice to the degree now required has not been adaptive to this point. It has not served survival. If some such adaptation is now required, it will not come about by "spontaneous" biological evolution. Only a cultural adaptation can conceivably be developed in time, and it is this consideration that wins religion an at least preliminary hearing.

My friend Jared Diamond, the author of the recent, Pulitzer Prize-winning *Guns, Germs, and Steel: The Fates of Human Societies*, cautions me that nothing so tied to the existing social order as organized religion can be expected to retain much efficacy if and when the famine, epidemic, and anarchy that are already seething in parts of Africa spread round the world. This is surely true, and yet it also seems to be true that religion is what survives when the *rest* of an existing social order collapses. As Diamond himself puts it: "First, shared ideology or religion helps solve the problem of how unrelated individuals are to live together without killing each other—by providing them with a bond not based on kinship. Second, it gives people a motive, other than genetic self-interest, for sacrificing their lives on behalf of others. At the cost of a few society members who die in battle as soldiers, the whole society becomes much more effective at conquering other societies or resisting attacks" (p. 278). But does "religion or shared ideology" only operate in the ranks of an army? Can it not operate in civilian society as well and function for the defense of the human habitat as a whole rather than only of a given nation's territory?

A religion functioning in defense of the human habitat would be a world religion rather than, as in Diamond's understanding, a national religion. Its holy land would be the planet, and its holy people the human race. But who would be its enemy—its gentiles or pagans or infidels? Clearly, it could function only by making its practice radically reflexive. Ecologically, humankind has quite literally become its own enemy. A religion responsive to this ecological crisis would give ideological, ethical, and ritual expression to this unprecedented turn of events.

But this is surely the tallest of tall orders. Historically, the universalization of religious values may have tended to secularize and subordinate national identity. Against this tendency, however, national conflict, whatever its proximate cause, has tended to re-sacralize the nation and re-particularize religion, subordinating it to or fusing it with nationalism. The prospects for a religion that would subordinate national interests to species survival cannot be called good.

Though this point can be illustrated from within several different religious traditions, Judaism over the past century and a half, in particular the comparison of Reform Judaism and Zionism, offers an especially pertinent example.

Reform Judaism arose in Germany in the mid-nineteenth century as an attempt to separate Jewish ethnicity from Judaic religion. The "Pittsburgh Platform," adopted by Reform Judaism after its arrival in the United States, continued and extended this program, proclaiming with regard to the Orthodox Judaism from which Reform Judaism wished to distinguish itself:

> Today we accept as binding only its moral laws and maintain only such ceremonials as elevate and sanctify our lives, but reject all such as are not adapted to the views and habits of modern civilization.
>
> We hold that all such Mosaic and Rabbinical laws as regulate diet, priestly purity and dress originated in ages and under the influence of ideas altogether foreign to our present mental and spiritual state.
>
> We recognize Judaism as a progressive religion, ever striving to be in accord with the postulates of reason.

Elsewhere in the same document (discussed in Stephen Steinberg, "Reform Judaism: The Origin and Evolution of a 'Church Movement,'"), the separation of ethnicity and religion is made even clearer: "We consider ourselves no longer a nation but a religious community."[1]

To say all this was not, of course, to say that there were no longer nations, only that, with regard to nationality, the speakers were content to be American. Moreover, they held their religious option open, by implication, no less to all their fellow Americans than to themselves. Historically, Reform Judaism has welcomed non-Jewish converts, while Orthodox Judaism has not.

Modern Zionism as a self-consciously secular, nationalistic movement began and, in principle, remains an equal and opposite dissolution of the Jewish religio-ethnic fusion. A Jewish Israeli need not be a practitioner of Judaism to be a citizen of Israel any more than a Jewish American need be a practitioner of Judaism to be a citizen of the United States. The state is officially secular. Jewish and Arab Israelis do not differ—at least in principle—in their legal status any more than do Jewish and Irish Americans.

Interestingly, however, during the last decades of the twentieth century, a re-ethnicization of Jewish identity in the United States has been mirrored by a re-sacralization of Jewish identity in Israel. The reasons for this double reaction may be several. Chief among them, however, is surely the fact that European anti-Semitism, culminating in Nazi Germany's attempt at genocide in the 1940s, has undermined the confidence which Jews had begun to develop in the late nineteenth and early twentieth century that they could be welcome individually as full citizens of other nations (Reform Judaism) or collectively as a state with full rights among the other states (secular Zionism). In both the United States and Israel, the earlier, repudiated fusion of religion and ethnicity has come to seem a refuge, while those who would separate the two have come to seem a threat. Thus, members of the religious right in Israel disparage the secular majority of their country as *goyim dobrey 'ivrit*, or "Hebrew-speaking gentiles." Thus, again, Orthodox Jews in the United States disparage Reform Jews as "Unitarians." The prospect, in the one case, that secularity should be no bar to citizenship or, in the other, that ethnicity should be no bar to conversion is regarded as repugnant or ominous or both.

Nations that share a religion are perfectly capable of going to war against each other. The fusion of religion and ethnicity must not be regarded as the root of all strife. It may, however, be regarded as a frequent exacerbating factor. The point of this closing digression on Jewish and Israeli identity is only to note that the prospects for either eliminating religion as an exacerbating factor in national conflict or employing it for the mobilization of the species against a peril facing it as a species are decidedly modest. It is a commonplace of contemporary political commentary that the end of the Cold War has brought about an intensification of religio-ethnic identity in one region after another. Ethnic divisions that had been secularized into insignificance in federations like the Soviet Union and Yugoslavia have been re-sacralized; religious divisions that had been similarly subdued beneath an official atheism have been revived and pseudo-ethnicized (thus, for the Serbs the Muslim Slavs are "Turks"). One is forced to infer that it is psychologically easier to subordinate local differences in the face of a perceived military threat than to do anything comparable simply for the common good. It is easier, by that token, to imagine how religion might aggravate the ecological crisis than to imagine how religion might alleviate it.

Still, to say that a thing is difficult to imagine is not to say that it is impossible. The current moment merely throws the under-valorized role of imagination within religion into newly stark relief. A problem that religion may well make worse may yet be one that cannot be solved without religion. The challenge, though posed by science, is artistic as much as it is theological, a breakthrough of the imagination in the service of religion in the service of the human species in the service of life itself. We would be fools to predict such a breakthrough, but worse fools not to hope for it.

Notes

1. Stephen Steinberg, "Reform Judaism: The Origin and Evolution of a 'Church Movement,'" *Journal for the Scientific Study of Religion* 5 (1965): 117–29.

10

The Altar of Sin: Social Multiplicity
and Christian Conversion
among a New Guinea People

EYTAN BERCOVITCH

ON THE morning of February 16, 1985 a group of people gathered inside
a leaf-roofed hut in a mountainous, rain-forested valley near the center of
the island of New Guinea.[1] The hut served as the local Christian church
for a community of the Atbalmin people; the occasion was a confession
of sins. One by one, individuals walked up to the handmade table that
served as an altar and spoke. A young man talked about insulting and
quarreling with others, about his jealousy of other people's wealth and,
especially, about his lustful thoughts. A thirteen-year-old girl confessed to
arguing and fighting with other children. One of the last persons to speak
was a man in his sixties who was an important leader in the area.[2] With
visible anxiety on his face, he said:

> I lied. When the talk of God came here I lied to you. I did ancestral rituals, I
> did spirit exorcisms [to cure sickness]. . . . It was because the pastor was away
> and the men and women would have died otherwise and so I kept doing
> that. . . . When the pastor came back I had a dream. And in it, the pastor
> approached me and said "What you have been doing . . . is a bad water that
> you have drunk so that you have been sick all of the time." I thought about
> this and now I have come here to cast out my sin. "I have slung a net bag of
> sin on my head," I said to myself. "I will go and speak of it and then I will give
> it up."

Kupsep went on for a long time to confess additional sins. Some involved
fights, killings, or plots to cause harm that had occurred in his long life.
Interspersed with these he mentioned his role in initiations and rituals of
the indigenous religion.

The individuals who made these confessions, and who allowed me to
record them, had not been Christian long. Indeed, the Atbalmin began
to convert to Christianity in earnest only in the late 1970s. Yet by the
time I began fieldwork among them in 1981, they had become deeply
committed to their Christianity. I had gone to study their indigenous

religion, but I found that I also had to contend with Christianity. During the three years I lived among the Atbalmin, I attended many of the church services that were held almost every Sunday and sometimes also at other times of the week. Outside of church, I heard people express concern on a daily basis about Christian morality, about Heaven and Hell, and about the life, death, and the coming return of Christ. Despite their apparent piety, the Atbalmin were deeply dissatisfied with themselves as Christians. They often affirmed their conviction, whether in church confession or in ordinary conversation, that they were terribly sinful in relation not only to their pre-conversion past but also to their Christian present.

Christianity has become a powerful force in many parts of the world that are most deeply associated in the popular Western imagination with indigenous cultures and religions. The vast majority of people of Papua New Guinea now profess to be Christians, as do 95% of the people living in the other new island nations in the areas of Melanesia, Micronesia, and Polynesia.[3] Christianity is likewise thriving in remote parts of sub-Saharan Africa, the Amazonian region of South America, and aboriginal Australia. By necessity and choice, anthropologists who study such areas are increasingly making Christianity a focus of their research.[4] This is a challenging task, for the beliefs and practices of Christian converts are, in most cases, a complex synthetic product of Christianity with indigenous religion. Equally important, conversion is usually tied to situations involving complex social connections and cultural exchanges. These connections and exchanges, in turn, are spurred by a variety of social and historical processes, including capitalism, colonialism, missionization, and nationalism. There is ongoing debate about how best to distinguish these processes and their intricate interrelations.[5]

Like many other anthropologists, I have been forced to think about what it means for a group of people to convert to Christianity. It is important to make clear that I am not a specialist on this subject, which spans a vast period of time and many disciplinary fields. In this paper my aim is to indicate certain analytic directions I have found useful in this task which may be of interest to others who are concerned not only with Christianity or conversion but also with the comparative analysis of religions in social and historical terms.

In particular I will argue for the usefulness of an analytic concept that I will call *social multiplicity*. I use this term to refer to a situation where people possess several, often contradictory sets of beliefs and practices. I will suggest that Christianity among the Atbalmin owed much of its character and success to its particular relation to such a contested reality. The concept of social multiplicity draws on long-standing concepts framed to account for conditions of coexisting cultural practices: social change, acculturation, pluralism, syncretism, and compartmentalization. However, while many of these concepts suggest an untroubled coexistence or synthesis, social multiplicity stresses the conflicted character of life when people live with a number of very different sets of social and economic forms and forces.

The main body of my paper explores how Christianity among the Atbalmin was dynamically constituted through its relationship with various non-Christian aspects of life, some indigenous and others exogenous. I will provide evidence suggesting that Atbalmin Christianity was at once one among several social contexts of Atbalmin life and a vital way in which people related to their entire conflicted reality of multiple social contexts. The Atbalmin found in Christianity a source of both desires and fears; a new way of living but also a disturbing ongoing critique of their lives, individually and collectively. These tensions were amplified when, in March 1985, two movements swept the area. The first was an apocalyptic Christian movement, which prophesied the coming of Christ and the need to purge life of all non-Christian elements. The second movement, spreading from Irian Jaya, made the contradictory assertion that ancestors would soon return, bringing with them the wealth and power of Europeans for all those who upheld indigenous social and religious practices.

In the latter part of the paper, I turn to the broader implications of the analysis, especially the way in which Atbalmin Christianity was organized in precisely such a way as to benefit from social multiplicity. Building on the evidence of the Atbalmin case, I distill some general features of social multiplicity that may help illuminate processes of conversion to Christianity in other places and times. I suggest that a capacity to draw strength from social multiplicity may be a basic part of Christianity. Christianity may not be the only religion organized in this way. This may help explain the capacity of certain religions—sometimes called "world religions"—to extend their influence over many areas and periods of time.

Ethnographic Contexts of the Atbalmin

About three thousand people who call themselves Atbalmin (and also Nalumin) live in the Star Mountains of Papua New Guinea, next to the border with Irian Jaya, the Indonesia-controlled west half of the island of New Guinea. They subsist on shifting cultivation of sweet potato and taro, supplemented by hunting and gathering. They live in widely scattered settlements, each averaging only 30–40 persons and three to four ordinary huts. Most settlements also have a hut for menstruating women, and a hut reserved for men. A few settlements have a far more sacred men's temple. The two kinds of men's houses play a central role in the indigenous religion, which centers around a complex system of rituals, myths, and sacred objects from which women are largely excluded and to which men gain access only through a long series of initiation rituals.

The indigenous Atbalmin social organization is shaped by kinship, exchange, and religion. Settlements generally consist of people closely related through either parent. At a higher level of organization, the Atbalmin divide themselves into larger scale groups based on ties to a distant (possibly mythical) ancestor. There are about twenty such major descent groups among the Atbalmin, each averaging 100 persons and encompassing a number of settlements and claiming a sizable territory. Relations between individuals and settlements are also created and sustained through practices of trade and marriage. The indigenous religion also shapes social relations at both the local and broader level. Houses of the more common kind, where men sleep and hold minor rituals, serve as community social centers. The special temples and their higher rituals require and promote the active cooperation of men across large areas. Underlying connections between communities are also a key theme of the sacred narratives that are learned in rituals.

In addition to indigenous social and religious forms, Atbalmin social life reflects the increasing influence of several non-indigenous sets of forces and influences. Direct experience of European forces came only in 1950s, when representatives of the Australian colonial government began to enter the Atbalmin area from the nearest government outpost at Telefomin (ten days' walk away).[6] Government officers visited the area on "patrol" three times in the 1950s and an average of once every two years in the 1960s. These patrols consisted of one or two Australian officers, accompanied by a force of fifty or more New Guineans acting as police, carriers, and translators. They focused their work mostly on determining population numbers and bringing an end to armed warfare between communities. Through the patrols, the Atbalmin developed a growing relation to those they referred to as the *tabala*, a term encompassing both Europeans and the government.

In the years following Papua New Guinea Independence in 1975, several key events increased connections to these new forces. Around 1976 the first airstrip was opened among the Atbalmin. Though limited only to single-engine planes, the airstrip made government access to the area much easier, allowing the introduction of a health clinic (1977) and eventually a primary school (1980). In the late 1970s construction also began on a multinational gold and copper mine at Ok Tedi. Some Atbalmin men made the seven-day walk to the mine site, bringing back detailed reports of what they saw. The Atbalmin associated the mine with both the national government and Europeans.

Around the same time another set of forces emerged which directly challenged the indigenous religion. A station of the Australian Baptist Missionary Society had been in Telefomin since 1950, but it was not until the 1970s that it had a little success—even in its immediate area—in persuading people to convert to Christianity. The change came when it began to rely much more on "pastors"—young men who were recruited locally, given a brief training, and then sent out to proselytize in areas they were from or at least knew well. In the case of the Atbalmin, the mission depended on a handful of pastors recruited from the Urapmin and Tifalmin peoples, who lived immediately to the east of the Atbalmin and who had close social and linguistic ties with them. In just a few years, from 1976 to 1979, these pastors persuaded the majority of the Atbalmin to convert and to see themselves as part of a much larger Christian community that encompassed Europeans as well as Melanesians. Unlike the representatives of the government and business, they demanded that people give up their indigenous religion.

In the early 1980s, yet another group emerged to make demands on Atbalmin loyalties. This was connected with the arrival of "West Papuans," refugees who had fled from conflicts with Indonesian military forces, and who built communities just to the west of the Atbalmin. The leaders of these refugees sought to unite all Melanesians against outside forces, a category that included not only Indonesians but also Christians and the existing Papua New Guinea government (which was seen to serve outside interests). They emphasized the need to reject new influences and return to ancestral Melanesian social and religious practices. They also said that they had special ties to the dead ancestors themselves, who would ensure their victory. Though the Atbalmin did not know this, the West Papuans were part of a larger set of movements that have contested Indonesian occupation of the former Dutch colony of New Guinea. At the center of these movements is an organization called the Organisasi Papua Merdeka—the "Free Papua Movement"—often known by the acronym OPM.[7] But the struggle has also been carried out by numerous local resistance movements, such as the one encountered by the Atbalmin.

Atbalmin Christianity in the Early 1980s

I had little idea of this complex and tense reality of partially distinct social contexts when I flew into the Atbalmin area in September 1981. My aim was to pick out a site for a study of how the indigenous religious system had historically shaped inter-community relations, a subject that seemed well suited for a remote area of Papua New Guinea that had gained a reputation among anthropologists for complex ritual systems.[8] People living near the airstrip suggested that I visit Bomtem, a settlement where they said there was a particularly important temple that had long served as a regional religious center. The way to Bomtem proved difficult, involving a three-day walk along rugged trails that crossed three mountain divides. The settlement I found at the end of this journey was built on an open ridge and offered a breathtaking view down to the distant lowlands. The temple was built of wood and vine on the highest part of the settlement. With the temple, eight other houses, and over sixty people, Bomtem was the largest settlement I had seen among the Atbalmin. It was the heart of a fertile valley that had a total of ten settlements and about three hundred people. This was where I lived during my period of research among the Atbalmin, which totaled more than three years between 1981 and 1985.

Though my major focus remained religion, my findings led me in directions I had not anticipated. To my surprise, the people of Bomtem early on made clear that, despite the presence of the indigenous temple, they considered themselves Christian. They were eager to talk about Christianity and especially their conversion. They spoke often of a man named James, one of the pastors that had been sent by the Australian Baptist Missionary Society. As people recalled, James had arrived on foot in 1976, a tall young man with a genial but commanding bearing. People were pleased to find out he was from the neighboring Urapmin group. James was given a warm reception and he stayed for more than a year, preaching about the Bible and urging people to become Christians. By the time he moved on, he had baptized almost everyone in the valley. He had also appointed several young men as local church leaders and taught them to run services in his absence.

Four years had passed since James's departure when I arrived. Nonetheless his legacy was very much evident. Every Sunday morning people from settlements throughout the valley where I lived walked to a settlement located at the valley bottom. In this settlement, called Okbil, was a hut used as a church as well as another hut used by government patrols on their occasional visits. The Sunday service at Okbil was conducted in the Atbalmin language (except for a few special Christian words) and led by one of the local men who were church leaders. It began with singing of Christian songs, followed by a general prayer. Then one or more of the church leaders would tell Christian stories and explain their meaning. This part was often interspersed with additional prayers, Christian songs, and comments raised by people for discussion. Afterwards there sometimes was a ritual of communion, with people filing up to receive a piece of taro and make a contribution of food or money to the church. Services ended with a final general prayer for the sweet potato and taro gardens.

A limited number of themes were particularly prominent in the prayers, stories, and commentaries that I heard at the Sunday services. There was always reference to the omnipotence of the Christian God (in the three aspects of Father, Son, and Holy Ghost) over all other forces and over all people, whether Atbalmin or European. Church leaders urged people that they needed to have absolute belief in God, despite various temptations (ultimately connected to Satan) to doubt Christianity or to believe in non-Christian ways. Even more strongly, they warned people against the danger of sin. Hell was the fate of all those who were sinful, and everyone was sinful. The purpose of Jesus was to offer a way for people to find forgiveness for their sins and to go to Heaven. In learning these themes, people also became familiar with a new set of words, especially *Got* (God), *Spirit* (Holy Spirit), *Jesus, Satan, sin, bilip* (belief), and *laip* (generally meaning eternal life, that is, the soul). These were imported from Tok Pisin, the lingua franca of Papua New Guinea which derives many of its words from English.

Though these doctrines would undoubtedly seem predictable to anyone familiar with Christianity, they constitued a radically new context of life for the Atbalmin. Christianity for them had three partially distinct components. First, it was a *system of representations*, with both cognitive and affective dimensions. Cognitively, this system offered a new way of understanding people and spirit beings as well as their spatial and temporal contexts. In affective terms, it was linked with a new set of feelings, including a fearful sense of sinfulness and a desire for salvation. Second, Christianity involved a *distinct set of social relations*, the way people organized themselves into groups with internal distinctions and inequalities. Among these new social arrangements were the relations between pastors and the mission, between the pastors and their locally appointed officials, between church leaders and ordinary people, between members of the congregation, and between converts and all other Christians. Third, Christianity was linked to the *impact of other kinds of powerful external forces* on the lives of the Atbalmin, including not only the missions, but also colonialism and multinational capitalism.

Central to all these dimensions of Atbalmin Christianity was the concept of sin. Both at church services, which I attended, and in discussions outside of church, people were preoccupied with sin. They said that it was a sin to do wrong to others, such as by fighting, stealing, lying, or committing adultery. They also emphasized that many of their indigenous ways of life were sinful, especially their indigenous religion. It was a sin to seek or have great wealth, whether of traditional or newly emergent forms. It was sinful to have involvement with the ideas and practices of the West Papuans. Many, though not all, said it was a sin to send children to the government school or to use government medicine, both accessible only at the distant airstrip.

Sin was thus connected not only to a sense of doing wrong to others but also of doing anything that claimed a truth or power that had a non-Christian origin. Atbalmin Christians linked both of these sides of sin to concealment. Many of the practices that were deemed to do wrong to others involved a degree of concealment and duplicity, such as theft or adultery. Non-Christian ways of thinking and acting were seen to involve hidden roots, ultimately stemming from Satan's evil plans. Finally, concealment was seen as an everyday strategy that people used to appear to be Christian while actually being and acting otherwise. Indeed, many of the comments made in church during services focused on false Christians who "lied" about or hid their sinful ways. As the indigenous leader Kupsep's confession showed, people directed this accusation against themselves.

The concept of sin was an important part of how Christianity came to serve as a new basis for acting, understanding, and feeling. It worked to promote a different kind of personhood among the Atbalmin and to articulate a different social landscape for them to live in. In this respect, Christianity had the qualities of what might be called, following Foucault, a new regime of knowledge/power which incited distinct desires and fears in the subjects it helped to create.[9]

Multiplicity and Sin

But as people's confessions also made clear, more than Christianity was at work in Atbalmin life. It was apparent to everyone that they regularly acted as non-Christians, and for compelling reasons. Indigenous social and religious forms continued to offer an essential way for people to pursue desired ends, including food and shelter, fame, wealth, influence, security, love, retribution, and sacred knowledge. Meanwhile people pursued ties with the government and business for other, but equally compelling, reasons. The Atbalmin had come to depend on government intervention in their lives, particularly in the form of dispute resolution by patrol officers. Money and manufactured goods were increasingly entering the area through exchange, along with accounts of the way of life at the government outpost and gold mine. The Atbalmin were, finally, deeply impressed by the force of the West Papuans, with their large numbers, semi-military organization, and reputed possession of firearms. They considered it only prudent to maintain good relationships with them, and many actively hoped that these ties might yield wealth, power, and possibly even a reunion with deceased ancestors.

In the Christian concept of sin, the Atbalmin found a ready way to criticize each other for pursuing such a heterogeneous set of social relations and desired ends; ultimately, Satan could always be blamed. But I would suggest that analytic advantage can be gained by approaching the complex, conflicted reality of the Atbalmin through the concept of "social multiplicity," that is, the coexistence of different sets of forces and influences on people's lives. In the Atbalmin case, people recognized divisions between their indigenous practices, Christianity, government and business, and the West Papuans. They were able to situate themselves, in this way, in terms of a number of different kinds of social and symbolic landscapes. These were linked with different ways of understanding, acting, and feeling. To draw once again on Foucault, the Atbalmin lived with what might be called several quite different regimes of knowledge/power.

It was often remarkable to me how people could alternate between different perspectives. Despite their conversion to Christianity, people commonly seemed to situate themselves in an indigenous landscape of settlements, territories, and descent groups constituted from a long history of indigenous social and religious relations. Sacred narratives of the indigenous religion explained many features of this visible world, such as physical or social differences between people and the existence of prominent natural landscapes.[10] At other times, people showed their knowledge of a landscape defined by the government and business. It was marked by a profound difference in wealth and power between New Guineans and Europeans, and by a hierarchy of places beginning with the nearest government outpost and leading up through the provincial government capital at Vanimo, larger cities, the national capital at Moresby, and finally the place of Europeans. Temporally, this landscape involved a division between the period before and after the arrival of Europeans, and an anticipation of development. The West Papuans had contributed another landscape. It had its center far away in the lowlands of Irian Jaya, where the place of the dead was located. Its temporality was defined by the process by which Melanesians had lost their original autonomy but would someday regain it. The last landscape was provided by Christianity. It encompassed an even vaster world, including Christians as well as all pagans, Satan (and a host of devils) as well as God and Jesus, and Hell and Heaven as well as the visible world. Christianity also offered a distinct, dynamic temporality that began with God's act of creation and that would soon lead to apocalypse.

Each of these landscapes of space and time was connected to somewhat different notions of personhood. Indigenous notions of personhood stressed generosity and equality while also emphasizing that some people were better than others; this reflected the role of exchange in building social relationships and prestige. Emerging relations with the government and business introduced other forms of wealth and social power. To gain these, Atbalmin individuals believed they had to become more like Europeans, in their way of behaving, speaking, thinking, making their homes and communities, dressing, and so on. The West Papuans urged people to return to past ways of living, and also sought to change how people understood themselves and others. This was evident in the connections they emphasized between all Melanesians and, even more dramatically, between the living and the dead. Finally, the translocal kind of person-hood Christianity promoted was defined by notions of sin and salvation and a general reformation of conduct and thought. It demanded that people focus on "heaven" while renouncing "worldly" interests of either the indigenous or externally derived kind.

Though I have emphasized the distinctness in each of the Atbalmin's multiple social landscapes, it is important to keep in mind that there were significant connections between the landscapes. The different emergent understandings shared some of the same conceptual terms. The Christian cycles of religious services and Christmas celebrations, for example, gave concrete meaning to the secular temporality of years and weeks. In a similar manner, the West Papuans sought to recruit people into a coun-ter-organization that the Atbalmin saw as mirroring the government. Meanwhile, indigenous perspectives deeply informed people's under-standing of each of the emergent social landscapes.

Yet despite these connections, the various social landscapes could not be merged into one common synthesis. The conceptual frameworks of the emergent forces simply did not deal with many aspects of ordinary life, including the manner in which people locally claimed rights to land or kinship. The various emergent ways of acting and thinking, in turn, were opposed to fundamental aspects of each other and of indigenous life. Christianity warned against new forms of wealth and prestige even as it rejected many indigenous social values. The West Papuans rejected both the government and Christianity.

To some extent, people found such a reality of multiple social and symbolic landscapes explicitly contradictory. They found themselves in a situation where demands were made on them—by themselves as well as others—to reject values and desires to which they were genuinely at-tached.[11] Christian notions of sin were useful in addressing these tensions by portraying human existence as divided against itself, as the soul strug-gled against its own evil and wrong desires. Christianity, of course, did as much to heighten as to resolve such conflicts.

The Christian linkage of sin and concealment also made sense in the context of another aspect of the Atbalmin's conflicted social reality. An important way people dealt with contradictions was through the selective use of concealment and disclosure. They affirmed their loyalties differ-ently, depending on the time, place, and people involved.[12] Such strate-gies were not an entirely new part of Atbalmin life. It was clear that people had made selective use of concealment and disclosure in the past as well, in response to the conflicted aspects of their indigenous social life.[13] But these strategies had come to have new importance as a key means of dealing with emergent social contexts. Rather than choosing one context, people tried to maintain ties to several. In this way, they sought to keep their footing in a world that was always made up of multiple landscapes, landscapes which embodied, but also were embodied in, partially distinct sets of powers and meanings, fears and desires.

Though this strategy of disclosure and concealment had certain immediate advantages, it also led to anxiety, uncertainty, and dissonance. People saw themselves as failing their obligations and ties to the opposing aspects of their lives—to their indigenous religion, to the government and business, to Christianity, and to the West Papuans. The Christian concept of sin provided a means by which people related not only to their problematic relation to Christianity but more generally to their sense of being internally divided and at odds with themselves.

Rival Religious Movements

The intensity of conflicts and tensions in Atbalmin life rose to a peak in the last part of my fieldwork, when two rival millenarian movements occurred, one involving anticipations of the return of Christ and the other the return of the non-Christian ancestors. The two movements also helped me gain insights into a dimension of the situation among the Atbalmin which bears directly on the focus of my present discussion. There is a danger of conceptualizing social multiplicity merely as a convergence of a set of discrete external forces on a relatively passive indigenous world. The two movements provide evidence that social multiplicity can have an open-ended and active local dimension. In the course of the movements, the Atbalmin innovated new relationships with each other and redefined their relations with what they saw as the key external forces acting on their lives. They also revised their views of how the various external forces were related to each other. And they simultaneously did this in two competing ways.

The emergence of the two movements followed a series of developments that raised Atbalmin concerns with each of the emergent contexts of their life, intensifying conditions of internal and collective tensions. In the second half of 1984 there was a large increase in the numbers of refugees from Irian Jaya along the Atbalmin border. Interest in the government and business, meanwhile, was fanned by an administrative patrol in July, by an election carried out by helicopter in November, and by rumors about the imminent opening of a mine in Atbalmin territory.

Christianity in the area around Bomtem gained a major impetus when James—the Urapmin pastor who had originally converted people—returned early in September 1984. Around Christmas the area was swept by prophecies of a coming famine and by a series of rumors about miraculous events, such as a talking ax and a tobacco plant that metamorphosed into stinging nettles.

These rumors continued into early 1985, and people took them as serious evidence of Christ's imminent return. Such views helped inspire a series of rituals of confession, of which the one I attended on February 16, 1985 was typical. Another result was a baptism that was held on February 24. People were glad when James agreed to do this, because it would ensure that those not previously baptized would be readied for Jesus' return. The event proved an opportunity to remind everyone of the need to avoid all non-Christian ways. "Baptism," James made clear, "is not the end but the beginning of the struggle."

The apocalyptic Christian religious movement began on March 21, 1985. At night a powerful wind struck a settlement near where I lived and a number of women became possessed. This wind and its consequences were widely understood to be the work of the Holy Spirit. Over the next two days, women in other settlements became possessed by what they and others believed to be the Holy Spirit. In their possessed state, the women emphasized that Christ was about to return and that people had to prepare themselves for the apocalypse. Several of the women took an important role in religious services, which were held daily at the church.

"Finally," a number of people told me, "we will have our own Revival!" In saying this, they were drawing on their knowledge of another Christian religious movement known as the Rebaibel ("Revival") that had taken place in 1977–78 among people who lived east of the Atbalmin.[14] It had involved widespread possession by the Holy Spirit, most often by women, and destruction of many existing temples of the indigenous religion. Many Atbalmin had been disappointed when the movement had failed to enter their own area. Now, people felt they had another chance. I found that many individuals, both male and female, hoped and expected soon to be possessed by the Holy Spirit. They saw this not only as preparing for the return of Christ but actually as a way of bringing it closer.

On March 25, I awoke to find people ridding the settlement of things they linked with indigenous ways. They brought out the ritual objects used for promoting the growth of pigs and gardens that they kept in their ordinary houses and disposed of them in the forest. They also threw out many very old netbags and arrows, items associated with past traditions. A young man told me, "If we give up all the non-Christian ways and only go to church, they say God will send his spirit—the Holy Spirit, a new life—into all of us and heat us up."

The next day, on March 26, I attended an intense Sunday service at the church at Okbil. In a loud and dramatic manner, people confessed their sins and worldly desires and condemned the sins and desires of others. They declared all power to lie in the Christian God. There was a great emphasis on disclosing and ending forever the kinds of routine conceal- ment of non-Christian practices and beliefs that had been occurring. I was startled when a woman sitting quietly next to me suddenly became possessed and began beating the floor and yelling for people to rid their house of evil.

A few days later, the same possessed woman began to urge people to destroy the crucial temple at Bomtem. She said she was willing to enter it first herself to exorcise Satan. For the next week, I waited for the destruc- tion of the temple. Kupsep, who looked after the temple, expressed the mixed feelings most people had about the issue. On the one hand, he felt that since he had converted to Christianity, it had been wrong to keep the temple. But he also worried that destroying the temple would cause great harm, because of its power, as understood in indigenous terms, to sustain the fertility of the land, success in hunting, and the health of people in general. Others I spoke to expressed similar ambivalence.

This ambivalence had been one of the main reasons the temple had remained despite conversions to Christianity. The temple, in those years, had become a highly visible reminder of the uneasy, conflicted reality of living with opposing beliefs and practices. The Holy Spirit movement was driven precisely by the desire of many to resolve these kinds of tensions. Church leaders had always suggested that the tensions could be resolved if people became entirely Christian, renouncing finally and completely their non-Christian ties. Others accepted this view, but were unable or unwilling to comply with it. But as the Holy Spirit movement grew in strength, it seemed to most people that they were about to make the commitment, helped by the certainty that an entirely new reality was to be created with the return of Christ. There would be no tensions in this reality, because non-Christian persons and forces would have been purged. The temple was a final obstacle between them and this goal.

In the midst of expectations of the imminent destruction of the tem- ple, a very different movement came to influence the area. It began on April 5, when a man returned from a visit to a West Papuan community bringing word that ancestors were on their way back bringing the wealth and power that had been promised. "They [the West Papuans] say we will clap our hands," he reported, "and the Europeans will cry out once and will trade positions with us. They will carry things for us, they will work for us for money. We will look after them and pay them." The

Atbalmin who remained Christians after the return of the ancestors would not get any benefits and might perhaps be killed.

This millenarian message, followed soon by others of a similar kind, provoked a great deal of interest. I learned that some people, especially in communities closer to the West Papuans, were joining an organization concerned with making preparations for the coming millenarian events. Most people, however, never joined this organization. But they often discussed the meaning of the messages and they debated how to deal with the contradiction between the millenarian message's opposition to Christianity and the Holy Spirit movement's demand for absolute Christian devotion.

Much like the Holy Spirit movement, the West Papuan millenarian movement offered the Atbalmin an apocalyptic resolution of tensions. It drew, however, on a different set of tensions. It was fueled by the inability and unwillingness of many Atbalmin to renounce their non-Christian allegiances and to deny the social realities they reflected. An intensification of previous West Papuan messages, it promised immediate access to the wealth associated with Europeans and the government and which neither the church nor the government had seemed willing or able to make available to them. It also promised that people would soon see their own ancestors again, a hope suggested in the indigenous religion but denied in Christianity (which assigned all the heathen to a Hell which the converted would hopefully escape).

Significantly, the millenarian movement did not lead to an end of the Holy Spirit movement. For a period of several months, from April to June, both were active in the area at the same time. Not everyone was equally drawn to the two. Young women, for example, seemed to be far more drawn to the Christian movement than the millenarian concerns, while older men and women (who stood to lose their traditional authority) seemed less impressed with either. But most people were to some extent involved with both movements, taking seriously the claims of their rival messages. In the midst of these events, it became even more apparent that the same individual could act differently depending on the context. Kupsep, who normally acted as resolute leader and ritual specialist, became in church a submissive and self-reproaching Christian follower. A young woman who had always seemed to me quiet and even timid, proved to be a fearless and, to many, fearsome leader of the church. I routinely found that an individual who spoke in the morning about her desire to be possessed by the Holy Spirit, could speak critically about Holy Spirit movement later in the day. In this way, more dramatically than I had seen before, individuals seemed to be different people depending on context, with distinct characters and social and moral values.

Conceptualizing Social Multiplicity

In many respects, the religious situation that I have described for the Atbalmin resembles what has been reported elsewhere in Melanesia. It is common to find ancestral religions along with Christianity, just as it common to find gift exchange along with commodities, and local forms of authority along with state politics and power. Nowhere is the coexistence of indigenous and exogenous practices and beliefs more dramatically evident than in religious movements. There have been hundreds of these movements in Melanesia in the present century. Some have centered around the return of the ancestors bringing wealth, and others have emphasized distinctly Christian themes.[15] Research on these movements has contributed to moves by Melanesianists away from approaching the religions and societies they study as bounded entities. Most scholars now emphasize that people's lives at a local level reflect the influence of social forces operating at a much higher level, especially colonialism, capitalism, and nationalism.

The shift in research in Melanesia has contributed to, and also drawn on, a more general transformation of the field of social and cultural anthropology. There is growing ethnographic and analytic focus on interactions between different social systems or forces, often operating at different levels of scale. This has encouraged an expansion of perspectives so that social life even at a local level is analyzed in various ways in terms of national or transnational economic forces, exportable nationalisms, and other kinds of translocal or even global "cultural flows."[16] Another development has been a renewed interest in historical anthropology, which explores how local social forms both shape and are shaped by external sets of forces and influences over time.[17] These various ways of spatially and temporally broadening the field of analysis have proven of value in understanding Christianity and other religions.[18]

Such perspectives have informed my analysis here. But I have also sought to deal with what I perceive as a serious problem of how to conceptualize the nature and consequences of interactions between local social and religious forms and broader realities. For example, it is clear that concepts of "acculturation" and "culture change" emphasize too strongly a process by which one culture is replaced, in part or whole, by another culture; as a result they tend to simplify what is often a very complex kind of coexistence. The concept of "pluralism," while useful in acknowledging coexistence, often serves to detract attention from the conflicts that may and often do result from such realities. Likewise, the concept of "compartmentalization" may overemphasize the degree that people can keep different ways of acting and thinking comfortably isolated from each other.[19] Finally, the concept of "syncretism" can work against a recognition that there can be several rival kinds of syncretism (and anti-syncretism) that, in turn, lead to tensions and innovation.[20]

It is precisely in the face of such concerns that I have turned to the concept of "social multiplicity" as a way of approaching conditions of coexisting and often contradictory sets of beliefs and practices. Before going on to examine how this concept opens up perspectives on Christianity among the Atbalmin, I would like to explain the concept further. I will focus in particular on how it emphasizes multiple emergent engagements rather than a duality of the local and the external, and, by doing so, also provides insights into conflict and innovation.

In the Atbalmin case, and possibly many others, any attempted analytical opposition between the "local" versus the "external" is undermined by the heterogeneity of what is defined as external. The Atbalmin emphasized this dimension in their distinctions between the government and business, the Christian mission and the West Papuans. While I do not suggest taking these Atbalmin views literally—as indicating three objectively distinct sets of forces—they should be taken seriously. There were significant differences between the Christian pastors, government representatives, and the West Papuans that the Atbalmin met. This was made clear to them, for examples, in the pastors' criticism of those who would like to send their children to government schools or to amass new forms of wealth through cash labor. It was also made clear in the hostility of the West Papuans to the government and mission.

The Atbalmin case resonates with what has been reported in other ethnographic studies, as well as in recent directions of theory. It is now evident that Christian missions, in their actions as well as their doctrines, have often opposed as well as served forces of colonialism and capitalism.[21] More generally, there is increasing recognition of differentiation as well as homogenization in the global system, including the existence of discrete and even contradictory transnational "cultural flows."[22] Such differences in the field of power may be more dramatically evident from the perspective of marginal peoples such as the Atbalmin.[23]

But a people's perception of external forces should not be analyzed in terms of the nature of those forces alone. The specific way that people understand and relate to external forces can be deeply shaped by their indigenous social and religious forms. This became apparent in many accounts that I heard: that Europeans were the progeny of one of the original ancestors who had fled; that new forms of wealth had been made in the Underworld by the spirits of the dead; and that Adam and Eve were alternate names of their own mythical divinities. In more general terms, the indigenous salience of concealment—both in the deception of everyday life and in the graded initiations of rituals—led people to look for hidden dimensions of external forces. Many people, for example, believed that the Bible carried by the pastors was only a superficial version, and that there was somewhere (perhaps in the possession of the Telefomin Mission) a "deeper" version. Hopes for ultimate revelations had much to do with the millenarian quality that informed not only Atbalmin Christianity but also their views of the government, the mine, and the West Papuans.

Indigenous social and religious ideas also shaped the way the Atbalmin understood the differences between various external forces. As I have argued, Atbalmin Christianity distinguished itself from other external forces as well as from indigenous values by emphasizing that it was based on openness while they were based on concealment; in this respect it drew on a negative view of concealment that was central to indigenous life even as it sought to undermine many indigenous practices. Familiarity with indigenous kinds of partial and progressive disclosures informed people's views in other ways. It framed their speculation, for example, about whether what pastors were revealing was "deeper" than what was being revealed by the government officers or the West Papuans. It also led them to look for inconsistencies that might indicate what was being "left out" or "covered up" in the various disclosures that they received through their contacts with the various new forces.

In ways such as this, attention to multiplicity highlights the way that the "local" can provide an active basis for the constitution of what is "external." Among the Atbalmin, the interaction took on the form not of a dualism but of several ongoing processes of interaction, each a partially different way in which the local and external were being connected to each other. This multiplicity was the result of differentiation at a number of levels: within the external forces, within local social and cultural realities, and within the emergent syncretic products that developed in between.

Many scholars have emphasized how syncretism involves and encourages innovation and creativity in religion and other areas of life.[24] The Atbalmin case suggests that such effects may be even more pronounced where there are several different syncretic processes at work at the same time. This was especially evident during the period of rival religious movements, when people kept changing their lives and understandings.

But the rival movements also point to a bitter side of living in and between different religious and social contexts. Among the Atbalmin, this kind of social multiplicity posed severe problems, leading to conflicts and tensions and a sense of failing vital obligations and ties. People responded in a number of ways to this. They selectively concealed and disclosed parts of their lives. They also constantly innovated new meanings, as was especially evident during the rival religious movements. But none of

these means proved a solution; on the contrary, they often only intensified the problems and anxieties that resulted from them.

Christianity and Multiplicity

Tensions between alternative emergent contexts of social and religious
life may have been unusually severe among the Atbalmin. But the severity
of the case makes clear a condition that may be very common.[25] The case
suggests that there is analytical advantage in paying more attention to
multiplicity and the tension it leads to. It may help with recent moves to
recognize that people have an active part in their engagement with new
forces of colonialism, capitalism, and nationalism. Of particular significance to the present paper, attention to multiplicity and tensions may
contribute to a better understanding of how people relate to Christian
missionization.

The analytical limitations of a dualism between local and external is
obvious in the case of Christianity, a religion which encompasses many
sects, societies, and historical episodes. There is wide recognition that
conversion to Christianity is not just a one-way process by which people
adopt a new set of beliefs brought by missionaries. Scholars in anthropology, social history, and religious studies have called for a different view
that allows people a more active and creative role. They point to the vast
number of locally led Christian sects that have appeared in formerly colonized and missionized areas.[26]

Yet it is often not made sufficiently clear how and with what implications a people's form of Christianity can be called local and indigenous.
Certainly, much of what the Atbalmin believed and practiced as "Christians" was not of their own creation but had been passed on to them by
pastors who had been deeply influenced by Australian missionaries. It was
one of several new forces that had come to influence their lives, each
connected to a partially distinct set of practices and representations.

Here it is important to recognize that Christianity had another side. It
was a means through which people sought to understand their social lives
in its opposing dimensions, including indigenous as well as the various
emergent aspects. The Atbalmin judged themselves harshly in these
terms, as people who pretended to follow Jesus but who actually lived in
other ways. But despite, and indeed through these doubts, the Atbalmin
were deeply concerned with distinctly Christian concerns of sin and salvation. The existence of other beliefs and practices actually contributed to
the intense local meaning of Christianity.

What was indigenous in Atbalmin Christianity in the early to middle
1980s was thus not so much how they were Christian but how they were
both Christian and non-Christian at the same time. Being Christian

meant not only embracing a number of beliefs and practices but also rejecting many others, some of which were indigenous and others related to emergent exogenous influences. And the process of rejection was part of an inextricable engagement with these other ways of life. Likewise what was local, in a spatial and temporal sense, about Atbalmin Christianity was how it was located in and between several different social and historical landscapes.

Let me clarify how the Atbalmin case may offer some ways of thinking about Christianity more broadly. As the case suggests, Christianity can be fundamentally constituted in practice and imagination in relation to that which is not-Christian. Of particular importance is the way that the Atbalmin form of Christianity was organized to benefit from precisely such a predicament, through its focus on sin, temptation, desire, the flesh, and so on. This is arguably the case for many forms of Christianity that have existed in other places and times. Christianity thus may be a religion that is particularly well suited to deal with conditions of social multiplicity. This, in turn, may prove useful for those seeking to clarify the unifying themes in the many variants of Christianity that have existed. It may also explain, in more practical terms, the proven ability of Christianity to extend across the boundaries of presumably discrete regions as well as across the boundaries of different local histories.

This is not to say, of course, that Christianity everywhere has existed and does exist in relation to the same set of non-Christian realities. This variability can be seen clearly by returning to the Atbalmin case. The non-Christian for the Atbalmin was characterized by a particular kind of multiplicity, which emerged from the engagement of their specific indigenous context of life with a particular constellation of non-indigenous but also non-Christian forces and influences. Atbalmin Christians struggled to be Christians in relation to these realities. Despite their dramatic participation in a Holy Spirit movement, they were unable and unwilling to repudiate these other realities and become wholly Christians. Yet they were precisely Christians in these terms. Indeed, Atbalmin Christianity took on its most dynamic qualities from its demand that people reject parts of themselves they were unable and unwilling to reject. This was a source of considerable anxiety to them, but it may also have increased their opportunities for actively shaping their own lives. For in light of this impossible demand, people had to keep finding ways of reaffirming themselves as Christian, giving "conversion" a dynamic, ongoing, and locally based meaning.

Such a dynamic view may prove useful in examining Christianity in other places and times. Many other peoples have been and are being placed in situations where they feel they must reject parts of themselves. Christianity appears as one of the sources of such a demand, but also a way of responding. And it is precisely for such a reason that Christianity may thrive under such conditions. People find a significant resource in the Christian ideas and practices that have been taught to them by their pastor, such as by prayer, confession, and church meetings. But people are not limited strictly to what they have been given. Particularly in the face of impossible demands, people may turn to innovation. As among the Atbalmin, people may elaborate new forms of Christianity, drawing their inspiration not only from their indigenous culture but also from their emerging understandings of the new forces and influences on their lives (which for the Atbalmin included not only the mission but also the government and business and the West Papuans). In this way, in the midst of their struggle to live within these multiple social and symbolic landscapes, people may find a way of being Christians in terms, partly, of their own creation.

The unfinished, emergent quality of Atbalmin Christianity was particularly striking to me just before I left the field, in December 1985. By then the Holy Spirit movement and the West Papuan millenarian movement had both declined, leaving a situation that most regarded as deeply unresolved. The Atbalmin I knew had neither become purely good Christians, nor had they renounced Christianity and reaffirmed their indigenous ways. They saw themselves, more than ever, in the disturbing perspective of being poor Christians. Neither of the rival movements could resolve the Atbalmin's conflicted reality of multiple social contexts and allegiances. Yet, far from threatening their Christianity, these conditions seemed to assure its continuing hold on their lives. What I witnessed at an Atbalmin altar sheds light on how Christianity is a powerful and tenacious force in many parts of the world, overriding myriad indigenous religions.

As a final thought, it is worth noting that Christianity may not be the only religion so well suited for social multiplicity. Christianity arguably shares this quality with a few other religions, such as Buddhism and Islam. This may help account for the astonishing capacity of certain religions to persist through enormous historical changes, to cross cultural boundaries, and to encompass diverse populations within the same society. Some theorists have characterized these as "world" religions. They have linked their success with an emphasis on "world rejection" that creates "transcendental tension" leading to societal transformation.[27] Behind these so-called transcendental tensions, I suggest, may lie conditions of everyday social multiplicity; and the success of the religions may reflect their capacity to thrive under precisely such conditions.[28]

Notes

1. This paper is based on three and a half years of ethnographic fieldwork carried out among the Atbalmin of Papua New Guinea (August 1981–March

1982 and November 1982–December 1985). My research was funded by grants from the Fulbright-Hays program of the U.S. Department of Education, the National Science Foundation, and the Department of Anthropology at Stanford University. I would also like to thank the Institute of Papua New Guinea Studies for its sponsorship and the Sandaun Provincial Government for its support.

2. Kupsep is a pseudonym. I will use pseudonyms to protect the identity of individuals and specific communities (the pseudonyms, however, are based on common Atbalmin names). All other names and terms used in this paper are accurate to the best of my knowledge.

3. T. Swain and G. Trompf, *The Religions of Oceania* (London: Routledge, 1994), p. 193.

4. See, for example: T. O. Beidelman, *Colonial Evangelism: A Socio-Historical Study of an East African Mission at the Grassroots* (Bloomington: Indiana University Press, 1982); J. Comaroff, *Body of Power, Spirit of Resistance: The Culture and History of a South African People* (Chicago: University of Chicago Press, 1985); J. Comaroff, J. and J. L. Comaroff, *Of Revelation to Revolution* (Chicago: University of Chicago Press, 1991); J. Fabian, "Six Theses Regarding the Anthropology of African Religious Movements" in *Africa* 11 (1981): 109–26; R. Hefner, ed., *Conversion to Christianity* (Berkeley: University of California Press, 1993); R. Horton ("On the Rationality of Conversion" in *Africa* 45 (1975): 219–35, 373–99; J. Nash, We *Eat the Mines and the Mines Eat Us* (New York: Columbia University Press, 1979); V. Rafael, *Contracting Colonialism: Translation and Christian Conversion in Tagalog Society under Early Spanish Rule* (Ithaca: Cornell University Press, 1988); J. Schneider and S. Lindenbaum, eds., *Frontiers of Christian Evangelism* (special issue, *American Ethnologist* 14 [1987]); M. Taussig, *The Devil and Commodity Fetishism in South America* (Chapel Hill: University of North Carolina Press, 1980). Within the literature on Oceania, my area of specialty, Christianity is a central focus of many recent edited collections and ethnographic monographs. See, for example: J. Barker, *Christianity in Oceania: Ethnographic Perspectives* (Lanham, MD: University Press of America, 1991); J. A. Boutilier, D. T. Hughes, and S. W. Tiffany, eds., *Mission, Church and Sect in Oceania* (Lanham, MD: University Press of America, 1978); M. Huber, *The Bishop's Progress: A Historical Ethnography of Catholic Missionary Experience on the Sepik Frontier* (Washington, DC: Smithsonian Institution Press, 1988); G. White, *Identity Through History: Living Stories in a Solomon Islands Society* (Cambridge: Cambridge University Press, 1991).

5. An overview of the debates can be found in Nicholas Dirks, ed., *Colonialism and Culture* (Ann Arbor: University of Michigan Press, 1992) and N. Thomas, *Colonialism's Culture: Anthropology, Travel and Government* (Princeton: Princeton University Press, 1994). Current debates owe much to E. Said's earlier *Orientalism* (New York: Columbia University Press, 1979).

6. There were European exploratory parties entering areas near the Atbalmin as early as 1910 and 1914 (German), 1927–28 (Australian), and 1936–37 (American). They did not, however, enter areas of main habitation, nor did they engage in any significant communication with the Atbalmin.

7. Though the Atbalmin did not know this, the West Papuans were part of a larger set of movements that have contested Indonesian occupation of the former Dutch colony of New Guinea. At the center of these movements is an organization called the Organisasi Papua Merdeka—the "Free Papua Movement"—often known by the acronym O.P.M. But the struggle has also been carried out by numerous local resistance movements, such as the one encountered by the Atbalmin. Perhaps the best account to date of the situation is in R. Osborne, *Indonesia's Secret War: The Guerrilla Struggle in Irian Jaya* (Sydney: Allen & Unwin, 1985).

8. The work of F. Barth was especially influential in establishing the reputation of this part of New Guinea. See, for example, *Ritual and Knowledge among the Baktaman* (New Haven: Yale University Press, 1975), and *Cosmologies in the Making: A Generative Approach to Cultural Variation in Inner New Guinea* (Cambridge: Cambridge University Press, 1987).

9. See, for example, his discussion in *The History of Sexuality (Volume 1)*, R. Hurley, trans. (New York: Pantheon, 1978).

10. Explanations in the indigenous religious narratives generally take the form of mythic origin accounts. These origins are traced to the primordial actions of a few main divinities that took place in this world as well as in the Underworld.

11. The unwillingness of people to reject aspects of themselves is explored cogently in an African case by T. Ranger in "The Churches, the Nationalist State and African Religion" in E. Fashole-Luke et al., eds., *Christianity in Independent Africa* (London: Rex Collings, 1978). He emphasizes, as I do here, that it is wrong to look at conversion in terms of a simple break with previous ways of living. My analysis differs from his, however, in the way it emphasizes the problems people face in holding several conflicting perspectives.

12. Similar patterns of selective affirmation of religious loyalties have been noted among other Papua New Guinea peoples. A good anthropological analysis of one such case is provided by M. Kahn in "Sunday Christians, Monday Sorcerers: Selective Adaptation to Missionization in Wamira" in *Journal of Pacific History* 18 [1983]: 96–112.

13. I have discussed indigenous conflicts and their relation to concealment and disclosure relation elsewhere ("Mortal Insights: Victim and Witch in the Nalumin Imagination," in G. Herdt and M. Stephen, eds., *The Religious Imagination in New Guinea* [New Brunswick, NJ: Rutgers University Press, 1989]; and "The Agent in the Gift: Hidden Exchange in Inner New Guinea" in *Cultural Anthropology* 9 [1994]: 498–536).

14. This earlier movement has been described by anthropologists working in the Telefolmin area in that time. See D. Jorgensen, "Life on the Fringe: History and Society in Telefolmin," in R. Gorden, ed., *The Plight of Peripheral People in Papua New Guinea* (Cambridge, MA: Cultural Survival, 1981), pp. 59–79; and R. Brumbaugh, *A Secret Cult in the West Sepik Highlands* (Unpublished dissertation, State University of New York at Stonybrook, 1980).

15. There is a large body of writings on these movements. Most have been concerned with those movements that emphasize the return of the ancestors bringing wealth, which are sometimes called "cargo cults." The work of three writers is especially well known on this subject: K. E. O. Burridge (*Mambu: A*

Melanesian Millennium [London: Methuen, 1960]), P. Lawrence (*Road Belong Cargo: A Study of Cargo Movements in the Southern Madang District of New Guinea* [Manchester: Manchester University Press, 1964]); and P. Worsley (*The Trumpet Shall Sound: A Study of 'Cargo Cults' in Melanesia* [New York: Schocken Books, 1968]). But increasingly, movements with a Christian emphasis have received attention (see for example C. Loeliger and G. Trompf, eds., *New Religious Movements in Melanesia* [Port Moresby and Suva, 1987]; W. Flannery, *Religious Movements in Melanesia: a Selection of Case Studies and Reports* [Goroko: Melanesian Institute, 1983], D. Tuzin "Visions, Prophesies and the Rise of Christian Consciousness," in G. Herdt and M. Stephens, eds., *The Variety of Religious Imagination in New Guinea* [New Brunswick: Rutgers University Press, 1989]). Many groups of people have apparently experienced both kinds of movements over time, though the Atbalmin case of two simultaneous movements may be unusual.

16. Studies of nationalism in anthropology have been deeply influenced by the work of B. Anderson (*Imagined Communities: Reflections on the Origin and Spread of Nationalism* [Revised Edition] [New York: Verso, 1991]). A. Appadurai has had a pivotal role in making anthropologists more aware of the need to attend to translocal "cultural flows" (see, for example, "Disjunction and Difference in the Global Economy" in *Public Culture* 2 [1990]: 1–24; and "Global Ethnoscapes: Notes and Queries for a Transnational Anthropology" in R. Fox, ed., *Recapturing Anthropology: Working in the Present* (Santa Fe: School of American Research Press, 1991). The body of writings about national or transnational economic forces is too extensive and diverse to summarize here. A useful (though now dated) discussion of this literature is provided by G. Marcus and M. Fischer in *Anthropology as Cultural Critique: An Experimental Moment in the Human Sciences* (Chicago: University of Chicago Press, 1986), pp. 77–110.

17. M. Sahlins has argued for the important role of indigenous religious forms in the Hawaiian encounter with the West in his influential works *Islands of History* (Chicago: University of Chicago Press, 1985). The historical role of indigenous cultural forms has been highlighted by others, including R. Rosaldo, *Ilongot Headhunting 1883–1974: A Study in History and Society* (Stanford: Stanford University Press, 1981); J. Comaroff, "Dialectical Systems, History and Anthropology: Units of Study and Questions of Theory, in Journal of African Studies 8 (1981): 143–178.

18. See, for example, J. Comaroff, J. and J. L. Comaroff, *Of Revelation to Revolution* (n. 4 above); P. Van dar Veer, *Religious Nationalism: Hindus and Muslims in India* (Berkeley: University of California Press, 1994).

19. Many of these concepts have been so commonly used for so many years that it would make little sense to relate them to specific authors. An exception is the association of the concept of compartmentalization with the work of M. Singer (see especially *When a Great Tradition Modernizes* [New York: Praeger, 1969]).

20. Concerns about the limits of the concept of syncretism are cogently addressed in a recent collection, C. Stewart and R. Shaw, eds., *Syncretism/Anti-Syncretism: The Politics of Religious Synthesis* (London and New York: Routledge, 1994). Such concerns also play a role in the increasing popularity of the concepts

of "hybridity" and "double consciousness," both of which are used in a manner that places more stress on tensions and ongoing innovations (see H. Bhabha, *The Location of Culture* [London: Routledge, 1993] and M. Gilroy, *The Black Atlantic: Modernity and Double Consciousness* [London and New York: Verso, 1993]). For reasons of space, I do not explore here the relation between my approach and these other recent directions. While I draw on them, I also diverge in two main ways. First, I am concerned with the predicament of the members of a small, peripheral group, rather than focusing, as many do, on global diasporas and major postcolonial nations. Second, I am more concerned with multiplicity and with tensions and conflicts.

21. See Comaroff and Comaroff, *Of Revelation to Revolution* (n. 4 above).

22. This is Appadurai's main focus in "Disjunction and Difference in the Global Economy" (n. 16 above). On the one hand, he argues that there are a variety of partially distinct kinds of transnational flows, such as those of people ("Ethnoscapes"), technologies ("Technoscapes"), capital ("Financescapes"), images of the mass media ("Mediascapes"), and political and cultural symbols and ideas ("Ideoscapes"). On the other hand, there are ways in which difference is defined in terms of each of these contexts of transnational flow, not only in the sense of distinctions between centers and peripheries but also in the emergence of rival centers. For another cogent discussion of these issues, see A. Gupta and J. Ferguson "Beyond 'Culture': Space, Identity, and the Politics of Difference" in *Cultural Anthropology* 7 (1992): 5–24.

23. A. Tsing has made this point eloquently in a study of an Indonesian people (*In the Realm of the Diamond Queen: Marginality in an Out of the Way Place* [Princeton: Princeton University Press, 1993]).

24. The celebration of syncretism seems to have reached its height in recent work on hybridity. See, for example, H. Bhabha's comments in "Location, Intervention, Incomensurability: A Conversation with Homi Bhabha" in *Emergences* 1 (1989): 63–88.

25. There are many cases where people may hold different systems of practices or beliefs without so great an apparent strain (for a Melanesian example see M. Macintyre, "Christianity, Cargo Cultism and the Concept of the Spirit in Misiman Cosmology" in J. Barker, ed., *Christianity in Oceania* [Lanham, Maryland: Univ. Press of America, 1991]). I do not see this, however, as putting in question the basic perspective on multiplicity that I am developing here. Rather it points to variability in the extent to which differences between various social contexts become an area of explicit tension and confrontation in people's lives.

26. See, for example, J. Barker, "Introduction" in *Christianity in Oceania* (n. 4 above); E. R. Fasholé-Luke et. al., eds., *Christianity in Independent Africa* (Bloomington: Indiana University Press, 1978); G. W. Trompf, *Melanesian Religion* (Cambridge: Cambridge University Press, 1991).

27. A recent statement of this position is made by Heffner ("Introduction" in R. Hefner ed., *Conversion to Christianity* [n. 4 above], p. 8). Heffner draws on the earlier arguments of R. Bellah ("Religious Evolution" in *American Sociological Review* 29 [1964]: 358–74) and M. Weber (*The Sociology of Religion* [Boston: Beacon Press, 1956]).

28. This perspective opens up a potentially fruitful line of comparative study

which I do not have space to develop here. The central concepts of the Atbalmin case—sin, Satan, etc.—are worth comparing with Christianity in other sects, places, and times. Christianity often also seems to involve a duality, important in the Atbalmin case, between the institutionally defined relation of people to their church (and the mission) and their spiritual relation to the Holy Spirit.

It would also be interesting to take a comparative look at other religions besides Christianity with attention to concepts and thematic oppositions that might help people relate to conditions of social multiplicity. My superficial knowledge of Buddhism, Hinduism, and Islam suggests many examples of this. The important point would be not just to emphasize the equivalences but also to explore differences, with attention to how such concepts arise, persist, change; and what kinds of consequences they have for religions and peoples.

Such a framework might also illuminate religions that are less well known and of a smaller scale of influence. This includes, for example, some of the non-Christian African religions whose translocal dimensions are emphasized by T. Ranger (see "The Local and the Global in Southern African History" in R. Hefner, ed., *Conversion to Christianity* [Berkeley: University of California Press, 1993]). It also applies to some of the religious movements in Melanesia, including the West Papuan millenarian movement described here.

11

God On Line: Locating the Pagan/Asian Soul of America in Cyberspace

BRUCE B. LAWRENCE

IT IS IMPOSSIBLE not to think of religion on the cusp of a new millennium that is defined, above all, by a religious figure said to have lived about two thousand years ago. But what should we think about religion as it is understood today, especially on the cusp of not just a new period of time but also a new, rapid, and seemingly irreversible pattern of human inter-action? The label most often given to the content of the new era is the Information Age. It is the Information Age because huge amounts of data are now available, with a promise of meaning, to more people and at faster rates than was ever humanly possible in the Pre-Information Age.

But can we say, with any verifiable certainty, that with the advent of the Information Age we have entered a new era in thinking about religion? Some would hypothesize that what we have now is unlimited relativism: with so many options to believe, or disbelieve, to practice, or not to practice, can we say anything more definite than "any truth fits, choose your own, none is final"?

The older generation—whether Baby Boomers or Generation X—may doubt that religious truth has moved so far from the certainties of their youth, but to Generation Y-ers, it may often seem that what we now have is a cyber-shopping mall. It offers infinite choices in the netaphysi-cal/digital as well as the physical/material realm. The popular press echoes the cyber-slogan of all Generation Y-ers: "Today's excess is but tomorrow's finite past!"

Perhaps no single bimonthly journal better reflects the mood of the current American quest for choice than the *Utne Reader* (fig. 11.1). The *Utne Reader*, with a circulation well above 50,000 and a website that is second to none (*www.utne.com*), culls the best of over 2,000 alternative media, and then distills them for its readership. Not only Generation Y-ers, but many older Americans consult the *Utne Reader* to get beyond the crisis-oriented style of CNN or *Time/Newsweek*.

It was to mark summer 1998 that the *Utne Reader* featured an article

Figure 11.1 An *Utne Reader* cover (Summer 1998) accents the Asian elements of do-it-yourself religion.

that linked the rise of interest in Asian religions to the explosion of information about spirituality. The author posited as self-evident that a new era was dawning in American religious practice; it was to be a new era portending large-scale cultural changes. Even those not convinced by either the argument or the author's evidence had to agree with his assertion that the new era, if it is upon us, "began with the Immigration Act of 1965, which eliminated a long-standing bias against Asians and other people enforced through quotas based on national origin. The new immigrants included many spiritual teachers whose influence would eventually extend beyond their immediate followers into the popular culture."

For skeptics, this new blending of Asian spirituality and popular culture may seem limited to such niches of netaphysical indulgence as Greenwich Village, San Francisco, and Boulder, Colorado. Yet books by the Dalai Lama now stand near the top of the best-seller lists, while in shopping malls near major urban areas throughout North America one can find evidence of what the *Utne Reader* article calls "a kind of do-it-yourself spirituality. Esoteric texts once known to a privileged few now fill the bookstores, their myriad truths laid open to be read and recombined at will. And virtually every work of sacred art, from the caves of Altamira onward, circulates endlessly now, free for the appropriating. This robust spiritual marketplace perfectly suits the consumer mentality that has turned Americans into a nation of comparison shoppers. In an age when we trust ourselves to assemble our own investment portfolios and cancer therapies, why not our religious beliefs?"[1]

Such speculation may sound like outrageous oversimplification. After all, many immigrants are not Asian. They are Hispanic, and even among Asian immigrants, Filipinos tend to be Roman Catholics, while Koreans are Protestant, often evangelical Protestants. Moreover, many of the new Asian immigrants do not see themselves as providers of a new spiritual commodity for jaded Anglo-American consumers.

Yet even the demurrals must reckon with the ground level change in turn-of-the-century America. In the 1990s the United States has become a different place, and not just in cyberspace. "By most counts," note two astute observers of the American religious scene, "in the 1990s there were more Buddhists than Quakers, more Muslims than Episcopalians, more Hindus than Disciples of Christ. Columbus might not have found Asia, but five hundred years later Asia certainly had discovered America. In a land transformed by meeting and migration, Americans were struggling to remap the world—and reimagine the nation."[2]

To reimagine the nation in the new millennium requires the resources of the Internet, and it is on the Net that we find not only Asian voices, but also pagan voices. Pagan voices? To some, pagans would seem not only strange but anathema to the heritage of Abraham, Isaac, and Ishmael, but my argument is that the middle ground of the social imaginary is no longer limited by Abrahamic parameters. Even for those considerably older than Generation Y-ers, the resonance of other possibilities, including pagan and Asian possibilities, beckons.

After all, pagan others have claims to be historically ancient "world" religions. They do not occupy as many web sites as Abrahamic advocates in cyberspace, but they do occupy sites that are contiguous with the majoritarian religious communities of North America. They have become equivalent, without being equal. They claim virtual space as living and public religions. They project their message to cybernauts from all parts of the globe but especially, at least for now, from North America.

There may not yet be an Asian/pagan soul in America, yet I want to make the case in this essay that because of the Net we are forced to think the unthinkable. Because of the Net we are also led to imagine where we can chart religion and religions as we cross not only a temporal divide into another millennium but also a cognitive divide into the murky realm of netaphysics.

While the future remains opaque, we do at least have a guide. He is Manuel Castells, the Berkeley sociologist who has tried to theorize what the shift to an Information Society portends for our collective future. According to Castells, we have *already* crossed the line from one era to another, since "the network society represents a qualitative change in the human experience." Why? Because "the inclusion/exclusion in networks, and the architecture of relationships between networks, enacted by light-speed operating information technologies, configurate dominant processes and functions in our societies."

Yet Castells is no mere bleak reductionist or beady-eyed determinist. He does project the cultural consequence of the Information Age to be as transformative as its commercial or political edge, but at the same time, he posits culture as an independent variable. He affirms that culture will provide its own autonomous spin to the space of flows, for "while the eternal/ephemeral time of the new culture does fit with the logic of flexible capitalism and with the dynamics of the network society, it adds its own, powerful layer, installing individual dreams and collective representations in a no-time mental landscape."[3]

Individual dreams and collective representations wrapped into a no-time mental landscape?! That is a daunting option to consider. It means the collapse of an arithmetic notion of time that can sort out as past-present-future. The space of flows links all parts of the globe but also all moments of history and all future moments into its band of simultaneity. Nothing is except what appears, and then disappears.

If Castells's is a dazzling vision, the consequences of the Information Revolution remain penumbral. Not all netizens share Castells's unshakable optimisim. Some foresee a dystopia of cyber-segmentations or raw class conflict.[4] Yet the hopeful traces of his comprehensive rereading of the human experience are already evident in the actual patterns of pagan/Asian spirituality as it begins to be felt in turn-of-the-millennium American culture.[5]

Let us examine more closely how pagans and Asians become part of a spiritual imaginary that shapes even the naysayers who would exclude Asians, unless Christian (or Jewish or Muslim), and pagans of all stripes because they are—well—heathen! The heathen pagans have actually always been with us, part of the American—and also European—religious landscape, though not accorded official recognition. Asians, on the other hand, as the *Utne Reader* essay points out, have only been present in significant numbers since 1965. Moreover, they have been present mostly as a minority subset in the mega-cities where the majority choose to locate.[6]

It is to underscore the novelty of the Information Revolution for religious awareness in North America that I conjoin the "pagan/Asian" experience in cyberspace. Neither group is seamlessly whole: neither is inevitably conjoined with other "pagans" or other "Asians," much less with each other. But what is too often ignored in efforts to depict the internal diversity of both pagans and Asians is the way in which they are not only conjoined but ranked in the popular media. Even though the *Utne Reader* represents, or tries to represent, "the best of the alternative media," it still makes choices in what it offers as ingredients for pastiche spirituality. Asians are deemed "acceptable" religious others, pagans less so.

Arguably the Asian influx makes room for the pagan difference, but only for some pagans and even then, not without qualifications. The first, and necessary, step is to understand the character of the Asian influx. Since 1965 between 5 and 6 million Asian immigrants have come to the United States.[7] If their arrival makes of this country even more a patchwork society of disparate groups from far-flung parts of the globe than it was in prior decades of the long twentieth century, their presence has yet to be theorized in spiritual terms. Asian Americans do not merely bring old baggage to new places. They also interact with, and benefit from, the Information Age as depicted by Castells—but how?

It would be possible to chart the recent past and the near-term future of American Asian religious experience as a series of overlapping but discrete diasporas. Arjun Appardurai has favored this optic, elaborating it through a taxonomy gauged by the emotive tone of the displacement/relocation of new immigrants. He classifies these as diasporas of hope, diasporas of terror, and diasporas of despair. Collectively, in Appardurai's view, "these diasporas bring the force of the imagination, as both memory and desire, into the lives of many ordinary people . . . and not just as a counterpoint to the certainties of daily life. They move the glacial force of the habitus into the quickened beat of improvisation for large groups of people. [Today, unlike in the past,] those who wish to move, those who have moved, those who wish to return, and those who choose to stay rarely formulate their plans outside the sphere of ratio and television, cassettes and videos, newsprint and telephone [and also the Internet]. For migrants, both the politics of adaptation to new environments and the stimulus to move or return are deeply affected by a mass-mediated imaginary that frequently transcends national space."[8]

Appadurai's analysis hinges on a mass-mediated imaginary, but mass-mediated by whom, and toward what end? While Appadurai paints a grand picture, it is painted in chiaroscuro, with abstract code words, like memory, desire, and habitus, and oblique referents, like large groups of people and national space. We need to go beyond the "mass-mediated imaginary" if we are to understand the autonomous cultural variable hypothesized by Castells as integral to the Information Age. To make that crucial, next step we need to have a theory of religion as culture that reflects the multifaceted, interactive nature of cyberspace communication. That theory is provided by Stuart Hall *et al.* in the following pentagon. It offers an interlocking grid. Its key components are:

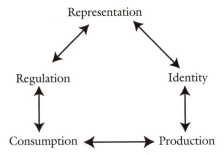

None of these five key terms stands on its own; all of them interact to form various patterns of Culture.[9]

While there is no automatic substantive correspondence, much less complete interchangeability, between culture and religion, they do overlap in their respective functions, and for the purposes of analyzing "God On Line," the model of Hall *et al.* offers a grid of deep processes that escape immediate notice at the same time that they signal crucial, long-term consequences.

To adapt Hall's model to religion, and above all, to the multiple religions of the recent Asian diasporas, some qualifiers are required. To complicate Representation, one must add the element of Contestation, since Representation always inscribes a choice, and often a conflictual choice, of what gets represented and for whom. Identity also needs to be problematized by its complementary other, Community, just as Castells has counterposed "individual dreams" to "collective representations." Nor can one avoid genderizing production; it is always shadowed by the parallel process of Reproduction. Consumption, however, is too tightly linked to Production in both the grid and Hall's analysis, for one must move beyond the material bases of the industrial assembly line imagery in order to grasp the imaginary as signaling Choice, with the space between Production and Reproduction camouflaged, yet no less real for being invisible.

But the most critical corrective concerns Location. It must be introduced into the grid when conceptualizing the outlook and experience of Asian immigrants. I would substitute Location for Regulation in understanding Religion generally and diasporic religious communities in particular. At the same time, Location cannot be projected as an inherently stable category. It is neither stable nor constant. One needs to reflect its malleability, and so I would always link it to its prepositional correlates: Dis-location, Re-location, Bi-location, all of which are crucial for studying diasporic groups, but also for understanding the mobile character of Information Age logistics.

It would then be possible to pursue a fivefold sequence, or five-node circuit of religion that helps us to see Asian religious experience in twenty-first-century North America as contingent both historically and contemporaneously. We could investigate how Asian "others" are mediated in several directions, but especially through cyberspace and the new marvels—at once magical and mischievous—of the Net or the World Wide Web.

Our new diagram would look like:

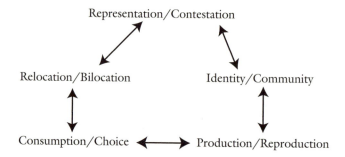

To highlight why this exercise is pivotal, we need once again to look at the hardwiring of virtual reality that is everywhere assumed but seldom foregrounded. If chips and computers are new and telematics (i.e., automatic telecommunications) ubiquitous, their growth is equally astounding and nearly unimaginable. Let me give as a case instance my own introduction to the network of global interaction called email. For those of you who do not take email for granted, it is good to remember the quip of a New York Bishop: "If Jesus were walking the earth today, I'm convinced He would have an email address."

Before 1990 that bishop would have been hooted out of the pulpit for such a "silly" remark. Now it seems, well, almost plausible. For me email was almost as remote as the Second Coming until summer 1993. It was then that I went to Oxford, England on a research project. One of my colleagues at the Oxford Centre for Islamic Studies introduced me to email so I could communicate more easily with office support staff back in North Carolina. It was remarkably easy and effective, but I still preferred the telephone, fax, and even occasionally, letters. Once back in North Carolina in the fall of 1993, I began using email there but never more than 40 emails per month, roughly one or two per working day. Eleven months ago, however, as I shifted over from Dec 98 to Jan 99 on my email ledger, I noted that from March 1998 on to the end of the year I averaged about 320 emails per month, an eightfold increase from my first, halting introduction some five years earlier. Now I seldom use the telephone except to contact family members or to surprise a colleague. I rarely resort to a fax, when I can instead attach a document to the email message, and I have given up letter writing except at holiday times or in extended postcards from overseas.

Is my experience with email unique? I doubt it. Will Jesus some day announce His return via email and, if so, who will be included in the listserve? Hard to tell, but either use of email pales next to the calculus of change suggested by Castells. Such are the advances in optoelectronics (fiber optics and laser transmission) that the Integrated Broadband Network (IBN), when it becomes fully available at a commercially viable price, will surpass the Integrated Services Digital Network (ISDN) that has been in place since the 1970s. The Internet as we now know it is, in effect, but the first stage of what it will become very quickly in the new millennium: a globally interactive system indispensable for all levels of communication. A new Production/Reproduction pattern of Consumption, featuring ideas as well as commodities, will emerge because the number of personal computers, estimated to have been 57 million worldwide in 1995, had already passed 100 million by the year 2000. If we accept Castells's calculus, the Internet has "the potential to explode into hundreds of millions of users by early in the twenty-first century."[10]

The dark side of netizenry is all too evident. Commercial forces, as represented by the W3C (the World Wide Web Consortium), an international organization of 250 companies, governments, and universities that sets the technical blueprints for many of the Internet's advances, will try to control how much access is provided to netizens, and at what cost. The increasing private appropriation of public electronic space, signalled by Saskia Sassen,[11] and the bifurcation of the multimedia world into two distinct populations, the interacting and the interacted, mapped by Manuel Castells,[12] both suggest that exclusion as much as inclusion will characterize the New Information Age.

But whether our gaze is from the bottom up or the top down, virtual and real will mesh in a way that up till now has seemed the realm of science fiction. Insofar as reality has always been virtual, insofar as it is perceived through polyvalent symbols, the culture of the Information Age will instantiate a system of real virtuality, or in Castells's words, "a system in which reality itself (that is, people's material/symbolic existence) is entirely captured, fully immersed in a virtual image setting, in the world of make believe, in which appearances are not just on the screen . . . but become the experience. It is no longer the medium as the message but the message as the message; it is no longer nature vs. culture (the premodern age) or culture vs. nature (the modern age) but culture as culture (the information age).[13]

God On Line escapes the net of analysis even while being itself the product of the Net; or better, God On Line becomes the representation of the Unrepresentable, the Surplus of Meaning that becomes the property of multiple "traditional" religions, and also others that are not traditional. It affects more than Asians and pagans, but its larger impact, in my view, cannot be assessed unless we take account of those who still count as "others" for most of the 87 percent of North Americans who self-identify as "Christian."

To understand the shift from Christian to non-Christian but also from traditional to nontraditional, we need to identify three projections of religion: cyber-religion, CD-ROM religion, and print-text religion, or rather religion *and* religions. As Hans-Georg Gadamer has indicated, it is not religion or religions but the conjunction of the singular with the plural that embodies the dilemma of the Information Age: not Religion or Religions but "Religion *and* and the Religions expresses the situation in which the problem of religion has become a central concern in the modern world."[14] And the problem derives from the imagining which is also the imaging of religion, for, as Gadamer also acknowledges, the deepest structure of religion is not cognitive but visual. "The transition from the stage of representation to that of the concept cannot be made without art."[15] And so while the Net would seem ideally suited to the religious imagination of netizens, the beauty of the Net is also its defeat: the multiplicity of images, like the diversity of religious options, offers a defiant range of choice.

While criteria remain elusive, one can at least acknowledge that hypertexts differ from print texts. Print-texts offer press catalogues and also compendia such as *Books in Print*. CD-ROMs also have an indexical flavor. But hypertexts, and above all, hyperlinks, test the ingenuity of each netizen to choose for herself, first, what matters (priorities), then, what counts (credentials of sources), and only later, what advances (critiquing, applying, and connecting hypertexts).

With respect to religions, the problem can be seen in the most basic of all exercises: naming, not only the naming of religion per se, to which Jacques Derrida has added yet another voice of anti-metaphysical lament,[16] but also the naming of religious communities that count either as Major or Minor or even count as Religions. Jonathan Z. Smith has uncovered, in numbing detail but near lyrical prose, the ideological fault line that renders suspect all notions of "world religions."[17] Smith's insights have to be constantly invoked in nuancing the taken-for-granted categories of not only the popular media but also academic textbooks. It remains standard practice to name certain religions as world or universal or living, whether in textbooks and dictionaries or in encyclopaedias.[18]

Consider the treatment of paganism. Paganism is a nontraditional religion, underrepresented in textbooks like *World Religions: Western Traditions/Eastern Traditions*, edited by W. G. Oxtoby, and omitted from others such as *The Religious Traditions of Asia*, edited by J. Kitagawa. When one comes to a CD-ROM such as *On Common Ground*, one does find an entire taxon or button that is labeled "Paganism." Yet in its CD-ROM projection as a single religious tradition, paganism is accorded "minor" coverage compared to the "major" traditions.[19] It is only with the expansion of the World Wide Web that one can now find multiple sites for paganism, or neo-paganism, or witchcraft/Wiccan. These sites luxuriate in the artistic and expressive dimension of paganism as feminine spirituality.

One might say that paganism has moved from the underrepresented or subjugated subcategory of print-text religion to the represented but understated single category of the CD-ROM and now to the equivalent, often ebullient multiple categories of the Net. There is no lost pagan or single pagan, but many, many pagans in cyberspace.

Consider two of the major search engines of the Net and their deployment of pagan sites. Is it but another illusion of cyber-optic overload that in July 2000 Yahoo.com, one of the top directories of websites, had in its Society & Culture Web directories for Paganism more than 580 links to choose from? This compares with a "mere" 381 for Hinduism, 614 for Islam (also a major Asian religion, as I have argued elsewhere[20]), and 743 for Buddhism. Even Hitbox.com, which surveys over 2000 sites for the number of hits each receives in the Religion subset of Society & Culture, posts a pagan site in the top 20. Is it mere cybermania that has produced over 2 million hits for www.witchvox.com, or have devotees of the Goddess begun to take a new life through the Net?

Erik Davis in *Techgnosis* explains this development as the natural convergence of magic with the Net. "Their experimental spiritual pragmatism has made it easy for Pagans to embrace new occult technologies: sophisticated astrological software, *I Ching* CD-ROMs, Tarot hypercard stacks. More important, it has led them to reimagine 'technology' as both a metaphor and a tool for ritual."[21] Durkheim called it "elective affinity," the seeming synergy of two opposite forces due to hidden traits or unacknowledged circumstances that matched each with its seemingly opposite other.

My argument foregrounds the emergent prominence of paganism not only for what it says about pagan practices in the Information Age but also for what the cybersuccess of paganism augurs for other religions, including Asian religions. Like paganism, the major Asian religions have moved beyond the familiar taxonomies of the past. No longer singly but cumulatively and collectively they are recited as part of the Generation X American imaginary. The newest image is now the smorgasbord (voluntarist), which surpasses the familiar metaphors of the past: the melting pot (assimilationist) or the common table/ground (integrationist). The concept of the melting pot goes back to the 1920s, while the common table/ground table is projected by Eck and others who support the grand liberal project.

Yet, increasingly, it is the smorgasbord which comes to the fore in popular culture, especially via journalism, where it is likely to have the greatest future impact. To see why, we need only look at a recent issue of *Life*. The December 1998 issue of *Life* features an unusual Religion special on its cover (fig. 11.2). GOD on the cover of *Life* is hardly surprising. After all, the huge Christmas market shapes all strategies for journal formatting and topic selection at the end of a calendar year. Especially inviting is the opportunity for increased sales that come in a calendar year one shy of marking the end of the second millennium in the Christian calendar, and the beginning of its third millennium. How many of us can say we don't think of that strange occurrence in our lifetime, whether with amusement, disdain, or awe? And so God is in the news as well as on our minds.

Nor is it surprising that the December 1998 cover of *Life* blends thought and sight, thinking and seeing: "When you think of God, what do you see?" To go back to the insight of Manuel Castells, a highbrow audience might not make this connection: thought is a reflective, and also a literary-based, activity, while image belongs to the lower world, the world of hoi polloi or undereducated folk. There persists, in Castells's words, "a social hierarchy between literate culture and audiovisual expression."[22] And the *Life* feature story acknowledges this same hierarchy even while trying to subvert it. Look at who answers the question: "When you think of God, what do you see?" It is not a theologian nor a film director but a man of letters. The person who answers the lead question is no less an authority on religion than Frank McCourt. McCourt is the renegade Catholic whose best-selling autobiography, *Angela's Ashes*, rebuts not only Trinitarian belief but also hide-bound institutional prac-

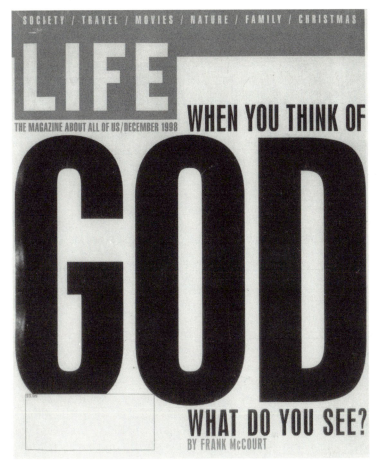

Figure 11.2 This cover of *Life* (December 1998) blends thinking *and* seeing, two related but separate reflexes.

tices. McCourt exposes all the pomp and circumstance that cloak the patriarchical, hieratic structures of his native church, and then concludes in the final paragraph: "I don't confine myself to the faith of my fathers anymore. All the religions are spread before me, a great spiritual smorgasbord, and I'll help myself, thank you."

Religion as a smorgasbord?! Has the "sacred canopy" of the 1960s really become the spiritual smorgasbord of the 1990s? Not for everyone, but for enough middle-class Americans to be a viable commercial strategy, and that is my point: if we take the Stuart Hall model of culture, it allows us to see how deftly all the edges of the puzzle do blur.

What is represented in *Life* are pictures, extraordinary pictures, pictures with captions, but pictures that are, above all, deliberate both in their selection and deployment (fig. 11.3). For *Life*, like the *Utne Reader*, mentioned earlier, is governed by consumer patterns. Its would-be purchasers dictate the production of familiar identities that are also unfamiliar, in that they all appear as equivalent options even when they have vastly different backgrounds, practices, and outlooks. Jews, Muslims, and Hindus—all appear in one image, yet Christians, though a perversely diverse group, do not bring the label "Christian" to the big table, the smorgasbord where all pick and choose, savor and relish, or ignore and forget. Instead, they bring Mormons, Evangelicals, and Russian Orthodox, to mention but a few.

We should not forget that the Asian faces remain marginal, even as the pagan—and also Native American and also atheist—faces do not exist, or at least are not deemed worthy of coverage, but that is because *Life*'s approach is dominated, above all, by consumerist strategies. Nor is *Life*'s marketing of global, polyanna, smorgasbord religion, the shopping mall approach to American-style spirituality, restricted to *Life*. Beyond the alternative it offers to the "On Common Ground" approach, it also mirrors a familiar commercial strategy: target your audience and its taste(s); evoke but don't provoke, and you will succeed.

Yet the *Utne Reader* also has to appeal in order to survive commercially. It is no coincidence that the cover of the July–August 1998 *Utne Reader* (fig. 11.1) outdoes all others in capturing what Homi Bhabha would call religious hybridity, or the rest of us might call syncretistic or creole expressions of American questing. It is the baby Buddha, probably Tibetan, springing off an invisible trampoline, or tossed into midair by invisible but gleeful parents. With designer pink silk pants and a mock brown monk's shirt, he sports three necklaces, with a cross, a crescent and star (Muslim), and a yin-yang (Taoist), and a toothy, leafy bracelet that could be Sikh. A Hindu tikka marks his forehead, a Jewish kippa and sidelocks adorn his smiling face—impish or beatific or both? Writ large across his piebald body is the phrase "designer God," and beneath, the question, "In a mix-and-match world, why not create your own religion?" The article that mirrors the cherubic pluriform baby god on the cover of the *Utne Reader* is titled: "God with a million faces" (thank you, Joe Campbell), and the subtitled message/thesis is: "Critics call it 'cafeteria religion', but the new mix-and-match approach to faith may be the truest spiritual quest of all." The body of the article addresses privatized faith in a way all too familiar to academics who have read, and tried to make sense of, Bellah *et al.*'s *Habits of the Heart*. The counterpart to Sheilaism there is Anne-Marieism here, the quest of a woman who forms her own religion of various beliefs and practices, pursuing the pastiche spirituality first made famous in California but now extant in many upscale communities of the U.S.A.

Figure 11.3 *Life* (December 1998) provides captioned pictures for seventeen groups representing "God in America." In addition to the Mormons, Evangelicals, and Russian Orthodox (here depicted side-by-side with Muslims, Jews, and Hindus), seven others are Christian.

In its content, if not its tone, the *Utne Reader* would seem to be prefiguring themes similar to those from *Life*, etched in Frank McCourt's lapidary prose. "Cafeteria religion," after all, is also a smorgasbord, though "not everyone thinks that smorgasbord spirituality is a desirable feature of life in the global village."[23] And the strength of the *Utne Reader* article is its inclusiveness of mainstream America: projecting be-

JEWS Ancient Hebrews founded their religion on reverence of a transcendent God who revealed Himself to Abraham, Moses and other prophets. Today there are six million Jews in the U.S., up 100,000 since 1996. Some 26,000 Orthodox Jews, including these celebrants, gathered at Madison Square Garden in September 1997 to mark the end of a seven-and-a-half-year reading of the Talmud.

EVANGELICALS Rev. Billy Graham's most recent U.S. crusade drew 263,000 Christians in Tampa. (The men seen here are part of an 8,000-member choir performing at an earlier appearance in Minneapolis.) When Graham first went abroad, in 1954, he preached his traditionalist view of the Bible to two million in London; in 1995 he reached one billion via satellite from San Juan, Puerto Rico.

Figure 11.3, *continued.*

yond the historical accent on the 1965 Immigration Act and the invocation of Net-based expanded resources, the *Utne Reader* article also underscores the changed climate for so-called traditional religions. In so doing, it introduces a dimension absent from most journalistic reporting and also from most popular writing about New Age spirituality. "We're living in what observers call an age of extreme 'religious pluralism,'" notes Jeremiah Creedon "[Yet] the same cultural forces that have driven

HINDUS A husband and wife pay homage at a shrine in their Newton, N.J., home on the Goddess Sri Saraswati's birthday. About 80 percent of India's one billion people consider themselves Hindu; there are perhaps 30 million Hindus elsewhere, including a million in the U.S. For Hindus, God is manifest in different forms and latent in all objects, so worship is appropriate on any occasion.

RUSSIAN ORTHODOX In Brooklyn's Cathedral of the Transfiguration of Our Lord, 300 communicants show up weekly, 1,000 on Christmas and Easter. They are among more than two million members of the Orthodox Church in America. Of all the Orthodoxies, Russia's has had the rockiest road: Since its 14th century split from Greek Orthodoxy, it has survived the persecution of czars and communists.

Figure 11.3, *continued*.

many to leave their inherited faiths have also affected others who have stayed. Almost all the major denominations now contain internal movements that are trying to transform them. Many traditionalists, of course, are trying to block them. . . . [Still] new hybrid modes of worship are constantly appearing, from the new Christian megachurches, whose mammoth services can resemble arena rock, to tiny garage religions hardly bigger than the average band."[24]

We may not then have a pagan soul or an Asian soul or a pagan/Asian soul pervading American spiritual life in the twenty-first century, though it is too early to make any but the most flimsy predictions. At least in the short term, we might deduce, the Asian turn has its limits. Although we see many more of the unfamiliar, and the non-Abrahamic, followers of other, often strange gods, it is the God of Abraham, Isaac, and Jacob, the God of Moses, Jesus, and Muhammad who will likely provide the dominant accent for popular American cultural norms for some time to come. We should not be surprised at this outcome, nor disappointed. It provides a riposte to all isolationists, modern-day monadists who see only their own view of the world as replicated on multiple stages, from the local to the transnational. To the extent that the new Asian presence blends with the New Information Age, many Americans will have more and more opportunities to explore—and also to appreciate—the religiously "other," who is not less American for being non-Abrahamic and also often non-Anglo. If cyberspace fosters the potential for mutual respect, beyond myriad options for pastiche or smorgasbord spirituality, it may yet justify some of the muted optimism of Manuel Castells, in company with devotees of the Goddess.

Notes

1. Jeremiah Creedon, "God with a Million Faces," in *Utne Reader* July–August 98:45.

2. Thomas A. Tweed and Stephen Prothero, *Asian Religions in America: A Documentary History* (New York: Oxford University Press, 1998), 10.

3. Manuel Castells, *The Information Age: Economy, Society and Culture* (Oxford: Blackwell, 1996–7), 3 vols.: *The Rise of the Network Society* (vol. 1), *The Power of Identify* (vol. 2), *End of Millennium* (vol. 3). Castells is the single most comprehensive theorist of the Net and the World Wide Web, and I draw on his insights frequently in the essay that follows. For the specific excerpts above, see especially vol. 1, pp. 477, 470, 463.

4. See, for instance, Saskia Sassen, *Globalization and Its Discontents* (New York: New Press, 1998) on the class struggles of the information economy. The dystopic outcome of cyber-segmentations has been graphically charted by Zillah Eisenstein in *Global Obscenities: Patriarchy, Capitalism, and the Lure of Cyberfantasy* (New York: New York University Press, 1998).

5. Castells himself accounts for the skeptic's refusal or demurral: even if one does not want to allow that "the universal society, based on a space of flows, and on timeless time, is historically new," one is still left with the incontrovertible fact that "our world has become the world of the Information Age."

6. In a forthcoming book, based on my 1999 American Academy of Religion Lectures in the History of Religions, and titled *New Faiths, Old Fears*, I will

explore just how significant is the urban relocation of the newest wave of Asian-American immigrants.

7. The actual figures, of course, are open to divergent reckoning. On the one hand, an advocacy group declares: "We, the American Asians, number 6.9 million, a 99% increase since the 1980 census. This report focuses on Asian Americans—Chinese, Filipinos, Koreans, Indians, Japanese, Vietnamese, Cambodians, Laotians Hmong, and Thai. Our dramatic increases are the result of increased immigration from China, India, Korea, the Philippines, and other Asian and Pacific Island areas following the adoption of the Immigration Act of 1965." See the website of welcome.to/virtualipinas, the website of Virtualipinas—the pearl of the infobahn, an innovative and comprehensive Filipino website. On the other hand, if one looks at county-by-county estimates of change in population, the figures for Asian immigrants would be lower but still significant; see www.rinconassoc.com/ for a Dallas-based company's report of the major U.S. government census figures.

8. Arjun Appadurai, *Modernity at Large: Cultural Dimensions of Globalization* (Minnesota: University of Minnesota Press 1996), 6.

9. Stuart Hall et al., *Culture, Media and Identities* (Sage: London, 1997), also summarized in a convenient outline by John Kraniauskas, "Globalization Is Ordinary: The Transnationalization of Cultural Studies" in *Radical Philosophy* 90 (July/August 1998): 13.

10. Castells, *The Information Age*, vol. 1, p. 351.

11. Sassen, *Globalization and its Discontents*, 190–91.

12. Castells, *Information Age*, vol. 1, p. 371.

13. Ibid., vol. 1, pp. 477–78. While this shorthand of history will disturb many, its catalytic effect is to force each reader/netizen to evaluate for herself what is continuous, as well as discontinuous, about the instruments and cultural production of the Information Age.

14. Hans-Georg Gadamer, "Dialogues in Capri," in Jacques Derrida and Giovanni Vattimo, eds., *Religion* (Stanford: Stanford University Press, 1998), 201.

15. Ibid., 209.

16. Jacques Derrida, "Faith and Knowledge: The Two Sources of 'Religion' at the Limits of Reason Alone" (Derrida and Vattimo, eds., *Religion*, pp. 1–78), which might be better subtitled "Religion Beyond Metaphysics, or Technoscience as Religious Belief, Calculation as Sacrosanct" (54). The difficulty with Derrida's logocentric approach to religion is his fixation with origins, in this case, Latin as source of *religio*, which leads him to talk about "globalatinization" as the counterpoint to tele-technoscientific reason. The basis for conflict and triumph is accented in the same phrase, as: "all the religions, their centers of authority, the religious cultures, states, nations or ethnic groups that they represent have unequal access, to be sure, but often one that is immediate and potentially without limit, to the same world market" (43). One is left gagging at the distance between "unequal access" and "potentially without limit access," all the more so since the cyber-segmentation of the Information Age (Sassen) is bound to have its religious, as also its commercial and political, consequence.

17. Jonathan Z. Smith, "A Matter of Class: Taxonomies of Religion," *Harvard Theological Review* 89:4 (1996): 387–403, but especially 399–401, where

"universal" and "living," along with "world" are shown to be terms that simultaneously denigrate hybridization and privilege the purity of originary belief characteristic not of all religion but of one above all others: Protestant Christianity.

18. See W. G. Oxtoby, ed., *World Religions: Western Traditions* (Toronto: Oxford University Press, 1996) and *World Religions: Eastern Traditions* (Toronto: Oxford University Press, 1996), where the West is limited to Islam, Judaism, Christianity, and Zoroastrianism, with the East comprising Buddhism, Chinese religions, Shinto, and Hinduism (together with Sikhism and Jainism). Yet Islam is as much an Eastern as a Western religious tradition, and increasingly the Eastern religions are represented in Western countries as competing and successful alternative traditions.

19. See Diana Eck, *On Common Ground: World Religions in America* (NY: Columbia University Press, 1997).

20. See *Shattering the Myth: Islam beyond Violence* (Princeton: Princeton University Press, 1998), especially pp. 33–36.

19. Erik Davis, *Techgnosis: Myth, Magic, and Mysticism in the Age of Information* (NY: Harmony Books, 1998), 183. Davis later goes on to qualify the technopagan fascination with cyberspace but without disavowing his central thesis: pagans were online long before the Web, and they continue to thrive as a subset of New Age spirituality through their use of virtual as well as physical space.

22. Castells, I:327.

23. Creedon, 47.

24. Except for the final accent on the internal transformation of mainline denominations, "Designer God" anticipates "The Age of Divine Disunity." It is as if the author of the *Wall Street Journal* article could've been a closet *Utne Reader* reader, so closely does the message of the February 10, 1999 article reflect the outline of the summer 1998 *Utne Reader* lead story. But one does not need to presume direct borrowing; the theme is so current that it could be gleaned from multiple media sources, and then recycled with a "personal" touch—in this case, the interviews which begin the *Wall Street Journal* and "hook" the reader.

Selected Bibliography

NOTE: This is not a comprehensive list of works cited in the collection's essays, but includes titles of interest to the general subject of religion and cultural studies. While many works cited in the chapters of this book appear below, complete citations can be found in their notes.

Alter, Robert. *The Art of Biblical Narrative*. New York: Basic Books, 1981.

Altizer, Thomas J. J., et al. *Deconstruction and Theology*. New York: Crossroad, 1982.

Anderson, Benedict. *Imagined Communities: Reflections on the Origin and Spread of Nationalism*. London and New York: Verso, 1991.

Andrews, William L., ed. *Sisters of the Spirit: Three Black Women's Autobiographies of the Nineteenth Century*. Bloomington: Indiana University Press, 1986.

Armstrong, Karen. *A History of God: The 4000-Year Quest of Judaism, Christianity, and Islam*. New York: Knopf, 1993.

Asad, Talal. *Genealogies of Religion: Discipline and Reasons of Power in Christianity and Islam*. Baltimore: Johns Hopkins, 1993.

Ashworth, William. *The Late Great Lakes: An Environmental History*. New York: Knopf, 1987.

Banton, Michael, ed. *Anthropological Approaches to the Study of Religion*. London: Tavistock, 1966.

Basso, Keith H. *Wisdom Sits in Places: Landscape and Language among the Western Apache*. Albuquerque: University of New Mexico Press, 1996.

———— and Steven Feld, eds. *Senses of Place*. Santa Fe: School of American Research Press, 1996.

Bell, Rudolph. *Holy Anorexia*. Chicago: University of Chicago Press, 1985.

Bercovitch, Sacvan. *The American Jeremiad*. Madison: University of Wisconsin Press, 1978.

————. *The Puritan Origins of the American Self*. New Haven: Yale University Press, 1975.

————. *The Rites of Assent: Transformations in the Symbolic Construction of America*. New York: Routledge, 1993.

Berger, Peter. *The Sacred Canopy: Elements of a Sociological Theory of Religion*. New York: Anchor, 1969.

Berlin, Isaiah. *The Crooked Timber of Humanity: Chapters in the History of Ideas*. Ed. Henry Hardy. Princeton: Princeton University Press, 1997.

Bhabha, Homi. *The Location of Culture*. New York: Routledge, 1994.

Booth, Wayne. *Modern Dogma and the Rhetoric of Assent*. Chicago: University of Chicago Press, 1974.

Bourdieu, Pierre. *Outline of a Theory of Practice*. New York: Cambridge University Press, 1977.

Brown, Karen McCarthy. *Mama Lola: A Vodou Priestess in Brooklyn*. Berkeley and Los Angeles: University of California Press, 1991.

Brown, Peter. *The Body and Society: Men, Women and Sexual Renunciation in Early Christianity.* Lectures on the History of Religions 13. New York: Columbia University Press, 1988.

———. *The Cult of the Saints: Its Rise and Function in Late Christianity.* Chicago: University of Chicago Press, 1981.

Browne, Malcolm W. *Muddy Boots and Red Socks: A Reporter's Life.* New York: Times Books, 1993.

Buber, Martin. *I and Thou* [1922]. Trans. Ronald Gregor Smith. New York: Scribners, 1958.

Burke, Kenneth. *The Rhetoric of Religion: Studies in Logology.* Berkeley and Los Angeles: University of California Press, 1961.

Burridge, Kenelm E. O. *Mambu: A Melanesian Millennium.* London and New York: Methuen, 1960.

Butler, Jon. *Awash in a Sea of Faith: Christianizing the American People.* Cambridge: Harvard University Press, 1990.

Bynum, Caroline Walker. *Fragmentation and Redemption: Essays on Gender and the Human Body in Medieval Religion.* New York: Zone Books, 1992.

———. *The Resurrection of the Body in Western Christianity, 200–1336.* New York: Columbia University Press, 1995.

Castells, Manuel. *The Information Age: Economy, Society, and Culture,* 3 volumes. Oxford and New York: Blackwell, 1996–97.

Certeau, Michel de. *Heterologies: Discourse on the Other.* Trans. Brian Massumi. Minneapolis: University of Minnesota Press, 1986.

———. *The Practice of Everyday Life.* Trans. Steven R. Rendall. Berkeley and Los Angeles: University of California Press, 1984.

———. *The Writing of History.* Trans. Tom Conley. New York: Columbia University Press, 1988.

Clifford, James. *The Predicament of Culture: Twentieth-Century Ethnography, Literature, and Art.* Cambridge: Harvard University Press, 1988.

——— and George E. Marcus, eds. *Writing Culture: The Poetics and Politics of Ethnography.* Berkeley and Los Angeles: University of California Press, 1986.

Collier, Peter, and Helga Geyer-Ryan. *Literary Theory Today.* Ithaca: Cornell University Press, 1990.

Comaroff, Jean, and John. L. Comaroff. *Of Revelation to Revolution.* Chicago: University of Chicago Press, 1991.

Csordas, Thomas J. *The Sacred Self: A Cultural Phenomenology of Charismatic Healing.* Berkeley and Los Angeles: University of California Press, 1994

Davis, Erik. *Techgnosis: Myth, Magic, and Mysticism in the Age of Information.* New York: Harmony Books, 1998.

Delbanco, Andrew. *The Death of Satan: How Americans Have Lost the Sense of Evil.* New York: Farrar, Strauss, and Giroux, 1995.

———. *The Puritan Ordeal.* Cambridge: Harvard University Press, 1990.

Dening, Greg. *The Death of William Gooch: A History's Anthropology.* Honolulu: University of Hawaii Press, 1995.

———. *Mr. Bligh's Bad Language: Passion, Power and Theatre on the Bounty.* New York: Cambridge University Press, 1992.

Deren, Maya. *Divine Horsemen: The Living Gods of Haiti* [1953]. New Paltz, NY: McPherson & Company, 1983.

Derrida, Jacques. *The Gift of Death*. Trans. David Wills. Chicago: University of Chicago Press, 1995.

—— and Gianni Vattimo, eds. *Religion*. Palo Alto: Stanford University Press, 1998.

Diamond, Jared. *Guns, Germs, and Steel: The Fate of Human Societies*. New York: Norton, 1997.

Dickens, Arthur G., and John Tonkin. *The Reformation in Historical Thought*. Cambridge: Harvard University Press, 1985.

Dillenberger, John. *The Visual Arts and Christianity in America: The Colonial Period Through the Nineteenth Century*. Chico, CA: Scholars Press, 1984.

Douglas, Mary. *Natural Symbols: Explorations in Cosmology*. New York: Pantheon, 1982.

——. *Purity and Danger: An Analysis of the Concepts of Pollution and Taboo*. New York: Routledge, 1966.

Dowie, Mark. *Losing Ground: American Environmentalism at the Close of the Twentieth Century*. Cambridge: MIT Press, 1995.

Dumont, Louis. *Homo Hierarchicus: The Caste System and Its Implications*. Trans. Mark Sansbury. Chicago: University of Chicago Press, 1970.

Dundes, Alan, ed. *Sacred Narrative: Readings in the Theory of Myth*. Berkeley and Los Angeles: University of California Press, 1984.

Durkheim, Emile. *Elementary Forms of the Religious Life* [1915]. Trans. Joseph Ward Swain. New York: Free Press, 1965.

Dyson, Michael Eric. *Between God and Gangsta Rap: Bearing Witness to Black Culture*. New York: Oxford University Press, 1996.

——. *I May Not Get There with You: The True Martin Luther King, Jr.* New York: Free Press, 1999.

Eck, Diana. *On Common Ground: World Religions in America*. New York: Columbia University Press, 1997.

Eliade, Mircea. *Images and Symbols: Studies in Religious Symbolism* [1952]. Trans. Philip Mairet. Princeton: Princeton University Press, 1991.

——. *Patterns in Comparative Religion* [1958]. Trans. Rosemary Sheed. Lincoln: University of Nebraska Press, 1996.

——. *The Sacred and Profane*. Trans. Willard R. Trask. New York: Harcourt, Brace, 1959.

Erikson, Erik H. *Young Man Luther: A Study in Psychoanalysis and History* [1958]. New York: Norton, 1962.

Evans-Pritchard, E. E. *Nuer Religion*. Oxford: Oxford University Press, 1956.

Feeley-Harnik, Gillian. *A Green Estate: Restoring Independence in Madagascar*. Washington DC: Smithsonian Institute Press, 1991.

——. *The Lord's Table: The Meaning of Food in Early Judaism and Christianity*. Washington DC: Smithsonian Institute Press, 1981, 1994.

Flew, Antony, ed. *David Hume: Writings on Religion*. La Salle, IL: Open Court, 1992.

Foucault, Michel. *The History of Sexuality, v.1: An Introduction*. Trans. Robert Hurley. New York: Vintage, 1978.

——. *The Order of Things: An Archaeology of the Human Sciences*. New York: Vintage, 1973.

Fox, Richard Wightman. *Reinhold Niebuhr: A Biography*. Ithaca: Cornell University Press, 1997.

———. *Trials of Intimacy: Love and Loss in the Beecher-Tilton Scandal.* Chicago: University of Chicago Press, 1999.

——— and Robert B. Westbrook, eds. *In Face of the Facts: Moral Inquiry in American Scholarship.* New York: Cambridge University Press, 1997.

Franchot, Jenny. *Roads to Rome: The Antebellum Encounter with Catholicism.* Berkeley and Los Angeles: University of California Press, 1994.

Frei, Hans. *The Eclipse of Biblical Narrative: A Study in Eighteenth and Nineteenth Century Hermeneutics.* New Haven: Yale University Press, 1974.

Freud, Sigmund. *Civilization and its Discontents* [1930]. Ed. and trans. James Strachey. New York: Norton, 1961.

———. *The Future of an Illusion* [1927]. *The Standard Edition of the Complete Psychological Works of Sigmund Freud,* ed. and trans. James Strachey, vol. XXI. London: Hogarth, 1961.

———. *Interpretation of Dreams* [1900]. *The Standard Edition of the Complete Psychological Works of Sigmund Freud,* ed. and trans. James Strachey, vols. IV, V. London: Hogarth, 1953.

———. *Totem and Taboo* [1913]. *The Standard Edition of the Complete Psychological Works of Sigmund Freud,* ed. and trans. James Strachey, vol. XIII. London: Hogarth,1955.

Frye, Northrop. *The Great Code: The Bible and Literature.* New York: Harcourt, Brace,1982.

Garber, Marjorie, and Rebecca L. Walkowitz, eds. *One Nation under God?* New York: Routledge, 1999.

Gaustad, Edwin S. *A Documentary History of Religion in America since 1865.* Grand Rapids, MI: William B. Eerdmans Publishing Company, 1983.

———. *A Documentary History of Religion in America to the Civil War.* 2nd ed. Grand Rapids, MI: William B. Eerdmans Publishing Company, 1982.

Geertz, Clifford. *The Interpretation of Cultures: Selected Essays.* New York: Basic Books, 1973.

Gilroy, Paul. *The Black Atlantic: Modernity and Double Consciousness.* London and New York: Verso, 1993.

Girard, Rene. *Violence and the Sacred.* Trans. Patrick Gregory. Baltimore: Johns Hopkins University Press, 1977.

Greenblatt, Stephen. *Marvelous Possessions: The Wonder of the New World.* Chicago: University of Chicago Press, 1991.

———, ed. *New World Encounters.* Berkeley and Los Angeles: University of California Press, 1993.

Grossberg, Lawrence, et al. *Cultural Studies.* New York: Routledge, 1992.

Gunn, Giles. *The Culture of Criticism and the Criticism of Culture.* New York: Oxford University Press, 1987.

———. *Thinking across the American Grain: Ideology, Intellect, and the New Pragmatism.* Chicago: University of Chicago Press, 1992.

Hackett, David G., ed. *Religion and American Culture: A Reader.* New York: Routledge, 1995.

Hall, David. *Lived Religion in America: Toward a History of Practice.* Princeton: Princeton University Press, 1997.

———. *Worlds of Wonder, Days of Judgment: Popular Religious Belief in Early New England.* Cambridge: Harvard University Press, 1990.

Hall, Stuart, et al. *Culture, Media and Identities*. London: Sage, 1997.

Harpham, Geoffrey Galt. *The Ascetic Imperative in Culture and Criticism*. Chicago: University of Chicago Press, 1987.

———. *Getting It Right: Language, Literature, and Ethics*. Chicago: University of Chicago Press, 1992.

———. *Shadows of Ethics: Criticism and the Just Society*. Durham, NC: Duke University Press, 1999.

Hatch, Nathan O. *The Democratization of American Christianity*. New Haven: Yale University Press, 1989.

Hawley, John Stratton, ed. *Saints and Virtues*. Berkeley and Los Angeles: University of California Press, 1987.

Hollinger, David. *Science, Jews, and Secular Culture: Studies in Mid-Twentieth Century American Intellectual History*. Princeton: Princeton University Press, 1996.

Hyman, Stanley Edgar. *The Tangled Bank: Darwin, Marx, Frazer, and Freud as Imaginative Writers*. New York: Atheneum, 1962.

James, William. *The Varieties of Religious Experience: A Study in Human Nature* [1901–2]. New York: Library of America, 1990.

Johnson, Paul. *A History of Christianity*. New York: Atheneum, 1976.

Jonas, Hans. *The Gnostic Religion: The Message of the Alien God and the Beginnings of Christianity*. Boston: Beacon Press, 1958.

Kahn, Joel S. *Culture, Multiculture, Postculture*. London: Sage, 1999.

Kermode, Frank. *The Genesis of Secrecy: On the Interpretation of Narrative*. Cambridge: Harvard University Press, 1979.

Knox, Ronald A. *Enthusiasm: A Chapter in the History of Religion with Special Reference to the XVII and XVIII Centuries* [1950]. Notre Dame, IN: University of Notre Dame Press,1994.

Kristeva, Julia. *Black Sun: Depression and Melancholia*. Trans. Leon S. Roudiez. New York: Columbia University Press, 1989.

———. *Powers of Horror: An Essay on Abjection*. Trans. Leon S. Roudiez. New York: Columbia University Press,1982.

Kung, Hans. *Does God Exist? An Answer for Today*. Trans. Edward Quinn. Garden City, NY: Doubleday, 1980.

Kuper, Adam. *Culture: The Anthropologists' Account*. Cambridge: Harvard University Press, 1999.

Lacan, Jacques. *Ecrits: A Selection*. Trans. Alan Sheridan. New York: Norton, 1977.

LaCapra, Dominick. *Rethinking Intellectual History: Texts, Contexts, Language*. Ithaca: Cornell University Press, 1983.

———. *Representing the Holocaust: History, Theory, Trauma*. Ithaca: Cornell University Press, 1994.

Lawrence, Bruce B. *Defenders of God: The Revolt Against the Modern Age*. San Francisco: Harper and Row, 1989.

———. *Shattering the Myth: Islam Beyond Violence*. Princeton: Princeton University Press, 1998.

Leonard, George J. *The Art of the Commonplace from Wordsworth to John Cage*. Chicago: University of Chicago Press, 1994.

Lerner, Robert E. *The Powers of Prophecy: The Cedar of Lebanon Vision from the*

Mongol Onslaught to the Dawn of the Enlightenment. Berkeley and Los Angeles: University of California Press, 1983.

Levi-Strauss, Claude. *The Savage Mind.* Trans. John Russell. Chicago: University of Chicago Press, 1966.

———. *Tristes Tropiques.* New York: Atheneum, 1961.

Levinas, Emmanuel. *Totality and Infinity.* Trans. Alphonso Lingis. Pittsburgh: Duquesne University Press, 1969.

Lewis, James R., ed. *The Gods Have Landed: New Religions from Other Worlds.* Albany: State University of New York Press, 1995.

Matt, Daniel C. *The Essential Kabbalah.* San Francisco: HarperSanFrancisco, 1995.

———. *God and the Big Bang.* Woodstock, VT: Jewish Lights, 1996.

Mauss, Marcel. *The Gift* [1925]. Trans. W. D. Halls. Chicago: University of Chicago Press, 1990.

——— and Henri Hubert. *Sacrifice: Its Nature and Functions* [1898]. Trans. W. D. Halls. Chicago: University of Chicago Press, Midway Reprint, 1981.

McDannell, Colleen. *Material Christianity: Religion and Popular in America.* New Haven: Yale University Press, 1995.

Miles, Jack. *God: A Biography.* New York: Vintage, 1995.

Miles, Margaret. *Image as Insight: Visual Understanding in Western Christianity and Secular Culture.* Boston: Beacon, 1985.

Miller, Perry. *Errand into the Wilderness.* Cambridge: Harvard University Press, 1956.

———. *The New England Mind* [1939, 1953], vols. I, II. Boston: Beacon, 1961.

Miller, Timothy, ed. *America's Alternative Religions.* Albany: State University of New York Press, 1995.

Mizruchi, Susan L. *The Science of Sacrifice: American Literature and Modern Social Theory.* Princeton: Princeton University Press, 1998.

Nietzsche, Friedrich. *"The Birth of Tragedy" and "The Genealogy of Morals"* [1872, 1887]. Trans. Francis Golffing. Garden City, NY: Doubleday, 1956.

Numbers, Ronald L. *The Creationists.* New York: Knopf, 1992.

Ong, Walter J. *The Presence of the Word: Some Prolegomena for Cultural and Religious History.* New Haven: Yale University Press, 1967.

Orsi, Robert. *The Madonna of 115th Street: Faith and Community in Italian Harlem, 1880–1950.* New Haven: Yale University Press, 1985.

———. *Thank You, St. Jude: Women's Devotion to the Patron Saint of Hopeless Causes.* New Haven: Yale University Press, 1996

Pals, Daniel L. *Seven Theories of Religion.* New York: Oxford University Press, 1996.

Patterson, Orlando. *Rituals of Blood: The Consequences of Slavery in Two American Centuries.* Washington, DC: Civitas/Counterpoint, 1998.

Peterson, Michael, et al. *Philosophy of Religion: Selected Readings.* New York: Oxford University Press, 1996.

Pratt, Mary Louise. *Imperial Eyes: Travel Writing and Transculturation.* New York: Routledge, 1992.

Proudfoot, Wayne. *Religious Experience.* Berkeley and Los Angeles: University of California Press, 1985.

Raboteau, Albert. *Slave Religion: The 'Invisible Institution' in the Antebellum South*. New York: Oxford University Press, 1978.

Ricoeur, Paul. *The Symbolism of Evil*. Trans. Emerson Buchanan. Boston: Beacon, 1969.

Sahlins, Marshall. *Islands of History*. Chicago: University of Chicago Press, 1985.

Said, Edward. *Orientalism*. New York: Pantheon, 1978.

Scarry, Elaine. *The Body in Pain: The Making and Unmaking of the World*. New York: Oxford University Press, 1985.

Smith, Jonathan Z. *Drudgery Divine: On the Comparison of Early Christianities and the Religions of Late Antiquity*. Chicago: University of Chicago Press, 1990.

———. *Imagining Religion: From Babylon to Jonestown*. Chicago: University of Chicago Press, 1982.

———. *Map Is Not Territory: Studies in the History of Religions*. Leiden: Brill, 1978.

———. *To Take Place: Toward Theory in Ritual*. Chicago: University of Chicago Press, 1987.

Smith, Theophus Harold. *Conjuring Culture: Biblical Formations of Black America*. New York: Oxford University Press, 1994.

Stewart, Susan. *On Longing: Narratives of the Miniature, the Gigantic, the Souvenir, the Collection*. Baltimore: Johns Hopkins University Press, 1984.

Tattersall, Ian. *Becoming Human: Evolution and Human Uniqueness*. New York: Harcourt Brace, 1998.

Taylor, Mark C. *Nots*. Chicago: University of Chicago Press, 1993.

———, ed. *Critical Terms for Religious Studies*. Chicago: University of Chicago Press, 1998.

Thompson, Robert Farris. *Flash of the Spirit: African and Afro-American Art and Philosophy*. New York: Vintage, 1984.

Todorov, Tzvetan. *The Conquest of America: the Question of the Other*. Trans. Richard Howard. New York: Harper and Row, 1984.

———. *Facing the Extreme: Moral Life in the Concentration Camps*. Trans. Arthur Denner and Abigail Pollak. New York: Metropolitan Books, 1996.

———. *Theories of the Symbol*. Trans. Catherine Porter. Ithaca: Cornell University Press, 1982.

Toumey, Christopher P. *God's Own Scientists: Creationists in a Secular World*. New Brunswick, NJ: Rutgers University Press, 1994.

Trilling, Lionel. *Sincerity and Authenticity*. Cambridge: Harvard University Press, 1972.

Turner, Victor. *The Forest of Symbols*. Ithaca: Cornell University Press, 1967.

Tweed, Thomas, and Stephen Prothero. *Asian Religions in America: A Documentary History*. New York: Oxford University Press, 1998.

Vidich, Arthur J., and Stanford M. Lyman. *American Sociology: Worldly Rejections of Religion and Their Directions*. New Haven: Yale University Press, 1985.

Weber, Max. *The Protestant Ethic and the Spirit of Capitalism* [1904–5]. Trans. Talcott Parsons. New York: Scribners, 1930.

———. *The Sociology of Religion* [1922]. Trans. Ephraim Fischoff. Boston: Beacon Press, 1956.

Weisenfeld, Judith. *African-American Women and Christian Activism: New York's Black YWCA, 1905–1945*. Cambridge: Harvard University Press, 1998.

——— and Richard Newman, eds. *This Far by Faith: Readings in African-American Women's Religious Biography*. New York: Routledge, 1996.

West, Cornell. *Prophesy, Deliverance! An Afro-American Revolutionary Christianity*. Philadelphia: Westminster Press, 1982.

Williams, Raymond. *Keywords: A Vocabulary of Culture and Society*. New York: Oxford University Press, 1976.

Wolfe, Alan. *Whose Keeper: Social Science and Moral Obligation*. Berkeley and Los Angeles: University of California Press, 1989.

Wosh, Peter J. *Spreading the Word: The Bible Business in Nineteenth-Century America*. Ithaca: Cornell University Press, 1994.

Wyschogrod, Edith. *Saints and Postmodernism: Revisioning Moral Philosophy*. Chicago: University of Chicago Press, 1990.

Index of Names